Ecuador

THE BRADT CLIMBING AND HIKING GUIDE

Fifth Edition

Rob Rachowiecki
Mark Thurber

Bradt Travel Guides Ltd, UK
The Globe Pequot Press Inc, USA

Fifth edition published 2004

First published in 1984

Bradt Travel Guides Ltd
19 High Street, Chalfont St Peter, Bucks SL9 9QE, England
www.bradt-travelguides.com
Published in the USA by The Globe Pequot Press Inc, 246 Goose Lane,
PO Box 480, Guilford, Connecticut 06475-0480

ISBN 1 84162 075 0

British Library Cataloguing in Publication Data
A catalogue record for this book is available from the British Library

Cover photograph Pete Oxford
Illustrations Carole Vincer
Maps Alan Whitaker

Typeset from the author's disc by Wakewing
Printed and bound in Italy by Legoprint SpA, Trento

Authors

Mark Thurber has lived in Ecuador for nine years and manages an environmental and archaeological consulting firm. He updated this edition with help from many other outdoor enthusiasts and conservationists who live full time in Ecuador.

After several years living in South America, including a long stint in Ecuador, Englishman **Rob Rachowiecki** moved to Arizona, where he now lives. He has three school-aged children. He returns to Ecuador and Peru every year both as a tour leader for Wilderness Travel, an adventure-travel company, and to research his other popular travel guidebooks.

Readers' comments can be sent directly to the authors by email – Rob Rachowiecki (robrachow@earthlink.net) and Mark Thurber (sun@ecnet.ec), or via Bradt Travel Guides at info@bradt-travelguides.com.

One cannot stay on the summit forever -
One has to come down again.
So why bother in the first place? Just this.

What is above knows what is below -
But what is below does not know what is above.

One climbs, one sees -
One descends and sees no longer -
But one has seen!

There is an art of conducting one's self in
the lower regions by the memory of
what one saw higher up.

When one can no longer see,
One does at least still know.

René Daumal

Contents

LIST OF MAPS

PUBLISHER'S FOREWORD

The first Bradt travel guide was written in 1974 by George and Hilary Bradt on a river barge floating down a tributary of the Amazon. In the 1980s and '90s the focus shifted away from hiking to broader-based guides to new destinations – usually the first to be published on those places. In the 21st century Bradt continues to publish these ground-breaking guides, along with others covering established holiday destinations, incorporating in-depth information on culture and natural history alongside the nuts and bolts of where to stay and what to see.

Bradt authors support responsible travel, with advice not only on minimum impact but also on how to give something back through local charities. Thus a true synergy is achieved between the traveller and local communities.

*

The volcanoes and hiking trails of Ecuador featured in one of the very first Bradt Travel Guides: *Backpacking in Venezuela, Colombia and Ecuador*, published in 1979. George and I had spent a thrilling three months exploring those countries on foot, but it was Ecuador that provided the best blend of spectacular snow-covered peaks, wonderful cloudforest, hot springs, and perhaps the most colourful markets in South America. Although there were plenty of trails (Ecuador is the most densly populated country in South America and the people travel on foot) finding them was a question of luck. We didn't always succeed. My description of the Volcán Antisana hike began: "I don't think we should write up this hike for our readers," I commented, watching George flounder towards a three-metre barrier of luxuriant growth. His technique was to fling himself full length on the tangle of vegetation, roll around for a while, then crawl over the top of the flattened bit, leaving me to follow. It didn't always work, and when it failed there were exciting drops down one-metre gaps in the lava floor.' I concluded: 'Antisana to Papallacta is the most difficult hike we've done, and the 18km took us two days. During that time we almost never walked; we either scrambled, jumped, or crawled.'

All that is in the past, and thanks to the passage of time and the skilful research of Rob and Mark, Ecuador's unchanged delights are now accessible to anyone with a reasonable degree of fitness. Lucky you! You won't be disappointed.

Hilary Bradt

Hilary Bradt

19 High Street, Chalfont St Peter, Bucks SL9 9QE, England
Tel: 01753 893444; fax: 01753 892333
Email: info@bradt-travelguides.com
Web: www.bradt-travelguides.com

Acknowledgements to the Fifth Edition

It has been seven years since I updated the fourth edition and many things have changed. I want to express my appreciation to all of the people who have helped me update existing routes and provided text on new ones. All of the people listed below are strongly committed to the conservation of Ecuador's wild areas. It is our hope that your visits will strengthen this effort. I also encourage readers to contact me directly about changes in routes for the next edition.

Wayne Lampier and Diana Morris introduced me to the waterfalls and native forests of the Río Pita and provided the description of the great day-hike close to Quito. Peter Ayarza provided updates on the mountaineering history and the new generation of Ecuadorian climbers and guides. Piet Sabbe updated his description of the Golondrinas trek. John Clark updated the section on natural history. Cindy Smith, the South American Explorers' manager, provided numerous updates on hotels, visas and other travellers' details. Peace Corps volunteers Jonathan Old and Mike Kraft provided updated details on the hike from Saraguro to Yacuambi, one of my favourite walks. Josh Busby, Raj Ayyagari and Nathan Brown explored many new routes with me in the Sierra, as well as bars in Quito and Cuenca. Ben Bellows introduced me to the idea of hiking from Gima to La Florida, which is another one of my favourite walks in Ecuador. Olmedo Mashqui, of the Café Paso del Inca, helped update the Trek of the Condor. Hillary Hammon hiked with me to the Laguna Encantada near the town of Oyacachi. Jairo Masaquiza and Edward Marshall helped edit the section on Salasaca and Teligote. Edward also hiked with me into Cerro Hermoso and lost my machete in a tapir tunnel on our crawl down to the Río Topo in the Llangantates; he still has not replaced it! Santos Calderon is the Director of Biodiversity for the provinces of Loja and Zamora-Chinchipe and helped update the Podocarpus section. Birder Jonas Nilsson also provided information on the Pododcarpus area. Andy Hammerman and Michelle Kirby, owners of the now famous Black Sheep Inn, updated hikes in the Quilatoa area. Molly Brown provided information on the Mindo area. Biologist Francisco Silva translated some information from Spanish to English. Aida Buidron, the owner of Casa Aida, added details on the Imbabura climb. Long-time resident of Ecuador and avid botanist Lou Jost updated the section on Baños and wrote the description of the hike to Sacha Llanganates. Russ Meehan and son Kerry Meehan have dragged me off to the mountains when I should have been working, and provided updates of climbs (Antisana and Sumaco) I did not get to for this edition. Chris Canaday wrote the section on the new community-run rainforest lodge in Añangu on the Río Napo. Kathy Jarvis of Andean trails wrote up the hike from Urbina to the Laguna Cocha Negra. Mike McComb updated the section on the Mache-Chindul range on the coast. Mark Haeg, Nick Hedgecoe, Andy Williamson, Jim Wyss, Stan Lanzano, Jason Bremner and Jane Letham accompanied me on many hikes and climbs in the Sierra. Jason Haberstadt provided information on internet resources. Rodrigo Peralvo helped with information on the Ilinizas. Jaime

Domínguez of ETAPA in Cuenca provided information on Cajas. Roberto Gutiérrez of AEAP updated the information on sport climbing in Quito. And finally a big thank you to my wife, Leonor Zambrano, who accompanied me on many of the hikes and climbs.

Mark Thurber

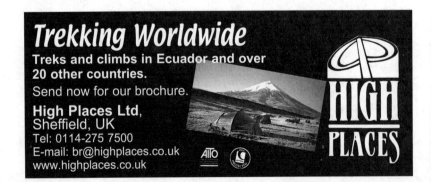

Introduction

Though one of the smallest countries in South America, Ecuador offers an incredible diversity of scenery, wildlife and people. The mountaineer and adventurous traveller have a choice of the ice-clad Andes, tropical rainforest, mountain trails leading to Inca ruins, and quiet beaches; all these attractions lie within a day's journey of Quito, the capital city. This accessibility makes Ecuador an attractive destination for climbers and hikers of all abilities, and avoids the long approaches and expedition planning often necessary in other high mountain ranges.

Mountaineers find Ecuador well suited as a high-altitude training ground. There are many technically straightforward ascents of 5,000m peaks. Climbers can gain technical experience in the lower ranges of Europe and North America and then learn about how the body functions at high altitudes in the Ecuadorian Andes. A combination of these abilities will produce climbers ready to challenge some of the world's most difficult high peaks.

Superb mountain scenery, however, is only one of Ecuador's attractions. It also has some of the best beaches in South America, colourful indigenous markets, and plenty of wildlife, especially birds. Come and see for yourself.

KEY TO STANDARD SYMBOLS

—·—·—	International boundary
······	District boundary
------	National park boundary
✈	Airport (international)
✈	Airport (other)
✛	Airstrip
🚁	Helicopter service
▬▬▬	Railway
··········	Trail/Footpath
--🚗--	Car ferry
--🚢--	Passenger ferry
⛽	Petrol station or garage
🅿	Car park
🚌	Bus station etc
🚲	Cycle hire
M	Underground station
⌂	Hotel, inn etc
🛆	Campsite
⬆	Hut
⚲	Wine bar
✕	Restaurant, café etc
⊠	Post office
☏	Telephone
@	Internet café
✚	Hospital, clinic etc
⚱	Museum
🐘	Zoo
i	Tourist information
$	Bank
⚱	Statue or monument
∴	Archaeological or historic site

⛫	Historic building
✝	Church or cathedral
🌲	Buddhist temple
⌂	Buddhist monastery
⛩	Hindu temple
☪	Mosque
⚑	Golf course
🏃	Stadium
▲	Summit
△	Boundary beacon
◉	Outpost
✕══✕	Border post
⌂	Rock shelter
🚡	Cable car, funicular
≍	Mountain pass
○	Waterhole
✳	Scenic viewpoint
❀	Botanical site
♧	Specific woodland feature
🗼	Lighthouse
⟂	Marsh
🌴	Mangrove
🕊	Bird nesting site
🐢	Turtle nesting site
~~ ~~	Coral reef
🦅	Beach
🤿	Scuba diving
🐟	Fishing sites

Other map symbols are sometimes shown in separate key boxes with individual explanations for their meanings.

Part One

General Information

ECUADOR AT A GLANCE

Location
Size 256,370km² (second smallest republic in South
America); 685km from north to south.
Climate Quito rainy season: September–May; average annual rainfall
1270mm. Mean annual temperature 13°C; average high temperature
22°C, average low temperature 7°C. Guayaquil rainy season:
December–May. Average high temperature 32°C, average low
temperature 20°C.
Status
Population 13,500,000 (2002 estimate). 65% Mestizo, 25% indigenous,
7% European, 3% others. 48% of the population live on the coastal plain,
47% in the Andean Sierra and 5% in the eastern lowlands (the Oriente).
Population growth 1.97% per annum.
Population density 53 per km² (highest in South America)
Capital Quito (population 2,000,000)
Other main towns Guayaquil, largest city and main port (population
2,000,000); Cuenca, main town of southern highlands (population 300,000)
Public holidays January 1 New Year's Day, Moveable Epiphany,
Moveable Carnival (Monday & Tuesday before Lent), Moveable Holy
Thursday, Good Friday, Holy Saturday, Easter Sunday, May 1 Labour
Day, May 24 Battle of Pichincha, July 24 Bolívar's Birthday, August 10
Quito Independence Day, October 9 Guayaquil Independence Day,
October 12 Columbus Day, November 1 All Saints' Day, November 2 All
Souls' Day, November 3 Cuenca Independence Day, December 6
Foundation of Quito
Time GMT–5, EST
International telephone code + 593
Electricity 110V (same as US)
Flag Tricolour (yellow, blue, red) with the national seal in the centre

General Information

A traveler. I love his title. A traveler is to be reverenced as such. His profession is the best symbol of our life. Going from-toward; it is the history of every one of us.

Henry David Thoreau

GEOGRAPHY

Geographically, Ecuador is one of the most varied countries in the world, despite its small size (256,370km², about the size of the United Kingdom).

The Andean range is at its narrowest here and divides the country into three distinct regions: to the east of the Central Sierra lies the tropical rainforest of the upper Amazon basin (known as the Oriente) and to the west are the more accessible but equally hot and humid coastal lowlands. It is barely 200km from the western lowlands to the eastern jungle, yet within this narrow area are found peaks of up to 6,310m forming two major *cordilleras*, or mountain ranges.

These two cordilleras run north–south and are 40 to 60km apart. Between them lies the fertile Central Valley, which is about 400km long and contains Quito and most of Ecuador's major cities, as well as almost half of the country's inhabitants. It is this Central Valley that was called 'The Avenue of the Volcanoes' by the famous German explorer and scientist, Alexander von Humboldt, who visited Ecuador in 1802.

GEOLOGY

Tectonically Ecuador is similar to other countries around the 'Pacific Ring of Fire'. A dense oceanic plate (the Nazca Plate) is subducting under a less dense continental plate (the South American Plate). The collision of the two plates has resulted in the uplift of the Ecuadorian Andes and partial melting of the mantle below the South American Plate. The melts or magmas forming at the base of the South American Plate migrate along weaknesses in the earth's crust, eventually erupting on the surface to form volcanoes. Consequently the landscape of Ecuador is quite dynamic, with numerous eruptions and earthquakes, as well as lahars (volcanic mud flows) and landslides all constantly reforming the geography. These geological events have also caused a tremendous amount of destruction and loss of human life throughout the history of Ecuador.

The core of the Sierra was first uplifted in the Palaeozoic era (230 million years ago), and divides the drainages of the Oriente and the coast. The visually dominant geologic features in the Sierra are the short-lived (in geologic time) volcanoes represented mostly as numerous eroded volcanic edifices. An example of one of these extinct volcanoes is the craggy peak Cerro Imbabura, near the town of Otavalo.

Eight volcanoes are active, towering above the landscape and occasionally throwing out ash and lava flows to counteract the erosive work of lahars, glaciers and rivers. Cotopaxi (5,897m) is a classic and famous example of an active cone-shaped volcano. There are four volcanoes which have erupted in the past five years: Volcáns Sangay, Guagua Pichincha, Tungurahua and Reventador. Unfortunately these peaks are dangerous to climb, but are nonetheless very interesting to observe from a distance. If these volcanoes become dormant again, they will be climbable. The Smithsonian Global Volcanism Program (www.volcano.si.edu) or the Politecnic University in Quito (www.igepn.edu.ec) have up-to-date information on the status of all active volcanoes in Ecuador.

The Sierra is really two geologically distinct mountain ranges: the Cordillera Real (eastern range) and the Cordillera Occidental (western range). A system of generally north–south lying valleys (eg: the Central Valley or 'Valley of the Volcanoes') separates these two ranges in the northern part of the country. These valleys are down-dropped blocks or grabens and are filled with a thick layer of sediments and volcanic ash. These ash-filled valleys make for very fertile soil.

The basement rocks of the Cordillera Real are older (Palaeozoic) and consist mainly of high-grade metamorphic rocks like gneisses and mica-schists. These rocks were once buried deeply in the crust and exposed to high pressures and temperatures, but now are being uplifted towards the surface. However, basement rocks are generally not exposed in the Sierra because they are covered by a thick layer of volcanic material. They can be observed in the 'fold and thrust belt' on the eastern slope of the Andes (first you need to cut through the thick cloudforest to actually see the rock!). The Alpine-looking Cerro Sara Urco is made of this hard crystalline rock and so is good for rock climbing.

The basement rocks of the Cordillera Occidental, meanwhile, are volcanic units from the Cretaceous to Upper Tertiary periods that probably developed originally as an 'island arc' (like Japan) and were subsequently sutured on to the South American Plate. Intense volcanic activity has also covered the basement rocks in the Cordillera Occidental, but interesting outcrops of bedrock (such as quartzite and conglomerates) can be observed in the river valleys cutting down the western slopes (eg: Angamarca).

The coast is a 'fore-arc sedimentary basin' but is probably underlain by oceanic crust from the Mesozoic age – a piece of the oceanic crust that was sutured on to the South American Plate and is now covered by sediments. The geography consists of wide, hilly terrain mostly drained by the Río Guayas and Río Esmeraldas. There is a low coastal range (about 600m high) that was uplifted in the Neogene era (two to 22 million years ago) and which harbours some interesting coastal forest. Parque Nacional Machalilla and the Reserva Ecológica Mache-Chindul protect some of the remnant forests in this range.

The Oriente is a 'back-arc sedimentary basin'. Sediments eroded from the Sierra have been transported by rivers and deposited in this basin for millions of years. The transition zone between the eastern slope of the Sierra and the Oriente is faulted and folded, resulting in several small cordilleras and hilly geomorphology. These largely unvisited ridges and peaks on the eastern slope of the Sierra extend into the Oriente (eg: Cordillera de Los Guacamayos or Vieja Cordillera de Cutucú). There are also several anomalous volcanoes – completely separated from the Sierra – that poke up through the jungle in the Oriente. The most important are Volcán Reventador (3,562m) and Volcán Sumaco (3,732m), both of which are active and relatively inaccessible.

Farther east in the Oriente, the sediments are more flat-lying and less deformed. This area was once a shallow inland sea that harboured swampy vegetation. As the organic material was buried and heated it was converted to oil and natural gas which has been trapped in fold axes and faults. Texaco discovered this oil near Lago

Agrio in the late 1960s, an event that has radically changed the environment of the Oriente. Towns, an infrastructure of roads and oil pipelines, and an alarmingly high rate of deforestation have resulted in profound changes to the ecosystem.

HISTORY

Very little is known of the earliest history of the area. In the early 1400s at least six linguistic groups were recognised in the highlands alone (the Pasto, Cara, Panzaleo, Puruhá, Cañari, and Palta) and by the middle of the century the Caras had gained a dominant position. They overpowered a minor tribe, the Quitus (hence Quito), forming the kingdom of the Shyris which was the major presence in the area at the time of Inca expansion from the south. Despite several years of resistance, the Shyris and nearby lesser groups were integrated into the Inca Empire by about 1490.

In 1525 the Inca leader Huayna Capac died, dividing his empire between two sons. Atahualpa, of Shyri descent on his mother's side, became ruler of the northern part of the empire, whilst Huáscar received the rest. Violent civil war between the two brothers followed and Atahualpa won. Thus, when the Spanish conquest began in 1532, the Inca Empire had been severely weakened by the civil war. Atahualpa was captured and paid a huge ransom in gold and silver for his release; despite this he was murdered by Spanish conquistador Francisco Pizarro and the Inca Empire effectively came to an end.

In 1534 Sebastián de Benalcázar founded Quito on the ruins of the old Shyri city. After the success of the Spanish conquest the area became known as the Audiencia de Quito, and (except for a period of six years) remained under the viceroy of Peru until 1740, when it became part of the Viceroyalty of Nueva Granada. The 16th to 18th centuries were characterised by peaceful colonialism. Agriculture was developed, the indigenous people were exploited, and Spain profited.

By the 19th century, in common with other parts of South America, a strong independence movement had developed. From 1809 several unsuccessful attempts were made at establishing independence, but it was not until May 24 1822 that Mariscal Sucre finally defeated the royalist forces at the Battle of Pichincha. Although free of the Spanish, the area then became part of Gran Colombia, and it took over eight more years before Ecuador became completely independent under the leadership of its first president, General Juan José Flores.

The rest of the 19th century was a continuous struggle between conservatives and liberals. By the end of the 1800s Ecuador was under the military rule of General Eloy Alfaro and much of the 20th century has seen a succession of unstable military governments. A civilian leader, President Jaime Roldós, was elected in 1979, and after his untimely death in an air accident was succeeded in 1981 by his Vice-President, Osvaldo Hurtado Larrea. Since then, the country has continued to elect civilian governments democratically, with the conservative León Febres Cordero serving from 1984 to 1988 and the leftist social democrat Rodrigo Borja Cevellos from 1988 to 1992, whose policies left the country in an economically weakened state. He was succeeded by the right-wing Sixto Durán Ballén, of the Republican Unity Party, who governed from 1992 to 1996. Durán attempted to strengthen the economy by privatisation and development of the country's Amazonian oil reserves, but ran into strong opposition from trade unionists and environmentalists.

The populist Abdala Bucaram, campaigning on promises to provide cheaper housing and food staples, was elected to the office of president to serve until 2000, but his presidency quickly became an economic disaster overseen by a carousing and incompetent leader. Bucaram was ousted by a congressional vote in early

1997 after congress claimed that Bucaram was mentally unfit to lead the country; he fled from Ecuador to Panama and now lives in exile. Fabián Alarcón, then president of the congress, served out Bucaram's term. After leaving office Alarcón was briefly jailed for corruption, but eventually released. Jamil Mahuad, a Harvard-educated economist of the Popular Democrat Party, was elected in 1998 (after early elections were called), but his term was tarnished by a banking scandal followed by a widely unpopular devaluation of the sucre and the dollarisation of the economy. This prompted a national strike in January 2000, which was led by representatives of the Confederation of the Indigenous Nations of Ecuador (CONAIE) along with some military officers. They forced Mahuad to resign and his term was served out by his vice-president, Gustavo Noboa, until January 2003. Army colonel Lucio Gutiérrez, one of the former coup leaders who ousted Mahuad, was elected and took office in 2003.

Chronology

1527   First Spanish contact; Pizarro's men land at Esmeraldas, in northern Ecuador
1535   Incorporated into the Viceroyalty of Peru; Ecuador is known as the Audiencia de Quito
1822   Ecuador gains independence from Spain after the Battle of Pichincha on May 24, under the leadership of Mariscal Sucre. Incorporated into Gran Colombia
1830   Becomes fully independent under first president, Juan Flores
1942   War with Peru; much of the Ecuadorian Amazon lost to Peru but Ecuador still claims this region
1979   First democratic elections in seven years
1999   Dollarisation of national currency
2003   President Lucio Gutiérrez elected until 2007

PEOPLE

The population in 2002 was estimated at 13.5 million. This is approximately ten times the number of indigenous people estimated to have been living in the area at the time of the Spanish conquest. The population density of 53 people per square kilometre is the highest in South America.

About 65% of this total are *mestizos* (mixed European-indigenous heritage), 25% are indigenous, 7% are of European descent and the remainder are black and other minorities.

The majority of the indigenous people are Quechua speaking and live in the highlands; they are the direct descendants of the inhabitants of the Inca Empire. There are also several small groups living in the lowlands and speaking their own distinct languages. These tribes include, among others, the Quechua, Shuar, Achuar, Huaorani, Cofán, Secoya, Siona and Zaparo of the Oriente and the Montuvio, Chachi, Awá and Tsachila of the coastal plain. The highland Quechua indigenous people are often bilingual, although Spanish is a second language and not much used in remote areas. Until the land reforms of the 1960s the majority of the Quichuas were little more than slaves to the big *hacienda* owners. Nowadays they live in self-governing co-operatives and own land, but nevertheless often still live at a subsistence level.

Some Quechua communities, notably the Otavaleños and to a lesser extent the Salasacas and Cañaris, have developed a reputation for being excellent weavers and craftsmen; their goods are in great demand, not only by tourists but also by export markets in Europe, North America and other South American countries. After some time in Ecuador you will notice the different styles of clothing that individual groups traditionally wear. The Otavalo men are characterised by their white, calf-length trousers, rope sandals, grey or blue ponchos, and a long single braid of hair. The women wear a colourfully embroidered blouse and a bulky gold-coloured necklace. The Salasaca men, meanwhile, wear distinctive broad-brimmed white hats, white shirts, and black ponchos. The indigenous people of the Saquisilí area are most often seen wearing red ponchos and little felt 'pork pie' hats.

Another interesting and attractive feature of indigenous life is the fiestas which often celebrate church holidays. One of the best fiestas is All Souls Day (November 2), when throngs of people visit cemeteries to pay their respects to the dead. Everyone does this, from rich Quiteños to poor *campesinos* (peasants), but the cemeteries near the indigenous villages are the most colourful. Hundreds of people show up in their best clothes and leave wreaths and flowers on the graves. To ensure that their departed friends and relatives also enjoy the day, people bring food and drink and leave some in remembrance and offering. The majority of the food and drink is, of course, consumed by the indigenous people themselves, and the atmosphere is generally festive rather than sombre.

CLIMATE

Most descriptions of Ecuador's climate agree that its most reliable aspect is its unreliability. Unfortunately, this really seems to be the case, so I can't give you foolproof advice on which months will be best for your visit. However, here are some generalisations.

In common with other tropical countries, Ecuador does not experience the four seasons known in temperate parts of the world. Instead there are wet and dry seasons. Despite its small size, Ecuador has several distinct climatic zones, with wet and dry periods varying from area to area.

The coastal areas are influenced by the cold Humboldt current which flows up from the South Pacific, but during December a warm current from the north, seasonably called 'El Niño' (the Christ Child) predominates. This marks the beginning of the coastal rainy season. The northern coast is wet from January to June and dryish for the rest of the year, while further south the coast experiences a shorter wet season and in the dry season, from May to December, it is much drier than in the north. The effects of el Niño are not yet fully understood, and in some years there are devastating floods in the coastal lowlands during the wet season.

Inland, the climate is completely different. It rains most of the time in the Oriente, though some months (January and August) are a little less wet than others. The weather in the mountains varies from east to west. The eastern mountains, especially Antisana, El Altar and Sangay, and to a lesser extent Cayambe and Tungurahua, are influenced by air from the Amazonian lowlands. Their wettest months are June, July and August. December and January are when the highest number of successful ascents have been made on the difficult El Altar. Ecuadorian climbers favour February for climbing Antisana, and October through to January are suggested for Cayambe.

The situation is reversed in the western mountains. Here, the dry season is from late June through to early September, with a short dry spell in December and early January. The wettest months are February to May, with April being the wettest of all. Edward Whymper claims to have spent 78 days in the vicinity of Iliniza during February to April of 1880 '…yet we did not see the whole of the mountain on any single occasion.' During the dry season temperatures tend to be very low at night and high winds can be a problem, particularly in August. The weather in October and

November tends to be variable. Snow build-up during these months sometimes provides quite good snow conditions for the short December–January season.

The temperature variation is mainly influenced by altitude. From sea level to about 900m it is generally hot, with an average temperature of 26–28°C. The warm zone is from 900m to 2,000m with an average temperature range of 20–26°C. From 2,000m to 3,000m it is quite cold with an average of 12–20°C (remember average includes warm afternoons and freezing nights). Above 3,000m is the *páramo* with temperatures averaging from 0–12°C, and above the lowest snowline at about 4,500m the mean temperature stays below freezing, although the strong sun sometimes makes it feel much warmer.

There have been historical changes in Ecuador's climate. Ecuador has been experiencing a period of relative drought and warming compared with a century ago (although this is difficult to believe when you are caught in a torrential Ecuadorian downpour). This has also contributed to the receding of the glaciers on Ecuador's mountains. Theories on this climate change are attributed variously to global warming, el Niño or the deforestation in the highlands of Ecuador.

Detailed records have been kept only since about 1900, but from these it is known that there have been el Niño events in 1900, 1912, 1922, 1919, 1925–26, 1932, 1940–41, 1953, 1957–58, 1965, 1972–73, 1976, 1982–83, 1986, 1992–93 and 1997–98. An el Niño event involves uncharacteristically wet weather, and is often followed by a la Niña event, which is much drier. The drier years cause a significant reduction or disappearance of glaciers. Many peaks mapped with permanent snow cover on older IGM maps are now only perennially covered. Examples include Iliniza Norte, Sincholagua and Sara Urco. After the wet year of 1998 more snow and ice were again found on these peaks, but the last few years have been considerably drier, as evidenced by the glacial recession on most of them.

Not only is there variation in the climate from year to year, but the daily weather is also highly unpredictable. There is a local saying that in the mountains all four seasons can be experienced in one day. As Michaux notes in his book *Ecuador: A Travel Journal* (1928):

> Morning summer.
> Noon springtime. The sky is beginning to get overcast.
> 4 p.m. rain. Freshness.
> A night cold and luminous like winter.
> For this reason clothing is a problem if you must be out for more than a few hours.
> You watch the accursed setting forth, armed with straw hat, canvas, furpiece, and umbrella.

It is amazing and confusing that so much variation can be found in such a small area. With windows of good weather and seasonal variations, climbing any given mountain in any given month is feasible. However, as a general rule of thumb, December and January are the best months to be in the Ecuadorian mountains and March to May the worst. If you're there in June through to September, avoid the east and climb in the west. In October through to February concentrate on the east. Cotopaxi lies in a strange dry micro-climate all of its own and can be climbed during most of the year.

MOUNTAINEERING – A HISTORICAL VIEW

Despite some legends there is no evidence, as found in the more southerly countries of South America, of any mountain ascents by the local indigenous people prior to the arrival of the Spanish conquistadors who contented themselves with noting major volcanic activity in their journals, their first records being of the eruptions of Cotopaxi and Tungurahua in 1534. The earliest recorded ascent is that of the Ecuadorian★ José Toribio Ortiguera, who reached the crater of Pichincha in 1582. There is a disputed record of an ascent of Pichincha by Padre Juan Romero in 1660, the same year that a major eruption buried Quito in 40cm of volcanic ash, but generally speaking during the first two centuries of Spanish occupation there was little interest in the geographical aspects of the country. The windfall of a treasure-laden Inca civilisation was something the Spaniards wished to exploit themselves and so all foreign visitors, including natural historians or explorers, were regarded with suspicion. It was not until well into the 18th century that a European scientific expedition was first permitted to make a serious attempt at mapping and exploring Ecuador and this led to an awakening of interest in the mountains of the country. By the beginning of the 18th century it had been established that the world was round, but controversy still raged over the concept of polar flattening. In an attempt to settle the issue, the French Académie des Sciences organised expeditions to the Arctic and the Equator. At this time Africa was still the 'dark continent', Indonesia was little known, and the Amazon Basin was virtually unexplored. Consequently Ecuador, with its capital just 25km south of the Equator, was the obvious venue for such an expedition. This took place from 1736 to 1744 and was led by the Frenchman Charles-Marie de la Condamine, accompanied by two countrymen, two Spaniards, and an Ecuadorian. Surveying was undertaken, and their calculations of the distance from the Equator to the North Pole became the basis of the metric system of weights and measures (a metre was originally defined as one ten-millionth of the distance between the North Pole and the Equator). The flora, fauna, geology and geography were also studied. The explorers were very interested in the highlands, and during the course of their investigations concluded that Chimborazo (6,310m) was the highest peak in the world – a belief which existed until the 1820s. They made the first serious attempt to scale this mountain, reaching an altitude of about 4,750m. The less important peaks of Pichincha (4,675m) and El Corazón (4,788m) were also successfully climbed and most of the country's major peaks were surveyed.

This expedition's surveys and measurements started a series of disputes which have not been resolved to this day. For example Cotopaxi, Ecuador's second highest peak, was measured at 5,751m by de la Condamine's expedition. Successive expeditions turned in considerably higher measurements: 5,753m by Humboldt in 1802, 5,978m by Whymper in 1880, 5,940m by Martínez in 1906, and the highest of all, 6,005m, was published by Arthur Eichler in his book *Ecuador – Snow Peaks and Jungles* in1970. His is the only figure of over 6,000m; the height most generally accepted today is 5,897m, as surveyed by the Instituto Geográfico Militar in 1972. Nevertheless many recent sources are still unable to agree on the correct elevation. The same perplexing situation exists with other peaks (see *Appendix 2*, page 249).

After the departure of the French expedition, the rest of the 18th century saw no more major exploration of the Ecuadorian mountains. It was not until 1802 that an expedition led by the famous German scientist and explorer Baron Alexander von Humboldt reawakened interest in the Ecuadorian Highlands. Humboldt visited and studied various peaks including Cotopaxi, Pichincha, Antisana and El Altar, but it is for his research on and attempted ascent of

---

★Note: We use 'Ecuadorian' for convenience here and later in the chapter although the country was not known by that name until 1830.

Chimborazo that his expedition is particularly remembered by mountaineers. Accompanied by the Frenchman Aimé Bonpland and the Ecuadorian Carlos Montúfar, he identified many plants – including some new species – as well as noting barometric data during his attempted ascent of the southern flanks of the mountain. He made a sectional sketch map of Chimborazo which shows the plant species, various geographical landmarks, the expedition's penetration beyond the snowline and finally, high above the surrounding *páramo* the comment, 'Crevasse qui empêcha les voyageurs d'attendre la cime' (crevasse which prevents travellers from reaching the summit). This indicates the point at about 5,875m where Humboldt and his companions, suffering from altitude sickness, with cracked and bleeding lips and badly sun-burned faces, were forced to turn back. This attempt is particularly noteworthy since despite their failure to gain the summit, they did reach the highest point thus far attained by Western man. Since Chimborazo was still considered the highest mountain in the world, other attempts on its summit soon followed. The Venezuelan liberator of the Andean countries, Simon Bolívar, climbed to the snowline in 1822 and nine years later Bolívar's colonel, the French agronomist Joseph Boussingault, managed to reach about 6,000m on Chimborazo's southern slopes, again increasing the altitude thus far attained by Western explorers. Boussingault also made several attempts on other peaks, but without notable success.

President Gabriel García Moreno, a much-criticised and despotic ruler, was nevertheless the first Ecuadorian leader to take an active interest in the environment. He enacted several conservationist laws, and in 1844 he climbed to the crater of Pichincha. In succeeding years several European expeditions arrived. In 1847 the almost forgotten Italian traveller Gaetano Osculati spent a year in Ecuador, and although he made no attempts to climb any of its peaks he left us with some interesting paintings and drawings of Ecuadorian mountains. 1849 saw the first recorded expedition to the highly active volcano Sangay (5,230m) where the Frenchman Sebastian Wisse counted 267 strong explosions in one hour. During the 1850s and 1860s several expeditions from various nations visited Ecuador but achieved little, and it was not until 1872 that the next major breakthrough in Ecuadorian mountaineering occurred.

In this year the German Wilhelm Reiss, accompanied by the Colombian Angelm Escobar, succeeded in reaching the 5,897m summit of Cotopaxi by climbing the southeastern flank, rather than the northern route which has since become accepted as the normal route. The following year another German, Alfonso Stübel, accompanied by four Ecuadorians, Eusebio Rodriguez, Melchor Páez, Vicente Ramón and Rafael Jantui, reached the summit via the same route: it was the first major peak to have been climbed by Ecuadorians. The two Germans then joined forces and in 1873 made the first ascent of the active volcano Tungurahua (5,029m) as well as attempts on other summits.

A disastrous volcanic eruption on June 26 1877 left the slopes of Cotopaxi bare of ice and snow, and several climbers took advantage of this situation and climbed the volcano by the northeast side. Then a remarkable expedition in 1880, led by the renowned English climber Edward Whymper, succeeded in reaching the summit and spending a night by Cotopaxi's crater. Whymper had already established his reputation as a climber by making the first ascent of the Matterhorn, at one time reputed to be impossible. His Ecuadorian expedition must surely rate as one of the most successful mountaineering expeditions ever undertaken: with the Italian cousins Louis and Jean-Antoine Carrel, Whymper proceeded to climb not only Cotopaxi but also made the first ascent of Chimborazo, a climb which raised a storm of disbelief and protest. To quell his critics Whymper repeated the climb later in 1880 accompanied by two Ecuadorians, David Beltrán and Francisco Campaña. Ecuador's third highest peak, Cayambe (5,790m), and Antisana (5,704m), the fourth highest, also fell to the ice axes of Whymper and the Carrels as did Iliniza Sur (5,248m), Carihuairazo (5,020m), Sincholagua (4,898m), Cotacachi (4,944m) and Sara Urco (4,676m). In addition to these eight first ascents, several other climbs were made by this expedition, including ascents of El Corazón and Pichincha and an unsuccessful attempt on El Altar (5,319m), which is Ecuador's most technical snow peak and which was not finally climbed until 1963. Edward Whymper is remembered in Ecuador to this day; there is a street named after him in Quito and the country's highest mountaineers' refuge, the new and well-equipped hut at 5,000m on Chimborazo's eastern slopes, has been named Refugio Whymper.

After Whymper's memorable exploits no important expeditions occurred until the 20th century. Whereas the 19th century had seen many important European expeditions to the Ecuadorian Andes, the 20th century saw an awakening of interest in mountaineering by national climbers. The father of Ecuadorian mountaineering is Nicolás Martínez, who in the first decades of this century succeeded in making many notable ascents. In 1900 Martínez climbed Tungurahua (5,029m), and in succeeding years climbed this peak several more times. His interest in mountaineering awakened, Martínez made first Ecuadorian ascents of many major peaks: Antisana in 1904, a failed attempt on Cayambe in 1905, and successful climbs of Cotopaxi and Chimborazo in 1906. Succeeding years saw various successes and failures in Martínez's climbing career. A particularly noteworthy ascent was that of Iliniza Norte in 1912; this 5,126m peak is the only one of Ecuador's ten 5,000m peaks which was first climbed by an Ecuadorian.

World War I and its aftermath left little time or money for new foreign expeditions to Ecuador and it was not until 1929 that a United States expedition, led by Robert T Moore, achieved the first ascent of Sangay (5,230m). This, the most continuously active volcano in Latin America, was experiencing a rare period of tranquillity at the time. Moore's expedition also made various other notable climbs, including the first US ascent of Chimborazo.

By 1929 all but one of the major Ecuadorian peaks (the ten 5,000m ones) had been conquered. The exception was El Altar (5,319m), Ecuador's fifth highest peak, which was not climbed until 1963 when an Italian Alpine Club expedition led by Marino Tremonti succeeded in reaching the summit. In the intervening years many repeat ascents of the major peaks were made by climbers of various nationalities and several minor peaks were conquered for the first time. These included Cerro Hermoso (4,571m) by four Germans in 1941 and Quilindaña (4,877m) by a large party of Ecuadorians, Colombians, Frenchmen and Italians in 1952.

In the 1940s two Ecuadorian mountaineering clubs (Quito Nuevos Horizontes and Ascencionismo del Colegio San Gabriel) were established, which ushered in the modern era of climbing for Ecuadorians. The founders of San Gabriel were Hernán Rodriguez Castelo, Luis Andrade Reimers and Padre Salvador Cevallos. Largely through the efforts of these clubs, Ecuadorians began to take a strong interest in climbing and numbers began to grow through the 1950s. Padre José Rivas has been instrumental in supporting the young climbers of the San Gabriel climbing club for over 50 years. He is famous for giving a mass on the summit of Cotopaxi in 1979. He also raised funds for the construction of the Cotopaxi and Cayambe refuges. He is now in his seventies and still climbs!

The 1960s and 1970s saw a new approach to mountaineering in Ecuador. With Tremonti's first ascent of El Altar in 1963 all the major peaks had been climbed and emphasis was laid on climbing new routes and lower summits of the more important mountains. El Altar's eight other virgin peaks provided great impetus and excitement to Ecuadorian mountaineering as, one by one, they were climbed between 1965 and 1979 by climbers of various nationalities, including three first ascents by Ecuadorian climbers. During these decades Ecuadorian mountaineers were consistently in the forefront of finding new climbs, such as the second and third summits of Antisana, new routes on Cayambe and Iliniza Sur, the Central Summit on Chimborazo, the first ascents of the minor peaks of Achipungo and Ayapungo, and many others too numerous to mention. In connection with these new climbs the names of the Ecuadorians Bernardo Beate, Marco Cruz, César Ruales, Carlos Oleas, Fausto Ayarza, Humberto Sanchez, Milton Moreno, Ramiro Navarrete, Romulo Pazmiño, Hernán and Mauricio Reinoso, Santiago Rivadeneira, Hugo Torres, Iván Rojas, Luis Naranjo, Sixto Rosero, Digna Mesa, Rogelio López, Patricio Loayaza, Jimmy Desrosiers, Paul Williams, Fabián Almeida, José Moreano, Roberto Fuentes, Marcos Suárez, Marcos Serrano, Fabián Cáceres, Marcos Cevallos, Ramón Gómez, Danny Moreno, Santiago Palacios, Omar Cevallos, Belisario Chiriboga, American James Desrossiers and Frenchman Joseph Bergé will long be remembered. Many Ecuadorian climbers also made notable ascents in different parts of the world. Particular mention should go to Fabián Zurita, who, perhaps more than any other Ecuadorian, has brought the mountains of Ecuador closer to its people through his frequent and non-technical articles in the Ecuadorian press and his summer mountaineering camps AIRE LIBRE.

This generation of climbers formed the provincial association of mountaineering clubs (AEAP) and founded the provincial mountaineering school (Escuela Provincial de Alta Montaña – EPAM) in 1974. This school helped bring new standards to climbing in Ecuador. Some of the clubs associated with AEAP are the Universidad Central (Ingeniería), ESPE and Universidad Catolica, which are all still active.

The leaders of the next generation of climbers who emerged in the 1980–1990s include Peter Ayarza, Oswaldo Freire, Gabriel Llanos, Oswaldo Alcocer, Pablo Fernandez, Galo Bustos, José Luis Peralbo, Mario Vásconez, Julio Mesías, Oswaldo Leiva, Jürg Arnet, César Román, José Landázuri, Javier Ruales, Margarita Arboleda, Arecely Buchely, Diego Castillo, Edison Salgado, Juan Espinosa, Fabricio Avilés, Edison Oña, Santiago Quintero, Fernando Benalcazar, Roberto Gutierrez, Danilo Mayorga, Jorge Peñafiel, Diego Zurita, Javier Cabrera, Jaime Avila, Pablo Cruz, Carlos Stacey, Gaspar Navarrete, Javier Herrera, Oswaldo Morales. These climbers were more focused on new technical routes. This highly ambitious and well-trained group of Ecuadorians have also ventured to other ranges in Peru, Bolivia and the Himalayas. Some of their accomplishments in Ecuador are listed below:

The north face of El Altar was summited from inside the crater by Oswaldo Morales and Gilles de Lataillade on December 10 1984.

The south face of Canónigo of Altar was summited from inside the crater by Luis Naranjo and Mauricio Reinoso on December 30 1984.

The west face of Tabernáculo of El Altar was summited by Luis Naranjo, Mauricio Reinoso, Fabián Cáceres and Peter Ayarza on December 28 1987.

The east face of South Peak of Rumiñahui was summited by Pablo Fernandez, Galo Bustos and Pablo Cruz on October 15 1993.

The very challenging southeast ridge of the south peak of Antisana was summited by Oswaldo Freire, Gabriel Llanos and Oswaldo Alcocer on December 28 1993.

All 12 of El Altar's peaks were summited during a single expedition in December 1995 by Oswaldo Freire and Gabriel Llano, assisted by Edison Oña and Oswaldo Alcocer.

The northeast face of Cotopaxi was summited by Jurg Arnet, Gabriel Llano and Gaspar Navarrete in May 1997.

The first ascent of the Yanasacha rock face on Cotopaxi was completed by Eduardo Agama, Edison Salgado, Jorge Peñafiel and Danilo Mayorga on May 1 1989.

The first solo ascent of the Yanasacha rock face on Cotopaxi was accomplished by Santiago Quintero in 2002.

Extremely difficult routes like Arista del Sol Canónigo of El Altar, Arista Helena of Cayambe, and a second ascent of the north face of El Obispo have been unsuccessful to date. These routes have been attempted by Jorge Anhalzer, César Román, Gaspar Naverrete, Edison Oña, Julio Mesías, Luis Naranjo and William Navarrete.

Gabriel Llanos, a prolific guide with hundreds of ascents of the major Ecuadorian peaks, tragically died guiding in Bolivia in 2002.

Sport climbing also became popular in the 1990s in Quito and Cuenca. This different breed of climber is more focused on artificial wall climbing, bolted routes and competitions.

A climbing group consisting of indigenous women (Huarmirazu, 'Women of the snow-capped mountains') was organised by Dana Platin. They climbed Chimborazo in 1999 and Cotopaxi in 2001.

Since the 1960s mountaineering in Ecuador has become an economically important tourist asset. Consequently refuges have been constructed to accommodate foreign as well as national climbers. The first of these was the now destroyed Fabian Zurita refuge built in 1964 at 4,900m on the northwest slopes of Chimborazo. Since then several more mountain huts have been built and upgraded on Chimborazo, Iliniza, Cotopaxi, Cayambe, Tungurahua, Sangay, Cerro Hermoso and Pichincha.

Today, with its network of climbing huts and their easy accessibility, Ecuador has become an important mountaineering centre attracting thousands of climbers a year. For professionals and experts it still provides the opportunity for good new routes, but it is of particular interest to intermediate climbers who wish to experience the excitement of high-altitude ascents on mountains that aren't necessarily technically demanding. It is also very useful as a high-altitude training ground for climbers wishing to test and improve their skills before attempting ascents in the difficult mountains of the more southern Andes.

Bradt Travel Guides is a partner to the 'know before you go' campaign, masterminded by the UK Foreign and Commonwealth Office to promote the importance of finding out about a destination before you travel. By combining the up-to-date advice of the FCO with the in-depth knowledge of Bradt authors, you'll ensure that your trip will be as trouble-free as possible.

www.fco.gov.uk/knowbeforeyougo

Preparations

A journey is a person in itself; no two are alike. And all plans, safeguards, policies and coercion are fruitless. We find after years of struggle that we do not take a trip; a trip takes us.

John Steinbeck

GETTING THERE

From Europe there are direct flights on major airlines but these are expensive. Discounted tickets are often available, and as Ecuador is well placed for overland journeys to or from Peru, look out too for cheap flights to those destinations. Bear in mind that there is a 12% tax on air tickets bought in Ecuador and a $25 departure tax (payable in cash) from Quito airport for international flights.

Tour operators
UK

Adventure Bound 19 Gloster Rd, Martlesham Heath, Suffolk IP5 3RB; tel: 01473 667337; fax: 01473 614566; email: info@adventurebound.co.uk; web: www.adventurebound.co.uk

Footloose Adventure Travel 3 Springs Pavement, Ilkley, West Yorks LS29 8HD; tel: 01943 604030; fax: 01943 604070; email: info@footlooseadventure.co.uk; web: www.footlooseadventure.co.uk

High Places Globe Centre, Penistone Rd, Sheffield S6 3AE; tel: 0114 275 7500; fax: 0114 275 3870; email: info@highplaces.co.uk; web: www.highplaces.co.uk

Journey Latin America 12–13 Heathfield Terrace, Chiswick, London W4 4JE; tel: 020 8747 8315; fax: 0120 8742 1312; email: sales@journeylatinamerica.co.uk; web: www.journeylatinamerica.co.uk. The experts in arranging discounted fares for this part of the world, and pleased to answer unusual travel queries from their customers.

Terra Firma Travel Eunant, Lake Vyrnwy, Powys SY10 0NF; tel/fax: 01691 870321; email: info@terrafirmatravel.com; web: www.terrafirmatravel.com

Windows on the Wild 2 Oxford House, 24 Oxford Rd, London W4 4DH; tel: 020 8742 1556; fax: 020 8747 4331; email: info@gofishingworldwide.co.uk; web: www.go-fishing-worldwide.com

White Peak Expeditions Hockerill AEC, Dunmow Rd, Bishops Stortford, Herts CM23 5HX; tel: 01279 654401; fax: 01279 654406; email: info@whitepeakexpeditions.co.uk; web: www.whitepeakexpeditions.co.uk

Ecuador

Ecuaviajes (tel: 2 2249810) or **Oriental** (tel: 2 2260900) in Quito are good at finding the cheapest way to travel from Ecuador to other parts of the world.

Julio Verne Travel Calle El Espectador 22–25 y Avenida Daniel Leon Borja, Riobamba; tel: +593 (0)3 2963436; fax: +593 (0)3 2963436; email: julioverne@andinanet.net; web: www.julioverne-travel.com

North America

There are inexpensive flights on both US and Latin American carriers. Try **ExitoTravel** (Latin America travel specialists located in the USA; tel: 1 800 655 4053; web: www.exitotravel.com) or if you are a student **STA** (tel: 1 800 329 9537).

Finally, passenger and cargo ships call at Guayaquil from all over the world, but voyages are often more expensive than flights.

Documents

All visitors need a passport valid for at least six months and a tourist card which is valid for up to 90 days and is available from any port of entry. On arrival, tell them you want 90 days, as occasionally the guards will put less time on your visa. You are legally required to be able to show evidence of 'sufficient funds' (as much as $20 per day) and an exit ticket out of the country, but this is rarely asked for, particularly if travelling overland. Your tourist card is easily renewed at the Dirección Nacional de Migración in Quito at the junction of Av Amazonas and Av Republica, and in other major cities, but tourists are allowed a maximum of only 90 days in any one calendar year. Obtaining permission for a longer stay, however, is relatively easy. Tourist visas can be renewed after the maxiumum 90 days for an additional 30 days at the Jefatura Provincial de Migracion on Isla Seymour and the Río Coca, tel: 2 2247510. There is no fee for this extension. Normally only three extensions (for a total of another 90 days) are granted. Technically the fee is a fine paid in advance to Immigration for overstaying the 'official' 90-day tourist visa. Under no circumstances should you allow your visa to expire while you are in the country; on-the-spot police checks are frequent and a trip to jail possible if you do not have your passport and visas in order. You can obtain a notarised copy of your passport at any Notary Public. These copies are recognised by Ecuadorian authorities. Usually the staff at the SAE in Quito can give you up-to-date advice on how to extend your stay in Ecuador.

WHAT TO TAKE

In the words of 19th-century explorer and mountaineer Edward Whymper, 'It is indeed true that nearly everything may be obtained in Ecuador. It is also true that we often had great difficulty in obtaining anything.' Although a good selection of climbing and backpacking equipment is available for sale and hire in Ecuador, it can be expensive. If you're large then you'll have difficulty in finding clothing – and particularly footwear – to fit you, since Ecuadorians are generally small. It is best to bring what you need with you. It is easy enough to find storage facilities for your excess gear whilst you are hiking or climbing.

The following checklists reflect the fact that while you may be a mountaineer one day, you'll be just a tourist the next. We have included everything we consider useful, but doubtless some people's needs will differ from ours.

Camping equipment
Backpack

Bear in mind that an external frame pack, while very comfortable in warm weather, is awkward if hitchhiking and liable to break during the rough treatment it will receive on planes, buses and trucks. External frame packs tend to snag on everything from hotel doors to tropical vegetation and to throw the climber off balance; an internal frame or frameless pack hugs the body better. Buy as large a pack as you can – when the weather's terrible and your hands are cold it's easier to stuff a sopping wet tent and gear into a large pack than to struggle with a small one which held everything so snugly when you were warm and dry in your hotel. Having said that, just because you have lots of space doesn't mean you have to fill it – avoid over-packing, and bear in mind that what feels comfortable in the aforementioned hotel may feel much heavier halfway up a mountain at altitude. It is better to avoid backpack designs with many pockets, zippers and other accesses that make it easier for thieves to steal your gear.

Sleeping bag

It gets cold in Ecuador, but not very cold. Even when mountaineering high above the snowline, temperatures below –10°C are not very common, so you don't need the most expensive sleeping bag money can buy. A medium-weight one is adequate, especially if combined with a bivouac sac (waterproof and breathable sleeping bag cover) or a down jacket. If you plan on doing a lot of backpacking then you should consider a bag with artificial filling, because it will stay fairly warm when wet, whilst a soggy down bag is almost useless. At present artificial fillings are cheaper than down, though they are heavier and bulkier, but lighter materials are constantly being developed.

Sleeping mat

This is essential. Any closed cell foam pad will do. A cheap light one works as well as more expensive ones for insulation (which is the most important thing), although for comfort you may want a more elaborate one such as a Therm-A-Rest, which is a combination air mattress/foam pad.

Tent

You can manage without a tent if you climb only the major peaks, as good mountain refuges are available. If planning extended hikes or climbs, however, you'll need a tent which is waterproof and withstands buffeting by high winds, although some climbers make do with bivouac sacs instead. All tent seams must be carefully waterproofed with seam-sealer before leaving home.

Stove

Three of Ecuador's climbers' huts have kitchens with stoves, but if you plan trips away from the huts you'll need a stove as there is little firewood in the highlands. The best stoves for high altitudes are manufactured by MSR; some models run on paraffin (or kerosene, sold as 'Kerex' in Ecuador), white gas (which is becoming easier to find in Ecuador), and even car and aviation fuel. Another very good stove is the Bleuet Gaz 200 which operates on gas cartridges which are obtainable in Ecuador as well as in Europe and the USA. If you use this stove don't litter the mountains with 'dead' cartridges, and remember that you can't carry them on aeroplanes.

Cooking utensils and cutlery

Bring your own or buy them in Ecuador; the locals use cheap, lightweight pans which are available in any town. Aluminium spoons and plastic cups are also easily found. For larger groups the weight of a pressure cooker is offset by the need to carry less fuel. You can also cook dry beans, potatoes and rice quickly, thus saving money on not buying instant meals. They are also great for 'steam washing' dishes on a cold evening.

Water bottle

Carry several light, plastic water bottles for water. Alternatively, you can purchase 2-litre soda bottles or 1-litre Gatorade bottles when you arrive, which work just as well as commercially available water bottles.

Light

Being on the Equator means you can be sure of one thing: 12 hours of darkness. So you'll be needing light more than in the northern summers. Torches (flashlights), headlamps and batteries are usually available throughout Ecuador, as are candles. Slow-burning candles are particularly useful but sometimes difficult to find in Ecuador. For large groups you can bring a lantern to fit Bleuet Gaz cartridges (available locally).

Food

With a little imagination you can find plenty of food suitable for backpacking and climbing in Ecuador's supermarkets and stores. Freeze-dried food can sometimes be purchased in the outdoor shops, but you can also find noodles, dried soups, chocolate, raisins, nuts, oatmeal, powdered juices, dried milk, cheese, crackers, biscuits, salami, cans of fish and peanut butter. Some of the large supermarkets like Supermaxi and Mi Comisario have close to the same selection you find in the States. If there is a special outdoor snack you prefer, it is better to bring it from home.

Shoes and clothing
Footwear

You can climb most peaks with heavy hiking boots although double mountaineering boots (with a soft inner and a hard, plastic outer) are warmer. Medium-weight hiking boots are adequate for all the hikes and some of the lesser peaks. Rock-climbing boots with smooth rubber soles are only needed if you plan to do some technical rock climbing at the limited sport climbing areas and artificial walls. By far the most common footwear for walking in Ecuador are knee-high rubber boots (*botas de gaucho*), equivalent to the British wellingtons. These are especially good for jungle and swampy *páramo* excursions. Once you get used to them they keep your feet cosy and dry, but beware of blisters (tape your feet or wear extra socks) and the lack of ankle support. The Venus brand is considered one of the best; a pair can be picked up for about $10. Field scientists who have been down here for a few years have been seen practising *salsa* in them! Also bring a pair of light shoes, trainers or sandals, for sitting around camp and walking in cities, and some rubber thongs (flip-flops) for use in dubious hotel bathrooms.

All footwear stops at English size 10 (43 metric) in Ecuador. This includes socks, so those with large feet should bring spares. Heavy woollen socks are best for keeping feet warm, and cotton and nylon liners help prevent blisters.

Clothing

The variability of weather conditions means that you should stay away from cotton and rely on wool and synthetic fabrics. Thermal underwear (both top and bottom) can be slept in and keeps you warm at high altitudes. Jeans can become useless in the mountains as they bind on your legs when climbing and offer no insulation when wet. They are also too hot to wear in the sun, heavy to carry, hard to wash and take ages to dry. (Despite this, they're the gringo item most frequently stolen from washing lines.) For climbers, synthetic fabric mountaineering trousers are excellent, or a pair of fleece trousers combined with rain pants to keep out the wind. One or two pairs of lightweight slacks are good for town and lowland use.

Bring at least one light, long-sleeved shirt to protect against the intense tropical sun. You can buy thick woollen sweaters (even in large sizes!) cheaply in the indigenous markets (generally under $20), so think twice about carrying sweaters from home. Fleece pullovers or jackets stay warm when wet, dry quickly, and are lighter than wool. Bring your usual assortment of T-shirts etc, and one warm synthetic shirt.

A down jacket (or one with artificial filling) can be very useful for mountaineering and high-altitude hikes. Up to 40% of your body heat can escape from your exposed head and neck so it really helps to keep warm if you wear a wool or synthetic hat, or better still a balaclava which also protects your face and neck. A wide-brimmed sunhat is good for calm, sunny days and in the lowlands. Two pairs of gloves are needed by mountaineers: a light inner pair and a heavier wind- and waterproof outer mitt. Hikers will get by with one warm pair. Shorts are comfortable for lower hikes in remote regions and for visits to the coast, rivers, and hot pools. Also bring swimwear. All trousers should have deep pockets, preferably secured with buttons, zips, or velcro (see *Security*, pages 38–9) and they're handy in shirts (and skirts) as well. You may have to add them yourself.

Mountaineering equipment

Rope, ice axe, climbing harness and crampons are the basic necessities for snow climbs. A second tool (ice hammer) is useful for some mountains (as detailed in the text). Protection may be needed for less-experienced climbers, particularly whilst descending and for crevasse rescue. Two long ice screws and two snow stakes (with their respective slings and carabiners) will normally suffice. Bring jummars or know how to make and use prussiks in case you fall into a crevasse. A helmet is essential on some of the rock scrambles where there is danger of rockfall. A bivouac sac is worth throwing into your pack just in case you get caught out by nightfall. A head torch is needed for the predawn departures which are standard features of most glacier climbs. Alkaline batteries are available everywhere. Lithium batteries, which can last for 60 hours of continuous use, are available at a few photo developing shops in the major cities.

Glacier cream (not ordinary suntan lotion), lipsalve and climbers' goggles are essential – the power of the equatorial sun bouncing off glaciers at 6,000m will astound you. A friend of Rob became snowblind while wearing ordinary sunglasses.

Footpaths in Ecuador are generally not signposted or marked in any way, so a compass or GPS is essential for following directions, particularly when hiking cross-country. Bring marker flags or wands (which can be made from sticks and strips of plastic from plastic bags). Gaiters and good climbers' gloves should also be packed. Other useful but not essential items are ski poles and an altimeter.

Miscellaneous small items
- small pocket torch (flashlight) with spare bulbs and batteries
- travel alarm clock
- Swiss Army style penknife or Leatherman
- sewing kit (including large needles and thick thread for heavy repairs)
- scissors
- duck tape
- a few metres of cord (for clotheslines, emergency repairs, spare shoelaces, tent guys, etc)

INTERNATIONAL CLIMBING DEGREE RATINGS

The climbing ratings used in this book are American. For comparison, these equate as follows:

UIAA	Dresde (Germany)	USA	UK	France
5+	VIIa	5.7	4b	5a
6–	VIIb	5.8	4c	5b
6				
6+	VIIc	5.9	5a	5c
7–	VIIIa		5b	6a
7	VIIIb	5.10		
7+	VIIIc		5c	6b
8–	IXa		6a	6c
8	IXb	5.11		
8+	IXc		6b	7a
9–	Xa		6c	7b
9		5.12		
9+			7a	7c
		5.13		
10–			8a	
10				

The grades listed above assume climbing experience, and technical equipment (such as ropes, harnesses and so on) are essential.

- spare glasses; sunglasses
- binoculars; camera; plenty of film
- plastic bags (including large bin liners to cover packs at night)
- toiletries: soap for clothes and body (in a soap dish); shampoo; toothbrush and paste, dental floss (great for emergency repairs); small towel; toilet paper (rarely found in cheaper hotel and restaurant lavatories); handcream
- earplugs for noisy hotels and buses
- insect repellent
- suntan lotion
- pens and pencils
- address book
- notebook for journal and letter writing
- paperback book (easily exchanged with other travellers when you've finished)
- pocket Spanish–English dictionary
- waterproof matches or cigarette lighter
- waterproofing for boots
- small padlock (for cheap hotel rooms or locking gear in storage)
- large lightweight nylon bag for leaving gear in storage
- first-aid kit (see *Health*, pages 23–33).

MONEY

The Ecuadorian currency is the United States dollar. As of January 1999, after several years of rapid devaluation, the Ecuadorian currency, the sucre, was replaced by the dollar to stabilise the economy and reduce inflation. Generally most prices have risen dramatically in the major cities, but it is still possible to find inexpensive meals and hotel rooms in the smaller towns and villages.

Pounds, euros and other major currencies can be changed in Quito, but it is best to arrive with US dollars. Non-dollar exchange can be made at Multicambio (main branch at Amazonas and St Maria, but other branches in malls) and Casa de Cambio Vaz Cambio, on Amazonas and Roca. You will need to show your passport for the exchange.

Credit cards are now accepted at many establishments, even in smaller towns. The most commonly accepted credit cards are Diners and Visa.

Travellers' cheques are the most convenient and safest way of carrying large amounts of money. Guard against robbery by dividing your travellers' cheques and keeping them in different places, and be conscientious about recording each cheque cashed so that if the worst happens you can get a quick refund. Be careful which travellers' cheques you buy. American Express are recommended because in the event of loss or theft refunds can normally be arranged within 48 hours if you report the loss promptly and back up your claim with a police report (easily obtained), the receipts to show you paid for the cheques, and some form of personal identification (eg: your passport). Other companies are less efficient.

If you run out of money it is relatively simple to have more sent from home. The one million Ecuadorians abroad frequently send money to family members, so even banks in small towns are set up to receive transfers from abroad. There are numerous Western Pacific offices around the country where you could receive a transfer from home.

You can also use credit cards to get money. The easiest way is to buy American Express travellers' cheques with your AMEX card. The charge is 1%, and the entire process takes about ten minutes. In Quito, the American Express office is at Ecuadorian Tours, Amazonas 339 and Jorge Washington. With MasterCard or Visa, you may get a cash advance up to US$1,000 at Banco Pichincha (on Amazonas and Colon), Banco del Austro (on Amazonas and Santa Maria), Produbanco (on La Prensa near airport), and Banco de Guayaquil (on Colón at Reina Victoria in Quito). There are also cash machines at the Quito airport that work with Cirrus.

Budgeting
Generally most prices have risen dramatically since the dollarisation in 1999 and Ecuador is now one of the most expensive countries in South America, with most costs only slightly lower than in the United States. Increased petrol prices (now higher than average US prices) and a higher standard of living in the capital city have forced costs up. The classic bare bones budget is now up to $20 a day in the city, with cheap accommodation at about $10 a day. In rural areas, basic accommodation can be had for as low as $4 a night and an overall daily cost of $12 is possible if you want to scrape along.

If you're broke and desperate, don't give up. You can always sell your climbing and backpacking gear. The same applies to your camera or cassette recorder, or whatever else you think might be worth a few dollars. Used but good equipment can often be sold for its original price – even more if you're a shrewd businessman or a smooth hustler, depending on your point of view. A good place to advertise is in the budget hotels (see *Accommodation* in *Chapter 3*, page 36). You can also approach climbers you meet on the mountains or go to climbing clubs. Another way of making money is by teaching English. This will at least leave your weekends free to hike and climb, and you'll still have the gear to do it with. There are several language schools and the turnover is high. Often you do not need experience; just act schoolteacherish!

INSURANCE

Carrying AMEX travellers' cheques insures your money but you should get comprehensive travel insurance against theft, accidents, and illness. Most travel agents will advise you of available policies but shop around and read the small print carefully. Often you'll find that certain activities, including mountaineering, aren't covered. In the UK, the British Mountaineering Council can supply a comprehensive and not too expensive climbers' insurance policy. This is available to members only. Write to the BMC Insurance Department, Crawford House, Precinct Centre, Booth St East, Manchester M13 9R2, and ask for Expedition Remote Area forms. The insurance company, after hearing your plans, will offer a policy to suit your needs.

In addition to hospital coverage, you should consider a policy that includes evacuation to your home country if you become seriously ill or injured.

PHOTOGRAPHY

This is worth thinking about before you go. Cameras are expensive in Ecuador so bring everything you'll need with you. Film prices are reasonable, and certainly less expensive than in most Latin American countries. The choice of film is limited, though, so bring your own if you have a particular preference. Slide films that are available are Ektachrome, Fujichrome, and Agfachrome. High-speed Ektachrome 400 is good for the jungle, which is always darker than you'd expect. Kodacolor print film and most black-and-white film is easily found but always check the expiry date; I've seen professional-looking camera stores selling film which is two years out of date. Film processing is sometimes shoddy.

Digital cameras are very popular in Ecuador, and can be purchased at most photo shops. If you bring your cable for downloading, pictures can be sent home from one of the numerous internet cafés throughout the country.

Shadows in the tropics are very dark and come out almost black in photographs. A bright cloudy day is therefore often better for photography than a very sunny one. Taking shots in open shade or using fill-in flash will help. The best time for photography is when the sun is low: the first two hours after dawn and the last two before sunset. At high altitudes a haze can spoil your pictures; using a UV filter will improve them.

The people of Ecuador are both picturesque and varied. From the handsomely uniformed presidential guard to a charmingly grubby child – the possibilities of 'people pictures' are endless. However, most people resent having a camera thrust into their faces without so much as a 'by your leave'. Indigenous people in markets will often proudly turn their backs on pushy photographers. You should ask for permission with a smile or a joke, and if this is refused don't become offended. Some people are fed up at seeing their pictures in magazines or on postcards – they realise that someone must be making money at their expense. People living in remote areas are occasionally superstitious about bad luck being brought on them by cameras. Sometimes a 'tip' is asked for; whether or not you concede to such a request is a matter of personal preference, but bear in mind that it sets a precedent that's very hard to reverse, and that getting to know people is always better than throwing money about. Taking photos from a discreet distance with a telephoto lens is another possibility. Be aware and sensitive of people's feelings; it is never worth upsetting someone for a good photograph.

It is possible that you may be asked to pose in a picture with locals or Ecuadorian tourists, who generally love to have themselves photographed with gringos in *banos* or at the beach.

HEALTH
with Dr Felicity Nicholson
Before you go

Normal precautions for tropical travel should be taken. Vaccinations against typhoid, hepatitis A, **diphtheria** and **tetanus** are recommended. **Hepatitis A** vaccine (Havrix Monodose or Avaxim) comprises two injections given about a year apart. The course costs about £100, but protects for ten years. The newer **typhoid** vaccines (eg: Typhim Vi) last for three years and are about 85% effective. They should be completed unless you are leaving within a few days for a trip of a week or less, when the vaccine would not be effective in time. Travellers intending to visit the jungle or coastal regions of Ecuador should also have a **yellow fever** vaccination. A single dose lasts for ten years and is fully effective ten days after administration. Yellow fever vaccine is not mandatory for Ecuador unless you are planning to travel into other 'yellow fever' countries (eg: Brazil, Bolivia, Columbia or Venezuela).

For trips of four–six weeks or longer then **hepatitis B** vaccine is advised. This course comprises three injections and can be given over a four-week to six-month period depending on the time available.

Likewise **rabies** vaccine should also be considered for trips of four weeks or more or where the traveller is likely to be more than 24 hours away from medical help, or for a trip of any length if you will be working with animals. Ideally three doses of vaccine should be taken over a four-week period, but if there is not enough time then having two doses, or even one, of vaccine is better than nothing. (See *Rabies*, page 29.)

Cholera vaccine is no longer available in the UK because it is ineffective and was associated with unpleasant side effects. Some countries in South America continue to ask for proof of cholera vaccine when crossing land borders (eg: Peru and Bolivia). Ecuador alone has no such requirement, but if your trip includes crossing land borders then you are advised to obtain a Cholera Exemption certificate either through your GP or from a specialist travel clinic. Without this certificate you may be refused entry or worse still be forced to take the cholera vaccine. The latter is definitely to be avoided as not only is the vaccine unpleasant, but there are no guarantees that the needles used will be sterile! Cholera, like hepatitis A and typhoid, is transmitted through infected food and water and is best avoided by following the guidelines under *Traveller's diarrhoea* (pages 28–9). Even if you do become infected, it is treatable with antibiotics and seldom presents a serious problem to immunocompetent, well-nourished travellers.

A full course of the necessary inoculations can take six weeks or more so be sure to see your doctor or a specialist travel clinic (see pages 25–6) well before departure. Carry, and keep up-to-date, your international vaccination card.

Malaria

If you're planning a visit to a lowland area, anti-malaria pills are recommended since the disease is on the increase in Latin America. If you stay above 1,000m you aren't at risk since malarial mosquitoes don't live this high.

Malaria in Ecuador varies from region to region and expert advice is needed to ensure the correct prophylactic treatment is given. For coastal regions and the Amazon basin then chloroquine and proguanil are likely to be recommended. These tablets should be started one week before entering a malarial area, taken whilst there and completed four weeks after leaving. They may not be suitable if you are epileptic, have severe psoriasis or are taking Zyban (anti-smoking drug).

However, in the north of Ecuador (Esmeraldas) a pocket of high-risk falciparum malaria exists. Chloroquine and proguanil are not appropriate for this area.

Each drug has its own particular set of advantages and disadvantages and advice should be sought from a reputable travel clinic as it which is the most appropriate for you and the trip you have in mind.

If mefloquine (Lariam) is suggested, start this two-and-a-half weeks (three doses) before departure to check that it suits you; stop it immediately if it seems to cause depression or anxiety, visual or hearing disturbances, severe headaches, fits or changes in heart rhythm. Side effects such as nightmares or dizziness are not medical reasons for stopping unless they are sufficiently debilitating or annoying. Anyone who is pregnant, who has suffered fits in the past, has been treated for depression or psychiatric problems, has diabetes controlled by oral therapy or who is epileptic or has a close blood relative who is epileptic should avoid mefloquine.

Malarone (proguanil and atovaquone) is a new drug that is almost as effective as mefloquine. It has the advantage of having few side effects and needs only to be continued for one week after returning. However, it is expensive and because of this tends to be reserved for shorter trips. Malarone may not be suitable for everybody. It has recently acquired a licence for children over 11– 39kg (after 40kg the dose is as for an adult).

The antibiotic doxycycline (100mg daily) is a viable alternative when either mefloquine or Malarone are not considered suitable for whatever reason. Like Malarone it can be started one day before arrival. It may also be used in travellers with epilepsy, unlike mefloquine, although certain anti-epileptic medication may make it less effective. About 3% of users may develop an allergic skin reactions in sunlight; the drug should be stopped if this happens. Women using the oral contraceptive should use an additional method of protection for the first four weeks when using doxycycline. It is also unsuitable in pregnancy or for children under 12.

The regime for each malaria tablet is different, but whichever one is recommended, the course should be adhered to unless there are specific contraindications. All anti-malarial tablets are best taken on a full stomach and washed down with plenty of fluids. Ensure that you discuss the medication in detail with your doctor and always read the leaflet given with the medication before you go.

No tablet is 100% effective and therefore protection against the *Anopheles* mosquito that carries malaria is paramount. This involves wearing cover-up clothing between dusk and dawn, using insect repellents containing DEET (eg: the Repel range) and ensuring that your sleeping accommodation is as mosquito-proof as possible. It is always safer to take your own mosquito net impregnated with permethrin.

Travellers intending to spend many months in a malaria region may prefer to take a treatment course, either as well as or instead of prophylaxis. The most likely treatment to be recommended is quinine plus doxycycline or Malarone, but that will depend on what other medication you are taking. It is best to discuss this with an expert and purchase the appropriate treatment before you leave. Malaria testing kits are also available and should be considered if you are likely to be a long way from medical help.

Fitness

Finally, think about your physical condition. If you are planning a short, intensive trip and hope to climb several major peaks you should carry out regular pre-departure exercises such as swimming, running, cycling or whatever you prefer. If planning a longer trip then doing some of the Quito area day-hikes will help get you into shape.

Travel clinics and health information

A full list of current travel clinic websites worldwide is available on www.istm.org/. For other journey preparation information, consult ftp://ftp.shoreland.com/pub/ shorecg.rtf or www.tripprep.com. Information about various medications may be found on www.emedicine.com/wild/topiclist.htm.

UK

Berkeley Travel Clinic 32 Berkeley St, London W1J 8EL (near Green Park tube station); tel: 020 7629 6233

British Airways Travel Clinic and Immunisation Service There are two BA clinics in London, both on tel: 0845 600 2236; web: www.britishairways.com/travelclinics. Appointments only at 111 Cheapside; or walk-in service Mon–Sat at 156 Regent St.

Fleet Street Travel Clinic 29 Fleet St, London EC4Y 1AA; tel: 020 7353 5678; web: www.fleetstreet.com. Injections, travel products and latest advice.

Hospital for Tropical Diseases Travel Clinic Mortimer Market Centre, 2nd Floor, Capper St (off Tottenham Ct Rd), London WC1E 6AU; tel: 020 7388 9600; web: www.thhtd.org. Offers consultations and advice, and is able to provide all necessary drugs and vaccines for travellers. Runs a healthline (09061 337733) for country-specific information and health hazards.

MASTA (Medical Advisory Service for Travellers Abroad), at the London School of Hygiene and Tropical Medicine, Keppel St, London WC1 7HT; tel: 09068 224100. This is a premium-line number, charged at 60p per minute. For a fee, they will provide an individually tailored health brief, with up-to-date information on how to stay healthy, inoculations and what to bring.

MASTA pre-travel clinics Tel: 01276 685040. Call for the nearest; there are currently 30 in Britain. Also sell malaria prophylaxis memory cards, treatment kits, bednets, net treatment kits.

Mediserve 27 Wimpole St, London W1M 7AD; tel: 020 7436 8978; fax: 020 7636 3834; email: mediserve@virgin.net

NHS travel website www.fitfortravel.scot.nhs.uk, provides country-by-country advice on immunisation and malaria, plus details of recent developments, and a list of relevant health organisations.

Nomad Travellers' Store and Medical Centre 3–4 Wellington Terrace, Turnpike Lane, London N8 0PX; tel: 020 8889 7014; fax: 020 8889 9529; email: sales@nomadtravel.co.uk; web: www.nomadtravel.co.uk. Also at 40 Bernard St, London WC1N 1LJ; tel: 020 7833 4114; fax: 020 7833 4470 and 43 Queens Rd, Bristol BS8 1QH; tel: 0117 922 6567; fax: 0117 922 7789.

STA Travel 40 Bernard St, London; tel: 020 7837 9666; web: www.statravel.co.uk

Thames Medical 157 Waterloo Rd, London SE1 8US; tel: 020 7902 9000. Competitively priced, one-stop travel health service. All profits go to their affiliated company, InterHealth, which provides health care for overseas workers on Christian projects.

Trailfinders Immunisation Centre 194 Kensington High St, London W8 7RG; tel: 020 7938 3999.

Travel Deals 70 North End Rd, London; tel: 020 7371 6570; web: www.traveldeals.uk.com

Travelpharm The Travelpharm website, www.travelpharm.com, offers up-to-date guidance on travel-related health and has a range of medications available through their online mini-pharmacy.

The Vaccination Clinic 131–135 Earls Court Rd, London; tel: 020 7259 2180; web: www.vaccination-clinic.cwc.net

Irish Republic

Tropical Medical Bureau Grafton Street Medical Centre, Grafton Buildings, 34 Grafton St, Dublin 2; tel: 1 671 9200. Has a useful website specific to tropical destinations: www.tmb.ie.

USA

Centers for Disease Control 1600 Clifton Rd, Atlanta, GA 30333; tel: 877 FYI TRIP; 800 311 3435; web: www.cdc.gov/travel. A comprehensive range of advice is available on the internet.

Connaught Laboratories PO Box 187, Swiftwater, PA 18370; tel: 800 822 2463. They will send a free list of specialist tropical-medicine physicians in your state.

IAMAT (International Association for Medical Assistance to Travelers) 417 Center St, Lewiston, NY 14092; tel: 716 754 4883; email: info@iamat.org; web: www.iamat.org. A non-profit organisation that provides lists of English-speaking doctors abroad.

Canada

IAMAT (International Association for Medical Assistance to Travellers) Suite 1, 1287 St Clair Av W, Toronto, Ontario M6E 1B8; tel: 416 652 0137; web: www.iamat.org

TMVC (Travel Doctors Group) Sulphur Springs Rd, Ancaster, Ontario; tel: 905 648 1112; web: www.tmvc.com.au

Australia, Thailand

TMVC Tel: 1300 65 88 44; web: www.tmvc.com.au. Twenty-two clinics in Australia, New Zealand and Thailand, including:

Auckland Canterbury Arcade, 170 Queen St, Auckland City; tel: 373 3531

Brisbane Dr Deborah Mills, Qantas Domestic Building, 6th floor, 247 Adelaide St, Brisbane, QLD 4000; tel: 7 3221 9066; fax: 7 3321 7076

Melbourne Dr Sonny Lau, 393 Little Bourke St, 2nd floor, Melbourne, VIC 3000; tel: 3 9602 5788; fax: 3 9670 8394

Sydney Dr Mandy Hu, Dymocks Building, 7th Floor, 428 George St, Sydney, NSW2000; tel: 2 221 7133; fax: 2 221 8401

New Zealand

TMVC See above

IAMAT PO Box 5049, Christchurch 5; web: www.iamat.org

South Africa

SAA-Netcare Travel Clinics PO Box 786692, Sandton 2146; fax: 011 883 6152; web: www.travelclinic.co.za or www.malaria.co.za. Clinics throughout South Africa.

TMVC 113 DF Malan Dr, Roosevelt Pk, Johannesburg; tel: 011 888 7488; web: www.tmvc.com.au. Consult the website for details of clinics in South Africa.

Switzerland

IAMAT 57 Voirets, 1212 Grand Lancy, Geneva; web: www.iamat.org

First-aid kit

Assuming there is no doctor in your party, the following basic first-aid kit is suggested:

- A good drying antiseptic, eg: iodine or potassium permanganate (don't take antiseptic cream)
- A few small dressings (Band-Aids)
- Moleskin for blisters

- Lipsalve/Vaseline
- Needle and syringe kit (obtained from a chemist or travel shop and not 'homemade')
- Throat lozenges
- High-factor sunscreen
- Insect repellent; malaria tablets; impregnated bednet
- Aspirin or paracetamol
- Antifungal cream (eg: Canesten)
- Imodium and rehydration sachets (eg: Electrolade)
- Water purification tablets or drops.
- Ciprofloxacin antibiotic, 500mg x 2 (or norfloxacin) for severe diarrhoea
- Tinidazole (500mg x 8) for giardia or amoebic dysentery (see below for regime)
- Antibiotic eye drops, for sore, 'gritty', stuck-together eyes (conjunctivitis)
- A pair of fine pointed tweezers (to remove hairy caterpillar hairs, thorns, splinters, etc)
- Condoms or femidoms
- Malaria treatment and diagnostic kit if jungle travel is anticipated
- Thermometer in a case (low-reading for hypothermia)

If you are on any regular medication ensure that you have sufficient quantities before you go, as it may not be possible to buy the same treatment in Ecuador. This should be obtained from your doctor or, failing that, from a travel clinic.

In Ecuador
Health facilities
If you get very ill, see a doctor. Many Ecuadorian doctors speak English, have been educated in the US, and are very good. Your embassy or hotel can recommend one. Both the Canadian and American embassies have detailed lists of recommended doctors, dentists and other healthcare professionals, which you can also pick up at the South American Explorers (SAE). Hospital Metropolitano on Occidental and Mariana de Jesús is the largest modern hospital and one of the best in Quito. The staff are professional and most of the specialists have some training and experience abroad. Clínica Pichincha on Paez and Veintimilla, Voz Andes, on Villalengua and 10 de Agosto are also good choices. Ambulance service in Quito can be arranged by ADAMI (tel: 593 2 2465020). Medivac by helicopter or plane can be arranged with Icaro (tel: 593 2 2450928) or on local phone numbers in Cuenca, Guayaquil, Lago Agrio, Coca and Loja.

Many prescription medicines are available in Ecuadorian pharmacies at a much lower cost than in the US or Europe and these are sold 'over the counter' without a prescription. These include a variety of antibiotics, cold medicines, pain relievers, etc. The availability of certain medications within the country may make it easier to put together a decent first-aid kit (see above) at a much lower price. However, extreme caution is advised against trying to treat yourself without the benefit of a professional medical opinion.

Symptoms and remedies for other travellers' maladies are easily found elsewhere, so we are concentrating on the more specialised area of mountain health.

Water purification
Since many diseases are caught by drinking contaminated water, it is very important to sterilise your drinking supply. The simplest effective method is

boiling for 20 minutes but this is both time consuming and uses a great deal of the precious fuel you've carried. Various water purifying tablets are available but may not be wholly effective against everything: hepatitis, for instance. There are a variety of filters, and chlorine- and iodine-based treatment systems. Treatment pills can be obtained at most pharmacies.

One effective method is using a saturated iodine solution. Take a small (28g/1oz) glass bottle and put about 2–3mm of iodine crystals in it. Fill the bottle with water and give it a good shake for about a minute, then let the crystals settle to the bottom. The resulting saturated solution is added to a litre of water and left for 15 minutes to produce clean drinking water. The advantage of this method is that the crystals can be used and reused hundreds of times; very few of the crystals actually dissolve and you pour only the iodine liquid into the water and leave the crystals in the 1oz bottle for reuse. This is more effective than water purifying tablets and doesn't taste as bad. The only danger is for people who have been treated for thyroid problems and for pregnant women (whose ingestion of iodine may cause thyroid problems in their babies). Otherwise this is a safe and recommended method.

Travellers' diarrhoea

The drastic change of diet you will experience during your stay means you'll probably be sick at least once. Stomach upsets are almost unavoidable but this is generally nothing to worry about.

Diarrhoea is the most common ailment. Drink plenty of fluids, rest, and fast or eat only bland foods such as dry biscuits, crackers, bread, boiled rice, etc, and the condition will normally clear up in about 24 hours. Many travellers find that eating

TREATING TRAVELLERS' DIARRHOEA

It is dehydration which makes you feel awful during a bout of diarrhoea and the most important part of treatment is drinking lots of clear fluids. Sachets of oral rehydration salts give the perfect biochemical mix to replace all that is pouring out of your bottom but other recipes taste nicer. Any dilute mixture of sugar and salt in water will do you good: try Coke or orange squash with a three-finger pinch of salt added to each glass (if you are salt-depleted you won't taste the salt). Otherwise make a solution of a four-finger scoop of sugar with a three-finger pinch of salt in a glass of water. Or add eight level teaspoons of sugar (18g) and one level teaspoon of salt (3g) to one litre (five cups) of safe water. A squeeze of lemon or orange juice improves the taste and adds potassium, which is also lost in diarrhoea. Drink two large glasses after every bowel action, and more if you are thirsty. These solutions are still absorbed well if you are vomiting, but you will need to take sips at a time. If you are not eating you need to drink three litres a day plus whatever is pouring into the toilet. If you feel like eating, take a bland, high carbohydrate diet. Heavy greasy foods will probably give you cramps.

If the diarrhoea is bad, or you are passing blood or slime, or you have a fever, you will probably need antibiotics in addition to fluid replacement. A single dose of ciprofloxacin (500mg) repeated after 12 hours may be appropriate. If the diarrhoea is greasy and bulky and is accompanied by sulphurous (eggy) burps, the likely cause is giardia. This is best treated with tinidazole (four x 500mg in one dose, repeated seven days later if symptoms persist).

yogurt (commercially available and pasteurised) helps the digestive system adapt more quickly to the new bacteria being introduced into the diet.

By taking precautions against travellers' diarrhoea you will also avoid typhoid, cholera, hepatitis, dysentery, worms, etc. Travellers' diarrhoea and the other faecal-oral diseases come from getting other peoples' faeces in your mouth. This most often happens from cooks not washing their hands after a trip to the toilet, but even if the restaurant cook does not understand basic hygiene you will be safe if your food has been properly cooked and arrives piping hot. The maxim to remind you what you can safely eat is:

PEEL IT, BOIL IT, COOK IT OR FORGET IT.

This means that fruit you have washed and peeled yourself, and hot foods, should be safe but raw foods, cold cooked foods, salads, fruit salads which have been prepared by others, ice-cream and ice are all risky. And foods kept lukewarm in hotel buffets are often dangerous. If you are struck, see box opposite for treatment.

Dengue fever

This disease, like yellow fever, is transmitted by the day-biting *Aedes* mosquito, which makes it essential to use insect repellents during the day as well as at night if you see mosquitoes around.

It may mimic malaria but there is no prophylactic medication available to deal with it. Symptoms include strong headaches, rashes and excruciating joint and muscle pains and high fever. Dengue fever only lasts for a week or so and is not usually fatal. Complete rest and paracetamol are the usual treatment. Plenty of fluids also help. Some patients are given an intravenous drip to keep them from dehydrating. It is especially important to protect yourself if you have had dengue fever before. A second infection with a different strain can result in the potentially fatal dengue haemorrhagic fever.

In Ecuador (including the Galápagos Islands), dengue is prevalent on the coast and in jungle areas. Again, the mosquitoes are rarely found above 1,000m so are not a risk at altitude.

Rabies

The incidence of dog bites in Ecuador has increased in the last few years, and the possibility of contracting rabies or tetanus from the most innocuous of bites cannot be overestimated. Mark was bitten while riding a bicycle in Otavalo, and although the doctor told him there had not been any reported cases of rabies in the province in the previous month, he immediately travelled to Quito to get a booster shot.

Rabies is carried by all mammals and is passed on to man through a bite, scratch or a lick of an open wound. You must always assume any animal is rabid (unless personally known to you) and seek medical help as soon as possible. In the interim, scrub the wound with soap and bottled/boiled water, then pour on a strong iodine or alcohol solution. This helps stop the rabies virus entering the body and will guard against wound infections, including tetanus.

If you are exposed as described, treatment should be given as soon as possible, but it is never too late to seek help as the incubation period for rabies can be very long. Those who have not been immunised will need a full course of injections together with rabies immunoglobulin (RIG), but this product is expensive (around $800) and is available only at the larger hospitals in the major cities. Another reason why pre-exposure vaccination should be encouraged in travellers who are planning to visit more remote areas!

Tell the doctor if you have had pre-exposure vaccine, as this will change the treatment you receive.

Hypothermia

Often known as 'exposure', this insidious killer occurs when the body loses heat faster than it can produce it. By definition, the rectal temperature falls below 35°C or 95°F. Heat loss leading to hypothermia often occurs at temperatures well above freezing, and is caused primarily by wet clothing and the loss of body heat from the wind. Over 40% of body heat is lost through the head and neck (including through breathing).

Prevention is better than cure. Put on rain gear as soon as it begins to rain and not after you're soaking wet. Wear several layers of clothing, which can be removed to regulate your temperature; one very thick layer may cause you to get wet through perspiration. If you do get wet, remember to wear a windproof layer; at least your wet clothes will stay a little warmer. Cotton clothes (eg: jeans) lose 90% of their insulating properties when wet, whilst wool loses only 50%. Artificial fibrepile (fleece) is also a good wet insulator and has the added advantage of drying much more quickly than wool. Remember to keep your head and neck warm. Exposed hands should be covered – use spare socks in an emergency.

If you take the above precautions you are unlikely to get hypothermia, but lack of judgement or an accident can soon change a normal situation into a dangerous one. The hypothermia victim will begin feeling tired and start shivering uncontrollably. At this stage one can still stop hypothermia by getting out of the wind and rain and wearing more dry clothes (camping, getting into a dry sleeping bag, and eating some warm food). If this is not done, the affected person will begin to lose co-ordination, have difficulty in speaking, and show a lack of judgement. By this stage the victim is in serious trouble as they can't get themselves warm and must be re-warmed by friends. Climbing into a cold sleeping bag is inadequate, as the victim won't have enough body heat to warm the bag. The bag must be warmed. The best way is for someone to share the victim's sleeping bag after first removing wet clothing. If you're alone then try to make a hot water bottle with your canteen and drink small quantities of warm liquids. The final stage of hypothermia is a lapse into irrationality and incoherence, with hallucinations and disorientation, and a slow irregular pulse. The skin becomes blue and cold, and drowsiness and dilation of the pupils follow, and finally unconsciousness and death. The whole process can take as little as two hours. The combination of cold, wet, and windy weather is common in the Ecuadorian Highlands, so be prepared; even on a day-hike carry hat, gloves, wind and rain jacket, and a spare warm sweater.

Frostbite

This occurs when any part of the body becomes frozen. Backpackers are less likely to experience it but snow and ice climbers are possible candidates. The usual ways of getting frostbite are by exposing or wetting skin or by cutting off blood circulation to the extremities. These problems can be avoided by always wearing gloves and balaclava helmet in extremely cold conditions. The nose and cheeks are more difficult to protect. A scarf or handkerchief wrapped bandit style around the face will help, as will re-warming your nose with your hand at frequent intervals. (Rubbing snow onto the area, the traditional 'cure', is actually dangerous.) Ensure good blood circulation in your feet by not lacing boots and crampon straps too tightly. Keep your socks dry and unwrinkled. Bear in mind that exposed flesh will freeze more rapidly in windy conditions (the 'wind chill factor').

Some people are more susceptible to frostbite than others. Frostbite is liable to recur in those areas of the body which have been previously frozen. Smokers are more susceptible as are people weakened by hypothermia, exhaustion, drugs, injury, or blood loss.

The first symptom is pain. Warm and protect the area with extra clothing or by putting in a warm place (eg: warm your face with your hands or put your hands in your groin). Restore circulation to your feet by stamping them and loosening your laces. The pain may often increase in intensity during the first minutes of re-warming but this will soon disappear. If the pain disappears without re-warming and numbness occurs, then the problem is getting serious. The area becomes whitish and hard. Even at this late stage a small frostbitten area can be re-warmed without damage. If your feet are involved then they could be re-warmed on a friend's belly or armpit.

If a whole finger or toe (or larger area) becomes deeply frostbitten then the situation is grave. This is because re-warming the part will cause it to become extremely delicate and sensitive so it cannot be used at all for several weeks. For this reason a badly frostbitten climber should be taken to hospital for treatment. Once a part has been frostbitten it can remain that way for several days without much more damage and so climbers with severe frostbite should be evacuated under their own steam as soon as possible. This is entirely feasible in Ecuador as most climbing areas are within a couple of days of Quito. Once in hospital, a badly frostbitten area must be gently thawed in water just above blood temperature or damage will result.

Heat exhaustion

A calm, sunny day in the high Andes can be extremely hot and heat problems are not uncommon, although they are more of a danger on lowland hikes. Lack of liquids aggravates this condition so drink as much as possible before setting off on a hike or climb, as well as during the hike. If you are unusually tired, thirsty, giddy, suffer from cramps, and are not urinating much (less than three good-volume pees in 24 hours), you're probably suffering from heat exhaustion or dehydration. Rest in the shade and drink as much as you can. Refrain from activity till you recover.

If symptoms of heat exhaustion are ignored, more serious problems such as heat syncope and heat stroke could develop. Therefore these warnings must be taken seriously. Ensure a high fluid intake and wear a wide-brimmed sunhat and loose, light clothes.

Sunburn

Sunburn is a major problem at the Equator and at altitude, particularly for climbers on snow or ice who may be unaware of the power of the equatorial sun at 6,000m. A few hours outside at midday without protection can cause serious burns. The sun will reflect from the glacier and burn in all sorts of surprising places such as behind the ears, under the chin, and in the nostrils. These areas are very sensitive and must be carefully covered with glacier cream or sun block. Lipsalve is needed to prevent cracked and bleeding lips. Ordinary suntan lotion is helpful but normally doesn't offer enough protection for climbers on a glacier. A sun protection factor of at least 15 should be used. When making a pre-dawn departure remember to stop when the sun rises and put cream on. Reapply frequently. Good glacier cream is readily available in Ecuador, as is the heavier zinc oxide. Don't be fooled by a cloud layer; the ultraviolet rays of the sun will burn you anyway. Wear a wide-brimmed hat when possible. Backpackers should also be aware of sunburn and use plenty of suntan lotion, especially at the beginning of a trip.

Snow blindness

Snow blindness is sunburn of the retina. Snow and ice climbers must use the glacier glasses or goggles with complete UV protection to protect from the strong reflection over the snow. The only cure for this is to have your eyes completely covered for a few days – obviously inconvenient at the top of a mountain!

Altitude sickness

Until the 1960s this unpleasant and often dangerous reaction to high altitude was medically unknown in the West and climbers suffering (and dying) from it were said to be suffering from pneumonia. Recent studies have shown this not to be the case and today altitude sickness is recognised as a major mountaineering problem and studies are continuing to increase our knowledge of this condition.

It is known that altitude sickness can be divided into three categories: acute mountain sickness (AMS), pulmonary oedema, and cerebral oedema (see opposite for symptoms). All three are caused not just by the lack of oxygen at high altitude, but by a too- rapid ascent to these heights. The best prevention is acclimatisation which means not climbing too high too fast. It is unusual for anyone to be seriously affected at elevations around 2,850m (Quito's), so using Quito as a base for acclimatisation is recommended. Spending about a week at this altitude is normally adequate acclimatisation providing you do not climb very high fast.

Research has shown that an ascent rate of about 300–500m per day is normally slow enough to prevent problems, but it is impractical to spend over a week climbing Chimborazo which at 6,310m is almost 3,500m above Quito. Once acclimatised in Quito, it is quite common for one-day ascents to be made with little danger. Remember that altitude sickness usually takes from 6 to 36 hours to reveal itself and so a quick ascent and descent can normally be made with few ill effects. The old maxim 'Climb high and sleep low' is a good one.

Despite these reassurances, one should bear in mind that cases of altitude sickness can occur even if precautions are taken. Every mountaineer should be able to recognise the symptoms described below and know how they must be dealt with.

Acute Mountain Sickness (soroche) is the most common of the three variations. The symptoms are severe headache, shortness of breath, nausea, vomiting, fatigue, insomnia, loss of appetite, and a rapid pulse. Irregular (Cheyne-Stokes) breathing during sleep affects some people but is relatively harmless, although disturbing to both the sleeper and his companions. The best treatment is rest and deep breathing and drinking lots of water. Analgesics may alleviate the headache (some doctors recommend non-aspirin based ones) and Diamox can also be used as treatment as well as prevention. An adequate fluid intake must be maintained. If a victim doesn't improve then a descent is called for – as little as 500m is usually enough. A climber should never force him- or herself to ascend when symptoms of AMS are present as the conditions will probably worsen.

Acetazolamide (Diamox) helps speed acclimatisation and many people find it useful; take 250mg twice a day for five days, starting two or three days before reaching 3,500m. However, the side effects from this drug may resemble altitude sickness and therefore it is advisable to try the medication for a couple of days about two weeks before the trip to see if it suits you.

Pulmonary oedema kills climbers in the Andes every year, but it is extremely rare in Ecuador. It is a more extreme form of AMS and in addition to the symptoms mentioned the victim suffers from increased shortness of breath when at rest and a dry, rattling cough. As the condition worsens, frothy bloodstained sputum is produced and the victim turns blue. Fluid collects in the lungs, literally drowning the person if the condition is not recognised. Victims must immediately be assisted to a lower altitude (at least 600m lower) and taken to hospital if necessary. Ecuador's mountains are steep volcanoes and descent can be accomplished in hours, reducing the risk of pulmonary oedema.

Cerebral oedema is even less common but equally dangerous. Here the fluid accumulates in the brain instead of the lungs and may cause permanent brain damage or death. Symptoms include an agonising headache, giddiness, confusion, and hallucinations. Anyone showing these signs must immediately be assisted to lower altitude. Poor judgement is also one of the symptoms so strong persuasion may have to be used to evacuate the victim.

Finally, remember that anyone may be prone to AMS and that youth and fitness make no difference. It is important for the less-affected members of a climbing party to keep their eyes on climbers who may be trying to push themselves beyond sensible limits. Climbers are often so determined to reach a summit that they can jeopardise the whole expedition by trying to cover up an attack of AMS. Being affected by altitude sickness is not a sign of inherent weakness. It often takes more courage to stop, rest, and acclimatise further than it does to keep pushing dangerously close to an attack of pulmonary oedema.

Crossing rivers
When crossing rivers it is important to unbuckle your waist-belt in case you are pulled into the current. If the river is fast moving and over waist deep, consider turning back. If you do fall into the river, let your pack go and swim to shore. Chances are you will be able to retrieve the pack downstream, and in any case it is not worth drowning trying to save your gear.

Accidents
These can vary from a simple twisted ankle on a hiking trail to multiple injuries caused by a major climbing fall. The most important advice here is never to hike or climb alone.

It is best to wait for help or rescue. If a person is injured on a frequently travelled trail or route then the partner should stay with the victim and ensure that the injured party is as warm, comfortable, and reassured as possible. If you are climbing an unusual route or hiking cross-country then waiting for help may be pointless. If you go for help make sure that you will be able to find the victim again – leave wands or markers and arrange a whistle or flashlight signal if the victim is conscious. Don't leave injured climbers alone unless it is totally unavoidable.

All climbers should have training in first aid and carry a booklet on the principles of first aid, particularly with reference to mountaineering injuries.

34

34

34

STOP

In Ecuador

I never travel without my diary. One should always have something
sensational to read on the train.

The Importance of Being Earnest, Oscar Wilde

ARRIVAL

Most visitors will fly into Quito International Airport. This is about 7km from the
new city or 10km from the old town. Taxis into town are cheap and should charge
about $3 to $4 (up to $5 if going further to the colonial section of town) during the
day and about a 25% more at night. Be aware that many airport taxi drivers, in the
finest spirit of capitalism, will ask as much as $20 to take you into town! Don't let
yourself be suckered in – there are more taxis than there are passengers to fill them,
so the advantage is yours. Within the city, taxis are required by law to use meters,
but from the airport fares may have to be negotiated. Those taxis waiting directly
in front of the international area will be harder to bargain with than the others
posted near the national section of the airport. If you don't have too much to carry,
walk left from the international exit about 25m and look for a taxi there. It is
normal to agree on the price beforehand. If you're really broke, take the
southbound bus (to your left) from outside the airport into town.

ACCOMMODATION

Accommodation is still relatively cheap all over Ecuador. You can always find a
basic hotel for under $5 per night, and if you want something a little more
luxurious than four walls and a bed you'll find plenty of reasonably priced
accommodation in all the major cities. Family-run hotels known as *pensiones* or
residenciales are usually good and economical.

The best first-class hotels in town are:

Swiss Hotel 12 de Octubre and Cordero, $200 per night; tel: 2 2567600; email:
eswq@swissuio.com. This is a centrally located hotel outside the crime-prone Mariscal
District.

Radison 12 de Octubre and Cordero, $120 per night; tel: 2 2233333; email:
quito@radisson.com.ec. Right next door to the Swiss Hotel and cheaper.

Marriot Amazonas and Orellana, $150 per night; tel: 2 2972000),
visnesscenter.quito@marriotthotels.com The newest and best hotel in Quito.

Sheraton Four Points República del Salvador and Naciones Unidas, $95 per night; tel: 2
2970002; email: hotel@sheraton-quito.com Located in the business district, caters to the oil
industry.

Hilton Colón Amazonas and Patria, $110 per night; tel: 2 2561333; email:
reser@hiltoncolon.com Located next to the Parque Alameda where artists sell paintings on
weekends, and right in Mariscal close to shops, restaurants and night clubs. While the
neighbourhood is crime prone, security in the immediate area of the hotel is good.

Several good mid-range hotels are:

Cafe Cultura Robles and Reina Victoria; tel: 2 2504078; web: www.cafecultura.com
Long-time connection with the SAE
Hotel Quito Gonzalez Suárez y 12 de Octubre, $50; tel: 2 2544600. Great views of the valley and Guapulo.
Villa Nancy Muros and 12 de Octubre (near Hotel Quito), $50; tel: 2 2550839; email: nancita@pi.pro.ec, bed and breakfast and friendly owners.

In the new town there is a wealth of lodging choices, which are constantly growing. If you like the idea of staying in a house with kitchen privileges and washing facilities, one good choice run by a friendly Argentine is **La Casona de Mario** at Andalucía, 213 and Galacía, tel: 593 2 2230129. Mark stayed here for three months when he first arrived in Ecuador in 1994. The **Magic Bean** at Foch 681 and Juan Leon Mera, tel: 2566181, email: bhunta@ecnet.ec or magic@ecuadorexplorer.com, web: www.ecuadorexplorer.com/magic/, offers shared accommodation for $7, is located in the heart of the tourist district and is a good place for leaving messages and meeting friends. **El Cafecito**, on Luis Cordero and Reina Victoria, tel: 593 2 2234862, email: cafecito@ecuadorexplorer.com is a popular place to stay, drink coffee and attend somewhat eccentric full-moon parties. The **Posada de Guapulo**, Leonidas Plaza 257, tel: 593 2 2220473, located on the old road to Guapulo below the hotel Quito, is a nice escape from the city.

In the old town, hotels tend to be very cheap but there are more occurrences of theft during the day and it can be risky walking around at night. The only recommended hotel in this area is the **Residencial Marsella** at Los Ríos and Castro just above Parque Alameda, between the old and new sections of Quito, tel: 593 2 2955884. Rooms with a shared bath go for $4 per night, while single/double rooms with private bath are $5 per night. The Australian and Ecuadorian-owned **Secret Garden**, located on Calle Jose Anteparra and Los Rios in the San Blas Sector on the outskirts of the old town, tel: 593 2 2956704, email: hola@secretgardenquito.com, has a marvellous terrace with a view of the Quito valley. All rooms have shared bathrooms and prices range from $3.50 for a dorm bed to $12 for a private room with double bed.

GETTING AROUND
By bus
The best way to travel in Ecuador is undoubtedly by bus. Quito has a slow, crowded, but cheap bus service which covers the city thoroughly. There are also two new ecological bus lines: the electric Trolebus that travels down Av 10 de Agosto to the old town and the Ecovia on 6 de Diciembre in the north, both of which are quicker but more expensive than the numerous other options. Traffic has got worse in Quito due to the elongated shape of the city and lack of urban planning, so expect delays during rush hour.

Travel to even the most remote locations is relatively easy, since there is a large population of Ecuadorians from the countryside who work in Quito during the week and commute back to their home towns on weekends. Quito's central bus terminal, the Cumandá Terminal Terrestre, is located in the old city on Av Cumandá, and scores of buses to all parts of the country leave here every day (be wary of pickpockets and rip-off artists). Buses heading north or south on the Pan-American Highway through The Avenue of the Volcanoes past Latacunga, Ambato and Riobamba are very frequent. If you can't get a direct bus to a less well-known destination, take one to the nearest big town and change; the construction of central bus stations in all major Ecuadorian cities means that if you have to change buses you don't have to go looking for out-of-the-way bus stops – all departures are usually from the same place.

Some of the 'luxury' bus lines like Sucre and Pan-American Highway now have terminals in the new town, with routes heading south to Cuenca, Guayaquil and the Peruvian border.

Using the bus system is easy but here are some suggestions to make your journey more enjoyable. If you go to the offices in the Terminal Terrestre the day before your departure you can nearly always buy a seat in advance; this also means you can choose your seat number, and obviously the front means better views, more leg room and a more exciting trip. With luck, you can get these front seats as late as an hour before departure; if travelling during long holiday weekends, however, everything may be sold out several days in advance, so book early.

Both small microbuses (holding 22 passengers, and generally used for the shorter journeys to small towns) and large coaches are used.

The drivers and their assistants usually run around yelling out their destinations and looking for passengers. Often you will be on a bus going your way within a few minutes of arriving at the terminal.

There is also a separate, inter-provincial bus area for departures to the small towns around Quito. This is located in the area of Plaza La Marin, and is not really a terminal but a central location from where buses leave. It is located around the end of Av Pichincha in the old town only a few blocks from the main bus terminal, Cumandá. Plaza La Marin is also the end of the line for scores of city buses. Look for any bus that has a La Marin sign displayed in the window or as part of its route name. A few other nearby bus destinations, especially for Machachi, leave from Villa Flora, a neighbourhood south of Quito. To get there you can catch any city bus marked 'Villa Flora' along Av 12 de Octubre south of Patria, or along Av Colombia above and west of Parque Alameda. It's called the Villa Flora bus terminal, though it is just a street where buses line up and depart for Machachi every 15 minutes.

By taxi

If you're in a hurry there are many yellow taxis which are required to use meters. Know the base rate and be sure your taxi driver starts the meter at this figure. A typical trip in Quito varies between two and four dollars. Make sure they have a registration number in the window; in recent years there have been some rogue taxis involved in robberies. At night and for trips outside the city, fares will have to be negotiated. In most other cities, meters are not used so fares must be agreed on in advance.

Hitchhiking

Hitchhiking is also possible and may be the only transportation option in more remote areas. Often you will be expected to pay the driver – arrange this beforehand. Free rides are more common on the major roads, but are not recommended as robberies are possible.

By train

A train service (slow but with great views) runs daily from Riobamba to Durán (near Guayaquil), and on Saturdays from Quito to Riobamba. See *Chapter 8* for more details.

By air

The popularity of air transportation is growing in Ecuador. There are daily flights out of Quito and Guayaquil to Cuenca, Esmeraldas, Lago Agrio, Coca, Loja,

Manta, Portoviejo, Machala and Tulcan. The major internal flight companies are TAME and Icaro.

SECURITY

Ecuador is increasingly becoming a more dangerous country to travel in, particularly in the north near the Colombian border, and in Quito. Typically crimes used to be limited to pickpocketing, petty theft and occasional robberies. Today, armed robbery, rape, kidnapping and even murder are on the increase, especially in Quito. Generally, however, tourists are not targets for these types of crimes, especially those who have the 'budget-traveller' look. Keep a low profile, do not advertise that you have a lot of expensive gear or a lot of money, and you should be okay. Generally the more you get away from the tourist areas the less likely you are to be a target for crime.

Petty thieves generally look for easy targets. Tourists who carry a wallet or a passport in a hip pocket are asking for trouble. Leave your wallet at home; it's an easy mark for a pickpocket. Carrying a roll of paper money loosely wadded under a handkerchief in your front pocket is as safe a way as any of carrying your daily spending money. The rest should be hidden. Always use an inside pocket or (preferably) a body pouch to protect your valuables. A money belt is good; so too is a neck pouch under your shirt, or a leg pouch (as available from the SAE in Quito – see opposite).

Bag snatching is another problem. Motorcyclists sometimes zoom past unsuspecting pedestrians and grab a shoulder bag or camera. Similarly, if you put luggage down it can be stolen in seconds whilst your attention is diverted.

Crowded places are the haunts of thieves and pickpockets. A bustling market or an ill-lit bus station are prime venues for robbery so be particularly alert in such places. Razor blades are sometimes used to slash baggage (including a pack on your back) for a grab-and-run raid. Don't wear expensive watches or jewellery, as this also invites snatch theft. Do not walk out on the beaches alone at night, especially in party towns like Montanita, Crucita and Atacames. Muggings and rapes do occur. The Mariscal district, unfortunately where many of the hotels and hostels are located, has a big problem with crime. If you venture out at night make sure you travel in a group and take a taxi back to your hotel to avoid problems.

There have recently been reports of another, extremely insidious form of robbery: gringos are offered biscuits or chocolates on a bus by seemingly friendly passengers and they wake up several hours later in an alley with just a T-shirt and a pair of trousers. Unopened packages are injected with horse tranquillisers using hypodermic syringes. So the lesson is … don't take sweets from strangers. Drugging of drinks in bars has also been reported.

When travelling by public transport watch your luggage being loaded to ensure that it's not left behind, and try to keep your eye on it during stops. Don't leave valuables in vulnerable places like the easily opened outside pockets of your pack.

Beware of theft from your hotel room. Many hotels have signs that they are not responsible for theft unless valuables are placed in a deposit at reception. If using cheaper hotels, you'll find you can often lock the door with your own padlock. A combination lock is more secure than a normal padlock. Some travellers carry a short length of chain for securing baggage in storage areas or on luggage racks. Camera or bag straps can be reinforced with thin chain or guitar strings to prevent slashing.

Before you leave home make a photocopy of your passport to show embassy officials should yours be stolen. Many embassies also allow you to register your passport if you are planning to live in Ecuador; this makes replacement much easier. Take out travellers' insurance.

When you're climbing or hiking you'll want to leave your excess luggage in a safe place. Your hotel is usually OK, but beware of other gringos claiming your luggage; not all travellers are honest! Many hotels will give you a numbered receipt – this way no one else can claim your bag. A small charge sometimes accompanies this service.

In some of the mountain *refugios* you'll be able to lock up your gear in one of the storage compartments provided, or in a spare room. Bring a small padlock for this purpose. When camping, it's best never to leave gear unattended. Some climber friends recently had everything but their tent stolen from the Italian basecamp on El Altar whilst they were scouting Obispo. Always leave someone to guard the camp. If your entire group wants to climb, we suggest you hire a local *mulero*, or muleman, to look after your gear.

Despite the increasing problems with crime, there is very little anti-foreigner sentiment. The average Ecuadorian usually has a relative who lives in the United States or Europe and is very interested in conversing with you.

TOURIST INFORMATION AND MAIL

The main **tourist office** in Quito is the Ministerio de Turismo, located at Av Eloy Alfaro and Carlos Tobar (between Av República and Av Shyris); tel: 2 2507555, 2507560. They are helpful for standard queries (museums, buses, restaurants, etc).

The main **post office** in the Old Town is between Calle Guayaquil and Venezuela. They will hold mail for you addressed Lista de Correos, Correos Central, Quito, Ecuador. In the new town, you may receive mail at the main post office located on Av Eloy Alfaro and 9 de Octubre. Have mail addressed Lista de Correos, Correos Eloy Alfaro, Quito, Ecuador. The **American Express** office will also accept mail for their clients and for holders of their travellers' cheques. Their postal address is Apartado 2605, Quito, Ecuador and their street address is Amazonas 339 and Jorge Washington. Members of the South American Explorers may have their correspondence sent to the clubhouse, Apartado 21-431, Quito.

The South American Explorers

Founded in 1977 by Don Montague and Linda Rojas in Lima, Peru, this club opened a branch in Quito in 1989 and in Cusco in 1999, much to the joy of many travellers who have made use of its services over the years. It is regarded as the leading source of information on Latin America and serves as a network for travellers, adventurers, students, volunteers and researchers, providing a wealth of advice about exploring, working and living in Latin America.

The club is a member-supported, non-profit organisation. Annual membership costs $50 per person ($80 for a couple), and includes a subscription to their excellent quarterly journal, *The South American Explorer*. In addition, members have full use of all clubhouses and their facilities that include: tips and advice, a guidebook reference library, a cultural and science reference library, book exchange, trip reports, volunteer resource centre, secure storage for equipment and valuables, mail service, weekly presentations, excursions with other members, and discounts in many hotels, restaurants, language schools and tour agencies throughout several countries. It's a relaxing place to have a cup of tea and chat with other members, and a great place to look for travel partners, gear, work and advice. Non-members are welcome to come by for a tour of the facilities and to obtain limited travel information, but must come up with the $50 membership fee to take full advantage of the numerous benefits that the club has to offer.

If you're in Quito, stop by the club and see for yourself what SAE is all about! It is open Monday to Friday, 09.30 to 17.00, and Saturdays from 09.00 to 12.00. On Thursdays the club stays open until 20.00 for Thursday Night Presentations!

Quito Clubhouse Jorge Washington 311 y Leonidas Plaza (near the American Embassy). Mailing address Apartado 21-431, Quito, Ecuador; tel/fax: 2 222 5228; email: quitoclub@saexplorers.org; web: www.saexplorers.org, which you can access with your laptop and cellular phone from the refuge at Cotopaxi!
Lima Clubhouse Calle Piura 135, Miraflores; mailing address Casilla 3714, Lima, Peru; tel/fax: 511 445 3306; email: limaclub@saexplorers.org
Cusco Clubhouse Choquechaca 188, No 4; mailing address Apartado 500, Cusco, Peru; tel/fax: 518 424 5484; email: cuscoclub@saexplorers.org
Ithaca Clubhouse 126 Indian Creek Rd, Ithaca, NY 14850; tel: + 1 607 277 0488; fax: +1 607 277 6122; email: explorer@saexplorers.org

Websites
For details of websites that provide information about Ecuador, see *Appendix 3, Further Reading*, page 255.

MAPS
All maps, ranging from Quito city plans to wall charts of Ecuador, are published by and available from the IGM (Instituto Geográfico Militar). Their offices and map sales department are on top of a hill on Av T Paz y Miño, off Av Colombia, behind the Casa de Cultura.

There are very few buses up this hill but it's not a very hard walk, or you can just get a taxi. A permit to enter the building is available in exchange for your passport at the main gate; it is open from 08.00 to 16.00 (without closing midday), Monday to Friday.

There is a single 1:1,000,000 chart of Ecuador available. Most of the country is now also covered by 1:50,000 and 1:100,000 topographical maps. The current price is $2 per map. All extant maps are displayed in large folders so they can be examined before buying. Topographical sheets are available within half an hour and if they are out of stock a photocopy can be purchased. Parts of the Oriente as well as the coast and border areas are restricted and maps can only be purchased with special permission, a procedure that can take up to two weeks. The 1:50,000 topographical maps are the most useful for hikers and climbers. Much of the highlands has also been mapped to bigger scales: 1:25,000 or even 1:10,000. You can also buy airphotos of most of country (about $10 per print), which must be ordered in advance; it takes a few days for prints to be made.

The SAE now has an excellent collection of maps which you can use as a reference. Usually some of the more popular maps are on sale by members who have left the country. If you do not need your maps when you leave Ecuador, it is a nice gesture to drop them off at the SAE for other travellers to use.

The sketch maps supplied with this book are made to complement rather than replace the IGM sheets, so details of the sheets needed for each hike or climb are given in the text. It is essential with almost all of the hikes to have the appropriate topographic maps. Some of these maps are available from Bradt Publications.

On an international level, ITM produces excellent maps to the continent. Their three-part map of South America is a little unwieldy but is likely to be the most accurate you'll find. In addition, a new 1:1,000,000 country map of Ecuador is now available and much better than the local IGM version. These can be purchased through the SAE, or direct from ITM, 530 West Broadway, Vancouver, BC V5Z 1E9, Canada; tel: +1 604 879 3621 fax: +1 604 879 4521; web: www.itmb.com

RENTING AND BUYING EQUIPMENT

There are many outdoor stores in Quito that have a variety of gear for hire and for sale. Some of the new equipment for sale is locally made, reasonably priced, but of lower quality than in the US or Europe. Many of the European and American brands can also be obtained, at a higher price. Rental items are a mixture of Ecuadorian-made products and imported equipment, some of which is sold to the shops by travellers who are either broke or tired of lugging the stuff around. The quality of rented gear is extremely variable. A friend of mine rented some locally made crampons but the front points bent downwards at his first attempt to climb a small ice wall. Ecuadorian ice axes are somewhat primitive, but boots and sleeping bags are OK.

Most of the outdoor stores are open from Monday to Friday, 09.00 to 13.00 and 15.00 until 18.00, and usually on Saturday morning. Renting equipment is relatively inexpensive but a sizeable deposit is required (travellers' cheques, or sometimes the return portion of your international flight coupon, will do). These outfits are also good sources for information on clubs and meetings etc. The following is a selection of those shops which have proven to be the most reliable.

In Quito

Altamontaña Jorge Washington 425 y 6 de Diciembre; tel/fax: 593 2 2524422, has equipment for rent and sale with a good selection of larger sized boots. They work with Compañia de Guias next door, a co-operative of guides specialising in mountain climbing.
Andísimo 9 de Octubre 479 and Roca, tel/fax: 593 2223030, has good quality outdoor equipment and rents climbing gear. They also organise treks and climbing tours.
Surtrek, Amazonas and Wilson, tel: 593 2 2500530, info@Surtrek.com
Moggely Climbing Joaquin Pinto y Amazonas, tel: 2 2554984, web: www.moggely.com. Camping and climbing gear for sale and rent; also kerosene and white gas available.
Antisana Sport El Bosque Shopping Centre; tel: 2 2467433. Good selection of larger sized footware for the mountains.
Camping Cotopaxi Colon and Reina Victoria, tel: 2 2251626
Equipos Cotopaxi 6 de Diciembre and Jorge Washington; tel: 2 2250038
Agama Expediciones Venezuela 1163 and Manabí, is run by Eduardo Agama, and rents and sells equipment and arranges trips into the mountains. It also offers a unique climb on the south side of Cotopaxi.
The Explorer Reina Victoria and Pinto, tel: 2 2550911
Los Alpes Reina Victoria 821 and Baquedano, tel: 2 2232362. Reasonable camping equipment at cheaper prices.
Safari Sports 6 de Diciembre and Orellana; tel: 2 2220647.Camping, fishing and hunting gear.
Marathon Chain that can be found at El Bosque, El Jardín, CCI, San Rafeal and Quicentro shopping malls.
Backpacker Reina Victoria and Foch. Manufactures fleece clothing.
Kywi 10 de Agosto y Cordero; tel: 2 2221832; email: kywi@pi.pro.ec. Complete hardware store; good place to buy rubber boots and machetes.

In addition to renting gear these shops also provide accommodation and guides.

Outside Quito

Outside Quito, equipment is harder to come by. Although gear can be hired in Baños, and the rates there are often cheaper than in Quito, beware of quality. Climbing guide Willie Navarette at Cafe Higueron, Noviembre 270 and Luis Martinez; tel: 9 9932411, can give good advice.

Don't forget the noticeboards at the SAE and the Andean Cup.

CLIMBING CLUBS IN QUITO

Most of the major colleges and universities have active mountaineering clubs. The best known and oldest of these is the Ascencionimo del Colegio San Gabriel group (men only) which meets at the school on Wednesdays after 20.00 at Rumipamba y Vasco, and also irregularly publishes *Montaña* magazine. The club at the Universidad La Católica sometimes has climbing films and lectures open to the general public. It also has outings almost every weekend which are open to newcomers. General meetings are held at 19:30 on Thursdays at the university. The Politécnica Climbing Club meets regularly on Wednesdays at 19.30 on the 8th floor of the civil engineering building, Ingeneria Cívil de la Polytécnica Nacional, across the street from the Universidad La Católica on Av Isabel de la Católica. The Universidad San Francisco de Quito has a new outdoor club, but not many technical climbers. There is also the Nuevos Horizontes Club located on Colón 2038 and 10 de Agosto (tel: 2 2552154) and you don't have to be a member to join their trips.

In addition, one of the main climbing organisations in Quito is the Asociacíon de Excursionismo y Andinismo de Pichincha, comprised of amateur climbers who meet irregularly at the climbing wall within the Vicentina sports complex, or Complejo Deportiva de la Vicentina, on Calle La Condamine and Manuel Cajías.

GUIDES

This book aims to get you to the top of most mountains without a guide. Many inexperienced climbers, however, will feel more confident with one to start with.

Climbing in Ecuador can be deceptive, especially to the novice mountaineer. A climb of only 8 to 10 hours to a summit nearing 6,000m may sound like a piece of cake requiring little commitment. This, however, is not necessarily true. The effects of high altitude combined with abruptly changing weather patterns and variable snow/ice conditions can put heavy demands on even the most experienced of climbers. In 1992 six people perished on Chimborazo, another ten (including three experienced Ecuadorian guides) were killed in an avalanche there in 1993, and yet Chimborazo is considered a technically easy climb. Every year climbers die on Ecuadorian peaks and the hazards of embarking on a climb should not be underestimated. For these reasons, guided climbs on the major peaks may be the best alternative for some.

Choosing a guide is as important as deciding whether or not you need one. 'A little knowledge is a dangerous thing' applies unequivocally to some locals who consider themselves capable climbers on any peak after one or two ascents of minor summits. Rob ran into one fellow at the Cotopaxi refuge who had been hired as a guide by a couple of Americans. He chatted in a casual way about the route up, wanting to know where it went exactly, and what time Rob was leaving. Perhaps he and his 'friends' could tag along, he suggested? It turned out that he had gone up Tungurahua a few times and decided he could climb anything, not to mention actually guide other people! Fortunately, the weather turned sour, and no-one got out of the hut that night. The thing to realise is that you get what you pay for. Some so-called guides charge as little as $30 per person to climb one of the major peaks, while the going rate for an experienced, professional guide is somewhere between three to four times that amount, depending on group size. The Baños area is especially notorious for inexperienced guides exaggerating their abilities and touting their services at bargain prices.

The best way to locate a reliable guide is to contact the climbing/rental shops. Many of these, as described in the previous section, are owned and operated by experienced climbing guides. You can also get recommendations from other travellers or contact the SAE, which keeps updated information about local guides and guiding services.

The Ecuadorian Guide Association (ASEGUIM – Asociación Ecuatoriana de Guias de Montaña), Wilson and Juan Leon Mera, tel: 2 2234109 is open Tuesday and Thursday afternoons. ASEGUIM has 'professionalised' the guiding service by licensing their mountain guides with the Ministry of Tourism. Members have years of technical guiding experience and overseas training. Hiring a licensed guide does not always guarantee expert quality; it does, however, provide a format for negotiation and registering problems, should any arise.

The following guiding agencies are recommended:

Compañia de Guias Jorge Washington and 6 de Diciembre; tel: 2 2504773
Surtrek (see *Renting and buying equipment*, page 41). Professional and popular guiding service.
Sierra Nevada Joaquin Pinto 4E-150 and Cordero; tel: 2 2553658; email: snevada@accessinter.net
Climbing Tour Av Amazonas and Roca; tel: 2 2557663, 2237840; web: www.climbingtour.com. A new guiding service, highly recommended.
Mogeley (see *Renting and buying equipment*, page 41). Professional and popular guiding service which is often the cheapest as well.
Safari Calama and Mera; tel: 2 2552505, email: admin@safari.com.ec. Long-time resident Jean Brown has a variety of guides and mountain excursions to offer.
Ecotrek (Cuenca) Larga and Luis Cordero; tel: 7 2834677

The following are all good guides: Diego Zurita, Edison Oña, Jaime Avila, Oswaldo Freire, Fabricio Aviles, Jürg Arnet, César Román, Gaspar Navarrete, Julio Mesias, Eduardo Agama, Iván Vallejo, Javier Herrera, José Luis Peralvo, Marco Suarez, Javier Cabrera, Mario Vásconez, Rafael Martinez, Pepe Landázuri, Diego Castillo and Juan Gabriel Carrasco. This is not an exclusive list; there are other good agencies and guides, but those listed here come highly recommended.

The Andean Cup is becoming a climbers' hang-out, offering up-to-date verbal and written information and occasional evening talks on outdoor opportunities. They specialise in organic, shade-grown Ecuadorian coffee, roasted freshly on a daily basis. They are located at 810 Guanguiltagua, half a block north of the Metropolitan park entrance.

In case of an emergency, ASEGUIM also organises rescues. The guides do not charge for their time, but they do ask that their expenses (food and transport) be paid. Donations are gladly accepted. Raul Yépez at Guias de Montaña is the current contact for the association.

PROTECTED AREAS

Ecuador has a protected area system that encompasses over 20% of the country. This system includes national parks, wildlife reserves, flora reserves, marine reserves, geological reserves, monuments, nature reserves, protected forests and wetlands. The protected areas are managed by the Ministerio de Ambiente, which is housed in the MAG (Ministerio de Agricultura and Ganadaria) on the corner of Amazonas and Eloy Alfaro in Quito. Many of the parks have alliances with international and local NGOs, which help in the funding and management of the protected areas. There are also regional offices of the Ministerio de Ambiente in the provincial capital cities. The current (2003) regional office locations are listed below:

Regional offices of the Ministerio de Ambiente

Galapagos Santa Cruz; tel: 05 2527410, 05 2527411; email: comunicación@spng.org.ec

Pichincha Guayaquil 616 e Ibarra 3er. Piso, Santa Domingo; tel: 2750322; email: ambientedfp@interactive.net.ec

Imbabura Calixto Miranda 1-10 y Obispo Mosquera, Ibarra; tel: 06 2643808; email: ambiente.imbabura@andinanet.net

Esmeraldas Malecón, entre Mejía y Manuela Cañizares, Edificio MAG, 3er piso, Esmeraldas; tel: 06 2723204, 06 2721781; email: ambiente@esmeral.net

Sucumbìos Av Del Chofer entre Cofanes y Venezuela, Nueva Loja (Lago Agrio); tel: 06 2830139, 06 2850528

Orellana Amazonas y Bolívar Edificio MAG, Coca; tel: 06 2881030, 06 2881050

Napo Barrio Aeropuerto No 2 Calle Rubèn, Cevallos y Yutzos, Tena; tel: 06 2887154, 06 2880973; email: ma_napo@andinanet.net

Pastaza 20 de Julio y Chimborazo, Puyo; tel: 03 2883085, 03 2883809; email: ambiente_pastaza@hotmail.com

Tungurahua Alfredo Baquerizo 603 y Pasaje Tamayo, ciudadel Presidencial, Ambato; tel: 03 2848453, 03 2416290; email: disfortung@andinanet.net

Cotopaxi Antonio Vela 7531 y General Maldonado, Latacunga; tel: 03 2812768; email: itritoforestalch@andinanet.net

Chimborazo Av 9 de Octubre Quinta Macaji. Edf. MAG, Riobamba; tel: 03 2963779; email: minambientebolivar@andinanet.net

Bolivar Calle 7 de Mayo 704 y Azuay, Guaranda; tel: 03 2981874

Azuay Bolívar 533 y Mariano Cueva, Cuenca; tel: 07 2827583, 07 2823074; email: forazuay@cue.satnet.net

Cañar Luis Cordero 704 y Tenemasa frente al Inst Tec Luis Rogelio Gonzalez, Azoques; tel: 07 2243141, 07 2243141

Morona Santiago Juan de la Cruz y Guamote junto al MAG, Macas; tel: 07 2700823

Guayas Av Quito 402 y Padre Solano Edf MAG piso 10, Guayaquil; tel: 04 2293131, 04 2397730; email: distritoregionalgleo_ma@hotmail.com

Los Rios Av Jaime Roldos A. y Décima Séptima Cdla San José, altos Ecuaquimica, Babahoyo; tel: 05 2757445

El Oro Junín, y Pasaje frente a Porta celular piso 2 Edf Armijos, Machala

Manabí Edf. MAG 2do. Piso Ramos y fuarte entre primera y segunda transversal, Portoviejo; tel: 05 2651848, 05 2638857; email: ambiente_manabi@yahoo.com

Loja Sucre entre Imbabura y Quito, Edf. INDA, piso 1, Loja; tel: 07 2571534, 07 586421, 07 2606606; email: drlzch_ma@easynet.net.ec, podocar@zamoranet.net

Zamora Av Loja Barrio 2 de Noviembre Edf. De la Direcciòn Nacional Agropecuaria 2do Pabellón, Zamora; tel: 07 2805315

There is still a two-tier system of entrance fees for foreigners and residents. If you have an Ecuadorian *cedula*, you can pay the national rate. The current fees (2003) are listed in the following table.

There are also over 100 Bosques Protectores (protected forests) that are protected by the Ministerio de Ambiente. Some of these are privately owned and permission to visit them must be obtained from the owner. The Ministerio de Ambiente (offices in the MAG building at Av Amazonas and Republica in Quito) sells an excellent and inexpensive map of the park system titled *Sistema Nacional de Áreas Protegidas del Ecuador*.

NATURAL HISTORY

The great variety of habitats in a country that rises from ocean to snow peaks and drops back to tropical rainforest ensures an abundance of wildlife. The best-known

ENTRANCE FEES FOR PROTECTED AREAS

Protected area	Fee for residents	Fee for foreigners
Parque Nacional Galápagos	$25/$50*	$100
Parque Nacional Cotopaxi	$2	$10
Area Nacional de Recreacion El Boliche	$2	$10
Parque Nacional Sangay	$2	$10
Parque Nacional Podocarpus	$2	$10
Parque Nacional Machalilla (Mainland)	$2	$12
Parque Nacional Machalilla (Isla de la Plata)	$3.50	$15
Parque Nacional Machalilla (Mainland and Isla de la Plata)	$5	$20
Parque Nacional Llanganates	$1	$5
Parque Nacional Sumaco-Napo Galeras	$1	$5
Parque Nacional Yasuní	$2	$10
Parque Nacional Cajas	$2	$10
Reserva Ecologica Los Ilinizas	$1	$5
Reserva Producción Faunistica de Chimborazo	$2	$10
Reserva Producción Faunistica de Cuyabeno	$5	$20
Reserva Ecológica Cayambe/Coca	$2	$10
Reserva Ecológica Cotacachi/Cayapas	$1	$5
Reserva Ecológica Cotacachi/Cayapas (only Laguna Cuicocha)	$0.50	$1
Reserva Ecológica Antisana	$1	$5
Reserva Ecológica Manglares Churute	$2	$10
Reserva Ecologica Mache-Chindul	$1	$5
Reserva Ecológica El Angel	$2	$10
Reserva Ecológica Limoncocha	$1	$5
Reserve Ecológica Cayapas-Mataje	$1	$5
Reserva Geobotanica Pululahua	$1	$5
Amigos de la Naturaleza – Mindo		$4
Pasochoa – Fundación Natura		$7

*$50 for residents of Andean Countries, $25 for students enrolled in Ecuador

wildlife reserve is the Galápagos Islands; the plants and animals found there are fully described in several good guidebooks. The mainland, on the other hand, is a relatively unstudied naturalist's paradise. Since there are no comprehensive field guides to the flora and fauna of the country, Ecuador offers wonderful opportunities for a field researcher but many frustrations for the ordinary traveller who has difficulty in identifying this bewildering array of wildlife.

Although Ecuador lies in the heart of the tropics you wouldn't call the natural history of the highlands tropical. Indeed, the vegetation here has been compared to that of the Arctic tundra. This is because altitude has more of an influence than latitude on the flora and fauna of an area. Pioneering work on this concept was done in Ecuador in 1802 by the German scientist Alexander von Humboldt. He related ecology to altitude and recognised three major ecological zones: lowland (hot), central (temperate) and highland (cold). This last zone is said to begin at about 3,200m and continue to the glaciated mountain tops. It can be further sub-divided into the snow region above about 4,700m, where insects and birds are occasionally seen, and the area below the permanent snow line, which is known as the *páramo*.

The *páramo* is a highly specialised zone unique to tropical America, and is found only from the highlands of Costa Rica at 10°N down to northern Peru at 10°S. Similarly elevated areas in other parts of the world differ in their climates and evolutionary history. Most of the hikes and climbs in this book will pass through the *páramo* and so this section concentrates on highland ecology rather than giving space to the overwhelmingly diverse flora and fauna of low lying areas which deserve a book to themselves (see *Further Reading,* page 251 for suggested books on the subject).

Páramo weather is typically cold and wet, with frequent rain often replaced by moist mists and clouds. Snow falls occasionally and strong winds are common. Night-time temperatures are often below freezing and glaring sunlight can be a hazard during short spells of fine weather. In short, conditions are harsh, and comparatively few animals are seen. Plants, on the other hand, have adapted well to this extreme environment and as a result the vegetation looks strange and interesting.

Flora

The Andean flora has evolved over many millions of years of uplift of the range. Thus, the vegetation has had adequate time to slowly modify itself. The major adaptations have been the formation of smaller and thicker leaves which are less susceptible to frost; the development of curved leaves with thick waxy skins to reflect or absorb extreme solar radiation during cloudless days; the growth of a fine hairy 'down' as insulation on the plant's surface; the arrangement of leaves into a rosette pattern to prevent them shading one another during photosynthesis and to protect the delicate centre; and the progressive compacting of the plants until they grow close to the ground, where the temperature is more constant and there is protection from the wind. Thus, many *páramo* plants are characteristically small and compact, some resembling a hard, waxy, green carpet. There are exceptions to this however, including the giant *frailejones* and the *puyas*.

Giant espeletia, locally known as *frailejones*, are a weird sight as they float into view in a typical *páramo* mist. They are high enough to resemble human beings, hence the name *frailejones*, which literally means 'greyfriars.' Despite their size they retain certain features of other *páramo* vegetation, such as downy hairs for insulation. *Espeletia* belong to the daisy family, and are an unmistakable feature of the northern *páramo* of Ecuador, particularly in the region of El Angel.

Further south the *páramo* is rather drier and here we often find the *puyas*, members of the bromeliad family which replace the *frailejones* of the wetter north. The *puyas* are some of the least understood of the *páramo* plants, having very few of the normal characteristics of the plants found here. They are very large (reaching a height of over eight metres in Peru) and have no typical downy insulation. Their leaves, though still in a rosette pattern, are not small and compact but long and spiky and grow on top of a short trunk instead of at ground level.

Another attractive plant of the dry southern *páramo* is the *chuquiragua*. In some ways it resembles a tall thistle topped with orange flower heads and with stems densely covered with tough, spiky leaves. This plant has medicinal properties and is used locally to soothe coughs, and for liver and kidney problems.

Apart from the flowering plants there is a great variety of other vegetation found in this zone. Everywhere you go you will encounter a spiky, resistant tussock grass (*ichu*) which grows in clumps and makes walking rather uncomfortable. In the lower *páramo* (below 4,000m) dense thickets of small trees may be seen. These are often of the rose family and a particularly common tree is the *quinua* (*Polylepsis spp*), locally known as *el colorado* (the red one) because its bark is a dull reddish colour. If you push your way into one of these thickets, which are common in the *páramos* of Las Cajas in the south of Ecuador, you will observe a variety of lichens, mosses, epiphytes and fungi.

Fauna

Animals have not adapted themselves quite as well as plants to this extreme environment and are never plentiful. You are most likely to see birds, toads and rabbits.

The most exciting **bird** species is the Andean condor (*Vultur gryphus*). This is the largest flying bird in the world. With its 3m wingspan and effortless flight it is indeed magnificent – particularly from a distance. Close up, its vicious hooked beak and its uncompromisingly hard eyes set in a revoltingly bare and wrinkled pink head identify it as a carrion eater. Often it soars hundreds of metres in the air and its huge size is difficult to appreciate unless there is another bird close by for comparison. It is best identified by its flat, gliding flight with 'fingered' wingtips (formed by spread primary feathers), silvery patches on the upper surface of its wings and a white neck ruff. The rest of the body is black. Condors are becoming much rarer now than in the days of English explorer Edward Whymper, who wrote after his visit in 1880 '...we commonly saw a dozen on the wing at the same time.' Good condor-spotting areas include El Altar and Parque Nacional Cotopaxi, while the largest population is reported to be found in the Antisana area. Nineteen have been counted there. The crags of the Pasochoa Reserve, only 20km south of the capital, support a pair of nesting condors that are sometimes spotted by climbing up to the *páramo*.

Smaller birds of prey are also seen in the *páramo*. The black-chested buzzard-eagle (*Geranoaetus melanoleucus*) is quite common, especially in the Papallacta area. At 58cm in length it is one of the largest of the Ecuadorian hawks (though small compared to the 108cm of the condor). It is identified by a very short, dark, wedge-shaped tail, a white belly finely barred with black, and the blackish sides of its head and breast. Its throat is almost white. The most common hawk is the variable (or puna) hawk (*Buteo poecilochrous*) which is limited to the open *páramo*. At some 52cm in length, its most distinctive feature is a white tail with a black band near the end. As its name suggests, its plumage varies; it is usually light-bellied and brown-backed. The fairly small (44cm) cinereous harrier (*Circus cinereus*) is also sometimes seen. It is mostly grey, with a white rump and belly barred with brown. Finally, the distinctive carunculated caracara (*Phalcoboenus carunculatus*), with its bright orange-red facial skin and legs, white belly and black above, is also sighted here.

One of the most common *páramo* birds is the Andean lapwing (*Vanellus resplendens*). It is unmistakable with its harsh noisy call and its brown, white and black striped wing pattern, which is particularly noticeable in flight. Of the ducks, the speckled teal (*Anas flavirostris*), with its blue-grey bill and brown head, is the most common. Lago Limpiopungo in Parque Nacional Cotopaxi is a good place for both of these species, as well as the yellow-billed pintail (*Anas georgica*), the Andean gull (*Larus serranus*) and the American coot (*Fulica americana*).

If you wake up in your tent during the dark early hours of the morning to hear a weird whizzing sound like a lost UFO, don't be too alarmed. It's probably a cordillera snipe, also known as the Andean snipe (*Chubbia jamesoni*). They often fly at night and produce this strange drumming noise with their outer wing feathers. Another night flier in the *páramo* is the owl. You may catch sight of the great horned owl (*Bubo virgianus*) or even the well-known barn owl (*Tyto alba*). More frequently seen, however, is the short-eared owl (*Asio flammeus*), because it hunts during the day.

Of the small birds found in the *páramo*, the most easily identifiable are the hummingbirds, at least 126 species of which have been listed as occurring in Ecuador alone. The Andean hillstar (*Oreotrochilus estella*) is one of the most common found at high altitudes. I've often been amazed to see one come humming past my tent at a snow-line camp at 4,700m. This tiny bundle of life survives the intense night-time cold by lowering its metabolism by as much as 95% and entering an almost lifeless state, similar to hibernation. Its body temperature drops dramatically; one researcher measured a decrease from 39.5°C to 14.4°C overnight. The bird passes the night in a protected crevice or overhang, and regains its day-time temperature in the morning sun with no ill effects. Hummingbirds are the smallest birds in the world and the most manoeuvrable. The Andean hillstar, at 13cm in length, is comparatively big; the short-tailed woodstar (*Myrmia micrura*), which is common on the coast, is a mere 7cm in length and this includes its needle-like bill. Hummingbirds' wings beat in a shallow figure of eight instead of the normal up and down; this, combined with its 'humming,' 80-beat-a-second wing-speed enables them to hover and even fly backwards, and speeds of up to 110km per hour have been recorded.

Swallows are frequently sighted in the *páramo*; look particularly for the brown-bellied swallow (*Notiochelidon murina*) and the blue-and-white swallow (*N. cyanoleuca*); both are common. Thrushes are represented in the *páramo* by the great thrush (*Turdus fuscater*); the only pipit found is the *páramo* pipit (*Anthus bogotensis*). Other small species tend to come under the category of 'small brown birds'; of these the cinclodes are the easiest to recognise with a distinctive white eye-stripe. The stout-billed and the bar-winged cinclodes (*C. excelsior* and *C. fuscus*) are among the commonest of all *páramo* birds.

Good places for highland ornithology are the Papallacta area and Parque Nacional Cotopaxi. Don't forget that this is a harsh environment, so you won't see birds flocking in their hundreds. In the Cotopaxi park station there is a small museum which displays several dozen species of stuffed *páramo* birds; this should help you with identification.

Looking groundwards instead of skywards you'll frequently find another animal in the *páramo*: the **toad**. At this altitude they usually belong to the *Atelopodidae* family and are recognised by their lethargic movements and diurnal activity. They are particularly active after heavy rain. On one walk in Parque Nacional Cotopaxi Rob saw literally hundreds of *Atelopus ignescens* toads almost falling over one another. They are jet black with bright orange bellies and are locally known as the *jambato* toad. In the more southerly *páramos* these black toads are less common and are replaced by more ordinary-looking green examples of the same genus.

When talking of wildlife, it is **mammals** that most tend to arouse the general observer's excitement and curiosity. Interesting and strange species live on the *páramo*, but most, unfortunately, are extremely rare and difficult to observe. The first species you will see will be rabbits (*Sylvilagus* spp) which need no description. Semi-wild horses and cattle range in the highlands, but llamas, perhaps the animals most closely associated with the Andean mountains and their people, are found only in domestic situations. An experimental herd can be seen in Parque Nacional Cotopaxi.

Three species of deer are found in the highlands. The familiar white-tailed deer (*Odocoileus virginianus*) occurs at various altitudes and is seen fairly often in Parque Nacional Cotopaxi. Two smaller species are infrequently observed. Between 3,000 and 4,000m you may see a small brocket deer (*Mazama rufina rufina*). It is about 50cm tall and of a rusty brown colour with a blackish face. Its horns are limited to tiny, 8cm-long prongs. One of the smallest and rarest deers in the world is the dwarf Andean pudu (*Pudu mephistophiles*) which averages under 35cm in height. It is a light, greyish brown and lives in high scrub over 3,000m, usually in the Eastern Cordillera.

Both felines and canines are represented in the *páramo*. The American lion or puma (*Felis concolor*) has been observed at around 4,000m, and the erroneously named Andean wolf (*Dusicyon culpaeus*), which is in fact a fox, is also occasionally seen.

The largest Ecuadorian land mammals are the tapirs. The mountain or woolly tapir (*Tapirus pinchaque*) is one of the rarest South American animals, and inhabits the high cloudforests and *páramo* of the Eastern Cordillera from 1,500 to 4,000m. It is comparatively common in the Papallacta and Sangay regions, but is extremely difficult to sight because it spends most of its time in thick cover. Its heavy brown body, relatively short legs, large ears and emphatically elongated nose make it unmistakable – if you ever see it! You're more likely to find its tracks; four toes in front and three on the rear feet.

Finally, the smallest bear in the world may be seen in the *páramo* by the extremely lucky and very patient observer. *Tremarctos ornatus*, the Andean spectacled bear, is extremely versatile and has been observed from just above Peru's desert coast to *páramo* at over 4,000m. It is called 'spectacled' because of its irregular, light-coloured eye patches on its otherwise almost black hair. In Ecuador it has been sighted on both the outside slopes of the Western and Eastern Cordilleras and, as with the woolly tapir, the Papallacta region is favoured.

MINIMUM IMPACT

One look at the areas around basecamps and huts on some of the more popular Ecuadorian volcanoes will show you that not all mountaineers are environmentally aware.

Minimum impact means that a place is unchanged by your visit: no rubbish, no fire-scars or other damage and no indigenous people taught to beg by thoughtless handouts of sweets or money.

Don't litter. All your rubbish should be burned, carried out with you, or disposed of properly at mountain refuges. If you can bring yourself to clean up after less considerate climbers, so much the better.

When nature calls, go well away from the trail, campsite or river, and dig a hole. Bring a light-weight trowel or use your ice axe for the purpose.

Conservation is promoted by many international, national and local non-governmental organisations (NGOs). Many of these NGOs are involved in environmental education campaigns and sustainable development projects. It strengthens their causes through good example if international tourists show stewardship of the environment (ie: by picking up litter, burying faecal waste, not cutting down vegetation, etc).

Don't build fires in the highlands where wood is scarce and is sometimes the only fuel for inhabitants of remote areas. Instead, bring a stove for cooking.

Ecuador's indigenous population are proud people with their own culture and beliefs. Gratuitous present-giving tends to impose your culture on theirs, so only give gifts or money in return for their help or work. Children are especially influenced, and gifts of sweets and 'school pens' will quickly establish a cycle of begging, and a view that the gringo is simply a walking 'handout'. If you want to do something for the village children you encounter, give a donation of supplies or money to the local school.

Indiscriminate photography will often alienate you from mountain dwellers. These people, although living under extremely difficult conditions, are as sensitive and intelligent as anyone else and resent being treated with arrogance by foreign visitors. Not only will a few exchanged words in greeting and a round of handshakes be more likely to get you that special photo, it will also bring you closer to experiencing a culture different from your own.

LAST WORDS ABOUT CLIMBING AND HIKING

Keep in mind that the conditions related to climbing and hiking, as detailed in this book, are *not* static. Things change constantly. Climbing routes, particularly on glaciers, will vary from season to season. Sometimes this is a minor variation of our description, but at other times the change is drastic enough to make the described route life-threatening. Since the last edition of this book, every major climb has seen a number of route changes. Also, we are not always right and there are often several ways to do a trek or climb.

It is always best to get verbal information about a route from someone who has been to your destination recently. Be a responsible climber. Go with as much information as you can and use your experience and judgement to evaluate climbing conditions. Treks will see less variation, but water sources may come and go, again depending on the season. New roads, constantly being constructed in Ecuador, will alter, if not completely ruin, some beautiful hikes. Always carry a compass, GPS and topographic maps of the area you're venturing into. Even on lower altitude hikes and climbs, clouds can roll in and obscure the most visible landmarks. It is hoped that this guide will be a valuable tool in getting you into a variety of incredible places and on top of a number of beautiful summits, but no guidebook can replace common sense or be a substitute for experience.

A final note is that there are many possible walks and climbing routes that are not described in this or any guidebook. If you really want to do some exploring, buy some maps and start walking. For most indigenous people the primary form of transportation is still on foot or horseback, and there are trails everywhere. Equally, many of the less used roads are great for trekking. There are still a lot of 'undiscovered' corners of Ecuador.

MOUNTAIN BIKING IN ECUADOR

One of the reasons Ecuador is such an attractive destination for adventure is that it's small enough for even out-of-the-way places to be accessible. Hikers and climbers appreciate the speediness with which they can get off the beaten track and into the remote highlands or up to 6,000m. For this same reason, mountain biking

THE TOP TEN: PEAKS OVER 5,000M IN ECUADOR

Chimborazo	6,310m	20,703ft
Cotopaxi	5,897m	19,348ft
Cayambe	5,790m	18,997ft
Antisana	5,752m	18,892ft
El Altar	5,319m	17,452ft
Iliniza South	5,248m	17,219ft
Sangay	5,230m	17,160ft
Iliniza North	5,126m	16,818ft
Carihuairazo	5,020m	16,471ft
Tungurahua	5,029m	16,500ft

has become increasingly popular. A short bus-ride away from major towns are trails and tracks leading up to isolated villages and natural areas of extreme beauty, all approachable by bicycle. Many of these areas are places ignored by the hiker/climber except as incidental approaches to their end destination. For the climber the reasons are obvious as he/she heads straight for the highest point; for the hiker, meanwhile, trudging along even infrequently used roads is not very appealing. Most hikers choose to eschew man-made tarmacs for the more rustic footpath. All of this leaves a very big area for exploring by mountain bike, especially since Ecuador seems intent on building the most roads per capita in the world! This is not to say that venturing off-road isn't possible or as equally rewarding, but the plethora of access routes makes almost anything possible.

Apart from the Pan-American Highway, very few of the roads in Ecuador are paved. The rest may vary from blissfully smooth, hard-packed dirt (best avoided during the rainy season) to bone-jarring, rock-strewn, cobbled track. These serve as better choices for biking than the Pan-American Highway, which can sometimes be hair-raising (and life-threatening) due to speeding buses and recklessly driven trucks. Because of the road conditions, mountain bikes are much better suited to Andean excursions than narrow-tyred road bikes, as punctures and bent rims tend to occur more frequently with less sturdy equipment.

Transport

These days, it could not be easier to transport your own bicycle by air. Airline personnel will rarely give you a second look as you approach the check-in counter lugging a cumbersome bike box. While I've heard of friends avoiding additional freight charges by holding their head the right way, generally expect to pay a reasonable fee from your home country. From the US it's about $8 a kilogram extra to ship a bicycle as accompanied baggage. Ecuadorian customs officials have recently become more picky about imports, and X-ray machines have been installed in Quito and Guayaquil airports. Don't bring a bike that looks new, otherwise you may get charged import duty.

Travelling with wheels on domestic flights can be challenging, because of the small size of the domestic planes (particularly to smaller cities) and baggage limitations. TAME is generally more flexible, but you will be asked to pay for excess weight. If you don't have a box, remove the pedals and disassemble the handle bar, attaching it to the cross bar with packing tape in order to prevent major damage. Be sure to call the airline office ahead of time to ensure there's baggage space available on the day you expect to travel. Always deflate the tyres prior to flying – unpressurised luggage holds have a way of causing inflated tyres to explode!

Within Ecuador, transporting your bicycle is relatively painless. Most of the inter-provincial buses have large roof racks which accommodate a variety of substantial belongings, from double-bed mattresses to bundles of live sheep. An ordinary mountain bicycle is not likely to attract much attention. You may be asked to pay a little extra, but never more than the price of a passenger ticket. Be sure to remove all easily detachable objects from your bike before storing it on top. Such things have a habit of disappearing.

Equipment

As with climbing and hiking equipment, bring what you think you'll really need from home in the way of spare parts and extra gear. As interest grows, more equipment and expertise becomes available, but the quality is not up to US and European standards. You'll at least need a spare tube, a pump, a basic tool kit, and the minimum knowledge to keep your bicycle in a reasonable state of repair. If something really goes wrong, there are a few bicycle repair shops in Quito that can get you out of a jam. One is located at the Quicentro shopping mall at the north end of Parque Carolina, and there are a few nestled together at the top of Av 6 de Diciembre just south of Parque El Ejido. Lightweight panniers, or at least a rack for attaching a daypack, are probably essential. Lastly, you'll want a reliable lock and chain for theft prevention. In the larger cities you can generally lock up your bike outside during the day and find it where you left it when you return. This is not true at night – bring it inside your hotel or secure it in an enclosed area of some sort. While camping out, it's best to affix your bike to some permanent object nearby. If this is not possible, lock it and consider attaching bells or other noise makers to alert you of any mischief.

At the end of your trip, you may consider selling your bike and spare the expense of packing it up and shipping it home. Secondhand mountain bikes fetch a good price in Ecuador.

Renting bikes in-country is not accomplished easily. The towns of Baños and Otavalo are about the only two places where you can rent bikes to pedal around on your own. The cost is about $7 per day and the equipment is usually of poor quality and inadequately maintained.

Guided trips

If you'd like to do a bike trip but find it's impractical to lug your own wheels along, there are a few outfits that specialise in mountain bike excursions ranging from one to several days. In many cases, personalised itineraries can be arranged; established itineraries have frequently scheduled departures, and generally the bikes are imported and of good quality. Guides always accompany the group, and often a support vehicle is used.

Biking Dutchman Foch 714 and Juan Leon Mera, Quito; tel/fax: 2 2542806; email: dutchman@uio.satnet.net; web: www.bikingdutchman.com. The Biking Dutchman has an approach which is indicated in the name, and is popular with the gringos; he specialises in downhill riding. He offers trips of one day and longer which are graded according to ability, and are vehicle-supported. Good-quality bikes are available, with helmets, gloves, and pads for knees, shoulders and elbows. A minimum group of four costs about $45 per person, per day.

Safari (see *Renting and buying equipment*, page 41) offers tours for about $45 per day.

Sierra Nevada (see *Renting and buying equipment*, page 41) offers tours.

New Life Travel Juan Leon Mera and Foch; tel: 2 2505363. Biking trips to Cotopaxi and Papallacta.

Porbici Ciclotour Riobamba; tel: 3 2941880; web: www.probici.com. Trips in the Riobamba area.

Arie's Bike Company Wilson 578 and Reina Victoria; tel: 2 2906052; web: www.ariesbikecompany.com. Offers a variety of bike trips in northern Ecuador.

Terra Diversa Hermano Miguel 446 and Calle Larga, Cuenca; tel: 7 2823782. The cost of $48 per person per day includes bike, equipment, lunch, guide, transportation and helmet.

There are numerous bike agencies in Baños, but the best one is Exotours, on Maldonado and Oriente; tel: 3 2274097.

On your own

Many of the approaches to the hikes and climbs described in this guide will also serve as excellent routes for mountain biking. Topographical maps of the area will (sometimes reliably) give indications of disused tracks suitable for two wheels. Locals are always free with advice, but just be sure to exercise the proper amount of scepticism. The more open you are to experiencing what happens as opposed to remaining fixed on achieving a particular experience, the more likely it is that you'll have a remarkable trip. Here, we've included a few detailed trips to give you an idea of what mountain biking in Ecuador is all about. This is not intended to be a fully fledged guide to the art of mountain biking; this is, after all, a hiking/climbing guide. However, the beauty of biking cannot be ignored and perhaps a few details here will be of some value.

Mountain biking Salinas–Guaranda–Riobamba

Distance Approximately 115km
Altitude 2,700–4,200m
Rating Moderate
Time 2 days
Start Salinas
End Riobamba
Maps IGM 1:50,000 Riobamba, Guano, Guaranda, Chimborazo, Guarando Oeste and San José de Cameron
Other essential notes Good high elevation ride around Chimborazo and through cheese capital Salinas

Approach From Quito, take a bus to Ambato and from there another to Guaranda, or catch a less-frequent Quito-Guaranda direct bus. Have the driver drop you at the turn-off for Chimborazo (see *Climbing Chimborazo*, page 123 at what is described as the white house (covered in graffiti).

Route description Rather than following the dirt path that leads into the Chimborazo area, look opposite to the other side of the main road and you'll see a track leading off into the *páramo*. Follow this as it veers to the right, passing through several small communities (Panchanco and Yuracsha). Initially the track is uncomfortably stony, but soon levels off into a nicely packed dirt road, gently rolling. Behind you, if the weather co-operates, you'll have great views of Chimborazo. When you come to a junction in the track, take the left turn to ride into Salinas. The right turn will carry you along the road towards Facundo Vela and stunning views, but you'll have to backtrack to get to Salinas. From the roadhead, without diversions, it's about a three-hour ride to Salinas.

Salinas is a delightful village which is run as a co-operative, producing salt, hard cheeses, mushrooms and other commodities. The setting is impressive, tucked under a sheer cliff face. (If you are in no hurry, you may opt to stay overnight in the co-operative hostel and partake of the guided tours available through the salt mines and cheese-making plants.) After a lunch stop in the plaza restaurant, ask for the road to Guaranda, a gentle, chiefly downhill ride. This first day is about 50km (7 hours including the lunch stop). There are several hostels in Guaranda, the best of which is Residencial Bolívar on Sucre y Roca Fuerte.

The next day, take the old road out of Guaranda towards Riobamba. It immediately begins as a steep climb and doesn't let up until you reach the pass about five to six hours later. The road is hard-packed dirt, but can often be muddy and the weather can also be windy at 4,000m. The views are spectacular if you can relax a moment from the exertion and have a look around. From the pass, it's about two hours of downhill rolling into Riobamba. The first hour is on dirt to the village of San Juan where the tarmac takes over. Watch for the cement factory where you'll take the left fork into Riobamba. It's a tough 66km ride with an altitude gain of 1,300m, but the views are great and the severity of life on the *páramo* becomes a little more real.

Mountain biking Saquisilí–Zumbahua–Quilotoa–Sigchos

Distance 141km
Altitude 3,100–4,050m
Rating Moderate to difficult
Time 3 days
Start Saquisilí
End Sigchos
Maps IGM 1:50,000 Latacunga, Pilaló and Sigchos
Other essential notes Colourful ride through indigenous communities and Andean landscape, lots of hills.

Approach From Quito bus terminal get an infrequent bus direct to Saquisilí, or a more frequent bus to Latacunga from where you can catch a regular bus direct to the village. You can also have the Latacunga bus driver let you off at the Saquisilí turn-off, which comes up about 20 minutes before reaching Latacunga. From the Pan-American Highway it's a flat 12km ride into town on good secondary road, but this is best avoided on chaotic market day (Thursday).

Route The first section of the ride, Saquisilí to Pujilí, covers about 19km in two hours along mostly good dirt roads. From the Saquisilí plaza head south on the paved road to the edge of town where you'll see several prominent signs to the Muller Ranch. Follow the signs to the right down a cobbled track for about 200m. Here you'll encounter two roads forking to the left. Take the road furthest to the right (keep right, avoiding going straight into the woods) and continue until you can take a left turn past a military base. When you come into the village, you'll go left up a road just past the church. This leads to the old monastery of Tilipulo, which was recently bought by a local municipality and is being restored. The caretaker, Santiago, will be happy to provide a guided tour if you request. A tip is appreciated.

From Tilipulo continue along the road until you reach a cobbled junction where you'll head right. Cross a small river and take the dirt road up the hill to the left, avoiding the impossibly steep-looking section of the hill directly in front of you. You'll roll through a couple of small villages; in the first one take the right-hand exit, and continue on straight ahead until you hit paved road. Turn right on to the tarmac. About 200m along you'll come to a junction with a statue of a potter. Keep to the left and head into Pujilí. There is a lively market here on Sundays. With a start from Quito the same day, an overnight stop here would be just about right.

The second full section is from Pujilí to Zumbahua, beginning with 28km of uphill riding on paved road, and then a shift from tarmac to compacted dirt with continuous up and down along high *páramo* for a further 29km. This takes about seven to eight hours. If you're in a hurry and want to continue on through Pujilí, the best alternative is to catch a bus to Zumbahua (irregular) or hire a truck to carry you and your bike up along the Zumbahua road to the Guangaje turn-off. This will cut 29km and four to five hours off the trip, making it feasible to get there from Saquisilí in one day. At the Guangaje turn-off, continue along the main road (not the turn-off) to Zumbahua, about 29km and three hours away.

This area is high, dusty, stark *páramo* that is stunning to behold and fascinating thanks partly to the primarily indigenous communities that are settled throughout the area. In many ways life here has been relatively untouched by the modern world. Zumbahua is especially appealing for its Saturday market, which is considered by some to be the most traditional in the country. Much of the produce and other saleable goods arrive on the backs of llamas, transported from smaller villages higher up on the *páramo*. This and a visit to nearby Quilotoa, a volcanic crater filled by a beautiful emerald lake enhanced by several snowcapped volcanoes in the distance, are said to be the best excursions in the country.

Overnight facilities in Zumbahua include several basic hotels and the more comfortable Condor Matzi hostel (3-814610) on the main square.

The following day the route carries on from Zumbahua to Quilotoa and then on to Sigchos, covering a distance of about 65km. Prepare for an early start out of Zumbahua by arranging for one of the restaurants to open up early for breakfast. Take the main road out of town north to Quilotoa, first descending from the village to cross the river. After a few kilometres along a dusty road turn right, crossing over the bridge at the fork in the road. Have a local point it out if there is any confusion. As the landscape opens up at the top of the hill there will be a small road to the right leading up to the crater rim. There is a small settlement nearby and an overnight stay with a local family is possible, but you'll need a sleeping bag and extra food, which the family can prepare for you.

From the lake you'll be able to see the road as it continues through the hills towards Sigchos. This smooth dirt track skirts the edge of a canyon and first passes through Chugchilán, a rustic village in one of the most scenic areas of Ecuador, some 20km from Quilotoa. Continue another 25km to Sigchos where a couple of basic hostels and a restaurant are available. Buses to Quito depart daily at 04.00 and 14.30.

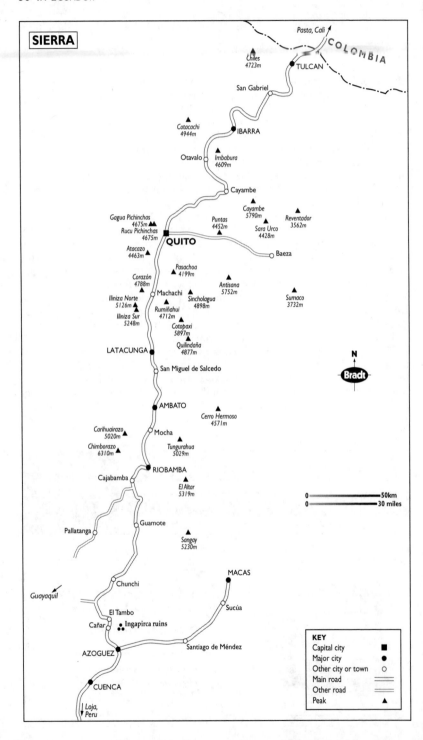

SIERRA

Pasta, Cali
COLOMBIA

Chiles
4723m

TULCAN

San Gabriel

Cotacachi
4944m

IBARRA

Otavalo   Imbabura
4609m

Cayambe

Cayambe
5790m   Reventador
3562m

Gagua Pichinchas
4675m   Puntas
Rucu Pichinchas   4452m   Sara Urco
4675m   4428m

QUITO

Atacazo
4463m   Baeza

Corazón   Pasachoa
4788m   4199m

Iliniza Norte   Machachi   Antisana
5126m   5752m

Iliniza Sur   Rumiñahui   Sincholagua   Sumaco
5248m   4712m   4898m   3732m

Cotopaxi
5897m

Quilindaña
4877m

LATACUNGA

San Miguel de Salcedo

N

Bradt

AMBATO

Cerro Hermoso
4571m

Carihuairazo
5020m   Mocha

Chimborazo   Tungurahua
6310m   5029m

RIOBAMBA

Cajabamba

El Altar
5319m

0   50km
0   30 miles

Guamote

Pallatanga

Sangay
5230m

MACAS

Chunchi

Guayaquil

Sucúa

El Tambo

Cañar   Ingapirca ruins

Santiago de Méndez

AZOGUEZ

CUENCA

Loja,
Peru

KEY

Capital city   ■
Major city   ●
Other city or town   ○
Main road
Other road
Peak   ▲

Part Two

The Guide

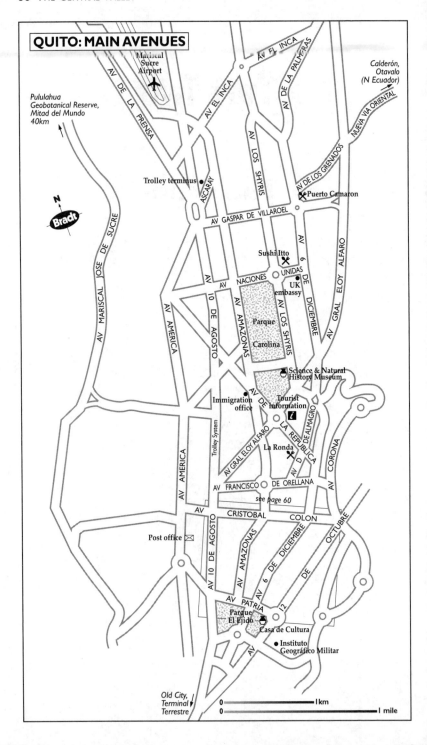

QUITO: MAIN AVENUES

Mariscal Sucre Airport

AV EL INCA

Calderón, Otavalo (N Ecuador)

AV DE LA PALMERAS

AV DE LA PRENSA

NUEVA VIA ORIENTAL

Pululahua Geobotanical Reserve, Mitad del Mundo 40km

AV EL INCA

N

Bradt

AV LOS SHYRIS

AV DE LOS GRENADOS

Trolley terminus

ASCARAY

Puerto Camaron

AV MARISCAL JOSE DE SUCRE

AV GASPAR DE VILLAROEL

AV GRAL ELOY ALFARO

Sushi Itto

AV 6 DE DICIEMBRE

AV NACIONES

UNIDAS

UK embassy

AV 10 DE AGOSTO

AV AMAZONAS

AV LOS SHYRIS

AV AMERICA

Parque Carolina

Science & Natural History Museum

Immigration office

AV DE

Tourist information

AV AMERICA

Trolley System

AV GRAL ELOY ALFARO

LA REPÚBLICA

AV DE ALMAGRO

La Ronda

AV CORONA

AV FRANCISCO

DE ORELLANA

AV D

see page 60

AV CRISTOBAL

COLON

AV DE OCTUBRE

Post office

AV 10 DE AGOSTO

AV AMAZONAS

AV 6 DE DICIEMBRE

AV DE

AV PATRIA

12

Parque El Ejido

Casa de Cultura

AV

Instituto Geográfico Militar

Old City, Terminal Terrestre

0   1 km

0   1 mile

The Central Valley

I live not in myself, but I become
Portion of that around me; and to me
High mountains are a feeling, but the hum
of human cities torture.

Byron

Lying in the middle of Ecuador, the Avenue of the
Volcanoes is not only the geographical heart of the
country but also contains most of its major cities and
almost half of its 13.5 million inhabitants.

The most important city of the Central Valley is of
course Ecuador's capital, Quito. Its high mountainous setting is marvellously
invigorating and, with its well-preserved old town full of narrow cobbled streets
and red-tiled colonial buildings, it is arguably the most attractive capital in Latin
America. Quito is proud of its 86 churches, which, with their intricate wood
carvings, superb colonial paintings, and lavish use of gold leaf decoration, are
amongst the most splendid in the continent. The church of La Compañía and
the monastery of San Francisco, both in the old town, are perhaps the most
extravagantly gorgeous. There are also some fine museums. The Casa de
Cultura at Av Patria and Av 12 de Octubre houses the collections of the Banco
Central, which chronicle the history of Ecuador through a well-conceived series
of four galleries featuring pre-Columbian artefacts, colonial art, republican art,
and finally the modern paintings of Guayasamin and Kingman which explore
the indigenous struggle for freedom. Information on tourist sights and a map of
the city are available at book stores, IGM and tourist agencies.

You'll probably find yourself staying in Quito for some time as it is not only
a charming city but it's also well located as a departure point for other areas.
Despite being only 25km from the Equator, its altitude (about 2,850m) gives it
a pleasant climate. This is an excellent elevation to begin acclimatising for high-
altitude mountaineering and the following easy day-hikes near Quito are
described with this in mind. These are followed by longer and more difficult
hikes and climbs.

Public telephones are rare in Ecuador. There are some stationary cellular phones
which can be used by purchasing phone cards. Some small stores may let you make
a local call for a fee. For long-distance calls use one of the numerous internet cafés
or go to the telecommunications building, Andinatel, at 10 de Agosto and Colon
in Quito (there are Andinatel offices in most major towns). Also, several North
American long-distance companies now offer service from Ecuador and collect
calls can be made from most hotels.

There are thousands of internet cafés throughout the county. Quito was
estimated to have the highest density of internet cafés in the world, since there are

QUITO: MARISCAL DISTRICT

so many Ecuadorians overseas and net-to-phone or email are much cheaper than a long-distance call.

SHORT WALKS IN THE QUITO AREA
Parque Metropolitano
The Parque Metropolitano of Quito is a large forested park in the north of Quito with numerous trails for walking, running and mountain biking. A walk through the park is a good introduction to the Sierra with excellent views of the Tumbaco Valley and several glaciated peaks, including Cayambe, Antisana, Cotopaxi and Iliniza Sur. The main entrance to the park is on Guanguiltagua in the neighbourhood of Batan Alto. You can get a bus along Eloy Alfaro, get off at Portugal and walk 5 minutes uphill to the entrance. There are several marked routes up to 10km long and numerous other side trails to explore. Walking here at night, however, is not recommended due to recent security problems. Enquire at the Andean Cup, near the entrance, for current conditions.

Loma Lumbisí (3,045m)
For those just arriving, this is a good way to test out your lungs at altitude on a 3 to 4 hour walk up a hill lying just east of the city. Below and to the west is the Río Machángara, once a pleasant river, but unfortunately now carrying most of

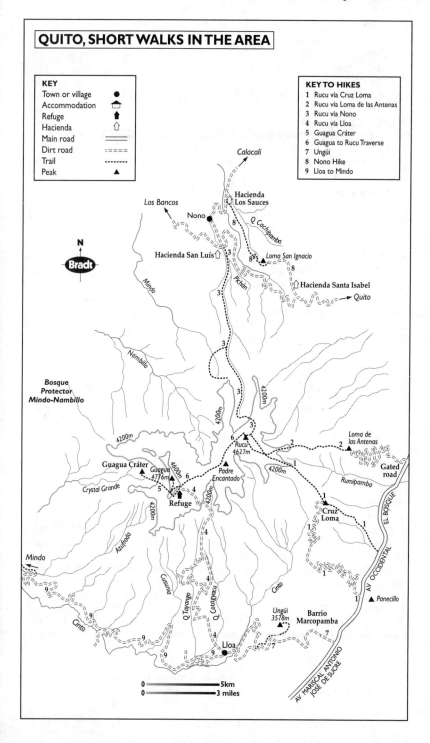

QUITO, SHORT WALKS IN THE AREA

KEY
- Town or village ●
- Accommodation
- Refuge ▲
- Hacienda
- Main road ═══
- Dirt road ═════
- Trail ┄┄┄
- Peak ▲

KEY TO HIKES
1. Rucu vía Cruz Loma
2. Rucu vía Loma de las Antenas
3. Rucu vía Nono
4. Rucu vía Lloa
5. Guagua Cráter
6. Guagua to Rucu Traverse
7. Ungüi
8. Nono Hike
9. Lloa to Mindo

Calacalí

Los Bancos

Hacienda Los Sauces

Nono

Q Cachipamba

N

Bradt

Hacienda San Luís

Loma San Ignacio

Pichán

Hacienda Santa Isabel

Quito

Mindo

Nambillo

Bosque Protector Mindo-Nambillo

4200m

4200m

Loma de las Antenas

Rucu 4627m

Guagua Cráter

Guagua 4776m

Padre Encantado

Gated road

Rumipamba

Crystal Grande

4600m

Refuge

4200m

Cruz Loma

EL BOSQUE

Mindo

Azufrada

4200m

Cusunia

Cinto

AV OCCIDENTAL

▲ Panecillo

Q Tayango

Q Cotagpicu

Ungüi 3578m

Barrio Marcopamba

Cinto

Lloa

AV MARISCAL ANTONIO JOSÉ DE SUCRE

0 ═══ 5km
0 ═══ 3 miles

> **Distance** Approximately 9km
> **Altitude** 2,700 2,900m
> **Rating** Easy
> **Time** 4 hours
> **Start** Las Monjas (Quito)
> **End** Hotel Quito
> **Maps** IGM 1:25,000 Tumbaco or 1:50,000 Sangolquí
> **Other essential notes** Good acclimatisation walk on the eastern edge of Quito

Quito's sewage untreated to sea. This hill is a partially protected area and preserves rural lifestyles a stone's throw from Quito. There are several very steep gullies on the west side of the hill that have escaped cultivation and are good birding spots.

Access You can catch a bus from Universidad Central going direct to Las Monjas, or any of the Chillos valley buses leaving from Plaza La Marín or Hotel Quito, and get off at the new Via Oriental interchange.

Hiking directions From the interchange, head east up the hill. You will cross fields then connect with a dirt road which switchbacks up the hill, although it is also possible to take short cuts. A dirt road reaches the top of the hill and runs north-northeast along the summit ridge for over 1km before dropping back down. Allow about an hour from the toll booth to the highest point.

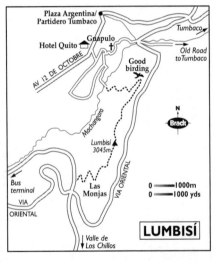

Continue on this dirt road before it begins descending into Eucalyptus forest and you find a dirt road that turns back to the south (if you go too far on the ridge you will eventually come to the new Via Oriental – a six-lane highway!). Follow the dirt road that switchbacks down to the Río Machángara. Cross the bridge to the other side and follow a cobbled road up past several small factories to the paved Avenida de Los Conquistadores. There is a set of stairs up to the Hotel Quito, a few metres to the left of where you meet Avenida de Los Conquistadores. A right turn takes you to the famous Guapulo church and plaza, usually crowded with university students (Universidad SEK). From the plaza you can walk up the steep cobbled road through the historic neighbourhood of Guapulo to the Hotel Quito. Frequent buses also head uphill from the plaza to the La Floresta neighbourhood.

This hike can also be done in the opposite direction from Guapulo to the hilltop and back – allow approximately 2 hours (see *Lumbisí map*, above).

Río Pita hike
Diana Morris and Wayne Lampier

Distance Approximately 7km
Altitude 2,800–2,900m
Rating Easy-moderate
Time 4–5 hrs
Start Río Pita bridge
End Río Pita bridge
Maps IGM 1:50,000 Pintag
Other essential notes: Good escape from Quito with remnant cloudforest and waterfalls.

This lovely river walk can be done as an easy day-hike from Quito or as a half-day trip if you have your own vehicle. The Río Pita descends from the Sincholagua–Cotopaxi area and is accessed through the town of Selva Alegre in Valle Los Chillos. The Río Pita is a beautiful clean river full of chutes, small waterfalls, cascades and deep pools set in a box canyon with native vegetation (including an abundance of epiphytes) covering the cliff walls. There are rainbow trout in the deeper pools (some over a pound, but mostly small), good birding opportunities, and great views. Pause at the swimming holes for relaxation and to refresh your spirit. The climax of this hike is a spectacular 50m-high waterfall 2½ hours upstream from the parking area – a fine reward for your efforts.

Access From Quito catch the 'Vingala' bus that runs along 12 de Octubre and take this to the end of the line in Selva Alegre (45 minutes). Near the bus stop in Selva Alegra you can hire a *colectivo* pick-up for about $12 to take you the remaining 20 minutes (13km). Follow the cobbled road that leaves from behind the Enkador fabric plant (behind Selva Alegre) and passes through the small town of Loreto.

There are two trailheads that join together; one starts where the road crosses the Pita River bridge, about 10 minutes past Loreto, and the second starts about a kilometre past the bridge.

Hiking directions From the first trailhead (at the bridge) you walk along and through the river (knee deep) to gain the trail that follows the right bank of the river for 15 minutes, before wading through the river again to gain the trail on the left bank for the next 15 minutes and then finally crossing back to follow the right bank. After a few minutes more you connect with the main trail identified above (small barbed wire fence to cross here) which continues along the right bank of the river until you reach the big waterfall. Your return is by the same trail. Total round-trip hiking time is 4 to 5 hours.

The second trailhead is an established trail managed by the local environmental association Fundación Madre Tierra, which has the mission of protecting the Río Pita ecosystem and promoting public awareness of the Pita waterfall ecological trail. There is a sign and small parking area at the trailhead. A 5-minute walk brings you past a large house where an entry fee of $1 per person is charged. From here the trail descends into the box canyon of the Pita River valley and follows along the bank of the river. You can explore downstream for several kilometres.

Ungüi (3,578m)

Distance Approximately 6km
Altitude 3,260–3,578m
Rating Easy
Time 3–4 hrs
Start Pass above Lloa
End Marcopamba
Maps IGM 1:50,000 Quito
Other essential notes Good short day-hike with views of Quito.

This small rounded hill can clearly be seen in a west-southwest direction from the Panecillo. The beginning of the walk takes you through Marcopamba, which is one of Quito's outlying suburbs and has a rural rather than an urban feel to it. You may even see a couple of llamas wandering by with loads of straw or firewood on their backs. The walk ends with some particularly fine views of the capital. It takes about 4 to 5 hours round-trip, and there is some traffic on the road if you need a ride back down.

Access Start by taking a No 8 Tola–Pintado bus to its western terminal at Cuartel Mariscal Sucre. Just before the end of the line there is a road at your right called Angamarca (maps show this as Chilibulo). Follow this road up the hill past a hospital on your left to the end where it makes a left turn to the southwest, and continue along its zig-zagging route out of town. At any intersection take the major cobbled fork and follow the road through the countryside for about 1½ hours of steady walking, which brings you to a pass. You can also get a taxi or bus up to the pass on the main road to Lloa from the neighbourhood of Chillogallo. The road down from the pass will eventually bring you to Lloa, which is a possible starting point for climbing Guagua Pichincha.

Hiking directions To climb Ungüi, however, you turn right at the pass. A dirt road heads right and goes around the back of the hill. In the crotch between the dirt road and the road you came up on there is a wide grassy lane which contours the east side of the hill and parrallels an aqueduct (marked *acequia* on the IGM map). The aqueduct runs underground at first but soon flows in an open canal at the surface. Follow the aqueduct until you reach the point where there is a full view of Quito. Here you'll find rough tracks heading up and down Ungüi. Note: paths which appear to lead to the top before there is a full view of Quito are just water run offs. At the top of Ungüi there is a tiny stone building.

If you continue following the aqueduct it will, after some 3km, join with a rough dirt road which heads down the hill towards the neighbourhood of Marcopamba, or you can make shortcuts downhill through fields if you wish. Half a day is perfectly adequate but if you bring a picnic lunch you'll probably enjoy a full day gazing down on Quito (see *Pichinchas map*, page 95).

Pululagua crater

The extinct volcanic crater of Pululagua is located about 20km north of Quito and is said to be the largest crater in South America. It is about 4km wide and 300m deep; its flat and fertile bottom is used for agriculture. The floor of the crater is at 2,500m, and there is a resurgent volcanic dome in the centre, Loma

Distance 2¹/₂km
Altitude 2,500–2,800m
Rating Easy–moderate
Time 2¹/₂ hrs
Start Crater Entrance or Calicali Entrance
End Crater Entrance or Calicali Entrance
Maps IGM 1:50,000 Calicalí, Mojanda, El Quinche
Other essential notes Pleasant walk close to Quito in a volcanic landscape.

Pondoña (2,975m). The area is protected by the Ministerio de Ambiente as a geobotanical reserve.

Access To get there take any Mitad del Mundo bus which runs from Plaza La Marin, through the old town and north on Av America. About an hour's ride will bring you to Mitad del Mundo, where a huge monument marks the Equator – though it should be mentioned that the correct Equatorial line as determined by the most recent surveys lies several hundred metres away. Get off the bus at the monument and take the road towards Calacalí. Walk, get a ride or catch a bus to the marked turn-off for the Reserva Geobotánica Pululagua which is a tarmac road to the right, some 4km beyond the Mitad del Mundo. Less than 1km later this road ends at a parking area at the very edge of the crater. Usually there are kiosks to buy snacks and someone to guard your car.

Hiking directions From here you can walk down a very steep and winding footpath to the crater floor, then walk around on several field roads, or climb the Loma Pondoña in the centre. The descent into the crater takes about half an hour, and it takes an hour to climb back out.

Alternatively you can continue on the main road past the first entrance to the second entrance to the reserve, about 1km before Calicali. This entrance road covers about 10km to the crater and makes a nice 2 to 3 hour walk or mountain bike ride on a gravel road.

Nono hikes

Nono is a sleepy little village located about 15km as the crow flies northwest of Quito, but vehicles travelling on the beautiful winding mountain road from Quito to Nono cover twice that distance. The village is interestingly situated on the western flanks of the Western Cordillera, and from Nono the road continues to the coast, dropping through lush tropical forests. This road and the surrounding forest are particularly interesting for the number and variety of their bird species. The road is little used so makes a good mountain biking route. Nono itself is the centre of a fine network of jeep tracks and foot trails going into the surrounding hills, all making good day-hikes or longer trips if desired. One day-hike is described below but armed with the IGM topographical maps you will be able to find plenty of other possibilities, including a northern approach to Rucu Pichincha (see *Pichinchas map*, page 95). It is also one of the access routes to the Tandaya area described on page 67.

You can reach Nono in a couple of hours from Quito. First take the No 7 Marin-Cotocollao bus northbound. Get off at the end of the line, which is the Cotocollao plaza. Wait at the corner of the plaza by the taxi stand for a ride to

Nono. There are occasional buses, and often trucks will stop at this corner and pick up passengers for Nono and beyond. Most of the transport to the coast will take the main highway through Calicali, though a few continue to go along the old road. This ride is very interesting because after you leave Quito you go past several kilometres of brickworks. These family-run brickworks are not the smoke-belching stacks of Britain's industrial midlands; here you can see *campesinos* mixing, pouring, forming, drying, firing and stacking the mud bricks which are so commonly used in the construction of houses in Andean villages. The mountain road continues climbing through pine and eucalyptus plantations until it reaches a pass at nearly 3,400m, before dropping down through farmland to Nono at 2,700m.

From Nono there is a jeep track heading south to the Hacienda San Luis and a footpath, which continues south to Loma Yanayacu. You could also continue south, walking cross-country to Pichincha. The route is shown on the Pichinchas map (see page 95). There are trails east and west of this footpath, including an eastbound trail that goes to Quito. Trails also lead to the northwest of Nono to Cerro Chiquilpe, and to the north to San Francisco and beyond. Finally, a mixture of tracks and trails climbs southeast out of Nono over Loma San Ignacio and to the pass on the Quito–Nono road. This is the hike described below.

Nono to Loma San Ignacio

Distance 7km
Altitude 2,700–3,325m
Rating Easy–moderate
Time 3 hours
Start Nono
End Nono road near the Hacienda Santa Isabel
Maps IGM 1:50,000 Nono and Quito
Other essential notes One of many walks from Nono, a small village northeast of Quito.

Hiking directions Begin walking northwest for about 1km into the village from where the bus or truck drops you off outside Nono. Continue on the main road until you come to the church plaza at the north end of town. Turn east on a road which twists and hairpins for over 1km to the Hacienda Los Sauces, and here take the right-hand track (which is still wide enough for a jeep), skirting the *hacienda* and climbing steadily southeastwards for 2–3km to the Finca La Florida (which is wrongly marked on the IGM map). After the *finca* the track changes into a narrow grassy footpath climbing south and southeast almost to the top of the hill known as Loma San Ignacio. Go through two gates and near the top turn right through a third gate. The trail now widens out again and soon becomes a jeep track which continues for 3–4km past the Hacienda Santa Isabel and onto the main Quito-Nono road.

The whole hike will take about 3 hours of steady walking and is mostly uphill. It could be done in reverse which would be easier. The beginning of the jeep track is marked by a sign for the Hacienda Santa Isabel on the right-hand side of the Quito-Nono road. The uphill route, however, climbs steadily but gently, and provides good exercise and acclimatisation for those planning more strenuous trips into the mountains.

HIKES AROUND TANDAYAPA AND MINDO

Richard Parsons

The Tandayapa and Mindo areas (down the road from Nono) have become very popular destinations for ecotourism and birding. The cloudforests are well preserved or recovering, unlike in other areas of Ecuador where locals are cutting back the forests. There are a number of hikes in the area, including paths that follow *coluncos* (prehistoric trails eroded into the soft volcanic pumice layers).

Access

There are two ways to reach the Tandayapa Valley:

From Nono Continue down the generally little-used road from Nono to Tandayapa (consider this as a possible continuation of the Nono hikes, since there is little traffic on this road). The road follows a beautiful stream and has some excellent cloudforests along the way, as well as fabulous views on a clear day towards Pichincha. This is also an excellent mountain-biking route, known for its downhill thrills! Crossing a bridge as you reach the village of Tandayapa, the hiking route described turns left up the hill towards Bellavista, and eventually Mindo.

From Nanegalito Take a bus from Quito (Flor del Valle, Kennedy) that heads for Mindo, Nanegalito, or Los Bancos. Four kilometres before Nanegalito, just after a bridge at Km 52, a dirt road turns to the left with signs for Pesca Deportiva and Hosteria Bellavista. It is 6km from the main road to Tandayapa. The hike on this road is pleasant, but there are also opportunities for a ride with local visitors to the Pesca Deportiva trout farms along the route.

Tandayapa to Bellavista and Mindo

Distance 5–35km
Altitude 1,200–2,300m
Rating Easy–moderate
Time 2–8 hours
Start Tandayapa
End Bellavista or Mindo
Maps IGM 1:50,000 Mindo
Other essential notes Good cloudforest and birding on gravel road.

Hiking directions This hike climbs about 500m from Tandayapa to the Bellavista Lodge, which is almost at the top of the ridge. The first 4km follow the road, which is little used, and has ever-more magnificent panoramic views of forest-cloaked mountains as you climb. The trail through the forest starts at a sign pointing to Discovery Falls – the 'C' trail. Follow this C trail up past a small wooden house, and then past a larger wooden house surrounded by a sea of flowers. After a further 200m uphill, you come out on to the road again. Follow the road 100m, then turn in to the C trail again. Ten minutes' climb brings you to Bellavista Lodge.

Bellavista (tel: 2 2116232, web: www.bellavistacloudforest.com) is also a private reserve with 9km of trails, and three respectable waterfalls. (The trail-use fee is $5 per person, althought there is no cost if a full meal is taken or if you stay overnight at the lodge. Seeing hummingbirds at amazingly close quarters is just one of its many attractions.)

It is possible to continue to the town of Mindo along the road from Bellavista. At some point in the near future, a trail may be opened that takes you directly down to the Río Mindo from the Tandayapa-Bellavista-San Tadeo road.

Other short walks in Mindo
These are several day-hikes in the Mindo area; enquire locally for specific directions.

Nambillo waterfall
An all-day hike up out of the Mindo Valley, taking 6 to 8 hours. Great views of the valley and incredible birdwatching (especially at higher elevations) leads up to the Nambillo waterfall, where you can jump off the falls into a deep pool as well as wade in the shallow parts. It's owned and operated by the Narvaez Family, who charge $3 for access to the waterfalls.

Cascada Primavera
Another all-day hike with an option for camping, taking 8–12 hours round-trip. It follows the road out of the Mindo valley into a beautiful section of primary cloudforest. The three waterfalls (Cascada Primavera) at the end of the hike are spectacular. Although wading at the falls is somewhat limited, there are a few nice pools to bathe in along the way. They're owned and operated by the Nelson Toapanta family, who charge a $4 entrance fee.

La Isla
A nice hike down in the Mindo valley itself. If you are looking for adventure you can find it here, climbing a few different waterfalls; guides and climbing equipment are necessary. The path is owned and operated by the Patino Family. You need a guide, and the cost is between $10 and $15 depending on group size.

Mindo Lindo
Up in the higher parts of the Mindo cloudforest, Pedro Penafiel and his wife Heike have created a wonderful area where tourists can come and observe numerous species of hummingbirds at close range. Visitors can hike the interpretive trails on their property and stay in *cabañas*. The entrance fee is about $5, and coffee and tea are served. Overnight stays are about $25 per person per night.

YANACOCHA RESERVE (JOCOTOCO FOUNDATION)
With Volcán Pichincha as a backdrop, this 960ha reserve is set in high-Andean pristine forest; its steep slopes and spectacular views are easily visited along a surprisingly level trail that was built in 1992 and is maintained by EMAP. This was originally a pre-Incan irrigation system that provided villages and towns in the entire region with water from the upper slopes of Pichincha – this irrigation system was taken over by EMAP and now supplies the city of Quito with fresh and pure drinking water. The reserve boasts *páramo* grassland and *Polylepis* woodland (some very old and huge trees remain) along with elfin and cloudforest. The flora is spectacular, with stunted moss-forest and huge *Gunnera* leaves; the floral diversity is also impressive and explains the great diversity of hummingbirds in the area. Puma and spectacled bear along with other high-Andean mammals are present too. It is also home to the critically endangered black-breasted puffleg.

Access

From Centro Comercial El Bosque travel north on Avenida Occidental for 6km (you will have to U-turn to reach the entrance to the old road of Nono). Travel along that road (cobble stone and dirt surface, but year-round usage) until you begin to get to the summit (after 10km or so) – look for a sign (to Yanacocha) and dirt road on the left (public transportation will take you only this far). Climb the first part of the road and make the sharp right at the top (keep following signs to Yanacocha) – you will pass a fenced gate of EMAP (municipal water company). Continue to the end of the road, where you will come to a guard station and a circular toilet facility. The road forks here – a guard will open the left gate to allow you to continue to the first wide area for parking.

Entrance fees

Foreigners $5; nationals $2; children $1.

Hiking directions

The Inca trail which is the main trail of the reserve is relatively flat and extends for 3.5km, passing through a number of tunnels built by EMAP. There are hummingbird feeders placed along the first section of the trail (approximately 1.8km) – these are very active, with at least ten species of hummingbirds seen, including sword-billed hummingbird and the rare endemic black-breasted puffleg, among many others. Another forest trail ('Oso de Anteojos'), which branches off from the Inca trail and connects back by the first tunnel, is about 2.5km long. There is also a trail that goes up into the *páramo* section of the reserve. It is about 3km long and is somewhat steep in parts,

Cerro Ilaló (3,185m)

> **Distance** 10–13km
> **Altitude** 2,300–3,185m
> **Rating** Moderate
> **Time** 4–6 hours
> **Start** Tumbaco
> **End** Tumbaco, San Pedro del Tingo or La Merced
> **Map** IGM 1:50,000 Sincholagua
> **Other essential notes** This extinct volcano next to Quito offers several routes through secondary forest, and pastures with views of the snow-capped peaks.

Ilaló is a long-extinct and deeply eroded volcano located next to the Quito suburb of Tumbaco. It is about a 45-minute bus ride to Tumbaco, located 10km east of and 400m lower than Quito. Climbing Ilaló makes a good half-day escape from Quito. Tumbaco is a rapidly growing suburb of Quito, but is still a delightful place. Although essentially Ecuadorian in character, it is home to many expatriates working in Quito. Its climate is rather like a warm summer's day in England and its gardens are full of bright tropical flowers, flashing hummingbirds and lazy butterflies.

Access and hiking directions To get there take a bus heading north on Av 6 de Diciembre or Eloy Alfaro to one of the towns in the valley (Tumbaco, Pifo or

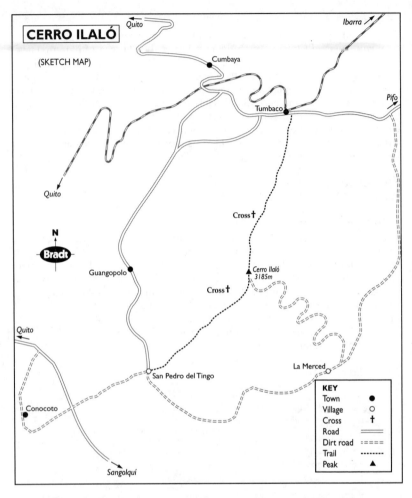

Yaruqui). Make sure that the bus goes as far as Tumbaco, as some buses wander around Cumbaya and never reach Tumbaco. Get off at the main traffic light in Tumbaco and walk east along the main road for 200m or so until the first right turn on pavement. Walk up this road for over 1km until the road forks. Take the right fork on a paved road to Centro Comunal Tumbaco where there is a church with blue domes. A few hundred metres further on you come to a major junction above several volleyball courts, where you turn left onto a cobbled road – this is a good place to park if you are in your own vehicle. Continue up this track staying on cobble until it turns to dirt and eventually deteriorates into a footpath on top of a ridge. This trail eventually becomes a grassy track zigzagging up the hill to the left. A few minutes later you reach a huge white stone cross which has been visible on and off from the beginning of the walk. You should allow 2 to 3 hours to reach this cross from Tumbaco.

This is a good place to stop and admire the view but you need another hour of hiking to reach the true summit. Continue past the cross on a narrow but well-defined trail which leads up a ridge, along a minor saddle and up another ridge to a white triangulation marker at the summit. Occasionally the trail forks, in which case you should always take the upper trail. The trail fades into grass at times but is generally easy to follow. From the top there is an interesting view of Quito to the northwest, nestled in the valley below Pichincha. To the southwest another white stone cross can be seen; a trail leads past this, complete with enchanting tunnels through scrub, and down to San Pedro del Tingo. To the southeast there is a dirt road, which zigzags its way down to La Merced. Either of these can be used as alternative descent routes. If you want to do this hike in reverse, buses ('La Merced', 'San Pedro', or 'Transportes San Rafael') leave frequently from Plaza La Marin in the old town for Tingo (see *map* opposite). There are virtually dozens of other routes up this mountain from all sides utilising farmer's trails.

THE THREE PEAKS OF EL CHAUPI
John and Christine Myerscough

> **Distance** 12km
> **Altitude** 3,000–3,945m
> **Rating** Moderate
> **Time** 5–6 hours
> **Start** El Boliche
> **End** El Chaupi
> **Map** IGM 1:50,000 Machachi
> **Other essential notes** Expansive views of snow-capped volcanoes and panoramic vistas of lush and fertile valleys.

If you enjoy walking across rough open country and are not particularly interested in altitude records, this walk could be for you. It offers expansive views of snow-capped volcanoes and provides panoramic vistas of lush and fertile valleys without taking you over 4,000m. The three hills are usually free of cloud even when all the surrounding mountains are hidden, making this a useful walk during periods of unsettled weather. The walk can easily be completed from Quito within a day, being only 12km long with just under 1,000m of ascent. It is therefore possible to travel light with only a day pack. However, there is no water along the trail, so it must be carried.

Access Take a Latacunga-bound bus from the Terminal Terrestre in Quito. They leave every 10–15 minutes. Ask to disembark at the El Boliche entrance to Parque Nacional Cotopaxi. The ride takes about 1 hour from Quito and on the way you will notice three rounded hills ahead and to the right of the road forming a horseshoe. These are the 'three peaks' of this walk.

Hiking directions On the opposite side of the road from the entrance to Cotopaxi Park there is a dirt road leading in the direction of the first hill, Loma Santa Cruz Chica, with the smaller mound of Loma Sal Grande in front of it. Walk down the dirt road passing under electricity cables and by a small conifer plantation. On your left, after about 15 minutes, you pass underneath another set of pylons and beyond them take the gravel road to the left. This road brings you to the foot of Loma Sal Grande. Heading in a southwesterly direction you should be able to find small paths to take you towards the summit. Keep heading upwards, crossing occasional tracks which skirt around the hill side. Eventually the fields end and you have to continue up through *ichu* grass. Within about 1 hour of leaving the Pan-American Highway you should be on the top of Loma Sal Grande.

Even if you only get this far the view is incredible. Cotopaxi rises majestically to the east, along with the crags of Rumiñahui. If you have made an early start you may also see the morning train from Quito wind its way across the miniature landscape below.

From this crest you can view the rest of the walk. Follow the ridge to the south over a shallow col and pass the edge of a young conifer plantation, then climb steeply up Loma Santa Cruz Chica, keeping to the left high above its craggy western side. It will take about another 45 minutes to reach the trig pillar on the top (3,890m) from where you may catch a glimpse of Tungurahua and El Altar away to the south if it is still clear.

From here descend a steep, grassy gully on the southwest side of the hill to the col between Loma Yuruquira and Loma Santa Cruz. Skirt below the southeast face of a small rocky knoll in your way and continue up to the summit of the Laguna Yuruquira, then descend once more westwards, crossing a col before beginning the ascent of Loma Santa Cruz, which at 3,945m is the highest of the three peaks.

Crossing the last col is a small but well-used path. If the weather is bad or if you wish to shorten the walk, turn right and follow this path, which soon turns into a dirt road. It skirts around the north side of Loma Santa Cruz Chica and eventually brings you back to the Pan-American Highway near the Cotopaxi Park entrance. From here you can get a bus back to Quito.

Going up Loma Santa Cruz you may find a narrow path to take you part of the way. It fades out about halfway up and the remainder of the climb is over tussocky *ichu* grass. From the top of Loma Santa Cruz Chica to the top of Loma Santa Cruz takes about 1½ hours.

From the top of Loma Santa Cruz head northwards following the steep ridge downwards. There is no path, but head for the dirt road that passes between this hill and your next peak, Loma Saquigua. On reaching this road turn right and follow it for approximately 400m before commencing your final ascent. Loma Saquigua, at 3,830m, is the lowest of the three hills and has the gentlest slopes to climb. From the road to its grassy summit will take about an hour. The top gives a spectacular close-up view of the ice-capped volcano Iliniza Sur, and also enables you to look back with satisfaction along the whole length of the walk.

Finally descend to the northwest to join a clearly visible track which will take you to the small town of El Chaupi, whose church can be seen some 3½km away to the north. In El Chaupi there is a store which can provide a refreshing and welcome drink.

Small buses leave every 30 minutes to Machachi. The ride takes about half an hour. From Machachi buses leave frequently for Quito. The ride back along the Pan-American Highway takes about half an hour.

ROCK CLIMBING AROUND QUITO

For the most part, the geology of Ecuador is not conducive to good rock climbing nor has the sport of rock climbing taken hold with Ecuadorian climbers in general. Nonetheless, we include some rock routes up smaller peaks in various chapters of this guide.

In the Quito area there are a couple of interesting rock climbing possibilities. Most noteworthy are two man-made climbing walls found near the Centro Deportivo in the barrio of La Vicentina, run by the Associacion de Excursionismo y Andinismo de Pichincha (AEAP); tel: 2 2508463), aeap@interactive.net.ec.

There are two climbing structures located on the south side of the roundabout at Toledo and Ladrón de Guevara, just a few blocks east of Av 6 de Diciembre and Patria in the new town. AEAP currently charges to use the walls: $0.20 for members, $1 for resident non-members and $2 for foreigners. The older and smaller castle-like structure has short routes of varying difficulty which are good for an afternoon of muscle-building. Next door is the new (2002) 19m-high structure with sport climbs ranging from 5.8 to 5.11. The facility is open daily from 08.00 to 19.30. There is also equipment for rent and sale.

On the closed Tumbaco road, about 1km down the hill from the Plaza Argentina roundabout on Av 6 de Diciembre, are some volcanic rock slabs on the left suitable for bouldering. You can't miss them because the obvious lines of ascent have been made more obvious with large painted arrows showing the route! Scrambling around in this area will turn up more slabs with more arrows, and hence more climbs.

A better alternative is to take the road towards Papallacta, and about 10km past Pifo (45 minutes from Quito) are several outcrops which are suitable for rock climbing. Most rock faces have not been exploited since the rock surface can be loose and rotten and requires cleaning. However, there is one small outcrop of adequate andesite on the north side of the road directly behind a small restaurant and below a power line. Here there are numerous bolted routes that are rated above 5.9 and are up to 20m long. Most weekends climbers use this cliff. A little further up the valley of the north side are some cliffs called 'El Castillo'. However, the rock here is not great as it tends to exfoliate, althought there are some climbable cracks.

LONGER HIKES AND CLIMBS
Cerro Imbabura (4,609m)

Distance Approximately 24km round-trip
Altitude 2,630–4,609m
Rating Moderate–difficult
Time 10–12 hours
Start La Esperanza
End La Esperanza
Maps IGM 1:50,000 San Pablo del Lago
Other essential notes Long acclimatisation (2,000m elevation gain) climb with some rock scrambling and fantastic views of Otavalo and Ibarra.

This long-extinct volcano is located about 60km northeast of Quito and northeast of the town of Otavalo and the pretty lake of San Pablo. It can be climbed in one long day and although not technically difficult, the extremely rotten rock at the top can make the last few metres treacherous. Its first ascent is uncertain; it used to be climbed by local indigenous people who collected ice and delivered it to the town of Ibarra. There are no longer glaciers on Imbabura and so this industry is now discontinued.

Access There are several routes approaching from different sides of the mountain. The most common and straightforward approach, however, is from the village of La Esperanza which lies about 8km northeast of the mountain. La Esperanza is easy to get to: buses leave frequently from Ibarra. La Esperanza can also be reached from

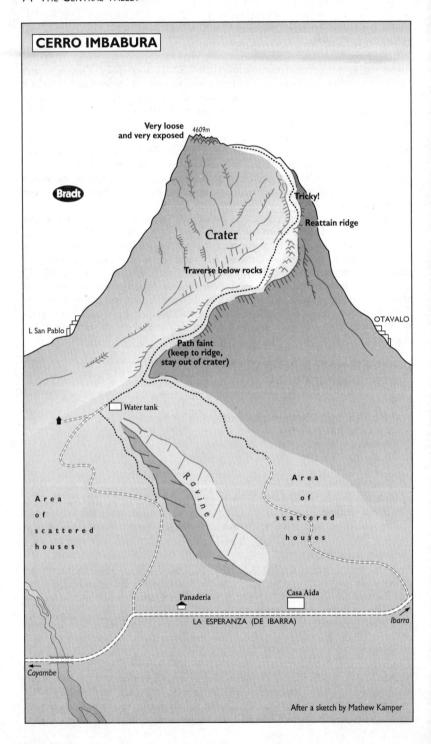

CERRO IMBABURA

Very loose
and very exposed

4609m

Bradt

Tricky!

Reattain ridge

Crater

Traverse below rocks

OTAVALO

L San Pablo

Path faint
(keep to ridge,
stay out of crater)

Water tank

Ravine

Area
of
scattered
houses

Area
of
scattered
houses

Panaderia

Casa Aida

LA ESPERANZA (DE IBARRA)

Ibarra

Cayambe

After a sketch by Mathew Kamper

Cayambe by way of the town of Olemeda. There are a couple of very cheap and basic hostels in the rather strung-out village. The highly recommended Casa Aida (tel: 6 2642020) has been operated by Aida Buidron since 1975; there are rumours Bob Dylan once stayed here. The cost for a bed is about $5 per night with shared bath (hot water). The restaurant serves mostly vegetarian food for $2 a meal. They have great pancakes for breakfast, tasty pack lunches for the hike and vegetarian dinners.

Climbing To begin the climb head south 100m from Casa Aida on the main road to a right turn on a cobbled road just before the bridge over boulder-clogged Quebrada Rumipamba. The road climbs past a school and soon after becomes a dirt track. Stay on track with a wide ravine (Quebrada San Clemente) on the right. It's best to ask for 'el camino para la cumbre de Cerro Imbabura', as this way you'll get on the correct path without a lot of guesswork. As the Quebrada San Clemente ends, switchback up through *páramo* grass and scrub to a cement water tank. Here is where most climbers get lost. Do not descend into the valley to your left. Switchback up the steep grassy ridge to your right. The trail is initially faint but soon becomes obvious. Follow the ridge until an elevation of 4,200m where you need to drop down to the left below some rocks. After regaining the ridge climb up a moderately exposed but easy rocky trail to the northeast edge of the U-shaped rim of the mountain. If there is clear weather, from here you can see the summit pyramid about 1km away on the southwest side of the mountain. Continue around the rim and scramble on loose and exposed rock to the summit. The round-trip from La Esperanza takes about 8 to 9 hours of steady climbing.

From the Otavalo side, there are several ways to go, but the routes are difficult to follow and more technical. From the village of San Pablo del Lago (accessible by frequent buses from Otavalo) leave town from the main square on the road to the right of the church. After about 2km the road turns right (east) and you continue up a track to the north with the mountain some 5km directly ahead of you. Where the road ends head across some fields for the highest point. Find a gully to take you up to the craggy rim. The rock here is extremely loose and rotten. The summit is to your left on the southwest corner of the U-shaped rim. Most people that Mark talked to have got lost on this route, so take care with your map-reading.

You can also get to this route by starting from the village of Peguche (take a taxi or walk along the train tracks from Otavalo). Ask for the trail to Agato in Hostal Aya Huma, which straddles the train tracks. From Escuela Agato head more or less straight up the slope to where it eventually meets up with the track out of San Pablo. For both routes it takes about 6 hours to reach the summit and 4 hours to return (see opposite).

Imbabura circuit

Distance Approximately 45km
Altitude 2,400–3,380m
Rating Moderate
Time 2 days
Start La Esperanza
End La Esperanza
Maps IGM 1:50,000 San Pablo del Lago
Other essential notes Cross-country around Imbabura, walking through Quechua villages.

If going around a volcano rather that up one sounds more appealing then try this circuit of Cerro Imbabura. Rather than cross-country *páramo* hiking, this route follows a cobbled path for much of the way and can be completed in one long day. It is an excellent introduction to life in small communities as it wanders through one village after another on its way around the volcano.

Hiking directions The hike starts in a counter-clockwise direction from the village of La Esperanza, described in the Cerro Imbabura climb. For an early start you might decide to stay overnight here; Residencia Aida is basic yet comfortable, and popular with hikers. From La Esperanza the cobbled track heads north to Caranqui and then angles west past Chorlaví to Tahuarin. Here it begins to turn south passing through the important weaving villages of Ilumán, Peguche and Agato. Beyond Agato you'll connect up with the paved road which circles Lake San Pablo and leads to the village of the same name. In the plaza of San Pablo a road goes up left to Tañahualu Chico where it ends. Above Tañahualu a clear trail ascends towards the pass between Imbabura and Loma Cubiliche offering splendid views of the San Pablo area. Beyond the pass the trail drops down to Las Abras where, just below this village, a left fork takes you down Quebrada Rumihuaycu to the cobbled road leading back (north) to La Esperanza.

This circuit has been a favourite of a group of dedicated Ecuadorian hikers who have turned it into an informal competition. The hike has taken as little as 7 hours and 20 minutes, though the most recent 'best time' can be ascertained at Café María in La Esperanza.

Loma Cubiliche (3,802m)

Distance Approximately 10km round-trip
Altitude 3,000–3,802m
Rating Moderate
Time 5 hours
Start Zuleta
End Zuleta
Maps IGM 1:50,000 San Pablo del Lago
Other essential notes Steep climb up pastures with views of hill south of Imbabura.

Loma Cubiliche can be hiked up from La Esperanza or from San Pablo in a day. The slopes are grassy, so there are numerous routes to the top. One good walk begins in Zuleta. Take the bus from San Pablo or Esperanza to Zuleta and get off about half a kilometre south of Aguas Guaraczapa. Here there is a good track which climbs southwest around the southern flanks of Loma Cunrru. It continues west along the ridge to Loma Cubiliche which has several small lakes in its crater. There are cows on the summit, but the views of Cerro Imbabura are great.

Laguna Mojanda
South of Otavalo is Cerro Fuya Fuya and the high *páramo* lakes of Mojanda. There are many hiking possibilities in this area. It's difficult to get tired of the ever-changing, yet always spectacular, views from the high, wide-open *páramo* and the three lakes near the summit. A good road with occasional transportation goes all the way up to the lakes from Otavalo and footpaths can be followed across the pass

and down several sides of the peak. You can easily pick your own route with the help of a topographic map. Trail maps and descriptions, plant guides and even guiding services are occasionally available at the small rustic tourist information office at Km 3.5 on the road coming up from Otavalo, although this office is often closed. From the north end of the main lake allow 2 hours to reach Fuya Fuya summit and 3½ hours to make a complete circuit of the main lake (be careful of the dogs at the trout farm on the southeast corner of the lake). If you are planning a day-hike it is good to leave Otavalo early, hiring a taxi ($10–15) to go the 16km up to the lakes. You could walk, but would have to plan to camp at the lake. The southern end of the main lake is suitable for camping.

Laguna Mojanda to Esperanza

Distance 10km
Altitude 2,880–4,263m
Rating Moderate
Time 4–5 hours
Start Laguna Mojanda
End Esperanza
Maps IGM 1:50,000 Mojanda, Cayambe (Otavalo and San Pablo del Lago for other routes on the north side of Mojanda)
Other essential notes There are many routes around the lakes and plenty of beautiful camping spots.

Hiking directions One idea for a hike is the 5 to 6 hour walk (about 10km) from the main lake to Esperanza (*not* the town at the base of Imbabura) near Tabacundo. From the lake climb south to the top of a low pass. Here there are three roads – follow the middle road which ascends the western slope of a hill. At the top, as the road begins to drop steeply down the valley, take the vague trail which angles off left (east). It's easy to follow this trail east across the open *páramo*, first contouring under a ridge, then crossing shallow ravines. In the distance the twin towers of Esperanza's church will come into sight. The trail eventually begins to descend a forested ridge and continues through fields before reaching the Esperanza. A good sidetrip is to head to Cochasqui, a tiny village above Esperanza which is known for the pre-Columbian pyramids of Tolas de Cochasqui. There are frequent buses from here back to Otavalo, which is 1 hour away.

There is a popular annual hike from Quito to Otavalo called Mojanda Arriba which generally coincides with Otavalo's annual festival at the end of October. A considerable number of hikers gather at Plaza Cotocollao in north Quito at 06.00 on the Saturday of the festival and hike all day, camping that night in the village of Malchingui. The next day's hike continues over the pass and down into Otavalo where the town band plays a cacophonous welcome. This hike is not recommended for those solitary spirits wanting to get away from it all!

Cerro Pasochoa (4,199m)

This mountain is an ancient and heavily eroded volcano which has been inactive since the last ice age. It is located 30km south of Quito and is easily identified from the Pan-American Highway by its crater open to the west. It is an easy ascent and has been climbed many times from all directions, except up the west face, where the crater walls are extremely steep and rotten.

Climbing Cerro Pasochoa
Canal Río Pita route

Distance 12km round-trip
Altitude 3,300–4,199m
Rating Moderate
Time 4–5 hours
Start Canal Río Pita
End Canal Río Pita
Maps IGM 1:50,000 Píntag, Amaguaña
Other essential notes This route from the north side of the mountain is the most direct.

Access The most frequently done route is from the Canal Río Pita on the north side of the mountain. You will need to have a car, to hire a taxi or to do a little road walking to get to the start of the climb. Find the turn-off to the 'Central Hidroelectrica Pasochoa' on the Tambillo-Sangolquí road; careful attention to the topographic map is essential here. The turn-off is unsigned but there is a basic restaurant at this corner; ask if you're unsure, since this area is developing quickly. Follow this cobbled road and make a left turn just past a soccer field. Climb steeply on a good cobbled road for about 20 minutes to a fork. Stay left here; do not descend to the hydroelectric power plant. Continue uphill 2km to where the road switches back onto small ridge, where it levels-out and contours around Pasochoa following the Canal Río Pita. A taxi can get you this far. At the point where the road levels out you can turn right onto a steep dirt track for another kilometre (possible with 4WD) to a car park. This dirt track is guarded by a gate which may be locked; if so, you may need to leave your car parked along the main road and walk up the track to the car park.

Climbing From the car park cross a stream to the east and head southeast up pastures and trees to a dirt track. Turn right and up the dirt track (with a short section of cobble) as it contours up and to the east side of the summit. (Note: You can also find the turn-off to this track in the farming area of Runahuaycu, on the Canal Río Pita Tambo road, but there is a gate that is usually locked and it is a longer walk.) There may be some bulls wandering around, so give them plenty of room.

At the end of the track, head up a trail through *páramo* grass to a saddle between two rocky peaks. The north summit is easier and slightly lower than the south summit which requires a traverse to the south side. It takes approximately 2 to 3 hours to hike to the summit from the car park.

Machachi route
Access Take a bus to Machachi (frequent buses leave from Quito's Villa Flora bus terminal).

Climbing From the town square follow the east-northeast road heading towards Güitig (pronounced wee-tig) where the famous Ecuadorian mineral water comes from. After two hairpin bends and a bridge you reach Güitig some 3km from Machachi. Turn left at the main store, then right almost immediately (just before the church). If in doubt ask for Güitig Alto. Continue on a cobbled road until

Distance 24km round trip
Altitude 3,000–4,199m
Rating Moderate
Time 10–12 hours
Start Machachi
End Machachi
Maps IGM 1:50,000 Píntag, Amaguaña, Machachi
Other essential notes Long route which passes through the mineral-water producing town of Güitig.

just beyond the Hacienda Mamijudy, where you turn left. At the next major fork head right and keep going uphill until you come to a left turn for the Hacienda San Miguel. Go through the cobbled and gated paddocks and continue on a dirt road down to a stream. Just before the stream there is a fork; take the left track which leads to a footbridge. Cross the stream and zigzag up the hill, then traverse northeast and head for a saddle south of the mountain. From here head north passing two smaller peaks to your left before reaching the main summit. You can descend the same way or continue due north descending to the Tambillo–Sangolquí road by the first route.

Bosque Protector route

Distance 16km round trip
Altitude 2,800–4,199m
Rating Moderate
Time 5–7 hours
Start Machachi
End Machachi
Maps IGM 1:50,000 Píntag, Amaguaña, Machachi
Other essential notes Long route, but passes through mineral-water producing town of Güitig.

On the northwest side of Cerro Pasochoa a forest preserve/environmental education centre has been established. It was declared a Bosque Protector in 1982 by the Ministerio de Agricultura y Ganaderia and turned over to Fundación Natura, a privately run conservation organisation, for management. There is also a very basic hostel by the information centre (take a sleeping bag). This area is unique in that it preserves some of the last of the original forest and other vegetation that once covered the Quito basin area. There is a park entrance fee of $7 for non-residents, and $10 for a camping permit.

Access To get to the Bosque Protector Pasochoa, take a bus to Amaguaña (buses leave frequently from Quito's La Marin bus area), about 1 hour away. Walk along the main road out of Amaguaña for about 1km until you get to the Pasochoa park entrance. From here it's about 6km and 1½ to 2 hours' walking to the information centre. If you feel competent with topo maps you can cross fields and streams and make it in a shorter time. Alternatively, trucks can be hired for the trip to the reserve in Amaguaña for about $6.

Hiking and climbing Several self-guided loop trails have been set up and the area claims almost a hundred species of birds. It is also possible to reach the summit from here but it takes 5 to 7 hours round trip.

Salasaca–Teligote hike

Distance 15km round-trip
Altitude 2,740–3,640m
Rating Moderate
Time 5–6 hours
Start Salasaca
End Salasaca
Maps IGM 1:50,000 Ambato and Quero
Other essential notes Pleasant walk in Andean forest on a mountain sacred to the indigenous village of Salasaca

Teligote (labelled Padre Loma on the IGM map) is an intra-Andean hill located south of the Quechuan village of Salasaca. The upper 300m of the hill are covered by an impressive secondary cloudforest. Clouds hover over the peak while the surrounding countryside and valleys are hot and dry. According to older members of the community of Salasaca the forests previously extended much lower and the climate in Salasaca used to be more moist. There are legends of Andean spectacled bears, and some households have deer hooves, suggesting that the forest supported large mammals in the recent past. Settlers on the slopes continue to cut and burn the remaining forest both for firewood and to clear more agricultural land. There are efforts underway by the community of Salasaca to preserve the area as a Bosque Protector.

Access Take a bus towards Baños and get off in Salasaca (about 20 minutes from Ambato). There is a small market on the north side of the road in Salasaca where villagers sell woven tapestries and sweaters to tourists. The Salasacas are friendly people but they are often shy. Visitors should be respectful of their privacy and should always ask permission before taking photographs. Currently there is only one hostel, Hostal Salasaca, run by a friendly, industrious weaver, Alonso Pilla. The hostal is modelled on traditional Salasaca dwellings and offers dramatic valley and river view.s Adventurous visitors can also arrange homestays with families. A great place to eat is Sanarina, just off the plaza, run by the Masaquiza family.

Hiking directions There are numerous routes to the top of Teligote. Generally it is best to contract a guide in Salasaca to take you through the maze of farmland trails leading up to the base of the cloudforest. If you decide to head out on your own, one route is to head for the community of Teligote where there is a church and a small store. From Teligote follow trails up to a road that contours around the base of the forest. From there you will need to locate a trail that snakes though the forest. Towards the top the vegetation can be thick and it is easy to get lost. On the summit is a very small pond called Guaguacocha. There are interesting legends about this water source. Some Salasacans believe is contains a secret passage into the Llanganates. The hike from the main road in Salasaca takes 5 to 6 hours round-trip.

Another route is to follow the contouring road to Quebrada Masabacho and climb the peak labelled Cerro Llimpi (3,732m) which has a radio tower on the top. It may be possible to continue south along the ridge and end up in the villages south of Quero.

Giant espeletia

The Western Cordillera

Never journey without something to eat in your
pocket, if only to throw to dogs when attacked by them.

E S Bates

INTRODUCTION

The Central Valley described in *Chapter 4* is flanked by
the Western and the Eastern Cordilleras. (These are
often called the Cordillera Occidental and the
Cordillera Real.) The Western is lower and less massive,
although it does contain Ecuador's highest mountain, the
extinct volcano Chimborazo, at 6,310m. This mountain range is about 360km long
and 30–40km wide and its average height is 3,000–3,500m above sea level. All the
major mountains and some hikes within the Cordillera will be described
systematically, beginning with the northernmost mountain.

GOLONDRINAS TRAIL
James Attwood and Piet Sabbe

Distance 30km
Altitude 1,000–4,000m
Rating Moderate
Time 3–4 days
Start Socavones
End Las Juntas
Maps IGM 1:25,000 La Plata, Río Chutín, Estación Carchi, La Concepción
Other essential notes Great *páramo* to subtropical forest hike passing
through friendly communities.

The high *páramo* above the township of El Angel in the Carchi Province is the
starting point for a 3 to 4 day, 30km hike down the western slopes of the Andes,
beginning at 4,000m, passing through three distinct ecosystems and finishing at the
Ibarra–San Lorenzo road, in the subtropical Mira Valley, 3,000m below. There are
several trails which follow this route but the Golondrinas trail is the most
accessible.

Access From the main plaza in El Angel (4 hours' bus drive north of Quito) you
can organise a ride in a pick-up truck to Socavones in the *páramo* (about 90
minutes). You will pass the small village of La Libertad, *haciendas* and trout farms

83

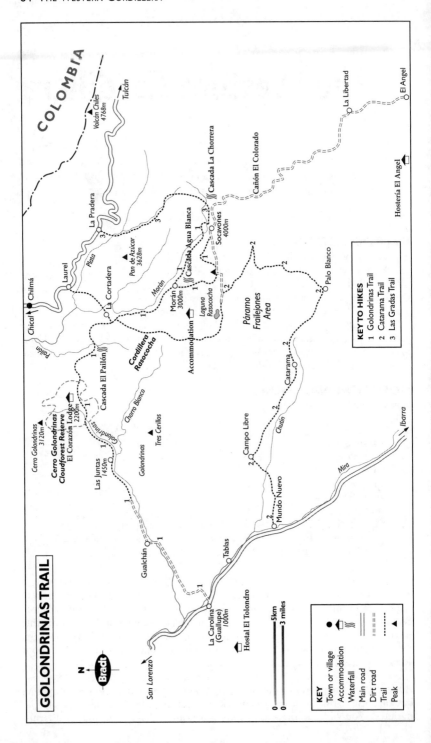

GOLONDRINAS TRAIL

COLOMBIA

Volcán Chiles 4768m
Tulcán
La Pradera
Laurel
Chical
Chilmá
Pailón
Pinta
La Coradera
Pan de Azúcar 3628m
Morán
Cascada Agua Blanca
Cascada La Chorrera
Socavones 4000m
Cañón El Colorado
La Libertad
El Ángel
Hostería El Ángel
Morán 3000m
Laguna Rasococha
Accommodation
Páramo Frailejones Area
Palo Blanco
Cordillera Rasococha
Cascada El Pailón 2200m
Cerro Golondrinas 3120m
Cerro Golondrinas Cloudforest Reserve
El Corazón Lodge
Chorro Blanco
Tres Cerillos
Golondrinas
Las Juntas 1450m
Catarama
Chuin
Campo Libre
Mundo Nuevo
Mira
Gualchán
Tablas
Ibarra
San Lorenzo
La Carolina (Guallupe) 1000m
Hostal El Tolondro

KEY TO HIKES
1 Golondrinas Trail
2 Catarama Trail
3 Las Gradas Trail

N
Bradt

KEY
● Town or village
⌂ Accommodation
≋ Waterfall
Main road
===== Dirt road
···· Trail
▲ Peak

0   5km
0   3 miles

along the way to Socavones, which is merely the name of the highest point on the road to Morán (no sign indicates the place, but there is a sign warning not to set fire or to hunt). Sr Fernando Calderón (tel: 6 2977274) is recommended as a driver. He leaves for Morán every day at 06.30 to collect the milk there. With advance notice, he can take your luggage to the village of Morán, while you walk from Socavones further west through the *páramo* and the Agua Blanca Valley.

Hiking directions From Socavones, pass the sign and walk down a dirt road on your left for about 300m, where a small walking track breaks off to the right, crossing about 50m of swamp, surrounded by the furry-leafed *frailejones* and *achupallas* plants. This leads to El Mirador, a look-out offering spectacular views of the lunar-like *páramo* at 4,000m and the pockets of cloudforest in the Morán Valley below. From El Mirador, backtrack about 200m and follow the path to the right and southwest for half an hour or so, until you reach a small pond, called El Cebadal (which is empty in the dry season). Walk round the pond and keep walking southwest, staying more or less at the same altitude. This leads to part of an old track to Las Juntas, carved out some generations ago. Follow this track for about 1½km to where it stops. Here you veer sharply down to the right, into a grassy valley. This leads you to the edge of the *páramo*, where you enter the forest. After 15 minutes of careful walking (it's very steep) you reach the Agua Blanca waterfall. After about 4 hours' walking through the forest, interrupted by some clearings, you arrive at the ten-family village of Morán.

Here the Castro or Quintanchala families may be able to put you up. If not, stay in the community guesthouse, a brick cabin, which offers more privacy. Villagers may ask you to register and to pay a small entrance fee ($1.5) to their valley. They are seeking financial support to get their 3,000ha territory declared Bosque Protector.

In Morán you can also organise guides and horses for the next day's trip to El Corazón. Hiring guides in Morán (Hugo and Arturo Quintanchala or Carlos Castro can help) is recommended, both to make the 7-hour hike to El Corazón more interesting and to involve locals in tourism and environmental issues. This part of the trail is enjoyable on horseback from Morán to the El Pailón waterfall. On your way you may want to stop in La Cortadera for a bowl of soup with Gonzalo Meneces's family.

From El Pailón to El Corazón the path may in parts be very muddy, especially in the rainy season, and physically demanding. There are several side tracks that veer off from the main trail. As a rule stay on the widest trail and keep going downhill. The cabin in El Corazón is owned by Sr Sabbe and may be occupied by volunteers working in the Golondrinas Reserve. You will have to make arrangements to share the bunkbeds or you may have to sleep on the porch, if the cabin is full.

The rich biodiversity of the wet evergreen forests surrounding El Corazón and covering the steep slopes of nearby Cerro Golondrinas have been the topic of much interest within the international scientific community. The highest of Golondrinas's three peaks, at 3,120m, is three machete-swinging days away; out of most people's reach. However, several existing paths make memorable day excursions from the cabin. Continuing on the trek to reach the village of Las Juntas, where the road to El Limonal and the Mira Valley begins, take the main track downhill, surrounding the valley, first heading north and gradually turning south. After 2 hours you will cross the Río Golondrinas. Keep the river on your left hand, past corn, yuca and naranjilla fields, eventually arriving 4 hours later at Las Juntas. You may arrange a meal with the villagers. You can organise a lift here to El Limonal (1,000m). Daily buses leave at 05.30 to El Limonal, Ibarra and San Lorenzo on the coast.

It is highly recommended to contact the man who made the trail, Piet Sabbe (email: bospasforest@gardener.com). He will give you details about the condition of the trail and can help you get in touch with locals along the way. He also organises research and volunteer programmes in his Bospas Forest Farm. You will find him 800m uphill from the village of El Limonal (www.ecuativer.com/bospas).

RESERVA ECOLÓGICA COTACACHI-CAYAPAS

The Reserva Ecológica Cotacachi-Cayapas was established in 1968 and preserves 204,420 hectares of Andean western slope terrain ranging in elevation from the summit of Cotacachi (4,939m) to coastal rainforest (300m). Access to the reserve is difficult since most of the area is covered by thick cloudforest, montane or rainforest vegetation except the eastern edge which is in *páramo*. A walk from the *páramo* to the coast would be interesting but challenging. Most people visit the margins of the reserve from the Otavalo-Ibarra area. The Piñan Lakes Trek, the Laguna de Cuicocha and Cerro Cotacachi are located within the reserve.

It is also possible to access the park by travelling up the Río Cayapas from the coastal African-American community of Borbón, though few tourists do this. Remember if you travel to the northwest coast it is important to have malaria protection.

Piñan Lakes trek

Distance 30–45km
Altitude 2,700–4,535m
Rating Moderate
Time 3–4 days
Start Irubincho (Irunguichu)
End Irubincho (Irunguichu)
Maps IGM 1:50,000 Imantag and Ibarra. 1:25,000 Cerro Yanaurco is necessary for this description.
Other essential notes Classic *páramo* hike to lake region west of Ibarra.

The Piñan Lakes are northwest of Ibarra, a bit off the beaten track, yet are worth a visit for their beautiful setting on the high *páramo* below the twin peaks of Yanaurco de Piñan (4,535m). The 3 to 4 day trek begins from the small settlement of Irubincho (Irunguichu), northwest of Ibarra.

Access Transport direct to the Irubincho (Irunguichu) leaves Ibarra several times a day, or you can take a bus to the larger village of Urcuquí and get a ride to Irunguichu from there (see map opposite).

Hiking directions From Irubincho (Irunguichu) a trail leads out of the village northwest towards a prominent hill called Cerro El Churo (marked Cerro Churoloma on the IGM 1:50,000 Imantag map). The steep ascent goes through small farming areas and forest and eventually skirts around the northeast side of El Churo. The trail then flattens for a short while as it picks up and follows west-northwest alongside a small stream for about 2km. This is likely to be the first water you'll encounter after leaving Irubincho (Irunguichu). There is good camping here

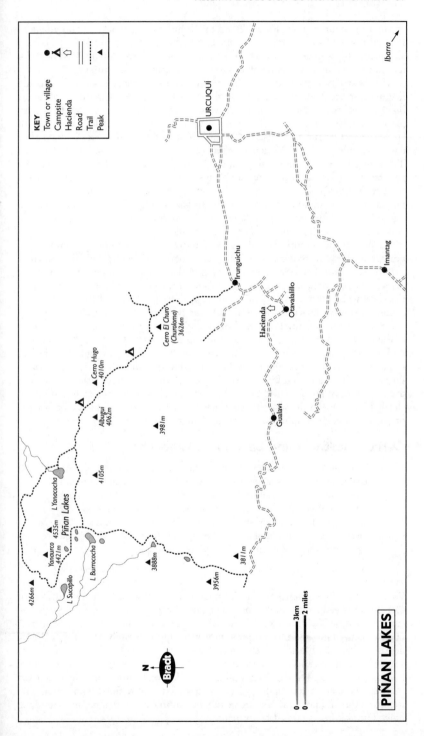

PIÑAN LAKES

or you can continue along for another 2 to 3 hours to a small lake/stream junction. Beyond the flat area, the trail leaves the stream and angles north for another steep ascent towards a low pass between Cerro Hugo and Cerro Albugui. Past here the terrain flattens somewhat and you can find an area suitable for camping.

The next day head northwest up to the Laguna Yanacocha or across to the Laguna Burracocha to the west. Both of these lakes are good basecamps for short hikes in the area. It can be a little boggy around the lakes, but you can find a dry place to pitch a tent. The area has much to offer – herds of wild horses, lots of lakes, spectacular *páramo* vegetation, trout fishing in the streams, etc. With an extra day, a circuit of the Yanaurcu volcano can be hiked in about 6 to 7 hours. Traversing below the mountain in a clockwise direction will bring you to a low pass beneath the west peak. The trail begins as a wide cattle track and narrows to a footpath as it reaches the backside of the volcano. Several trails meander in and out but the route is straightforward. The circuit is a rolling affair – up and down the entire way around Yanaurcu – littered with a variety of wild flowers, and there's a good chance of seeing wildlife such as white-tailed deer and condors.

A climb to the summit will take about 5 to 6 hours depending on your starting point. The views from the top are some of the best in Ecuador. With clear weather the whole of the Ibarra/San Pablo valley is visible along with more than 40 lakes scattered across the *páramo* below. There's not much of a trail but the route up to the summit is not difficult. Head northwest across a relatively flat area of *páramo* keeping left (northeast) of a small hill. On the IGM 1:25,000 Cerro Yanaurco map this is left of the area marked Tatacho. Ascend the scree along the southeast ridge of the volcano. As usual, the rocks near the top are unstable, so watch your footing.

The route out goes south from the Laguna Burrococha, descending along the ridge. Keep west of the Quebrada Pucará valley (passing Loma de La Ciénaga, Loma del Churo and Piguburu) eventually connecting to a track that heads east to the Hacienda El Hospital and Otavalillo. This ought to take about 5 to 6 hours of steady hiking. From the *hacienda* there may be transportation all the way to Ibarra, or you can hike 3km uphill to Irubincho (Irunguichu).

Cerro Cotatachi and Laguna de Cuicocha

In no other part of Ecuador is there anything equalling this extraordinary assemblage of fissures, intersecting one another irregularly and forming a perfect maze of impassable clefts. The general appearance of the country between the villages of Cotacachi and Otavalo is not very unlike that of a biscuit which has been smashed by a blow of the fist. The cracks are all V shaped, and though seldom of great breadth are often very profound, and by general consent they are all earthquake *quebradas*.

Edward Whymper, 1892

Cerro Cotacachi (4,944m) and the Laguna de Cuicocha are located northwest of Otavalo. A paved road leads to the Laguna de Cuicocha. It is a collapsed volcanic crater now filled with a deep lake which averages 3km in diameter and is over 200m deep. The volcano erupted violently approximately 2,000 years ago, depositing angular blocks (which can be seen in the road cut at the crater rim) and a thick layer of volcanic ash into which streams have cut box canyons on the slope leading to Otavalo. During the eruption the volcano collapsed into the evacuated magma chamber creating a deep depression which is now filled with water. The islands in the middle of the lake are resurgent volcanic cones that began to refill the hole. The volcano is currently dormant.

Access To get there take any bus from Quito to Otavalo. In Otavalo, *busetas* (small buses) leave regularly for the 30-minute ride to Quiroga, where the Syndicate Cuicocha *camionetas* (pick-up trucks) wait at the square to take passengers up to the laguna. The cost is about $7 for the vehicle. Walking to the lake from Otavalo along the road takes about 2½ to 3 hours and hitchhiking is also a possibility, but not dependable.

Once at the lake you'll find a restaurant and amenities such as boat rides around the islands. A path circles the rim, giving marvellous views of the deep blue lake with the snowy peaks of Cayambe and Cotopaxi in the distance. Among the many flowers growing by the path are several species of orchid and puyo with bright green flowers. Giant hummingbirds visit the lupins and condors are sometimes seen.

Laguna de Cuicocha circuit

Distance 11km
Altitude 3,070–3,400m
Rating Easy
Time 5 hours
Start Laguna de Cuicocha entrance
End Laguna de Cuicocha entrance
Map IGM 1:50,000 Otavalo
Other essential notes Loop trail around the lake with great views, although there has been problems with security.

Climbing The path begins at the reserve guard station and runs counterclockwise around the lake; allow 4 to 5 hours. This trail has steps in the steeper parts, handrails provided on the precarious sections and a bridge spanning the river. There are information plaques and picnic benches placed at two scenic lookouts. There have been robberies in the more remote sections of this trail, so it is recommended to walk only to the lookout, unless you are walking with a large group. Enquire at the guard station for current information on safety.

The trail is easy to follow since there are signs at all the major intersections. Head for the highest point on the north side of the lake along a well-used trail on the crater rim – you will see the road to Cerro Cotacachi below and to your right. The trail veers to the backside of this hill and regains the rim on the other side. Here there are spectacular views of the two islands in the centre of the lake. These are the resurgent domes that began to fill in the crater after the catastrophic collapse of the mountain.

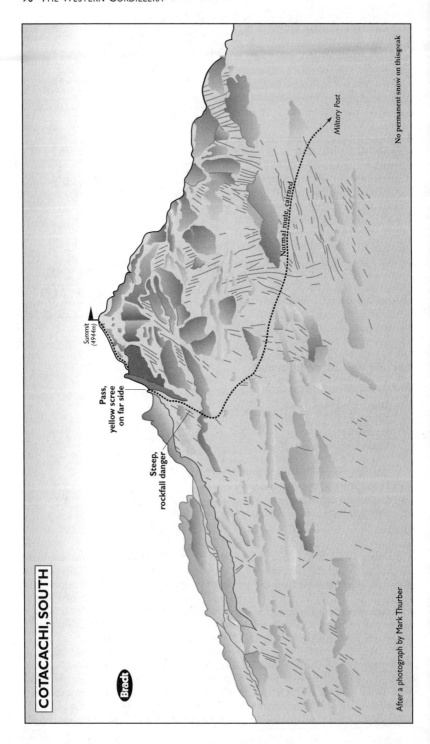

COTACACHI, SOUTH

Summit (4944m)

Pass, yellow scree on far side

Steep, rockfall danger

Normal route, cairned

Military Post

No permanent snow on this peak

After a photograph by Mark Thurber

Continue to a point where the trail meets the road to Cerro Cotacachi; keep on the trail to a covered veranda complete with rubbish bins! From here you descend to a bridge over a rocky streambed which may be dry. After contouring in and out of several valleys that drain Cerro Cotacachi you eventually reach the rim again. Follow the trail to a fence and head right to a dirt road. Take a left on the road and descend back to the reserve guard station. Just before you get to the station there is a basic but nice restaurant overlooking the lake directly above the visitors' centre. To the left of the restaurant are some cabañas that cost about $8 per person.

Climbing Cotacachi
Map IGM 1:50,000 Imantag
Cerro Cotacachi rises impressively above the northern shore of the Laguna de Cuicocha, but the weather is often misty, thus obscuring visibility. Whymper and the Carrels claimed the first ascent in 1880 (see pages 10–11). This climb can be done in one long day if you have transport to the end of the road. A more pleasant climb would be with a camp at the base of the peak, with the possibility of spotting a condor. The climb involves some exposed scrambling and may require the use of an ice axe if the slopes are covered with snow (see opposite).

Approach Continue up the road to the Laguna de Cuicocha; take a sharp right (north) just before the Laguna de Cuicocha guard station up a cobbled road which quickly deteriorates to loose gravel. This road is gated and locked at night, so it will only be possible to drive up this road during daylight hours. The road ends 13km from the guard station at a military post with a radio tower. This post is staffed during the week and can help with emergencies – however it is not set up as a refuge. If walking you can take a short cut by following the power lines, and it takes 2 to 3 hours from the Laguna de Cuicocha. A hired vehicle from Otavalo takes about 1½ hours and costs $25.

A couple of hundred metres before you reach the military post, the road crosses a ridge and turns sharply south. At this hairpin curve you'll find a trail that heads north up the grassy *páramo* ridge to the base of Cotacachi. Camping is possible after about an hour's walk up this ridge, with excellent views of Imbabura and Cayambe. Water can be found in a swampy area to the west of ridge.

Normal route From the base of the peak you need to corkscrew clockwise to the northwest side of the mountain. Stone cairns mark the way as you head west and up. This section of climbing up and across the slope is particularly dangerous because of rock and ice falling from above. A helmet is imperative. Look for a prominent col on the southwest side of the peak. From the col drop down to the yellow scree (or snow) in a basin and scramble up to rock benches. To avoid loose scree it is possible to stay on rock to the right – it's a little exposed but not too technical. At the top of the benches climb up 10m of easy class 5 to the summit ridge. At the top of this, it's a 10-minute scramble to the summit along a knife-edged ridge of rotten rock with drops on either side. There is an anchor rock at the top of the 10m wall which can be used on descent as an abseil anchor. Allow about 3 to 5 hours from the military post to the summit, 2 hours for the descent.

Northeast ridge A more technical alternative to the above route follows the northeast ridge to the summit. It consists of more rotten rock and for all this punishment you'll need a helmet, rope, climbing harness, carabiners and a few slings, and a figure of eight or similar device for abseiling. Follow the trail up the ridge to the base as previously described. Rather than angle left, continue straight ahead, either up a river gully or along the grassy slope on the right of a bedrock layer. Aim for a small saddle and continue up the slope to the right. At this point look for the cairns which mark the route straight up the ridge. Follow a series of 'saddles' until you're confronted by an impossible-looking, rotten rock wall. Take extreme caution as the handholds rarely stay put. Manoeuvre up a 15m chimney and follow up a short rock wall to the summit scree slope. Returning along the same route, it's a little easier to briefly follow the sandy ridge on the left to the point where you can cross over to the top of the rock wall for a short abseil to the saddle. From here it's a matter of retracing your steps (and continuing to avoid loose rotten rock!).

Laguna de Cuicocha to Laguna Mojanda

Distance Approximately 30km
Altitude 3,000–3,700m
Rating Moderate
Time 2–3 days
Start Laguna de Cuicocha entrance
End Laguna Mojanda
Map IGM 1:50,000 Otavalo, Mojanda
Other essential notes Cross-country route between two volcanic lakes; requires route-finding.

Armed with the IGM 1:50,000 maps of Otavalo and Mojanda, this 2-day hike will take you past several villages, through forested areas and across *páramo* from one crater lake to another. The route will require asking directions along the way. There are interesting changes in vegetation zones which range from bromeliads to tree ferns to wild orchids. The trek more or less heads due south from the Laguna de Cuicocha and the village of Ugshapungu. Continue on a variety of footpaths towards Cerro El Quinde (Loma Quinde Pucará). The stream on the east side of the main paved road would be a good camping place. The trail crosses the paved road before Cerro El Quinde and angles southeast towards Cerro Blanco. Head southeast, keeping Cerro Blanco on the left (east); there will be stunning views of the whole area. The route continues southeast until you finally reach the Laguna Mojanda; here you will need to do some route-finding, or ask locals if in doubt. On weekends there is traffic to Otavalo from the lakes, but do not count on a ride. It takes 3 or 4 hours to walk down from the lake on the cobbled road to Otavalo.

LA DELICIA TO APUELA

This day's outing northwest from Otavalo combines forested valleys with *páramo* ridges in an area superb for birdwatching. The trails can often be muddy and suitable waterproof boots may be desirable. (See map opposite.)

Access The hike starts from the small village of La Delicia (also known as Las Delicias) which consists of a school, a tiny store and some 4 houses, about 2 hours from Otavalo. There is no direct transport but buses and trucks bound for the villages of Apuela and García Moreno pass through the settlement. Departing from Otavalo at the corner of 31 Octubre and Colón, the earliest truck leaves at 07.15 except Tuesdays, and several daily buses (Transportes Otavalo or Transportes Cotacachi) go until mid-afternoon.

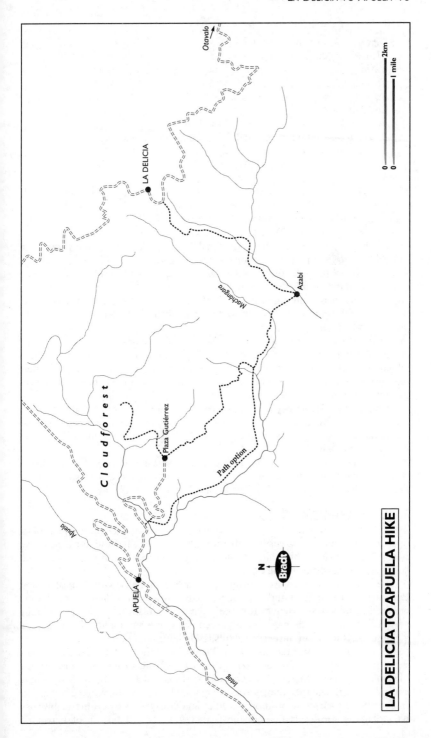

Otavalo

LA DELICIA

Azabi

Mochängara

Cloudforest

Plaza Gutiérrez

Path option

Apuela

APUELA

Intag

N

Bradt

0   2km
0   1 mile

LA DELICIA TO APUELA HIKE

> **Distance** Approximately 15km
> **Altitude** 1,600–2,760m
> **Rating** Easy
> **Time** 5–6 hours
> **Start** La Delicia
> **End** Apuela
> **Map** IGM 1:50,000 Imantag, Apuela and Otavalo
> **Other essential notes** Route passes through cloudforest villages on pre-Columbian trail to hot springs.

Hiking directions From the store in La Delicia (where you'll be dropped) walk 200m back up the hill and around the bend to the last house. Here you'll find the beginning of the trail to the community of Azabí which is visible down the valley.

The descent begins through polylepsis forest which is a good area for birdwatching. Once in the valley of Quebrada Agua Azul, the trail follows the river to Azabí. Here, just past the school, the track divides. Keep right for a short yet steep climb up the side of the valley where a good wide trail leads to Plaza Gutiérrez. As it descends the ridge to this hillside village there are some impressive views of the neighbouring valleys. In Plaza Gutiérrez there is a wonderful panorama of the entire area from the old church which is situated on a large (likely pre-Columbian) terrace.

Leaving Plaza Gutiérrez, a good jeep track winds west down into the valley and crosses the river. Halfway down to the valley there is a steep, narrow shortcut which eliminates half a kilometre and crosses a rustic suspension bridge. It then rejoins the main track following the Río Toabunchi into Apuela. From La Delicia this hike takes about 5 to 6 hours.

Occasional transport from Apuela makes the return trip to Otavalo in about 3 hours. There are two hostels in town if you decide to stay overnight. Hostal Veritas is rather basic, and is on the plaza, and Hostal Don Luis (probably better) is 200m up the hill.

This area is full of lovely walks. To the southwest is the village of Vacas Galindo where several trails lead up into the hills. To the northeast a road winds up to Peñaherrera and on through Cuellaje to the Cordillera de Toisan.

THE PICHINCHAS

The Pichinchas are two volcanoes known as Guagua and Rucu, located some 10km due west of Quito and so easily visible from the capital. They are normally snow free but an occasional high-altitude storm will cover them with a brilliant white layer – a pretty sight from the capital.

The two volcanoes are very distinct. Guagua Pichincha, which means baby Pichincha, is the highest and is presently active. Rucu (old) Pichincha is lower, closer to Quito, and inactive. Rob and Mark have read half-a-dozen different versions of their elevations; the most recent IGM measurements put Guagua at 4,675m and Rucu at an unspecified but slightly lower elevation.

In 1983 a refuge was built on Guagua Pichincha by the Defensa Civil. Although the refuge is mainly used by scientists, the caretaker will normally allow small groups of climbers to stay the night. A fee of about $5 is charged and equipment lock-up is available. The refuge is extremely cold at night, so bring a warm sleeping bag.

Because of their close position to Quito and Guagua's activity, the Pichinchas have played a great part in both the factual and fictional history of Ecuador's

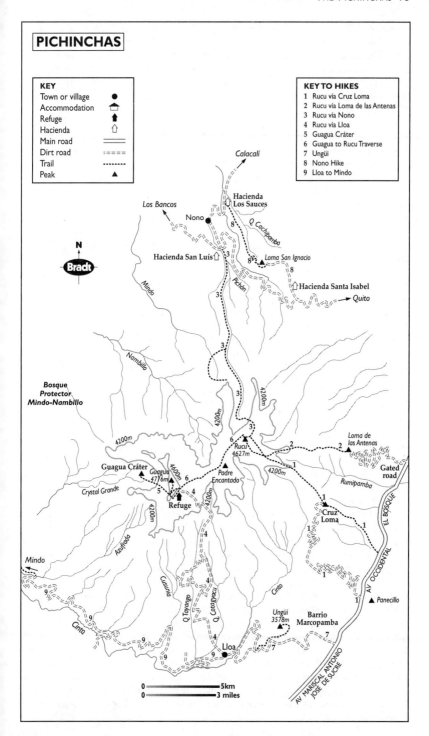

PICHINCHAS

KEY

Town or village	●
Accommodation	⌂
Refuge	↑
Hacienda	⇧
Main road	══
Dirt road	====
Trail	····
Peak	▲

KEY TO HIKES

1 Rucu vía Cruz Loma
2 Rucu vía Loma de las Antenas
3 Rucu vía Nono
4 Rucu vía Lloa
5 Guagua Cráter
6 Guagua to Rucu Traverse
7 Ungüi
8 Nono Hike
9 Lloa to Mindo

Calacalí

Los Bancos

N

Bradt

Hacienda Los Sauces

Nono

Q Cachipamba

Hacienda San Luís

Loma San Ignacio

Hacienda Santa Isabel

Quito

Mindo

Pichán

Nambillo

Bosque Protector Mindo-Nambillo

4200m

Loma de las Antenas

Rucu 4627m

Guagua Cráter

Guagua 4776m

Crystal Grande

Padre Encantado

Refuge

Rumipamba

Gated road

Cruz Loma

Azufrada

Mindo

Cusunia

Q Tayango

Q Cotogracu

Cinta

Ungüi 3578m

Barrio Marcopamba

Panecillo

AV OCCIDENTAL

EL BOSQUE

Cinta

Lloa

AV MARISCAL ANTONIO JOSÉ DE SUCRE

0 ═══ 5km
0 ═══ 3 miles

mountains. They are mentioned by the first Conquistadors and activity is recorded as far back as 1533. The greatest eruption was in 1660 when ash fell up to 500km from Quito, and the capital itself was covered with 40cm of ash and pumice. The sky was filled with incandescent clouds and the sun was blotted out for 4 days – it must have been a terrifying time for the inhabitants of Quito and the surrounding highlands. Two centuries of inactivity followed. Minor eruptions occurred in 1868, 1869 and 1881.

In 1998, the Guagua Pichcincha volcano once again became active after many years of relative dormancy. On July 12 2000, the volcano sent an ash column five miles into the sky, which appeared on the front pages of many newspapers around the world. A portion of the crater collapsed and Quito was a mess, with ash everywhere. The volcano began to quieten down by the end of 2001, but no-one has predicted the next eruptive period.

Volcanologists claim that the volcano continues to be potentially dangerous, although Quito is unlikely to be affected by anything more serious than an ash fall; the topography of the area would cause lava flows and lahars (avalanches of heated snow, earth and mud) to be diverted to the relatively uninhabited areas to the west and south of the volcano.

The climbing history of the volcano goes back further than other Ecuadorian mountains, with 1582 seeing the first recorded ascent by a group of locals led by José Ortiguera. All the famous scientific expeditions of the 17th and 18th centuries made successful ascents; first La Condamine and Bouguer of the French Geodesic Expedition in 1742, then Humboldt in 1802, and Ecuadorian President Gabriel García Moreno in 1844. The American photographer C Fardad spent a week taking photographs in the crater in 1867, Reiss and Stübel (the conquerors of Cotopaxi) spent several days there in 1870, and of course Whymper and the Carrels made an almost obligatory ascent in 1880. There were several other ascents during this period. Climbing in the 20th century has been dominated by Sr Pedro Esparza, who began climbing in 1926 and has made well over a hundred ascents of the mountain, often alone, thus earning for himself the nickname 'the solitary of Pichincha'. In 1959 Ecuador's first mountain refuge was built on Pichincha by Fabian Zurita at 4,300m, on the northeast side of the mountain. Unfortunately vandals destroyed this soon afterwards and today the shelter is mainly used by scientists, but the well-worn footpaths from Quito make this an easy and popular climb.

Various legends have been told about the mountain. One goes back to early colonial days when the inhabitants of Quito didn't dare to climb the volcano because of frequent explosions and eruptions. At last three adventurous Franciscan friars decided to explore, but high on the volcano's slopes became lost in a thick fog. Cold and frightened, the three found a cave to shelter in and the bravest went out to investigate the area and look for the way down. A long, terrifying storm followed and the friar became hopelessly lost. The storm ended and his two companions left the cave in search of their lost brother, shouting and yelling but with no result. Despondently, they returned to the cave to spend the night. The next morning they went looking for him once again and were overjoyed to see him kneeling in prayer on a high summit. Happily they rushed up to embrace their friend, but their joy turned to terror when they discovered that he'd been turned to stone. They fled back down the mountain and reported to their superiors that the brother had become a rock pillar, praying eternally to God on a peak close to heaven. To this day, Pichincha's third highest peak, lying about halfway in between and a little north of Guagua and Rucu, is named El Padre Encantado (the bewitched priest).

Climbing Rucu Pichincha
Maps IGM 1:50,000 Quito and Nono

The approach to Rucu is becoming increasingly dangerous due to robberies in *barrios* on the west side of the city that you must cross in order to reach the peak. Aggressive dogs in the inhabited areas at the base of the mountain below Cruz Loma have been responsible for numerous bites. Armed assaults along Av 24 de Mayo and in the area around Cruz Loma (including rape) have happened all too frequently. Be wary of dogs, avoid altogether the walk up Av 24 de Mayo, and inquire as to the safety of climbing up to either set of antennas before you decide to go. Hike together in a group of five or more and carry no valuables. Contact the SAE for the latest information.

There are numerous approaches from the city but the safest way to climb Rucu is by hiring transport or driving to Cruz Loma. It is also possible to climb to another set of antennas located to the north known as Loma de las Antenas (Antenna Hill). This hill can be reached from the neighbourhood of El Bosque, but hikers and bikers have been robbed and you cannot drive to the top because there is a locked gate a third of the way up the road. Any route starting in the city will take about 10 hours round-trip. (See *Rucu Pichincha route diagram*, overleaf.)

Cruz Loma Take a bus to San Roque market located directly west of the Panecillo, then hire a pick-up truck for about $20 to take you past a military monument (Templete de Los Heróes) to Cruz Loma. If you arrive on a weekend day you will see other cars parked at Cruz Loma so you may be able to arrange a ride back down. If you have access to a car, you can drive up to Cruz Loma by following the Occidental Highway through the tunnels to Av Libertadores. Turn right and continue up to Cima de La Libertad. About 100m before the military monument there is a dirt road turn-off to the left that switchbacks for 45 minutes up to the antennas.

If you decide to walk up to Cruz Loma (it takes about 3 hours) head up Avenida La Gasca towards Via Occidental. At the on-ramp for Av Occidental turn left on cross street Enrique Ritter. Walk four blocks south to a dirt road that passes under Av Occidental. Walk through the tunnel – the road swings right on the other side. You should climb out of the road-cut and cross a fence in front of you. Now you are on the edge of a eucalyptus grove; follow a road up through the grove to a clearing (¹/₂km). From here there are numerous routes; follow your nose or the description below. From the clearing find a path that switchbacks left (south) back into the grove. This path leads counter-intuitively away from Rucu but soon plants you on Cruz Loma's shoulder. From here you can eyeball it to the antennas through pastures and small patches of brush.

From the antennas at Cruz Loma you head up an obvious northwest trail on a grassy ridge towards the base of the rock which is about 1¹/₂ hours away.

Loma de las Antenas Take one of several buses northbound on Av América to Calle Mañosca. Walk up this street for about 15 minutes until it crosses the Via Occidental. Directly opposite Mañosca is a signed road leading to a fertiliser factory; ignore this and take the unsigned road some 50m to the right (north). Follow this road and take your first left up the hill and then continue taking the uphill fork whenever the road divides. Four-wheel-drive vehicles and good pick-ups can negotiate this road as far as the locked gate of a *hacienda* about a third of the way up. The road continues up to the antennas, but the *hacienda* owner has closed the access road to private vehicles. Walkers will have no problem passing the gate.

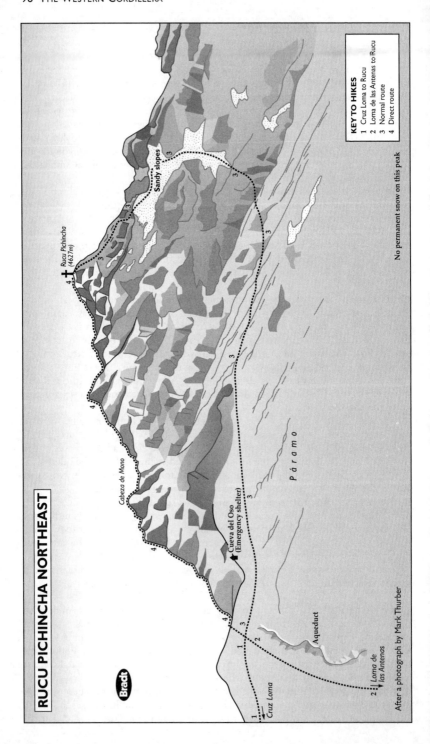

RUCU PICHINCHA NORTHEAST

Rucu Pichincha
(4627m)

Sandy slopes

Cabeza de Mono

Cueva del Oso
(Emergency shelter)

Páramo

Aqueduct

Cruz Loma

Loma de
las Antenas

KEY TO HIKES
1 Cruz Loma to Rucu
2 Loma de las Antenas to Rucu
3 Normal route
4 Direct route

No permanent snow on this peak

After a photograph by Mark Thurber

Bradt

To reach Rucu Pichincha from the Loma de Las Antenas you take a path which goes over the hill behind the car park. This path follows a ridge, which after 2 hours meets the trail from Cruz Loma.

Summit Where the paths from either set of antennas meet you have two options: (1) head right traversing the base of the cliffs to a sandy slope which leads to the summit (the easiest way) or (2) head straight up the rocks which are marked with paint splashes or white arrows in places. This second route is more direct although perhaps a little hair-raising for beginners. The route more or less follows the ridge, but you need to drop off the crest in places. The summit will take a further 1½ hours from the trail junction on both routes. There is also rock climbing to be had on Rucu's summit pyramid if you are so inclined.

Descent You may be able to hitch a ride back to Quito from Cruz Loma or the Loma de Las Antennas (a local paragliding group has keys to the gate at the *hacienda*). If you are walking, however, the quickest route is straight down from Cruz Loma to the city, following a faint path underneath the electricity pylons from the TV and radio antennas. This will bring you out in the La Gasca area north of the route previously described. There are other paths if you feel in an exploratory mood, but remember descending on foot alone or in a small group puts you at risk of being robbed.

Climbing Guagua Pichincha
Maps IGM 1:50,000 Quito and Nono

Guagua is accessed from the village of Lloa and is literally a walk-up. You can get there with a 4WD vehicle arriving at the refuge just a 30-minute stroll from the crater rim. The walk up the road, however, is peaceful, with great views, and so far has none of the dangers of assault associated with climbing Rucu.

Approach Take a bus (No 8) or cab south on Avenida Mariscal Jose Antonio de Sucre to Calle Angamarca (shown as Chilibulo on maps) where transport departs west to the village of Lloa (this is also the beginning of the walk to Ungüi described in *Chapter 4*, page 64). From here you can walk to Lloa (2 to 3 hours) or buses depart several times a day (when full), and more often on weekends. You may also be able to hitch a lift from a truck that is returning to a mine several kilometres beyond Lloa. The road winds up through the growing barrio of Santa Barbara to a pass, then descends 4km to the agricultural village of Lloa. If you are walking it is quicker to take the old cobbled road just beyond the pass on the left down to Lloa.

Once you get to Lloa ask for directions to the refuge. Follow the track west out of town as it passes through some cultivation and eventually meanders up through *páramo*. Track junctions are signposted for the route to Guagua, but when in doubt, take right-hand forks. Allow about 5 to 6 hours of steady hiking to reach the refuge. The facilities are minimal but it has bunks and foam mattresses, and you can use the stove if the caretaker is there. If staying overnight, bring a sleeping bag and a stove, just in case.

By car, you can get up to just below the refuge, but there are many rough sections along the road, and a 4WD vehicle is essential in all but the driest of seasons. The dirt track turns into a mud wallow after a bit of rain. If you have any doubts about the strength of your car engine, burn super (higher octane) for the trip up to the refuge. It can really make a difference in the power output, and you'll need all you can get! You can hire a truck from Quito for about $40.

The easy route to the summit is to follow the obvious trail on the pumice slope to the crater rim. Head right along the rim for about 20 minutes to reach a metal cross which is slightly lower than the true summit further along the rim. There are more interesting routes to the summit up the rock to the right of the refuge as well, but they are exposed in places. For rock-starved climbers, this area is loaded with possibilities. A huge slab at the base of a rock face has several lines of solid climbing that can be top-roped, and the face itself may have potential, though we haven't tried it out.

The crater contains several new domes and numerous fumeroles caused by the eruptions in 1999 and 2000. Although eruptions are now rare it is not considered safe to descend into the crater because of the volcanic gases and the chance of an ash eruption. Tragically, volcano seismologist Diego Viracucha of the Instituto Geofísico died in the crater in 2001 during an eruption.

There is also an approach to the summit of Guagua from the north, although we haven't met anyone who has done it. Head to the village of Nono (see *Nono hikes* in *Chapter 4*, pages 65–6) and then head south on a jeep track to the Hacienda San Luis and continue south on paths and then cross-country to the Pichinchas.

Guagua to Rucu traverse From the refuge you can return to Quito via Rucu Pichincha in one long day. It's a beautiful hike because the west side of Rucu has a large variety of flowering plants. From the refuge traverse north then east. Follow the ridge past Padre Encantado and then climb up a basin that looks steep and long with a lot of loose rock. It's much easier than it looks and takes about half an hour to climb. Rucu is just beyond. If you look carefully you'll be able to follow a faint path for most of the way. The traverse takes approximately 4 to 5 hours. Carry water as it is usually not available unless the peaks are covered with snow or it is raining.

LLOA TO MINDO TRAIL

Distance Approximately 45km
Altitude 1,300–3,040m
Rating Moderate
Time 2–3 days
Start Lloa
End Mindo
Maps IGM 1:50,000 Quito, Nono and Mindo.
Other essential notes Great Sierra to coast hike with birding opportunities

This is a 2 to 3 day trek for hikers and perhaps a 4-day trek for birders and botanists. The eruptions of Guagua Pichincha 1999 to 2002 have altered parts of this trail and there is some risk of debris flows if Guagua becomes active; check for current conditions on the trail before hiking.

The route takes you from the agricultural town of Lloa through cloudforest into western slope rainforest, skirting the southern edge of Bosque Protector Mindo-Nambillo. There has been some clearing in the river valleys for cattle, but a large amount of primary forest remains. It is amazing to think this area is so close to Quito! In the late 1980s a road was planned and partially constructed for this route but was abandoned when it became clear that the construction maintenance costs

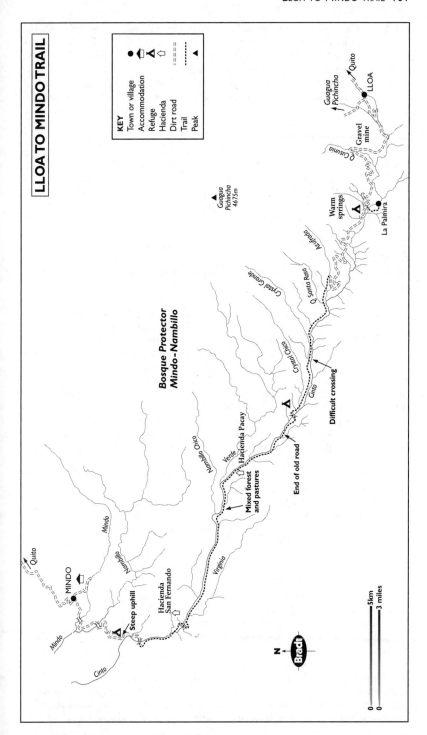

LLOA TO MINDO TRAIL

KEY
● Town or village
⌂ Accommodation
▲ Refuge
⌂ Hacienda
=== Dirt road
···· Trail
▲ Peak

Bosque Protector
Mindo–Nambillo

Guagua
Pichincha
4675m

Quito
LLOA
Guagua
Pichincha
Gravel
mine
Q. Cusuniu
Warm
springs
La Palmira
Azulrodo
Q. Santa Rosa
Crystal Grande
Crystal Chico
Cinto
Difficult crossing
End of old road
Hacienda Pacay
Verde
Mixed forest
and pastures
Nambillo Chico
Virginia
Hacienda
San Fernando
Steep uphill
Nambillo
MINDO
Mindo
Quito
Mindo
Cinto

Bradt

N

0 ___ 5km
0 ___ 3 miles

due to unstable slopes and frequent landslides were not worth the benefits the road would provide. Undoubtedly the area would have been deforested if the road had been constructed and, hopefully, the road will now never be completed.

There is plenty of water but remember to treat it. You quickly drop to warmer elevations so one sweater is probably sufficient, but proper raingear is essential. The trail is very muddy, so rubber boots are recommended. Though not essential, a machete may come in handy. There are places to camp along the river or it may be possible to arrange to spend a night in a wood shack at one of several *fincas*. Bring all your food from Quito.

Hiking directions You begin by making your way to Lloa (see *Climbing Guagua Pichincha*, pages 99–100). The hike can begin here or you can arrange transport at least as far as Palmira. There should be some traffic as far as the second gravel mine (1 hour walking from Lloa), but beyond here catching a ride could prove difficult. The walk along the road is quite pleasant. You will reach a turn-off to the left to the Hacienda La Palmira. Just beyond this turn-off is a dirt road up to 'warm' springs. The springs are really only tepid and a bit grungy, but this makes a nice spot to camp. Landslides along the road make it difficult to drive more than a few more kilometres. The road eventually enters primary cloudforest with views of the box canyon of Río Azufrada – here you might smell sulfur from the vents upstream on Guagua Pichincha. This is probably the most dangerous place to be when Guagua Pichincha erupts again since lahars and toxic gases may pour down this drainage. Not to worry though; the chances of you being here when Guagua goes off are slim.

Wade across the thigh-deep river. Continue on the road across several small streams until you reach the Río Crystal Grande. During high water this stream is a difficult crossing – narrow but waist deep. There is usually a log footbridge across the river since the route is used by locals. Find the streambed/road on the opposite side, which eventually becomes road again. Follow to a well-constructed bridge across the Río Cinto. There should be a sign that says Bosque Protector Mindo-Nambillo on your right. Cross to the south side of the Río Cinto and follow the road past several *fincas*; you will cross into the Hacienda Pacay which extends several kilometres downstream. Soon you reach the end of the road and begin on a trail leading to the right into forest.

From here the trail stays on the south side of the river, but it is difficult to find at times because you will be alternating between muddy pastures and forest. When in the forest you should be on a more less obvious track. About an hour past the road end you reach a large ranch house (also the Hacienda Pacay). It is about 6 hours from Palmira to the Hacienda Pacay. Here we saw about 30 red-billed parrots flying in a flock. The steep slopes on the opposite side of the Río Cinto are uncut since the river blocks access to farmers and consequently has abundant birdlife. Continue on a trail on the backside of the large ranch house that leads past a corral and into the forest.

Again stay on the left side of Río Cinto – you do not have much choice since the river is wide and rapid. Do not be discouraged if you lose the trail in the pastures – the key is to find the correct gate at the far end of each pasture where the forest begins. Birding is great in this section so take your time as you walk up and down the ravines feeding into the Río Cinto. About 2 hours from the ranch you pass over a waterfall in dense forest. Another hour brings you to a small ranch house on the left. Continue down to the lower pasture on the right, enter the forest and you soon cross landslide debris with a 50m high cliff on the left. You are now entering *fincas* with tropical fruits such as bananas, guayabas and lemons – the lemons are quite sour but are a great addition to the water you are drinking.

You soon arrive at a covered bridge across the Río Cinto to the Hacienda San Fernando. A sign indicates it is 9km to Mindo and 22km to Lloa, probably as a toucan flies – it's certainly farther on foot. Do not cross this bridge; instead continue downstream on the left side of the Río Cinto. About an hour later you will come to another bridge (logs with planks, but no railings) across a box gorge. Cross this. Continue downstream, now a gravel road on the right side of the Río Cinto for 30 minutes, before crossing an ankle deep stream, then take a right-hand turn uphill. There should be a house in front of you with a concrete pad surrounding it. The road to the right is the end of the aborted Lloa–Mindo road project. Continue up the steep hill – you have to cross the small ridge 200m above you. The views from the pass are incredible. From here it is about 2 hours to Mindo and the road is driveable, so if you are lucky you might be able to hitch a ride. In total it is 8 to 10 hours from the Hacienda Pacay to Mindo.

In Mindo (1,300m) there are numerous options for sleeping and eating. Mark likes the Mindo Orchid Garden (2 2765471, mindo_mundo@hotmail.com), which does good vegetarian food and provides information about hikes in the area. Mindo has become a ecotourism attraction, particularly for birders. It is also known for its guayaba orchards (the locals will complain that the numerous parrots wreck havoc on their crop). A jam is made from this fruit which is quite tasty. Buses leave from Mindo daily and take about 3½ hours. You can hire a taxi to Quito for about $70 or take a taxi to the main road (7km) for $7, where there is traffic and frequent buses from the coast back to Quito. Buses from Mindo to Quito leave twice daily. From Monday to Friday the bus leaves Mindo at 06.30 and 14.00. On Saturday and Sunday the bus leaves Mindo at 06.30, 14.00, 15.00 and 16.00.

You can arrange to do this trek with an excellent bird guide out of Mindo – Vinicio Perez and Jane Lyons are both recommended. They charge $45.Contact them at the Bird Watchers' House in Mindo, or email jlyons@pi.pro.ec.

CERRO ATACAZO (4,457m)
Map IGM 1:50,000 Amaguaña

Atacazo is an extinct and eroded volcano located about 20km southwest of Quito. With a 4WD vehicle you can get to within an hour of the summit. It is not a difficult climb and, unusually in Ecuador, the rocky summit is not composed of rotten and dangerous rocks but is quite solid. Because transport is somewhat of a hassle, this area is rarely visited, but worth the effort to get there. The spectacular summit views are of Quito and the Pichinchas to the northeast, and the countryside dropping down to the lowlands to the west. (See map overleaf.)

There are numerous routes up Atacazo – it is just a matter of picking a line from the Pan-American Highway and heading for the summit. Perhaps the most straightforward is to take a bus south out of Quito on the Pan-American Highway to the turn-off just before the turn-off to the Estación Experimental Santa Catalina and begin hiking towards the summit. This dirt road eventually peters out to trails and fields – follow your nose to the summit.

The way to drive to the summit is a jeep track from the tiny village of San Juan on the old Santo Domingo road, which also makes a pleasant walk. You can also get to San Juan by catching a bus at Plaza La Marin in Quito's old town to Chillogallo or La Libertad on the old Santo Domingo road. From here you will find occasional trucks (or you can walk or hitchhike) as far as San Juan, 10km to the west. This beautiful mountain road climbs and hairpins steeply from La Libertad (3,000m) to San Juan (3,450m). Continuing westward from San Juan the old highway descends, offering fascinating opportunities to observe the ecological

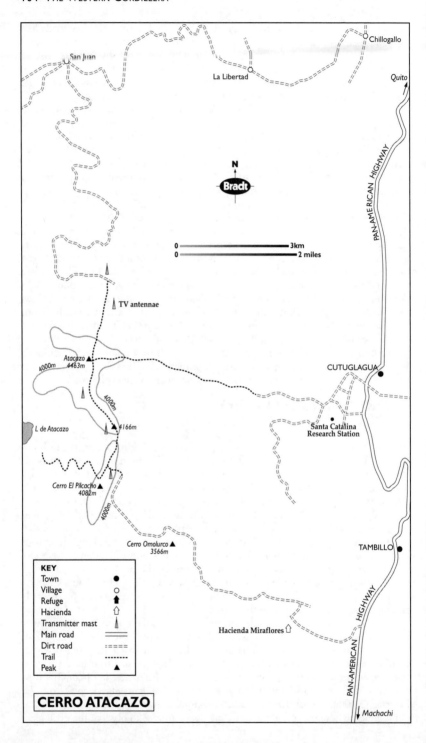

CERRO ATACAZO

changes from *páramo* to coastal rainforest, with excellent birding. This route is also great for mountain biking since all the traffic to Santo Domingo now goes through Machachi.

To climb or drive to Atacazo from San Juan take the southbound jeep road heading towards some TV and radio antennas. Anyone in the village will point out the road; it reaches the antennas in 10–12km. If you need drinking water you'll pass near the last streams about 2–3km before the end of the road.

From the antennas head south up gently sloping, grassy *páramo* to an obvious notch in the crater rim. It is an easy walk which will take a little over an hour. From here the highest point is to your left: a gentle scramble over grass and rocks. Below you is the delicately coloured crater, wide open to the west, and filled with pastel shades of sand and lava and brighter splashes of vegetation. It is not difficult to scramble down and explore 'These dwarf plant Japanese gardens', as Henri Michaux's poem described them.

The descent can be made in different ways. The shortest is to head almost due east for 7km until you reach the Estación Experimental Santa Catalina. A more interesting descent is to head south on the crater rim for about 1km beyond the highest point, then head southeast along an obvious ridge to a small hill (4,166m) about 1km away; from here head south-southwest along another ridge to a long flattish hill (Cerro El Pilcacho, 4,082m) almost 2km away. A series of antennas dot these prominent points and can be used as landmarks for the descent. A short distance before you reach the top of El Pilcacho you'll find a trail crossing the ridge. Westward, it winds through interesting-looking *páramo* to the Laguna de Atacazo some 3km away; eastward it soon joins a trail heading southeast towards Cerro Omoturco, 3,566m high and 2km away. From Omoturco a dirt road winds 7–8km to the Hacienda Miraflores, from which a road continues a further 2–3km to the Pan-American Highway. If you go north along the Highway for about 3km to Tambillo, it will be easier to catch buses to Quito.

EL CORAZÓN (4,788m)
Map IGM 1:50,000 Machachi

El Corazón is yet another eroded and extinct volcano located about 40km southwest of Quito. Like Atacazo it is a good place to stretch your legs and lungs for a day if you have recently arrived in Quito. The route is straightforward and requires no rock-climbing equipment or experience. The first recorded ascent was in 1738 by La Condamine and Bouguer, and this easy peak has been climbed many times since. Pre-conquest ruins have been reported on the northeast slopes, but they are very overgrown and have yet to be investigated. The name El Corazón means 'heart' in Spanish and is said to refer to two gullies on the northwest slopes which, when seen from a distance, appear to join together roughly in the shape of a heart. (See *Ilinizas and El Corazón* map, page 107.)

Access To get to El Corazón take a bus from the Terminal Terrestre heading south on the Pan-American Highway and ask the driver to drop you at the turn-off to Aloasí. Go through Aloasí on a good cobbled road for 2.8km as far as the railway station. You can take a bus from Machachi or the Pan-American Highway as far as the station; they run every few hours between 08.00 and 18.30.

About 100m past the station, take the dirt road going left. If travelling by car, this road will get you within 2 hours of the summit, but the gate is frequently locked. Check at the Hosteria La Estacion (2 2309246) near the railroad station for an updated status of this route.

Climbing El Corazón The road winds its way through *páramo* – to get to the end you will need a 4WD vehicle, although at the time of writing it was a very difficult drive, since it has become overgrown. On foot, you'll have to keep pretty much to the road for the first few kilometres. Fenced off, cultivated fields make heading cross-country fairly difficult lower down. Up higher, look for trails leading west up across the *páramo*; otherwise it's probably easier to keep to the switchbacking road, as tramping through the dense *ichu* grass is tiring and time-consuming. The road ends in the *páramo* on the northeast side of the summit rock in a valley. From here an irrigation canal leads towards a saddle between El Corazón and a minor peak to the north. Follow alongside this canal until it runs out, then head up rocky scree slopes to the summit. If you stay on the ridge you will avoid the scree. The trails through the scree, however, are useful to speed up the descent. There is no rock climbing except an easy 10m-high class 3 rock band just below the summit. Rock cairns and a few rocks painted with arrows mark the way. Allow about 5 to 7 hours of steady hiking to reach the summit from Aloasí and 2 to 3 hours to descend.

There is another route from the north. Follow the main road from Machachi to Santo Domingo for 3km to Alóag and just outside of town near the railroad station take the left fork down a dirt road. About 12km down this road you'll find the Hacienda La Granja, where it is possible to hire mules. From here head south across the *páramo* another 6km to the peak, reaching the saddle on the north side as described in the first route. On foot it will take about 5 hours to walk from the highway to the saddle.

THE ILINIZAS
Map IGM 1:50,000 Machachi

These are two peaks located about 55km south-southwest of Quito. Iliniza Sur (5,248m) has the distinction of being the sixth highest mountain in the country whilst Iliniza Norte (5,126m) is the eighth highest. Prehistorically they were one volcano but today the two peaks are separated by a saddle and are about 1km apart. Jean and Louis Carrel's Whymper's expedition logged the first ascent of Iliniza Sur in May 1880, but Whymper himself never reached the summit despite two attempts in February and June of the same year. The first ascent of Iliniza Norte was interesting in that it was one of the few first ascents made by Ecuadorian climbers and the only Ecuadorian 'first' of one of the country's ten peaks over 5,000m. Ecuador's Nicolás Martínez accompanied by Alejandro Villavicencio reached the summit in March 1912.

There is a simple refuge known as Refugio Nuevos Horizontes at 4,650m just east of and below the saddle linking the two mountains. The refuge is managed by Bladimir Gallo, who takes the route up to the refuge every few days on an old motorcycle. The refuge has 15 bunk beds, fireplace, gas stove, and sometimes a few basics like sodas and crackers for sale. There is a small generator for electric lights, although it's often not working. A nearby stream provides water that must be treated. Overnight stay for non-residents is $9 per night. Free camping is possible but the area is exposed to the weather.

The twin peaks of the Ilinizas offer some of the more enjoyable climbing in Ecuador. For the hiker, Norte is a challenging but fun scramble when free of snow. For the experienced climber, Sur provides several interesting and demanding technical steep snow and ice routes.

Access About 40km south of Quito and 8km south of Machachi on the Pan-American Highway there is a turn-off – located approximately 50m before a bridge

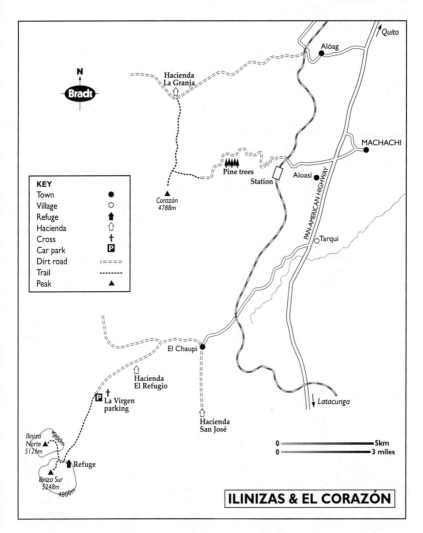

KEY
Town	●
Village	○
Refuge	⬆
Hacienda	⇧
Cross	†
Car park	🅿
Dirt road	=====
Trail	....
Peak	▲

ILINIZAS & EL CORAZÓN

and marked by a Vulcanizadora (tyre repair shop) and several shops – to the small community of El Chaupi. Buses north and southbound on the Pan-American Highway pass this turn-off. From here it is 7km of cobbled road to El Chaupi; there is enough traffic to hitchhike, and buses pass here from the main square in Machachi every hour on the way up to El Chaupi.

Those wishing to acclimatise for a few days can stay at the highly recommended Hacienda San Jose (3,400m). This bed and breakfast is a farmhouse with several rooms and a shared kitchen and bath. It costs $10 per night (including a big and delicious breakfast) and the friendly owner Rodrigo Peralvo can arrange horses to take you up a trail to the refuge ($20 for 4 hours). Transfers by car to La Virgen are $20, and to the parking area below the refuge at Cotopaxi they are $40. Rodrigo can be reached at 2 2891547 or 09 9737986, hacienda_sanjose@hotmail.com. If you are coming from El Chaupi, from the Pan-American Highway head straight through town (do not take the road to La Virgen) and follow the yellow and black arrows marked with 'Hacienda San Jose' for 3km. Aside from the hike up to Ilinizas there are also some shorter day-hikes to native and pine forests from the *hacienda*. To get up to the refuge turn right at the main plaza in Chalpi onto a road that passes to the right of the church. Walk or drive up this dirt road for 3km until you come to a left turn. If you come to a stream ford you have gone too far and need to backtrack 200m. This turn-off goes through fields, then crosses an avenue of pine trees where it forks (keep right) and eventually heads through a *hacienda*. About 3km from the turn-off it switchbacks up a hill. Occasional grazing bulls in this area are territorial and require a degree of respect. If encountered, you should move slowly and quietly. The road above the *hacienda* is eroded and only passable with 4WD vehicles – hired pick-up trucks may have difficulty depending on when the road was last graded. At 8.7km from El Chaupi you arrive at a flat grassy area (parking) and a shrine to the Virgin Mary with a blue cross. This is the normal drop-off point for hired transport. The track above the parking area could be navigated by a 4WD but it's probably not worth the effort. You can hire a pick-up truck in Chalpi; the trip will cost about $20. Note that it is not safe to leave unattended vehicles in the parking area as break-ins are common.

Above La Virgen the road switchbacks up to a broad rocky ridge eventually petering out into a footpath. The trail follows this flat crest to the base of a steep sandy ridge leading to the refuge which sits just below a saddle between the two peaks. The going is slow due to backsliding in the sand, but the way is marked by green paint dots on the rocks. At the top of the sandy ridge a well-established trail veers right to the refuge 'Nuevos Horizontes' (4,765m). From the parking area it is about 2½ to 3½ hours on foot to the refuge, or if you are walking from El Chaupi to the refuge it takes 5 to 7 hours. There is normally no water between the Virgen and the refuge.

Climbing Iliniza Norte (5,126m)

Despite the glacier marked on IGM maps, Iliniza Norte is a rocky mountain with no permanent snow. It can easily be climbed in 2 to 3 hours from the refuge. Technical equipment is unnecessary unless it has snow cover, in which case you will need at least an ice axe and perhaps crampons and a rope.

From the refuge walk to the saddle between the two peaks. Most of the route to the summit is marked by cairns. Climb up the southeast ridge, trying to stay high on solid rock. The trails below in the sandy scree are great for descent but hard work on the ascent. The ridge narrows; work your way up to the base of a false summit pyramid (5,060m). Traverse right on sandy ledges (this is the Paso de Muerte, or death pass, which is far easier to cross than the name implies, unless there is ice) to the base of the summit block. Follow the gullies with loose rocks to the summit. The true summit is marked by an iron cross. The climb is straightforward except for the danger of a rockfall in the last few metres, or when there is snow making the Paso de Muerte more true to its name. When Mark first climbed the peak in the mid-1990s the cross on the summit was buzzing, and his hair was sticking up in punk rock style from static electricity, so it's probably best not to climb here during a thunder storm.

Climbing Iliniza Sur (5,248m)

This relatively steep and crevassed mountain is one of the more difficult climbs in the country, and is not for beginners. There are two frequently climbed routes to the summit, the Normal Route and Direct Route. What was for years considered the normal route (Direct Route) has become even more difficult, especially when there's a lack of snowfall. Some of the steeper sections can approach 80° in certain seasons so front pointing is necessary. This is a tiring technique, particularly at over 5,000m, and should be learnt and practised at lower elevations if possible (in the Alps or the Rockies for example). It is best to bring an assortment of ice screws, flukes and snow stakes. Rockfall can be a hazard and a helmet is recommended. Avalanches occur often enough to pose a danger and a detailed route description is difficult due to constantly changing conditions. (See diagram overleaf.)

Direct Route (or the Ramp Route) The difficult direct route is via the north face. It begins from the Nuevos Horizontes hut then heads west into the saddle between Norte and Sur. From the saddle ascend the steep moraine, then climb on to a snow-covered 'terrace' – a flat area where the northern glaciers terminate. After gaining the terrace, you will be almost exactly below the direct route which looks like the bottom of an hourglass between two large rock outcrops. Slopes steepen from 30° at the bottom of the route to between 50 and 55° near the middle, with several 3m long sections of 65 to 70°. You exit this ramp to the left and then negotiate a crevasse field. Finally there is a rock band that needs to be negotiated – difficult if covered by recent snow. Above the rock band traverse/climb right to a ridge, then left to the Ambato Peak. To get to the Maximum Peak follow the ridge, bypassing a rocky outcrop known as 'el hongo' (the mushroom) and ascend Maximum. The descent is via the easier Normal Route described below, but it is easy to become confused if there are no tracks on the Normal Route. In good conditions the round trip can be done in less than 6 hours, but a full day is not uncommon. You should plan a pre-dawn departure to minimise rockfall and avalanche danger caused by the melting of the snow in the midday sun.

Normal Route This is an easier route to the summit, but still requires climbing experience and technical safety equipment. Follow the same route as the Direct Route up to the base of the steep north face. Traverse the glacier west (right) to the next snow ramp just beyond a low rock band. Take some caution here as rockfall is frequent. Ascend the slope as it winds right and to the northwest, then more or less west, traversing the mountain. This area is quite heavily crevassed, requiring careful route-finding depending on snow conditions. If there is deep snow, crevasses are not as much of a problem. After reaching a low angle bulge, continue cork-screwing right and up to the small rock outcrop, then head left and straight up the steeper snow slope (45 to 50°) to the Maximum Peak. From the hut, it is 3 to 4 hours to the summit.

Northeast Ridge This is a challenging mixed snow and rock route with exposure along an interesting ridge crest. Bring a rack of three or four ice screws, three pickets, slings, and a small rock rack. The rock is poorly consolidated agglomerate, so rockfall can be a problem in places. The rock is also difficult to protect, but with heavy snow cover you can place snow stakes. For the experienced mountaineer, this is a fun route.

From the refuge head up to the terrace, then traverse left to the northeast ridge. You can gain the ridge about a third of the way up by ascending to the right of the first knob on the skyline, following up snow fields and rotten 5th class rock to the ridge crest. Alternatively continue around to the base of the ridge and climb the ridge from the bottom. Just past the first knob follow easier class 3 rock and snow fields along the crest to the Ambato summit.

Celso Zuquillo (East ridge) Follow the east ridge through an area of snow, ice and loose rock, until it eventually becomes a snow and ice route. Cross over Ambato Peak and head to Maximum Peak.

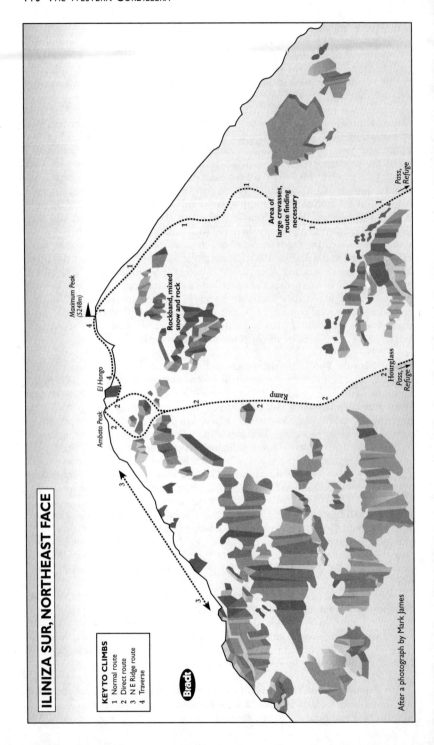

ILINIZA SUR, NORTHEAST FACE

KEY TO CLIMBS
1 Normal route
2 Direct route
3 N E Ridge route
4 Traverse

Maximum Peak (5248m)

El Hongo

Ambato Peak

Rockband, mixed snow and rock

Area of large crevasses, route finding necessary

Ramp

Hourglass
Pass,
Refuge

Pass,
Refuge

After a photograph by Mark James

South ridge The most difficult route of all was done by the French and Ecuadorian climbers, Joseph Bergé and Marco Cruz, in October 1973, and goes up the south ridge. A bivouac and highly technical ice climbing are required. The route was repeated by Martin Slater, Travis White and Peter Hall in March 1974 and again by George Gibson and Allan Miller in June 1977.

Southwest face The southwest face was climbed by Tom Hunt and Jorge and Delia Montpoli in September 1982. This route is approached from the 3,600m Loma de Huinza pass on the Sigchos road, south of the mountain. Head for the base of the westernmost glacier located just north of the prominent, crumbling rock towers that divide the south and west sides of the mountain (8 hours). Camp here. Climb the left side of the heavily crevassed glacier to a 40° snow ramp which bears further left and above the first rock walls. Ascend a steep couloir to the right (75°, 50m) and at the top angle right along a mild ridge to a 5m ice wall. Ascend the final 100m to the summit via the southwest knife ridge. Total climbing time from camp should be about 5 hours, for 900m of ascent.

HIKING IN THE ZUMBAHUA AREA

The high *páramo* and rocky peaks around Zumbahua are an undiscovered treasure that have maintained a character that is distinctly Andean and indigenous. There are remnant cloudforest patches, interesting *páramo* vegetation and walks into the coastal rainforest or back into the central valley. The people are mostly warm-hearted but sometimes distrustful of outsiders. A recent earthquake in 1996 which killed several dozen people and destroyed thousands of houses has instilled fear among the indigenous people. It is important to be respectful and sensitive when visiting this region. When choosing places to camp put your tent up away from villages unless invited to stay near or inside a *choza* (grass hut). We have described several routes here, but cross-country travel is possible with the appropriate maps. The best place to stay in Zumbagua is the Hostal Condor Matzi on the main square, with carefully crafted furniture from a workshop managed by Italian missionaries. The Italian missionaries also operate a small but well-stocked and modern hospital in town, with some foreign staff. (See *Zumbahua to Loma Tambo* and *Chugchilán area maps*, pages 112 and 117.)

Zumbahua to Angamarca hike

Distance Approximately 28km
Altitude 2,900–4,420m
Rating Moderate to difficult
Time 2 days
Start Zumbahua
End Angamarca
Maps IGM 1:50,000 Pilaló and Angamarca
Other essential notes Trek through traditional Andean villages.

This 2-day trek takes you from Zumbahua over rarely visited *páramo* to the isolated town of Angamarca. The area is mostly above 4,000m and is sparsely populated with Quechuan-speaking *campesinos* who raise llamas and mostly still live in *chozas*. The broad green valleys surrounded by rocky peaks and cold weather make you feel like you are in the more expansive cordilleras of Peru. Most llama populations in Ecuador were eradicated by the Spanish but we were told that the llamas in this

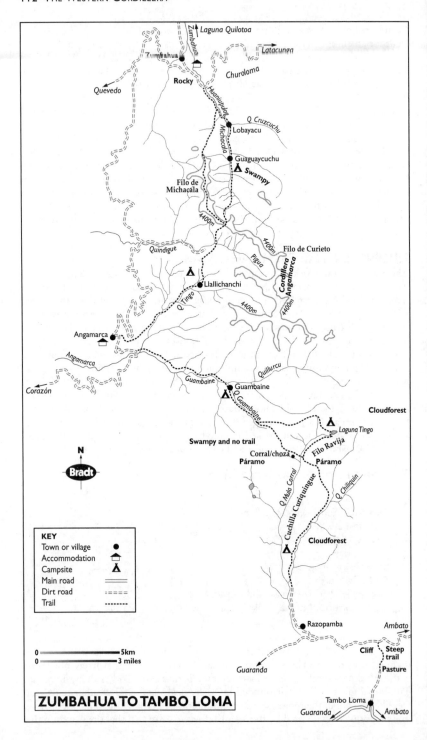

ZUMBAHUA TO TAMBO LOMA

region are original, pre-colonial stock. They have been purchased by US llama breeders because of their high quality. The highlights of the hike are views of the peaks of Ilinizas, Cotopaxi, the Laguna Quilotoa and Chimborazo. There is also an interesting canyon with remnant cloudforest vegetation. On this hike the people are incredibly friendly and do not beg. Do not give money or candy unless you are paying for a service!

Access Take a bus from Quito to Latacunga and get off at the traffic lights. Buses leave from here to Zumbahua every couple of hours. It is also possible to catch the more frequent buses to Pujilí and hitch the rest of the way to Zumbahua. After approximately 2 hours, or 2km before Zumbahua, get off in Misaruni (small store and bridge over Río Huaniupulog).

Equipment The weather is cold and snow is possible so bring sweaters or fleeces and a Gore-Tex jacket. You could arrange to stay in a *choza*, or camp; in either case bring a sleeping bag. There is plenty of water on the route but it must be treated.

Hiking directions Begin at the small store in Misarumi and walk south along a dirt path on the right side of the river. This is a beautiful canyon that narrows just before you arrive at the community of Michaca (1 hour). Continue right and south past the villages of Loayacu and Guaguaycuchu in a broad green valley. Just after the valley narrows again and turns southeast, leave the valley and head southwest up the prominent draw of Quebrada Saniahuaycu. There are only game trails but the walking is easy. Reach the pass to the west of Cerro Tixan. The views from this rocky ridge are incredible. Below you is the broad valley of the Río Pigua and the orange roof of the Hacienda Chinipamba. Drop down to the river. This is a nice place to camp, about 5 to 7 hours from Misarumi.

If you would rather walk on the ridge you can head up Quebrada Satram just before Michachi, to the pass between Cerro Sachacocha and Sachapata, and continue south. We came up the valley but this looks like an easy ridge-walk in stable weather.

The following day climb over a small pass and descend to the isolated community of Llallichanchi, mostly consisting of *chozas*. Arrive at the concrete school and contour over to the other side of the valley. Follow the well-defined trail down to the canyon, eventually getting to a narrows with good cloudforest and abundant birds. Follow this valley as it becomes wider and more agricultural, eventually crossing to the right side of the river. As you approach Angamarca it is best to stay high on the right side of the valley. From Río Pigua to Angamarca is about 5 to 6 hours of hiking.

There are no hostels in Angamarca but a bed can be arranged at one of the shops in the village square. Note the ornate carvings on the church doors – the work of artisans trained in a school set up by a respected Italian Catholic missionary living in the town. Buses come from the semi-tropical village of El Corazón and continue back to Zumbahua, usually leaving in the morning. However there is usually some form of transport in the afternoons or evenings. It is 3 hours by bus back to Zumbahua, with incredible views as you climb up from Angamarca.

Angamarca to Tambo Loma hike
You can extend the Zumbahua to Angamarca hike by continuing to Tambo Loma, a small community located on the paved Ambato–Guaranda road north of

Distance Approximately 40km
Altitude 2,900 4,200m
Rating Moderate to difficult
Time 3 days
Start Angamarca
End Tambo Loma
Maps IGM 1:50,000 Angamarca and Simiatug
Other essential notes Route passes up through an Andean village to the base of Chimborazo.

Chimborazo. It is possible to re-supply in Angamarca. Alternatively you can get a bus from Zumbahua to Angamarca – there are several a day – to begin this hike. It takes about 3 days and you will see very few people, so go prepared.

Hiking directions From the town of Angamarca walk or get a ride down the road to Barrio San Pablo (3km). Just past a school before you cross the river follow a narrow dirt road up a hill to the community of Shuyo Grande. From here find the main trail on the north side of the Río Guambaine – ask for the trail to the community of Guambaine. The trail is wide and obvious, with great views of the Guambaine valley and surrounding peaks. About 3 hours upstream you cross the Río Guambaine and climb for another half an hour to the community of Guambaine, which consists of a concrete school and several dozen *chozas* scattered on the hillside. The people of this village are friendly and may let you camp on the volleyball court.

The trail climbs along the south side of Quebrada Guambaine with some interesting hoodoos (rock towers) on the north side of the valley. The valley opens to a broad swampy basin called Hondonada de Yuracucha. Here you can continue on the north side of Cerro Chaso Carapungu, eventually dropping down to the Laguna Tingo, or take the more direct route to the pass on the west side of Loma Negro Huanuna. Taking the Loma Negro Huanuna route, drop to Quebrada Mula Corral past a circular corral and *choza* on your right. The route to the Laguna Tingo is longer, but there it is possible to camp below a large polylepsis forest. It takes about 4 to 6 hours to reach the Laguna Tingo or Quebrada Mula Corral from the village of Guambaine.

From the Laguna Tingo it is easiest to cross around to the north side of Filo Ravija and descend Quebrada Chiliquin. If you are camped in the Quebrada Mula Corral you can descend the valley through *páramo* grass to the confluence with Río Calamaca, or cross on the north side of Cerro Yanantzay and descend on a good trail to the Río Calamaca. This trail descends on the west side of the Río Calamaca valley and crosses the river just above the confluence with Río Sigsiyacu – about 4 to 5 hours from the lake. A new dirt track has been constructed to this point and it is an easy 2-hour walk from here to the Río Ambato and the old road between Ambato and Guaranda. Buses pass along this road four times a day and there is moderate traffic for hitchhiking.

You can complete the hike by walking downstream on the road for about 4km to a trail that heads south steeply up Cerro de Pailo Loma. This trail begins about 5 minutes beyond the bridge over Quebrada Paila Huaycu and immediately beyond the overhanging cliff next to the road. The trail climbs to a dirt track which brings you to Comuna Tambo Loma on the new Guaranda-Ambato road, with much more traffic. It is about 3 hours from Río Ambato to Loma Tambo. From here you continue cross-country to the refuge at Chimborazo, or catch a bus to Ambato (it's difficult to get a ride after dark).

Zumbahua to Sigchos

Distance Approximately 45km
Altitude 2,920–3,900m
Rating Moderate
Time 3 days
Start Zumbahua
End Sigchos
Maps IGM 1:50,000 Pilaló and Sigchos
Other essential notes Hike between Andean indigenous villages and by a volcanic lake.

This 3-day trek begins in the colourful indigenous town of Zumbahua, ascends to the crater rim of Quilotoa, passes the village of Chugchilán and ends in Sigchos.

Hiking directions From the village plaza in Zumbahua descend the hill to the bridge and continue on the road north to the Laguna Quilotoa. There is a large arch at the entrance to the village of Quilatoa. The walk is 12km and takes approximately 3 to 4 hours. The community charges a small entrance fee ($1) to visit the lake. There is usually some traffic so you can hitchhike if you do not want to walk this stretch.

The views of the barley fields and pumice plain along the way are spectacular. You can camp at the rim or stay in some basic huts, including Cabañas Quilotoa, Posada Quilotoa and Refugio Quilotoa. There is a small community here that sells *cuadros* (small, colourful, symbolic landscape paintings) and they have been known to wake campers early in the morning to peddle their wares. A more secluded option is to hike down to the lake at the bottom of the crater, which takes approximately 1 hour. The trail down starts in a notch in the rim to the left of the parking area and steeply descends on a dusty path. The lake water is alkaline so it is not recommended for drinking – bring enough water for your needs.

From the rim of Quilotoa you can walk or hitch a ride down the dirt road to Chugchilán. It is 22km away, and 6 hours of walking. The other option is to head around to the northwest side of the crater to Loma Quilotoa. Look for the third low sandy spot about 45 minutes along the west side of the rim. The most common mistake is to leave the rim too early. Follow a row of eucalyptus trees down to Huayama. In Huayama, walk through town past the cemetery and take the second right down to the canyon of Río Sihui. The trail is an eroded deep notch. The Río Sihui needs to be forded, before you hike up the trail on the other side to Chugchilán. This route to Chugchilán is 11km and takes approximately 5 hours.

Just half a kilometre beyond Chugchilán there is a pleasant eco-hostel, run by an American couple, called the Black Sheep Inn. This is a good place to check up on current trail conditions and other day-hikes in the area, such as hikes to the pre-Columbian ruins of Atalaya and a co-operative cheese factory (see below). There are also two basic hostels in town.

There are several ways to get from Chugchilán to Sigchos – again, the Black Sheep Inn has good information. One route is to head up to the Cordillera Chugchilán and back down to Sigchos. Follow the main road out of town for about 20 minutes, then take a left turn up a dirt road leading towards the cheese factory. This road switchbacks and you can find shortcuts. Continue to Gusumbinialto village church (3 to 4 hours), with views of the coast, Toachi valley and the Ilinizas. After the cheese factory take a right turn until it splits; stay left and you might find the track to the Ruinas Pucurá, 100m further to the right. Continue to the Hacienda San Gabriel (3 hours), where there is another set of nearby ruins and a good place to camp with a spring. From here find the path or take the road down to Sigchos (about 1 to 2 hours).

Chugchilán to Guangaje hike

Distance 21km
Altitude 2,720–3,750m
Rating Easy
Time 2 days
Start Chugchilán
End Guangaje
Maps IGM 1:50,000 Pilaló, Sigchos
Other essential notes Hike between Andean indigenous villages and by a volcanic lake.

Another option from Chugchilán is to head east across the *páramo* to Guangaje – a 2-day hike with views of the crater of Quilotoa. From Chugchilán walk down the road towards Sigchos and at the first road junction on the left take a path right into the canyon towards the villages of Chinalo and Itualo. Take the path through Itualo to the Río Toachi. Follow the riverbed upstream to a bridge, cross the river and head up the steep hill in front of you. Follow the path to Punteo, where you take the left fork to the pleasant village of Guantualo (where there's a market on Monday mornings). Head southeast to Salado. It is 3 hours from Chugchilán to this point. You can hike up from the church in Salado to a small lake where there is a good camping spot.

The next day follow the road south out of Salado for about 100m until a track veers up the ridge to the left. The trail brings you up to the Loma Malingua, with great views of the Laguna Quilotoa. Continue gently uphill. At Quebrada Malingua you join the road again. From there a path goes level to your right and later descends down to Quebrada Chinchil. To the south are the villages of Guangaje and Salamalec Chico. From Quebrada Chinchil head up the canyon until you reach a road at Salamalec Chico. From here you can follow the road to your right towards Guangaje, where there are buses to Latacunga. It is approximately 5 hours from Salado to Guangaje.

Chugchilán to Pucuyacu

Distance Approximately 30km
Altitude 650–3,400m
Rating Easy
Time 2 days
Start Chugchilán
End Pucuyacu
Maps IGM 1:50,000 Sigchos, Pucayacu
Other essential notes Hike from Andean highlands through cloudforest to coastal lowlands.

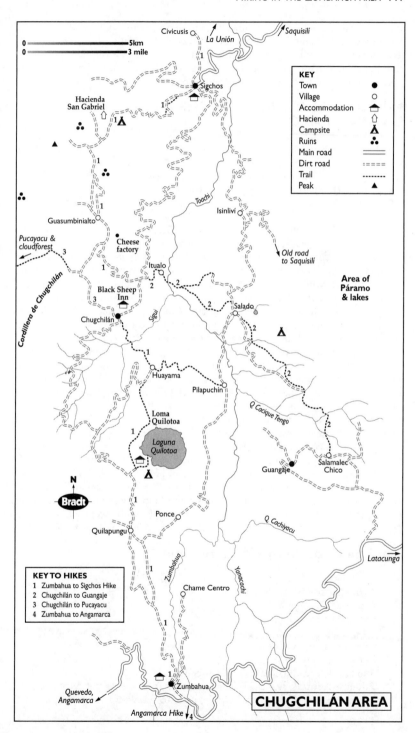

KEY

Town	●
Village	○
Accommodation	⌂
Hacienda	⇧
Campsite	⋀
Ruins	⋮
Main road	═══
Dirt road	═ ═ ═
Trail	- - - -
Peak	▲

KEY TO HIKES

1 Zumbahua to Sigchos Hike
2 Chugchilán to Guangaje
3 Chugchilán to Pucayacu
4 Zumbahua to Angamarca

CHUGCHILÁN AREA

Civicusis
Saquisilí
La Unión
Sigchos
Hacienda San Gabriel
Guasumbinialto
Pucayacu & cloudforest
Cordillera de Chugchilán
Cheese factory
Itualo
Black Sheep Inn
Chugchilán
Isinliví
Old road to Saquisilí
Area of Páramo & lakes
Salado
Toachi
Sigui
Huayama
Pilapuchín
Loma Quilotoa
Laguna Quilotoa
Q Cacique Tengo
Guangaje
Salamalec Chico
Ponce
Quilapungu
Q Cachiyacu
Latacunga
Zumbahua
Yanaachi
Chame Centro
Quevedo, Angamarca
Zumbahua
Angamarca Hike

Bradt

It is also possible to hike from Chugchilán to the subtropical village of Pucuyacu. You climb out of Chugchilán to the Cordillera de Chugchilán, then follow a track that turns to a better trail. The hike takes 2 days and you pass through some great cloudforest. We have not done the hike but the trail is not difficult to follow. Enquire at the Black Sheep Inn for details (see page 115).

HIKING AND CLIMBING IN THE CHIMBORAZO-CARIHUAIRAZO AREA

Señor, we understand perfectly, that in an affair like yours, it is necessary to dissemble – a little; and you, doubtless, do quite right to say you intend to ascend Chimborazo – a thing that everyone knows is perfectly impossible. We know very well what is your object! You wish to discover the TREASURES which are buried in Chimborazo...

Edward Whymper, 1892.

Chimborazo and Carihuairazo are two extinct glaciated volcanoes located about 150km south-southwest of Quito. Chimborazo is the tallest mountain in Ecuador at 6,310m, and for many years it was thought to be the highest mountain in the world. It still retains the distinction of being the point on the earth's surface which is farthest from its centre; this is due to the earth's equatorial bulge. It is higher than any mountain in the Americas north of it: McKinley, the highest peak in North America, is about 75m lower. Chimborazo's reputation as such a high mountain led to many attempts on the summit during the 17th and 18th centuries, before it was finally climbed by Whymper and the Carrels in 1880. Carihuairazo is also an impressively high peak; at 5,020m it ranks ninth in height in Ecuador and was conquered, also in 1880, by the Whymper expedition, with the Ecuadorians David Beltrán and Francisco Campaña. Padre Rivas of the San Gabriel climbing club gave the first mass on the summit of this peak in 1969.

The more deeply eroded peak of Carihuairazo is located 10km northeast. Despite its height and glaciers, it appears diminutive alongside Chimborazo.

Both mountains are heavily glaciated, and snow- and ice-climbing equipment and relevant techniques are required for their ascents. The normal routes are relatively straightforward but have claimed lives. For the non-climber, an excellent hike is from the Pan-American Highway to the Ambato-Guaranda road. This crosses the pass between the two mountains with beautiful views of these and other major peaks. For the mountaineer, combining the hike with ascents of both peaks provides an exceptional experience. (See *Chimborazo-Carihuairazo map*, opposite.)

Doce de Octubre to Vicuña Reserve

Distance Approximately 20km
Altitude 3,570–4,600m
Rating Moderate–difficult
Time 3 days
Start Doce de Octubre
End Vicuña Reserve
Maps IGM 1:50,000 Quero and Chimborazo
Other essential notes This classic trek provides great views of Chimborazo and Carihuairazo, and a chance to see skittish vicuñas.

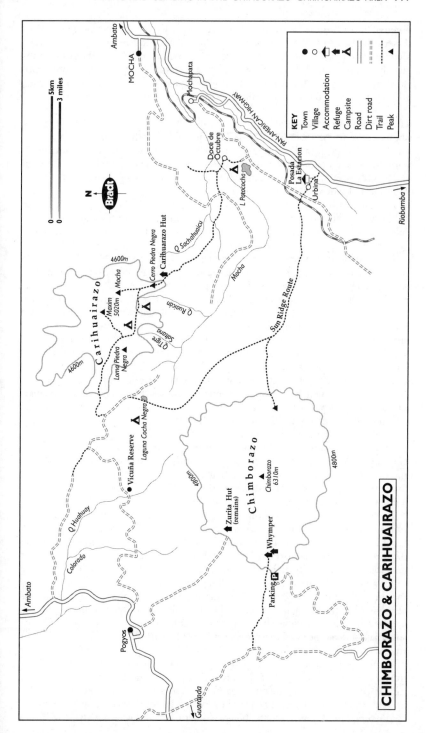

KEY

●	Town
○	Village
◖	Accommodation
◀	Refuge
▲	Campsite
══	Road
═ ═	Dirt road
· · ·	Trail
▲	Peak

5km
3 miles

N
Bradt

Ambato
MOCHA
Mochapata
PAN-AMERICAN HIGHWAY
Riobamba
Doce de Octubre
L Patococha
Posada La Estación
Urbina
Q Sachahuaico
Cerro Piedra Negra
Carihuairazo Hut
4600m
Carihuairazo
Máximo 5020m ▲ Mocha
Q Ruídchi
Mocha
Loma Piedra Negra ▲
Q Tigre Saltana
Sun Ridge Route
4600m
Vicuña Reserve
Laguna Cocha Negra
Chimborazo
Chimborazo 6310m ▲
4800m
4800m
Q Huchuay
Zurita Hut (remains)
Colorado
Ambato
Whymper
Parking P
Pogyos
Guaranda

CHIMBORAZO & CARIHUAIRAZO

Access From Quito's Terminal Terrestre take a Riobamba bus along the Pan-American Highway. About halfway between Ambato and Riobamba you will see a sign on your right for Mocha. Stay on the bus for a further 9km as the road climbs steeply past the turn-off to Mochapata, to the turn-off for Doce de Octubre. Doce de Octubre may not be marked, but it is also possible to start from Mochapata, adding an extra hour of hiking. Allow about 3 hours on the bus from Quito.

Hiking directions Walk off the road northwest from the Pan-American Highway about 1.5km to the town of Doce de Octubre, crossing the train tracks. You may be allowed to sleep in the village hall (four bare walls, no facilities). Alternatively continue about a kilometre along the steeply descending dirt road to the banks of the Río Mocha where you can camp. If you have a heavy load of gear, you can rent mules in Doce de Octubre.

In clear weather Chimborazo's steep and rugged southeastern flanks are visible to the west; this side provides the most difficult ascent routes and the view is splendid. Carihuairazo is seen to the northwest, but from this angle the major glaciers are not properly appreciated.

Hiking from Doce de Octubre to the base of Cerro Piedra Negra takes 6 to 8 hours. After crossing the Río Moche below the village, climb out of the river canyon and take the second left fork, passing a house and climbing north-northwest. Take the mud road that climbs the side of a hill above an area known as Mauca Corral. The road switchbacks up Loma Tulutuz and ends at two grass huts on the back side of the hill. Follow this for another 1km until you can see two sharp ridges heading northwest towards Carihuairazo. They are separated by a small river, the Quebrada Cachahuaicu. Cross a small stream and climb the left-hand ridge (Filo de Sachahuaicu), and follow cow paths along the gently rising ridge-top, which heads west and then curves northwest towards Cerro Piedra Negra (4,480m), which is a southern spur of Carihuairazo and about 4km away. Head to the east of Cerro Piedra Negra and right past the flank of a small conical hill to reach the area of the destroyed hut of Carihuairazo.

The ruins of the hut are difficult to see, but the surrounding area is suitable for camping and still used as a base to climb the Moche Peak of Carihuairazo (see *Climbing Carihuairazo*, page 122). From the camping area it is an easy scramble to the top of Cerro Piedra Negra, from which there are views of Ambato as well as four other major peaks: Carihuairazo to the north, Chimborazo to the southwest, Tungurahua to the east, and El Altar to the southeast.

From the camping area continue roughly westwards along the south flanks of Carihuairazo. First climb on to the ridge joining Cerro Piedra Negra with Carihuairazo and continue north along it for about a kilometre until you are near the head of the Aucacán river valley on your left. This ridge is narrow and exposed in places. Then drop down from the ridge, cross the Quebrada Aucacán high up the valley and scramble up the ridge on the opposite side. Crossing this valley is easier than it looks, especially if you follow the diagonal slash of vegetation, which is clearly visible on the far side. Beyond the opposite ridge of the Quebrada Aucacán are flat camping areas with snow melt streams. Other good campsites are found near small lakes at the head of the Quebrada Tigre Saltana valley, about half an hour roughly west from here. Both campsites are often used as basecamps for the ascent of Carihuairazo's main (Maxim) peak (see *Climbing Carihuairazo*). Allow a full day to reach this area from the hut. This is such a pretty area that it is worth camping early and exploring its interesting high Andean lakes, streams and bogs.

The next day the hike continues roughly north over a pass between Carihuairazo and Loma Piedra Negra (not to be confused with Cerro Piedra

Negra), a pyramidal peak west of Carihuairazo. There is a trail around the eastern and northern flanks of Loma Piedra Negra. The trail is rather indistinct in places, but frequent cairns are an aid. Once you have rounded Loma Piedra Negra the trail fades and you strike west down a gently sloping plain for about 3km until you come to a road. Follow this road to the right to a hairpin turn, with a sign to Vicuña Reserve, and take a hard right fork (not shown on map) to get to the Ambato-Guaranda road in 1½ hours. Here you can flag down a bus to take you into Ambato (turn right) or Guaranda (turn left). For ascents of Chimborazo, it is about 6km to the turn-off for the Whymper refuge in the direction of Guaranda.

The glaciers on the mountains are inaccurately represented; they have greatly receded in recent years and on Carihuairazo occupy barely half of the area assigned to them on the maps. Thus, part of the hike appears to cross glaciers but this is not so. Most of the other topographical features are accurate.

Urbina to Laguna Cocha Negra and Vicuña Reserve
Kathy Jarvis

Distance 20–24km
Altitude 3,615–4,400m
Rating Moderate
Time 2 days
Start Urbina railway station
End Urbina railway station or Vicuña Reserve
Maps IGM 1:50,000 Chimborazo and Quero
Other essential notes Good hike up to the glaciers of Chimborazo.

This route takes you around the northeast flank of Chimborazo, with fantastic views of the glaciers when the weather cooperates. Be warned that it is very easy to get lost on this route in poor visibility, as it crosses quite a lot of featureless *páramo*. Allow 8 to 9 hours from Urbina to reach the Laguna Cocha Negra.

Access Transport along the Ambato-Riobamba highway will pass the turn-off for the old Urbina train station just north of the provincial boundary at the pass. From the highway, get off at the Entrada a Urbina (there may be a sign, though they seem to come and go) and walk just over 1km up the dirt road to the station, which has been converted into a hostal, Posada La Estacion (3,615m). This place has plenty of character and lots of train artefacts decorating the walls. It boasts friendly staff and meals are available (although there is no camping food available), and visitors can also use the kitchen. Beds are $6 per night (there are several rooms). Muleteers and donkeys/horses are also available locally for $7 per day. The hostal is operated by Alta Montaña in Riobamba (tel: 3 2942215; email: aventura@exploringecuador.com).

Hiking directions From the train station walk southwest for 2km until you reach a dirt track to the right, just after the road goes over the railway line, and just before the small village of Santa Rosa de Chuquipogyos. Follow this road upwards for 2km to a fork (Hacienda Chuquipogyos) and turn left. Continue another kilometre and take another left. You should now be heading northwards towards the ridge of Loma Caparina, which is 2km ahead. From the ridge of Loma Caparina continue up the hillside on the same track, as agricultural land gives way to the grassy tussocks of the *páramo*. After 1km take a right fork and the path will soon head across a distinctive boulder field known as 'Rumipamba', turning into a much narrower, sometimes extremely muddy path. You cross several small streams (the route's first good water source). The path continues across the boulder field, then goes in a northwesterly direction, contouring round Chimborazo (elevation varies between 4,200 to 4,400m) above the Río Mocha, eventually reaching the Laguna Cocha Negra. The Laguna Cocha Negra is small (50m across); there is reasonable camping around the lake.

From the Laguna Cocha you can continue north about 0.75km to a road that connects with the Vicuña Reserve and the Ambato–Guaranda road (7km, 2 hours) or return to Urbina.

Climbing Carihuairazo

There are two main peaks, Maxim in the centre and Mocha to the southeast. Maxim is the highest at 5,020m (IGM figures) although some authorities put Maxim at 5,116m and Mocha at 5,030m. Whatever the correct altitude, both peaks are glaciated and require ice axes, crampons and a rope. The rotten rock at the top of both peaks is a little exposed.

Maxim

Access The most direct approach to the Maxim Peak is from the Ambato–Guaranda road. About an hour out of Ambato you'll see a large sign on the left side of the road which says Río Blanco. A short way down the road there are a group of buildings and a school, Colegio Manuela Cañzares, on the right. Have the driver let you off here. Follow the road going left from the community and this will take you up towards. The Laguna Negra (about 3 to 4 hours' walking) and beyond to Quebrada Tigre Saltana. You can drive this section of road with a 4WD vehicle, but it can be tricky since it is sloped in places. A drawback is that this route passes through a vicuña reserve and technically you should have permission from the Ministerio de Ambiente office in Cuenca. Some groups get stopped, others go through without seeing anyone. What seems to be the easiest solution is to 'pay' on the spot for permission to enter if you're stopped.

You can camp at a pleasant lake called the Laguna Negra, about a 45-minute walk up the *páramo* from the road (not to be confused with the Laguna Cocha Negra). It is best to hide your things or hire someone from the Ministerio de Ambiente office to watch them while you are climbing. Another hour higher up there is a camp just below the glacier, west-northwest of peak 4,698. To get to this camp head to the left of peak 4,698 and eventually up to the ridge behind this peak, then follow a cairned trail to a flat rocky field, usually trickling with water but possibly covered by snow. By camping here you reduce climbing time by about 2 hours, but it's risky leaving anything out and unattended anywhere in the area. It is also possible to camp at the head of Quebrada Loma Saltana where there is usually a lake.

Direct Route Maxim Peak is most easily climbed by the Direct Route, but there are numerous variations. From the flat area west northwest of peak 4,698 head up the moraine slope to the glacier. Once on the snow an obvious line leads to the right for the summit ridge. There may be a few crevasses depending on conditions. The last 100m may be a moderately steep, mixed snow-and-rock scramble. Once on the ridge, traverse left along a rotten and exposed knife-edged crest. The top few metres are loose and there is some danger from rockfall. Allow 2 to 3 hours for the ascent.

Mocha

Access The route up Mocha is steep and provides an interesting route-finding problem. It can be climbed directly from the destroyed Carihuairazo hut (described earlier) in 4 to 6 hours. A pleasant alternative is to place a high camp on the upper slopes below the Mocha glacier.

Glacier Route From the hut climb up onto the ridge joining Cerro Piedra Negra with Carihuairazo and follow the ridge towards Carihuairazo for about a kilometre. At one point, this section becomes rather narrow and steep, with large drop-offs. A rope may provide more security, or you can drop down and traverse below the ridge crest. Flat spaces are found at the end of the ridge for a high camp. From here there is no standard route because the glacier is constantly changing. You can try climbing up the scree along the left-hand side of the lower slope, then climb onto the glacier above the serac field at its tongue and skirt the large ice fall in the centre of the glacier (but beware of rock fall from the cliffs bordering the ice). Route finding through crevasse fields may be necessary. The summit is to the right and is composed of rather rotten rock.

Climbing Chimborazo

There are five summits: the Whymper (or Ecuador) summit at 6,310m, the Veintimilla summit at 6,267m, the North summit at about 6,200m, the Central (or Polytechnic) summit at around 6,000m, and the Eastern (or Nicolás Martinéz) summit of approximately 5,500m. The last, although the lowest, is the most difficult. The routes to the highest summit will be discussed more thoroughly. (See diagram overleaf.)

Access The best way to reach the mountain is by bus from Ambato to Guaranda. Sit on the left-hand side of the bus for the best views. About 56km from Ambato you will come to a dirt road on your left leading to the Whymper refuge. This road is marked by a deserted white house (often painted with colourful political slogans) of cement blocks on the left-hand side, immediately beyond the junction. It is the only house on the left-hand side for many kilometres. From the junction walk southeast on the dirt road for 3–4km until you come to a hairpin bend. Here you can turn left up a small gully and climb due east for a further 3–4km until you see the parking area and lower refuge below the larger Whymper refuge. (The lower refuge has some facilities, but most parties stay at the Whymper refuge some 200m above, and half an hour away.) Allow 3 to 6 hours from the junction to the car park at the lower refuge (the high altitude slows you down). If you don't want to go cross-country you can follow the road around to the parking area, but this is 10–12km. If you'd rather hire transport, a taxi can be hired in Ambato at the Terminal Terrestre for about $30. Better still is to go by taxi from Riobamba, especially if you plan to stay overnight before going to the refuge the following day. You ought to be able to get a taxi for $30 or less, and the road up to the refuge via the village of San Juan is straightforward. Riobamba has a better variety of accommodation and restaurants, and a lovely market on Saturdays.

At the parking area and lower refuge, a narrow trail takes off from the left of the refuge for the half-hour climb up to the Whymper hut. There have been recent break-ins in the parking lot but the military is now patrolling the area. The Whymper hut is well appointed with enough bunk beds and foam mattresses for about four dozen mountaineers (use your own sleeping bag), toilets, cold water, a kitchen with utensils and a propane gas stove (though this has been known to run out of gas during and after a busy weekend), a small supply of basic foods for sale, a fireplace, and a huge visitors' book with which to while away high-altitude storms. There is a hut guardian who will keep an eye on your belongings when you climb; he will also charge you a fee of $10 per day to use the hut.

Normal Route This route has become the normal approach to the Chimborazo summit over the past few years, replacing the Whymper Route. Its steepness is more continuous but it offers a direct line to the summit. The route will vary slightly from year to year, so it's best to check with the refuge guardian for the latest information. From the hut, follow the path which leads to the prominent scree slope to the left of the receding Thielman glacier. Climb up the scree to the huge horizontal snow ramp (El Corredor) just below a prominent rock outcrop (on the descent, this section ought to be negotiated quickly as danger from rockfall increases as the snow softens). Traverse El Corredor right up to the main glacier, then angle left up a steep snow-field to a pass above a rock outcrop called El Castillo. The area below El Castillo was heavily crevassed in 2003. As you ascend from El Castillo you will eventually begin to head northwest (right) towards the Veintimilla summit. There can be short but steep icy sections (40–45°) that may require front-pointing on the climb and abseiling (rapelling) on the descent. The snowfield is usually marked with flags and footsteps. There may be a large crevasse just below the Veintimilla summit which may be passed on the right. It is 6 to 8 hours to the Veintimilla summit. It is nearly 1km east over a gentle snow basin to the main summit – approximately 20 to 60 minutes, depending on the snow conditions. Late in the day this snow basin is filled with notoriously soft snow and at this altitude it takes great energy to wade through thigh deep snow. Therefore it is advisable to start as early as possible (midnight) so that the final slog to the summit is easier. Some climbers have spent the night near Veintimilla summit and finished the climb the next day – this is an adventure for experienced, acclimatised, and well-equipped climbers only. 8 to 10 hours are normally needed for the ascent (although one party we met took 20 hours!). Allow 4 to 5 hours for the descent.

The route should be marked with wands during the ascent, and it's not a bad idea to mark the path up the scree to the snow ramp in advance during daylight hours. It's surprisingly difficult to find the track up through the scree in the middle of the night.

Direct Route A variation on the Normal Route is to head straight up the Thielman glacier and meet the Normal Route where it exits El Corredor. This route is not recommended, however, since it is subject to avalanches and could be heavily crevassed.

Whymper Route Chimborazo with historical connections to boot, this line of ascent is no longer considered practical or safe. The icy traverse under the seracs has been the site of several deaths.

The route begins by following a trail to the right of the refuge to Agujas Whymper (Whymper Needles). Continue on the ridge crest and aim directly towards the Veintimilla summit. Pass between some rock out-crops where the snow begins to steepen. Depending on conditions, crevasses may be present. Continue directly up the steep snow slope to the left of the large rock face. From here two routes are possible to the Veintimilla summit. One is to follow the original Whymper route by traversing left and joining the Normal Route. A more direct variation may be followed, although only if the snow is stable, by continuing up the steep snow slope straight to the Veintimilla summit.

Murallas Rojas Route This is no longer a popular route, but we have retained the description in case conditions change.

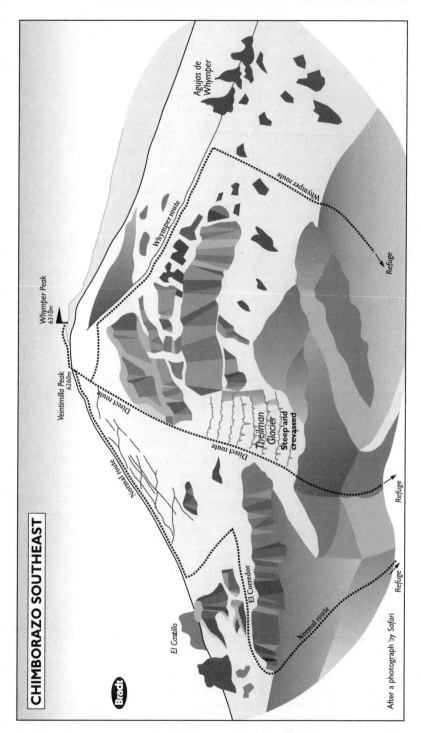

CHIMBORAZO SOUTHEAST

Whymper Peak
6310m

Agujas de
Whymper

Veintimilla Peak
6260m

Whymper route

Whymper route

Refuge

Normal route

Direct route

Direct route

Thielman Glacier

Steep and crevassed

Refuge

El Castillo

El Corredor

Normal route

Refuge

Refuge

After a photograph by Safari

Bradt

The old route begins at the village of Pogyos (also spelt Poggios or Pogyo) which is a tiny group of buildings on a bend of the road about 50km south of Ambato, on the old road to Guaranda. About 1km and 4km before Pogyos are two roads to the left, which may help you find it; the bus driver sometimes knows it.

Pogyos is the last place on the route where you can find water, but you'll probably want to sterilise it. Mules can be hired inexpensively to carry water and gear up to the remains of the Fabián Zurita refuge at 4,900m, about 900m above Pogyos. To get to the refuge cross the Ambato-Guaranda road and follow a dirt track that leaves the road a few hundred metres west of Pogyos and heads southeast across the sandy *páramo* to the hut, which is 3 or 4 hours' walk away.

The climb from the camp at the ruins of the Zurita refuge to the summit is becoming more demanding as the glacier recedes. The route goes up the loose scree above the hut to the snowline and then continues on the snow to the base of a large, red, rock band known as the 'murallas rojas' (red walls). At the base of the red walls traverse to your right and continue upwards on snow along or a little beyond the right-hand edge of the walls. Once beyond the walls head towards the peak above you, watching for crevasses which will be predominantly to your right. As you get high on the peak, start heading left and to the side of it – this peak is the second or Veintimilla Peak. The rounded summit is about 1km east of Veintimilla. The climb takes from 8 to 12 hours. A midnight departure is recommended as the summit snow plateau becomes very soft and slushy, and avalanche danger on the slopes increases after midday.

Piedra Negra and Sun Ridge routes

These two routes on the eastern side of Chimborazo involve rock climbing and mixed rock/ice climbing, respectively. This area is rarely visited but is located in a spectacular setting formed by a natural amphitheatre of rock and snow. Even if the climbing proves to be too challenging, the area is excellent for exploring and hiking.

Access

See *Access* in *Urbina to Laguna Cocha Negra and Vicuña Reserve*, page 121. From Posada La Estacion a trail leads up the *páramo* and begins a steep ascent to the terminal moraine at the foot of Chimborazo. At the top of the moraine there is a small lake with a flat area for camping, about 4 to 5 hours from the refuge. This is a good base for climbing both the Piedra Negra route and/or the Sun Ridge route. Another option for camping, particularly if you're not planning to climb, is to continue along the moraine to the right for another 1½ hours, where there are magnificent views of Carihuairazo and the surrounding area, and where there's plenty of water available from nearby streams.

Climbing Piedra Negra

This enjoyable climb is not to be confused with either Cerro Piedra Negra or Loma Piedra Negra, both of which are located across the valley on Carihuairazo. This route was first climbed in 1984 by the Polytechnic Climbing Club, but has not been repeated with much frequency. An assortment of technical rock gear is necessary. From the moraine camp you will see the entire east side of Chimborazo clearly – an impressive view. To the northeast (right) is a large rock formation, Piedra Negra, with a long moraine leading directly up to its base, about 1 to 2 hours from camp. At its base, traverse right (northeast) to the obvious ridge and climb to the summit. The difficulty is rated about 5.5 based on the Yosemite decimal system and takes a maximum of 2 hours from the start of the traverse.

A more difficult option, again requiring technical rock gear and experience, is the route up the east wall of Piedra Negra.

This climb, first ascended by Hugo Torres and Francisco Espinosa, begins on the east face just past the obvious overhanging junction of the east and southeast faces. A few metres to the right is a smaller overhang (good to belay below this) with the climb starting in a crack next to it. The crack runs out quickly, and you'll continue up, face-climbing between two large rocks to a small belay ledge. Because of the rarely climbed condition of the route, pitons may be more useful for securing belay stances than chocks or nuts, but several well-placed small nuts may do.

The second pitch continues up the face to another, larger ledge. Just below this belay the rock turns a little ugly with downward-sloping holds. From this belay, the third pitch climbs a chimney to the ridge, for about one rope length. At the ridge, the route goes left, in 4th class scrambling up and across some big loose rocks. The top is about half an hour to an hour away. There is no easy downclimb; you'll have to descend to the ridge and then abseil the rest of the way.

Above the second pitch, at the wide ledge, there are several alternatives for reaching the top. One is to go left at the chimney rather than climbing in it, and you'll find easy rock leading to the ridge.

Sun Ridge Route

This climb ascends to the Nicolás Martínez summit of Chimborazo and is considered by many climbers to be one of the most beautiful mixed rock/ice routes in all of Ecuador. It requires both rock and snow experience and equipment, along with regular camping gear. Carry an assortment of ice screws, stakes and various sizes of rock protection. A bivouac will more than likely be necessary below the summit, so you'll need to come prepared for that as well. From the moraine camp, follow the same route up to Piedra Negra. Traverse left under the rock and head for the main snow ridge. Once on the glacier, traverse across the snow-field towards the immense rock face of the Chimborazo summits. Camp is set up on the glacier well below and in line with the start of the rock face. Allow about 3 to 5 hours of hiking from the moraine camp.

From the glacier camp, you will see a wide snow ramp to the left on the rock face which leads up into a couloir. Ascend about halfway, to a logical point where you can begin a traverse left across the rocks. Be careful of loose rock in this section. The traverse continues across to an area of huge rock slabs/boulders stacked on top of each other. In spite of appearing ready to give way at any minute, this area is quite stable. Climb these slabs up and left to just below a ridgeline. Here the route begins another traverse across a mixture of steep snow and rock up and down across small ridges. (The feasibility of crossing this section depends on the season. If there has been little snow, you'll have to continue up to the main ridge to make the traverse, but this is more difficult.) The traverse continues left and flattens out at the top of a wide snow ramp. It should take about 5 to 7 hours from the camp to reach this point. Here you can make a choice. If the going has been difficult, or the group is moving too slowly, this ramp is an excellent escape route and provides an easy descent back to the lower glacier and camp.

If continuing, traverse a bit further to a snow-field which is the beginning of the upper glacier. Head left up the snow-field to a section of huge snow 'mushrooms' which begin the final approach to the summit. A bivouac is normally made just after gaining this part of the glacier. The snow and ice are steep and of poor quality, and some route finding is necessary to make your way up towards the summit. From the top of this snow-field you can look up left to pinpoint the final approach to the summit. It should take about 3 to 5 hours of climbing from the bivouac to reach the summit. The descent backtracks to the easy exit snow ramp for the fastest return to the lower glacier.

An easier alternative to this mixed route is to traverse from the snow camp below the rock face to the snow gully used for the descent in the above climb. Climb this to meet up with the other route, and continue up to the summit following the above description. From camp, this could take about 7 hours to the summit and another 3 for the descent.

Other routes Many new routes remain to be climbed on a mountain of this size. There are also routes which have had only one or two ascents. Among these are the following: the eastern summit via the Moreno glacier in the southeast, the main summit from the north, and the central peak via the Humboldt glacier in the south.

These routes are suggestions for highly advanced climbers only. Otherwise stay on the standard routes; if you need a guide, see *Chapter 3*, page 42.

Chimborazo can be and is climbed year-round, but June and July are considered the best months. August tends to be windy and September is not too bad, but October and November have long spells of bad weather. Late December and early January are good, but the rest of the year has predominantly bad weather, with April the worst month. A tent is only needed by hikers doing the full hiking route described.

PARQUE NACIONAL CAJAS
At the southern end of the Western Cordillera is found an enchantingly beautiful area of *páramo* and cloudforest. For the naturalist the principal attraction is the variety of plants on show, and a careful ornithologist will see a good number of bird species too. The hiker, meanwhile, is faced with a profusion of lakes of all shapes, sizes and colours; the area boasts 275 named lakes and countless minor ponds and tarns. This is Parque Nacional Cajas, a reserve of almost 29,000 hectares set aside for preservation in 1977 and named a national park in December 1996.

Parque Nacional Cajas is one of the best-managed conservation areas in Ecuador, which is probably due to local Cuencano pride in the area. On any weekend, hundreds of local anglers and recreationalists drive from nearby Cuenca into the park. Most visitors usually do not travel far from the road, so you can find solitude on an overnight backpacking trip into the centre of the park.

The preserve lies about 29km west of Cuenca. This charming city, the nation's third largest, is worth a few days' exploration. Getting a bus for the 9-hour trip to Cuenca from Quito's Terminal Terrestre is straightforward, or you can take one of the several daily flights. The offices of the Ministerio de Ambiente in Cuenca are located on 12 de Abril and Floriana Astudillo (Sector Puente Roto), second floor (tel: 7 2848543). You can also obtain more information on the area from the offices of ETAPA (Empresa de Telefonos Agua Potable y Alcantarillado) located at Km 8 on the highway to Azogue (sector Ucubamba; tel: 7 2890418, gambiental@emp.etapa.com.ec).

Access Buses leave every half hour from the main bus terminal in Cuenca on the Vía Molleturo, which passes right by the Centro de Información Toreadora (1½

PARQUE NACIONAL CAJAS

hours from Cuenca) in the northern part of the park. Here you need to pay the park entrance fee. There may also be buses that leave from Plaza San Sebastián at the corners of Bolívar and Talbot, so check locally. You can hire a taxi in Cuenca to Toreadora or Miguir for about $20–30. There is a refuge with a few bunks and a kitchen (a small fee is charged). Camping is permitted throughout the park and is free. Another route into the park is on the bus to Angas, on the southwestern border of Cajas. Enquire locally for bus schedules.

Once you get away from the immediate environs of the park station at Toreadora you will find that an effort has been made to mark some of the frequently used trails. Still, those markers which wander some distance from the main area usually peter out fairly quickly, so hiking here is largely a cross-country affair. A strong hiker with a good sense of direction can cross the park in 2 days. The vegetation is primarily *páramo* grasses, and trails exist up most valleys and to most lakes, so the walking is straightforward. Having said that, several people have died from exposure, so it is important to have warm clothes and rain gear. We describe several recommended routes here, although perhaps your best bet is to bring enough food for a week and just amble around gently; you'll see very few people and the scenery is really marvellous.

The major part of the land area is *páramo* and many typical *páramo* species may be seen here. Most exciting of all is perhaps the condor, which is still occasionally sighted. You will also hear as well as see the Andean snipe. Highland thickets of the dwarf quinua tree dot the landscape and are filled with a fascinating variety of primitive plant and fungal life: the trees and ground are covered with mosses,

ROUTES IN PARQUE NACIONAL CAJAS

Trail	Distance	Time	Difficulty	Alt range
Avilahuayco	1.6km	4 hours	Moderate	3,840–4,200m
Cucheros/Burines	3.0km	2 hours	Easy	3,880–4,100m
García Moreno	3.0km	3 hours	Easy	3,720–3,960m
Camino de Inca	20.0km	3 days	Difficult	3,100–4,050m
Osohuayco/Huagrahuma	10.0km	6 hours	Moderate	3,770–4,120m
Parada/Patul/Virgen	9.2km	5 hours	Moderate	3,650–4,250m
San Luis	2.0km	3 hours	Moderate	3,690–4,240m
Shayana/Burines	3.6km	2 hours	Moderate	3,880–4,110m
Toreadora Unidas	1.3km	2 hours	Easy	3,880–3,960m
Toreadora Soldados	30.0km	3 days	Moderate	3,300–4,150m
Tres Cruces/Huagrahuma	3.5km	3 hours	Easy	3,860–4,160m
Toreadora/Parada/Patul	8.0km	6 hours	Moderate	3,880–4,080m
Toreadora/Unidas/Virgen	5.2km	5 hours	Moderate	3,690–3,720m
Toreadora/Burines/Llaviuco	14.0km	2–3 days	Moderate	3,100–4,150m

Source: ETAPA

lichens, liverworts, mushrooms, toadstools and other fungi. One of the most colourful and common flowers is a small, bulbous, yellow and red flower known locally as sarazhima. You'll see rabbits and, with luck, a white-tailed deer or fox. The lakes are filled with trout and sport fishing is permitted. Towards and beyond the park's western boundaries are almost impenetrable cloudforests. There is one area of the park, however, which is known for its accessible cloudforest: the eastern part near the Laguna Llaviuco. This is one of the very few areas of cloudforest on the eastern slopes of the Western Cordillera. It is reached by a short, signposted dirt track leading from the main park entrance road about a third of the way between the village of Sayausi and the park station. Many more bird species are found here including the grey-breasted mountain toucan (*Andigena hypoglauca*), the multi-coloured masked trogon (*Trogon personatus*), and various tropical woodpeckers. Another park station is being planned for this vicinity.

The altitude of the park averages around 4,000m, with no area rising above 4,500m, so there is no snow, yet it can get rather chilly at night and in the early morning. The weather varies so much that it's best to be prepared for all temperatures. Mornings are usually clear with lots of sun (good T-shirt hiking), but by late afternoon clouds often roll in and rain is always a possibility. Visits can be made year-round, although April to June are said to be the wettest months and August and September the driest. ETAPA publishes a map to the park, which can be purchased at their office. They list the above routes through the park, which have not been tested by the authors. Two other treks are described below in some detail.

Miguir to Río Soldados hike

Hiking directions Begin on an established trail that leaves Miguir to the Laguna Sunincocha. You pass through second growth cloudforest to *páramo* vegetation. In this zone there are marvellous hummingbirds such as the shining sunbeam, veridean metal-tail, sparkling violet-ear, and the spectacular sword-billed hummingbird whose bill is three times the length of its body. The lakes also harbour Andean gulls, speckled teal and yellow-billed pintails. As the trail becomes less distinct, stay on the south side of the Laguna Sunincocha and follow the valley

Distance Approximately 20km
Altitude 3,240–4,150m
Rating Moderate
Time 2–3 days
Start Miguir
End Soldados
Maps IGM 1:50,000 Chaucha, Cuenca and San Felipe de Molleturo. At the entrance station in Toreadora pick-up a free planometric map of the area with trails and routes indicated.
Other essential notes Great views of lakes, but requires route-finding skills.

south past the Laguna Valeriana Yacu to a pass. From here you look down to the Laguna Inga Casa and the Río Soldados drainage basin. It is about 4 to 5 hours to this pass from Miguir and there are good camping spots next to the lakes on the opposite side of the basin. The walk out to Soldados the next day takes 4 to 5 hours. There are daily buses to Cuenca from Soldados.

Ingañan Trail

Distance 21km
Altitude 3,140–4,060m
Rating Moderate
Time 2–3 days
Start Miguir
End Laguna Llaviuco
Maps IGM 1:50,000 Cuenca, San Felipe de Molleturo and Chiquintad. At the entrance station in Toreadora pick up a free planometric map of the area with trails and routes indicated.
Other essential notes Follows an old Inca Trail through the park, but requires route-finding skills.

Hiking directions There is a portion of an Inca trail that crosses the park from the Laguna Luspa to the Laguna Llaviuco known as the Ingañan – it was probably a trading road from Cuenca to the coast. It is in ill-repair or lost in places, but there are some interesting ruins above the Laguna Mamamag that are presently being excavated. You can access the trail from several drainages near the park headquarters or from Miguir. Beginning in Miguir follow an established path to the Laguna Luspa. At the Laguna Luspa take a path on the left (north) side of the lake; this will bring you to a stream that flows into the Laguna Luspa. From here head east on a trail eventually ascending to a divide, from which point you will be able to see the Laguna Osohuaycu. Continue down to the Laguna Osohuaycu. The trail then passes north of the Laguna Osohuaycu, a large basin surrounded by rocky peaks in the centre of the park that makes a good base for day-hikes. It then descends to the Laguna Mamamag (Taitachugo), where you should stay on south side of the lake, cross over the small ridge near the mouth of the lake, and then descend through cloudforest on an established trail. Soon you reach a flat U-shaped, grassy valley-bottom and follow the wide Inca road to the Laguna Llaviuco and a gate where you should be able to get a ride with fishermen back to Cuenca. This trip takes 2 to 3 days. The area near the Laguna Llaviuco has recently been purchased by ETAPA. The entrance fee can be paid to the park guard if you plan on doing this hike in reverse. A good day-hike is from the Laguna Llaviuco to the Laguna Mamamag and back.

Rock climbing
Cajas
From the refuge at the Laguna Toreadora, you can look across the road and see a prominent rock block some 300m away. About 20 minutes of uphill walking will get you to its base. In the centre of the face is a large (35m) flake with three established routes and several other possibilities. The overhanging face on the main block can also be climbed, but bolting is necessary. A top rope can be set up on the flake.

Godzilla is a 5.10b, first ascended by Juan Rodriguez and Juan Carrasco. It begins near the centre of the flake at the base of a tree. Look for a finger crack leading up to a roof. Past this roof the thin crack continues up to a second and runs out to the right while the route angles left, up the face to a ledge. The descent is a matter of downclimbing a chimney (5.6) on the right side of the flake. Another chimney (5.7) on the left side can also be climbed, but both are somewhat dirty.

About 200m east (left) of Godzilla is another rock formation (25m) with an off-width crack starting in its centre which gradually narrows to a fist, then finger crack, called Salsipuedes (5.9).

In addition, there are many huge rocks scattered in this general area which would serve well for an afternoon of bouldering.

Cuenca area
In search for good rock a few stalwart Ecuadorian climbers have pioneered many routes and opened up several areas suitable for climbing. Of these climbers, Juan Carrasco and Juan Rodriguez seem to have been the most active, claiming many first ascents. While the majority of rock routes described here are not particularly noteworthy by American or European standards, at least for now they offer a sampling of the best available in the country. As mentioned previously, Ecuador is not a rock-climbing destination but if you're already here and longing for the feel of rock, the following suggestions and descriptions may be useful.

If you happen to be staying in Cuenca for a few days, you can get in a little climbing practice by 'buildering', or in this case, 'bridgering', near the Tomebamba river. Follow Av 3 de Noviembre southeast as it runs parallel to the river and crosses under a broken bridge (*puente roto*) just past Vargas Machuca. The three centre pillars on the west face of the bridge range from 5.7 to 5.8 and a top rope can be set up on the bridge railings.

About 6–8km outside of Cuenca, just before the village of Sayausi (buses leave from Plaza San Francisco), is a popular restaurant called Las Cabañas that serves the best trout (*trucha*) around.

After lunching here, continue along the road towards Sayausi until you come to a dirt road heading left. Follow this road down to a covered wooden bridge about a 100m away, cross over and backtrack along the river on the other side to just opposite the restaurant. Here you'll come to an 8m-high boulder called Piedra de las Truchas (trout rock) with two climbable faces and lots of routes.

The east face has several established climbs – Vía Murcielago (5.8) starts as an off-width crack leading off a flake near the centre of the face. It narrows to a finger crack near the top.

To the left of this climb is Cebiche de Trucha, a 5.11 climb which starts from a low rock ramp; it's overhanging and fun. Encebollado follows up the northeast

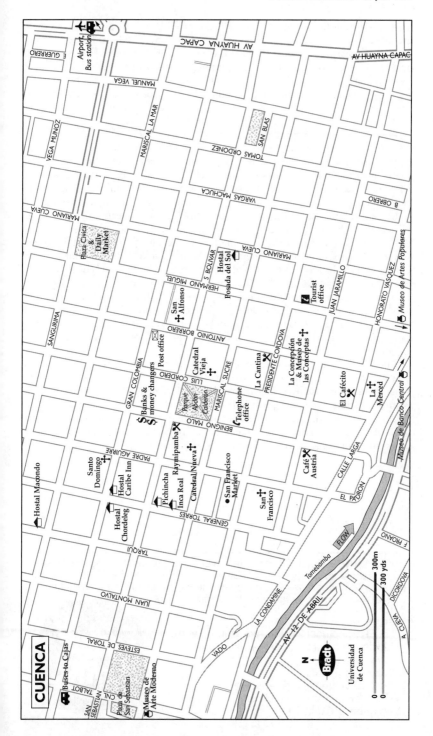

CUENCA

arête, and is not difficult at 5.8. Top roping is possible on the south side and there are other climbs and more possibilities on both the south and north faces.

Another nearby area is located outside the village of Cojitambo. Here you'll find a dome-shaped rock formation, spanning 800m with a 200m rock wall, overlooking the village. To get there, take a bus from Cuenca to Azogues (40 minutes) and get off at the end of the line. The bus for Cojitambo (25 minutes) passes nearby, at the hospital road junction. You'll have to ask where to wait. Once in the village you'll see the huge east face, about a 20-minute walk from town.

Dead centre in the wall is Ruta de la Gruta, a 5.7 crack that's dirty with vegetation; the second pitch is better. On the far left is Viuda Alegre, a nicer, wide, 5.10 hand-crack leading up to a roof. At the roof you can go left (dirty) or traverse right (nice) to a walk-off. Above this area, closer to the ridge and higher up, is a rose-coloured wall with two good cracks of about 30m running up to the south ridge. From here you can hike to the top and walk off via the easy west slope.

More climbing can be found to the south of Cuenca in a beautiful area near the village of San Fernando. To get there you first have to take a bus from Cuenca to the town of Girón on the road to Machala. Here take another bus to San Fernando, which is situated at the foot of the massive Mount Pablo. The area is loaded with climbing possibilities and is good for camping, hiking and birdwatching. Sometimes groups come up here for hang-gliding practice. From the village hike up to the Laguna Buza, 15 minutes away, where you'll find good camping. The approach to the base of San Pablo is somewhat difficult, requiring a steep bushwhack through dense vegetation and forest to reach the rock walls towering as high as 300m. This could take as long as 3 to 4 hours, but the area is worth exploring.

Another suggestion that may not offer world-class climbing but promises to get you off the beaten path is the gorge of Río Ridcay, about an hour down the Cuenca-Machala road near the village of Lentag. In Cuenca, hop on a bus from the main bus terminal going to Santa Isabel and ask to be let off at Lentag. From here find the dirt road that takes off left down to the river. After about half an hour's walk you'll come to a bridge. The rock walls of the gorge will be visible to the right. Cross the bridge and head down into the gorge. Climb on.

The Eastern Cordillera

The journey not the arrival matters.

T S Eliot

This is perhaps the most interesting region for the adventurous outdoor traveller. The Eastern Cordillera is, on average, higher and more massive than its western counterpart, and counts amongst its mountains the famous volcanoes of Cotopaxi, Cayambe, Antisana, El Altar and Sangay, which rank respectively second, third, fourth, fifth and seventh highest in the country. The last named is considered to be the most continuously active volcano in South America, if not the world.

The high eastern slopes of these mountains are bordered by a relatively thin strip of *páramo* which changes abruptly to almost impenetrable high mountain cloudforest on the lower slopes before merging into what is commonly called 'jungle', but is in fact the tropical rainforest of the lowlands. Hot air masses rise up the eastern flanks of the mountains depositing enough rainfall to make the high mountain cloudforest the wettest part of Ecuador; indeed, with some areas averaging over 5,000mm of rain per year, it is one of the wettest regions on earth. It is also extremely thickly vegetated and so the middle and lower slopes have been little disturbed by people. The story is often told of the *hacienda* owner who, upon being asked how extensive his land was, replied, 'I don't really know – as far as you can go to the east.' Even today the eastern slopes are so little explored that *haciendas* with ill-defined limits to the east still exist. These are the haunts of the rarely seen mountain tapir and the Andean spectacled bear, the two largest wild land mammals in Ecuador and both considered endangered species. Their rarity is due not only to hunting and land encroachment but also to the almost impenetrable nature of their environment – no-one really knows how many of these elusive animals are left.

The mountains themselves tend to be covered with more snow than those of the Western Cordillera because of the higher precipitation on the eastern slopes. The peaks are normally climbed from the western side, partly because the heavily populated Central Valley lies on this side and partly because the eastern side is difficult to get to, often clouded in, and the summits are more heavily corniced with potentially unstable snow. Adventurous climbers seeking new routes could look for eastern approaches to these mountains.

As with the Western Cordillera, the mountains of this range will be dealt with systematically from north to south; descriptions of both climbing and hiking routes will be given and walks into the rarely visited eastern slopes are also described.

RESERVA ECOLÓGICA CAYAMBE-COCA

The Reserva Ecológica Cayambe-Coca was established in 1970 and protects an area of over 400,000 hectares of diverse and largely unexplored forested and *páramo* wilderness. It occupies an area between Ibarra and Papallacta, straddling the Eastern Cordillera and extending down to the Oriente. Although some colonists and indigenous tribes live within the reserve, the inaccessibility of the eastern Andean slope has protected the unexplored centre from intrusion and development. On flights to the Oriente you pass over this maze of knife-edged ridges, frothing rivers, dense cloudforest and rainforest, and understand why not many people wander into this country. You do not have the wide navigable rivers of the lowland rainforest or the open *páramo* slopes of the Andes that make travel in these areas relatively easy. A wild adventure would be a traverse from the Eastern Cordillera down the eastern Andean slope to the Oriente using the good IGM 1:50,000 topographical maps that might help you from getting hopelessly lost. For the sane hiker and climber, however, there are numerous established routes that are accessible from the edges of the reserve.

The peaks of Nevado Cayambe, Cerro Sara Urco and Volcán Reventador (described in *Chapter 7*, pages 223–38) all lie within the boundaries of the reserve. There are many lakes in the *páramo* around the towns of Papallacta, Oyacachi, Olmedo and Sigsipamba which can be walked to on trails used by *campesinos* and fishers. There are also several short lowland rainforest walks.

The administration of the reserve is divided between Andean and lowland rainforest regions. The Ministerio de Ambiente office in Cayambe (located at km1.5 on Pan-Americana Norte) is managed by Luis Martinez and can provide information on road and trail conditions, guides, and weather conditions for the western side of the reserve. The two Ministerio de Ambiente offices in the Oriente are in El Chaco (located 2km along Via San Juan) and in the small town of Lumbaqui, and both can provide information on the eastern side of the reserve. Jorge Aguirre splits his time between these two offices. The staff for the reserve is small but friendly and helpful.

Laguna Puruhanta

On the northern end of the reserve is the Laguna Puruhanta, a large lake (3km long and 1km wide) which is popular with trout fishermen. The area is partly grazed, but still boasts a large amount of native cloudforest and *páramo* vegetation. There are several access points. The most common and shortest is to hike from Shanshipamba near the gorge of the Río Pisque. You can also walk from the village of Pesillo to the west or from the Laguna San Marcos to the south. (See *Laguna Puruhanta map*, page 137.)

Shanshipamba to Laguna Puruhanta

Distance 23km round trip
Altitude 2,760–3,450m
Rating Moderate–difficult
Time 2 days
Start Shanshipamba
End Shanshipamba
Maps IGM 1:50,000 Pimampiro and Mariano Acosta
Other essential notes Rough trail through good cloudforest to an Andean lake.

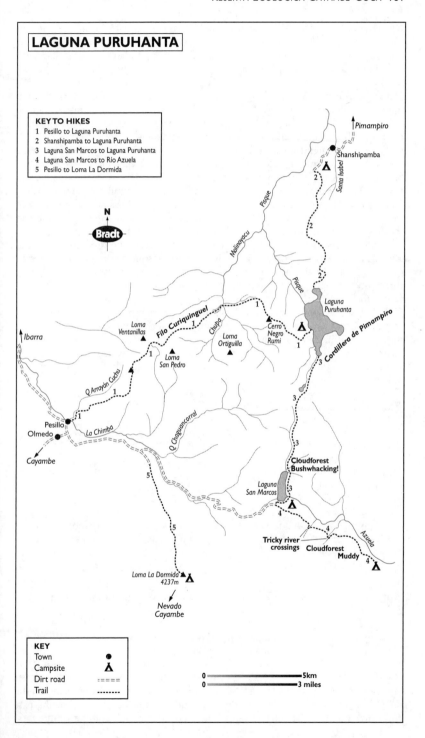

LAGUNA PURUHANTA

KEY TO HIKES
1 Pesillo to Laguna Puruhanta
2 Shanshipamba to Laguna Puruhanta
3 Laguna San Marcos to Laguna Puruhanta
4 Laguna San Marcos to Río Azuela
5 Pesillo to Loma La Dormida

Pimampiro

Shanshipamba

Santa Isabel

Pisque

Molinoyacu

Pisque

Laguna
Puruhanta

N

Bradt

Loma
Ventanillas

Filo Curiquinguel

Chuba

Loma
Ortiguilla

Cerro
Negro
Rumi

Cordillera de Pimampiro

Ibarra

Loma
San Pedro

Q Arrayán Cuchu

Q Chaguarcorral

Pesillo
Olmedo

La Chimba

Cayambe

Cloudforest
Bushwhacking!

Laguna
San Marcos

Tricky river
crossings

Cloudforest
Muddy

Azuela

Loma La Dormida
4237m

Nevado
Cayambe

KEY
Town ●
Campsite ⛺
Dirt road =====
Trail ·········

0 ———— 5km
0 ———— 3 miles

Approach Bus from Ibarra to Pimampiro (about 45 minutes). Reach Shanshipamba by hiring a taxi or catch an occasional bus from Pimampiro (1½ hours). It is a full day's (7 hours) walking from Shanshipamba to the lake, with camping possibilities along the way.

Hiking directions You have two options to get to the lake. The first is to climb up through the cloudforest to the ridge south of Shanshipamba. Not many people go this way unless they are hunting, and we could not find specific information on the route, though a trail is indicated on the IGM map.

The more straightforward route is along the Río Pisque gorge. Take the track out of Shanshipamba up to a flat pasture area with a dilapidated *hacienda*. Just before reaching the white house follow the main track to the right towards the Río Pisque. Follow a well-defined and sometimes muddy trail for approximately 3 hours to where you can see pastures on the opposite (west) side of the river. You can cross over to the furthest, upstream pasture near the confluence of the Río Palaucu to avoid a nasty stretch of trail on the east side of the river. The trail on the west side enters forest near a tin-roofed shack. You cross the Río Molinyacu and after an hour of hiking come to a log over the Río Pisque where you join the trail on the east side of the river. From here it is about 2 to 3 hours of muddy hiking through alternately swampy and cloudforest vegetation to the mouth of the lake where there is stream gauging station.

This hike has some of the best cloudforest vegetation of any intra-Andean trek, and spectacular views of the Río Pisque gorge and surrounding mountains. A good local guide is Juan Pupiales, who lives near the main square in Shanshipamba and charges about $15 per day for his services. He also may have a boat hidden somewhere on the shore of the lake that he will rent to his clients for about $8 per day. Rubber boots are highly recommended.

Pesillo to Laguna Puruhanta

Distance 35km round-trip
Altitude 3,120–3,953m
Rating Difficult
Time 3–4 days
Start Pesillo
End Pesillo
Maps IGM 1:50,000 San Pablo del Lago, Mariano Acosta, Cayambe
Other essential notes Good hiking along ridges and cloudforest to an Andean lake

Approach Take a bus to Pesillo from the town of Cayambe (see *Laguna San Marcos Access* opposite).

Hiking directions From the central *hacienda* of Pesillo, which is now a school and cheese factory, take the dirt road that heads up Quebrada Queseras Cuchu. After 5 minutes follow the trail on the left along powerlines, which soon joins a dirt track. You can see pine-covered Loma El Panecillo to the south and eventually will get spectacular views of Nevado Cayambe. Continue on the track (contouring on the south side of the hill) and when the track turns south, head left up to the pass following a trail up the ridge towards Loma Turupamba and contour on the west side of Loma Chafina to a pass east of Loma Ventana. On the other side of the pass you should see the Ventana (window), a natural rock arch, below you. Cross over to the east side of Loma Ventana and contour around to Filo Curiquingue Chupa. Pass a *choza* and ascend to peak 3953. From here you need to cross through cloudforest and a stream which separates Cerro Negro Rumi. It may be easier to head for the grassy slopes of Loma Ortiguilla. The slopes of Cerro Negro Rumi are open; descend the steep trail to the west side of the Laguna Puruhanta. It's 8 hours to the lake.

Laguna San Marcos to Laguna Puruhanta

Distance 20km
Altitude 3,430–3,800m
Rating Difficult
Time 3–4 days
Start Laguna San Marcos
End Laguna San Marcos
Maps IGM 1:50,000 Nevado Cayambe, Mariano Acosta
Other essential notes Cross-country hiking through cloudforest and swampy *páramo* to a large Andean Lake

Hiking directions From the Laguna San Marcos (see *Laguna San Marcos Access*, below), it is a long day or two short days of cross-country hiking to the Laguna Puruhanta. Once on the north side of the lake, stay to the right of the river, bushwhacking sometimes through thick forest, but mostly walking in the *páramo*. Bring a machete.

Laguna San Marcos

The Laguna San Marcos is located on the north side of Nevado Cayambe and is also a popular destination for trout fishers who drive to the lake. The lake is just across the continental divide and is strongly influenced by weather from the Oriente. Hence, when it is wet in the Sierra it is often dry in this area and vice-versa. The road into San Marcos was constructed for a water project to bring irrigation from the western slopes to the dryer central valley. The project has been put on hold, but if completed it will likely impact the level of the lake.

The Laguna San Marcos is the gateway to the seldom-visited cloudforests east of Cayambe. Luis Martinez, the highland director of the Cayambe-Coca Reserve, says it is beautiful but wild country with potentially dangerous river crossings and thigh-deep mud. There are also mountain tapir, Andean spectacled bear and deer here. A series of glacial outwash plains extend up to 15km east of the summit of Cayambe. These plains are covered with low heath vegetation and are swampy in places, but provide much easier walking than the surrounding cloudforest-covered ridges. You can also get to the edge of lowland rainforest where the rivers drop off these plains and descend on steep gradients (probably waterfalls) to unknown forests. For a well-prepared expedition this would be the jumping-off point for a traverse to the Río Aguarico in the Oriente.

Access Take a bus to the town of Cayambe (1½ hours from Quito), then take a bus to Olmedo (1 hour). Hire a vehicle to take you to the pass above the Laguna San Marcos or walk from town (3 to 4 hours). You can get to within ½km of the

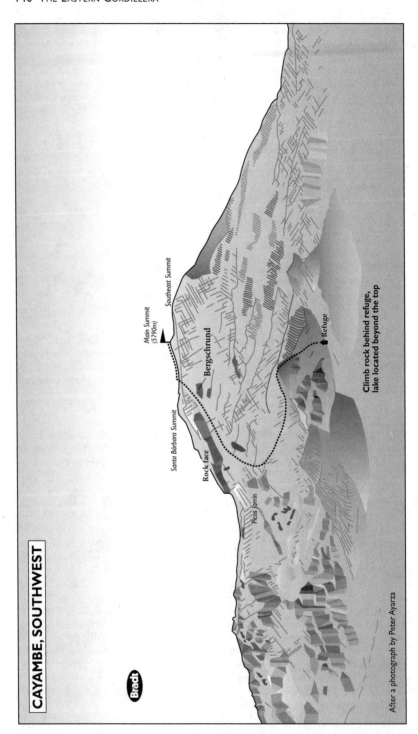

CAYAMBE, SOUTHWEST

Main Summit
(5790m)

Southeast Summit

Santa Bárbara Summit

Bergschrund

Rock face

Picas Jarrin

Refuge

**Climb rock behind refuge,
lake located beyond the top**

After a photograph by Peter Ayarza

lake in a car. You need to pay the entrance fee to the reserve and can camp for $3 per night next to the lake.

The weather is unstable and often rainy, but January through to March is said to be dryer.

Equipment Rubber boots, a machete and lots of plastic bags. You may have some tricky river crossings so bring extra food and a length of rope.

Hiking directions The Laguna de San Marcos is a pleasant spot to camp, fish and enjoy the forest. It is easy to see mountain tapir tracks near the lake.

If you are just camping at the lake there is a nature trail around the lake (2–3 hours), or you can continue down the Río Azuela on a washed-out road, crossing several deep river canyons cut into the flat glacial outwash plains of Nevado Cayambe.

Río Azuela to the Oriente

Distance 15–65km
Altitude 3,640–1,360m
Rating Difficult to very difficult
Time 1–10 days
Start Laguna San Marcos
End Laguna San Marcos or Río Salado confluence with Río Quijos
Maps IGM 1:50,000 Nevado Cayambe, Río Dué Grande, Volcán Reventador, Las Palmas
Other essential notes Very difficult route to the Oriente through the centre of the reserve, which has perhaps never been done.

For overnight and longer treks continue down the old road south of Río Azuela, which eventually turns into a muddy track. You can make an overnight camp in Toldadas (you'll need rubber boots but you do not need to cut a trail) or continue on longer treks to the lakes east of Nevado Cayambe.

Hiking directions From the guard station and turn-off to the Laguna San Marcos, walk on the road east to Quebrada San Pedro. This is the first of three river crossings on your way to Toldadas. If dry the water is ankle deep; if it has been raining heavily then water may be waist deep and dangerous. You follow the old road and ford across the Quebrada San Pedro past the broken-down buildings of an aborted hydro project. Continue on the road to the deep canyon of Río Boqueron; the road has been washed away so look for a trail on the left as the road begins to descend the canyon wall. Cross the river at a destroyed water gauging station and ascend to the opposite side. About 20 minutes later you need to descend to the Río Arturo canyon and climb to the other side. Soon you lose the wide road and the trail becomes a muddy path. It is frustrating but easy to follow. About 4 hours from San Marcos you arrive at Toldados, a beautiful plain with fern plants, a few palm trees and great views of waterfalls and surrounding hillside cloudforest. The area is soggy, but it's possible to find relatively dry spots to camp.

You can continue downstream to lower elevation forest along the Río Azuela, where the trail is said to peter out in La Chorra. Perhaps most adventurous hike is south along the Río Jeronimo to the Lagunas Patacocha, Yanacocha and the

Planada de La Virgen. There is supposed to be a hot spring on this plain with several lakes. Plan on at least 3 days to reach the Planada de La Virgen and 2 days for the return journey. The reserve office in Cayambe can help arrange a guide. There is no record of anyone dropping down to Río Salado and exiting at Río Aguarico in the Oriente. This looks like the best route on maps, but would be extremely difficult.

Nevado Cayambe (5,790m)

Maps IGM 1:50,000 Cayambe and Nevado Cayambe

Nevado Cayambe, a massive glaciated volcano, is located about 65km northeast of Quito and is both Ecuador's third highest peak and the third highest peak in the Americas north of the equator. It also enjoys the distinction of being the highest point on the earth's surface through which the equator directly passes (at about 4,600m on the south side). It was first climbed in 1880 by, you guessed it, Whymper and the Carrel cousins. Although technically not very difficult it is rather dangerous due to crevasses and avalanches. In 1974 an avalanche killed well-known Ecuadorian and French climbers Carlos Oleas, César Ruales and Joseph Berge. A refuge, which has been recently refurbished, is located on the southwest flanks of the mountain at 4,600m and is named after the three climbers. It has a permanent guardian, running water, a gas stove and cooking facilities, and toilets. It is now under the administration of the San Gabriel climbing club and the overnight charge is $15. (See map opposite and route diagram, page 140.)

Access Catch one of the many buses leaving Quito's Terminal Terrestre that go to the town of Cayambe. It is 25km from the town of Cayambe to the refuge, which can be driven most of the way with a normal vehicle and all of the way with a 4WD vehicle, or at least one with a strong engine and good clearance. There are no buses and hitchhiking is difficult except on weekends, when there are some daytrippers from Quito. A truck can be hired in the central square in Cayambe for a lift to the refuge ($20–25); all the drivers know the route. They will drop you off 2km below the refuge, where the road steepens and becomes quite rocky.

If you are driving your own vehicle, look for a sign on the southern edge of town which indicates a turn-off to the east towards Nevado Cayambe. Continue down this road for about 30m and then turn right. Now heading south, in approximately 200m you will cross an indistinct bridge; turn left just beyond this. There should be a rock painted with 'Cayambe' at this junction. The road from here is cobbled most of the way to the refuge. There are several turn-offs but the locals know the way. You will pass through a short tunnel at the Hacienda Piedmonte Bajo (6km) and continue up to the Hacienda Piedmonte Alto (14km). There is a guard station for the Cayambe-Coca Reserve which is presently unstaffed and does not charge an entrance fee, but this may change. The road flattens before reaching steep switchbacks. Usually this is where hired transport will leave you and from here it is about an hour's walk to the refuge (4,700m). There is so little traffic midweek that if hitchhiking you'll have to walk most of the way, which makes a good hiking trip even if you don't intend to climb the mountain. There are broad views of the ancient lava flows of this now extinct volcano as well as of the Glaciar Hermoso (the beautiful glacier) near to the refuge.

Climbing Cayambe To climb Cayambe, get as early a start as possible to take advantage of the frozen snow; a 23.00 departure is not unreasonable. It is essential to be back down on the lower glacier by 10.00, since later in the day the snow

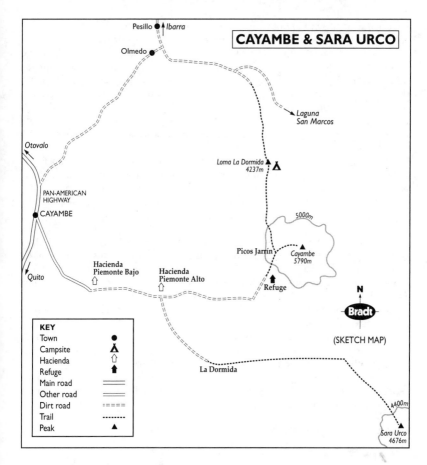

softens and may be prone to avalanches. There are numerous crevasses which – if hidden by a fresh snow fall – are extremely dangerous. It is important to carry wands for your descent.

Normal Route From the refuge scramble up the rocky hill. There are numerous trails, but it is easiest to stay to the right where there are cairns. After reaching the top of the hill in 45 minutes (4,830m) drop down slightly and continue to the right of a green tarn. If you want to avoid hut fees you can camp next to this tarn. Traverse around the right side of a rock outcrop to the base of the glacier. There are numerous small crevasses at the toe of the glacier, but they're not too much of a problem. From here head approximately northeast towards Picos Jarrin, an emergent rock outcrop on the ridge. A common mistake is to be too far to the right, where you must pick your way through a crevasse field. After about an hour of climbing before getting to the Picos, turn east towards another small emergent outcrop (5,200m). Pass either side of the rock and head east-northeast to gain possibly corniced snow on the flat ridge. There is a massive rock-and-ice cliff to your left and a crevasse field in front of you. Conditions are constantly changing so you need to pick your way through the crevasse field to the right of the ice and rock cliff. The crevasses are large and deep, but obvious.

Reach a bowl with a large crevasse or bergschrund at 5,600m. Route finding around the gaping bergschrund will be necessary. This is a dangerous spot and is where Berge, Ruales and Oleas died. There are two options: (1) descend into the bergschrund crossing a snow bridge and climbing steep snow to the ridge or (2) traverse across the very steep snow slope to the far right of the bergschrund and up the steep slope to the ridge. Option 1 is preferable when possible, since there is a high avalanche danger and exposure on the steep slope to the right. Once you reach the ridge it is a short hike to the summit (5,790m), with fantastic views. The bergschrund in recent years has presented difficulties and ice climbing may be necessary to the pass – bring some ice screws.

During good weather, Cayambe is frequently climbed despite its dangerous reputation, so you can sometimes follow footprints and wands from previous parties. Follow the same descent route and watch for avalanche danger and softening snow bridges. Expect it to take about 8 to 10 hours to reach the summit and another 2 to 3 hours to get back to the refuge.

Old Route The Old Route avoids the refuge completely. You head for the village of Olmedo about 10km northeast of Cayambe town. Mules and guides may be hired from the Hacienda La Chimba, in Olmedo's western outskirts. It takes 5 to 8 hours to reach Chiri Dormida where water is available. Camp here. From Chiri Dormida a further 2 to 3 hours are needed to reach Picos Jarrín, from where the route continues as on the new Normal Route. Since the construction of the refuge this route is rarely used.

Cayambe is one of the less explored of Ecuador's major peaks and new routes could be attempted by highly experienced climbers. The mountain has rarely been climbed other than by the Picos Jarrín route described above.

Snow storms and high winds are more frequent on Cayambe than on many other peaks. It can be climbed year round, although October through to January is said to be the best period.

Oyacachi to El Chaco hike

Distance 42km
Altitude 1600–3200m
Rating Difficult
Time 2–3 days
Start Oyacachi
End El Chaco
Maps IGM 1:50,000 Oyacachi and Santa Rosa de Quijos
Other essential notes Hike on overgrown pre-Columbian trail from the cloudforest community of Oyacachi to the jungle town of El Chaco, with challenging river crossings.

This 2- to 3-day hike takes you from the small mountain village of Oyacachi (3,200m) located south of Nevado Cayambe, along the Río Oyacachi, to the frontier jungle town of El Chaco (1,600m). The local legend is that the Oyacachis fled the Incas in the 15th or 16th century, retreating from Cayambe to the Oyacachi valley on the eastern side of the Sierra. From here they persisted relatively unmolested, trading with people in the highlands and the jungle. The Oyacachis never came under the *hacienda* system, but the Jesuits had a mission in

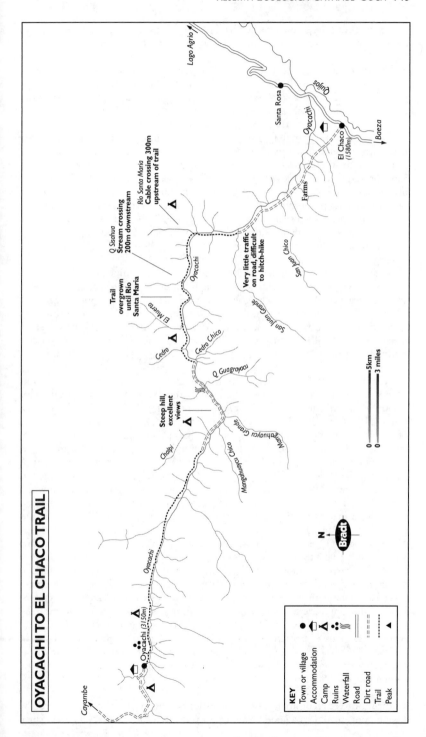

OYACACHI TO EL CHACO TRAIL

Cayambe

Oyacachi (3150m)
Oyacachi

Chalpi

Manzanuayca Chico

Manzanuayca Grande

Steep hill, excellent views

Q. Guagrayacu

Cedro Chico

Cedro

El Muerto

Trail overgrown until Río Santa María

Q Sisahua Stream crossing 200m downstream

Río Santa María Cable crossing 300m upstream of trail

Oyacachi

San Juan Grande

San Juan Chico

Very little traffic on road, difficult to hitch-hike

Farms

Santa Rosa

Oyacachi

Quijos

Lago Agrio

El Chaco (1580m)

Baeza

N

Bradt

0   5km
0   3 miles

KEY

● Town or village
◨ Accommodation
Δ Camp
∴ Ruins
≈ Waterfall
═ Road
═ ═ Dirt road
······ Trail
▲ Peak

Cangahua (until they were expelled by the King of Spain in the 18th century) and used this route to supply their missions on the Aguarico and Napo rivers in the Oriente.

This route to the jungle, therefore, is believed to be quite old – it is paved with cobblestones similar to the Inca Trail to Machu Picchu in Peru – but its exact age is not known. There are some interesting stone ruins called Huasipamba near the present town of Oyacachi that are at least a few centuries old. There are also several *fincas* below these ruins that are terraced and probably pre-Columbian.

The cobblestoned trail takes you through the heart of the Cayambe-Coca Ecological Reserve and this is truly wilderness hiking. The trail has fallen into disrepair in the middle section between two big river crossings (Río Cedro and Río Santa María) where bridges were destroyed by an earthquake in 1987. In 1996 the bridge across the Río Oyacachi also collapsed because too many cows were on it. Now only cables precariously stretch across the channels and it is necessary to have a pulley and harness to span the rapids below. The locals slide across on barbed-wire loops attached to their belts or makeshift rope harnesses, but cannot get their cattle across, so the area between these rivers is not deforested and there are good opportunities for birding and animal spotting.

A road was built to Oyacachi in 1995 and access is now much easier for hikers. This road, which has been extended about 10km down the valley, is hardly used and still pleasant for hiking. The government should restore the route down to El Chaco as a national archaeological and natural history trail. It is one of the most interesting walks in Ecuador and would attract people from around the world, as does the Inca Trail in Peru. As it is, however, the hike is for the prepared and intrepid. (See map on previous page.)

Access Take a 1½-hour bus ride from Calle Manuel Larrea and Portoviejo in Quito to the town of Cayambe. These buses run every 30 minutes until about 19.30. In Cayambe hire a taxi for approximately $20 to take you the 1½ hours on a dirt road to Oyacachi. Alternatively, you can get a bus as far as Cangahua and perhaps find a pick-up truck to take you the distance to Oyacachi. There may be a daily bus soon to Oyacachi; enquire in Cayambe or Cangahua. Walking from Cangahua would take a full day. Above the village is a community-run control station for the Reserva Ecologica Cayambe-Coca; currently there is no charge but this may change. They are mostly concerned with illegal hunting, fishing or wood harvesting in the reserve. If you get permission from the reserve office in Cayambe, it may be possible to walk or bicycle from here on the EMAP-managed gravel road to Papallacta.

The village of Oyacachi currently has no hotels, but you can arrange to stay with a family or camp next to the hot springs on the far side of the river. There is great fresh bread in the carpentry shop on the main street near the church, and basic supplies in several small shops. You can pay a visit to the cheese factory up the hill and there are several restaurants in town. Oyacachi is known for its woodworking, and spoons, bowls and sculptures can be purchased. Trout fishing is possible in the streams.

You may want to hire a guide and mules to carry your gear as far as Río Cedro. Mules cost about $7 per day and a guide charges $10 per day plus his food. David or José Parión have experience guiding and are the ones to contact – they live near the carpentry shop. You can also send a message to them by way of HCJB radio by calling 593 2 266808.

Equipment We recommend rubber boots for the mud but, since it is quite rocky, hiking boots would be a good idea for those with weaker ankles. A tent and stove are not absolutely necessary if you plan to stay in one of the wood shacks along the trail. Definitely bring good raingear, though, and at least one sweater, gloves for vegetation, a machete and insect repellent. For cable crossings you need a strong iron pulley that can pass a ⅘ inch steel cable and that can be disassembled (a normal climbers pulley would be chewed up by the steel cable). You can purchase a pulley at Kywi on Av 10 de Agosto in Quito for about $15. Also bring 45m of cord and a climbing harness.

Hiking directions The trail is always on the left side of the Río Oyacachi. Do not try to cross to the other side, even though the map (incorrectly) shows a trail on that side of the river. There used to be a large suspension bridge that you could not miss downstream of Río Santa María, that crossed the Río Oyacachi several hours before you got to the town of El Chaco. Now it has collapsed into the river and you need to look for a cable! Several other rivers may also be difficult to cross; enquire in Oyacachi.

Find the new road (under construction in 2004) that leaves the east side of the village of Oyacachi. The first day you will walk along the road alternating between pasture and forest. About 30 minutes out of Oyacachi you will encounter an abandoned group of three-sided stone structures with window frames. This is the old location of the town that was abandoned in the 1960s after a landslide destroyed several houses. The road currently goes as far as the Río Cariaco (not named on the map), where there is a suspension bridge (1½ hours from Oyacachi). The Oyacachi valley soon narrows from a broad, U-shaped glacial valley to a steep-sided, V-shaped valley. The Río Chalpi is reached after another 2½ hours and can be waded during moderate flow, when its only ankle deep. A cable may be located downstream that can be used during high water. From here the trail narrows, becomes more rocky and involves more up and down hiking. About 8 to 9 hours from Oyacachi you arrive at the Río Cedro, which is as far as mules can normally go. There are two streams to cross. The first you need to cross on a log, the second involves a cable crossing. You can stay in wood shacks on either side of rivers. It is customary to leave some food or money for the owner. Camping is best on the far side of Río Cedro.

If you have not tried the technique of cable crossing an explanation is in order. Depending on the type of pulley you are using it may need to be disassembled and reattached to the cable, so you may need pliers or spanners to unscrew some bolts. Tie a rope or some strong cord to the pulley so that it can be retrieved from the opposite side of the river after each person has safely crossed. Put on a climbing harness and loop it over the hook on the pulley – do not tie it to the pulley! If for some (very unlikely) reason you are swept into the water you do not want to be attached to the cable because you won't be able to swim to shore. For the same reason do not clip the hip belt on your pack to the pulley. Once safely on the other side the next person can retrieve the pulley and climbing harness with the cord. We found that with a pack it was easier to maintain a sitting position with one hand on each side of the cable. If you fall in, get yourself free of the cable and your pack and swim to the shore. I do not recommend using the barbed-wire loops that the *campesinos* attach to their belts.

The trail from the Río Cedro has numerous hills and is overgrown and difficult to find in places. It is also the most beautiful section of the hike, with great views of primary forest on the opposite bank of the Oyacachi. In two spots you are walking along the bouldery bank of the Río Oyacachi. You are confined to a narrow valley so if you loose the trail it must be somewhere on the slope above or below you. The trail is never more than 100m above the Río Oyacachi. About an hour from Río Cedro you reach Quebrada El Muerto. The next landmark is

Quebrada Sisahua (4 hours from Río Cedro), a gravel-clogged channel where you need to walk downstream to about 200m from the confluence with the Oyacachi to find the faint trail up the bank. About 6 hours from the Río Cedro there is a wood shack with a view of Río Santa María just beyond. You will reach the banks of this river an hour later to see the ruined foundations of a suspension bridge and a 15m-wide river with Class 5 rapids. Do not try to wade across this river unless it is low water! There may be a cable 300m upstream. If this river is too high you may be forced to walk back to Oyacachi. Camping is best on the opposite side of this river.

The trail leaves the gravel banks below the old bridge foundations and from here is well travelled. In about 30 minutes you need to look for a cable crossing which may be tricky, since the river is quite wide here. Note: ask in Oyacachi about this crossing as there are plans to repair the bridge. Once across to the right side of the river it is about 1½ hours to the end of the road. The walk on the road to the town of El Chaco takes about 3 hours depending on the soreness of your feet. Frequent buses pass through the town of El Chaco on their way back to Quito (4 hours).

Oyacachi to Laguna Encantada

Distance 21km round-trip
Altitude 3,200–4,100m
Rating Moderate–difficult
Time 2 days
Start Oyacachi
End Oyacachi
Maps IGM 1:50,000 Oyacachi
Other essential notes Hike up to a *páramo* lake with chance to see spectacled bears.

The Laguna Encantada is named after a hunter from Oyacachi who mysteriously disappeared while hunting deer in the vicinity. This area around the lake is known to have spectacled bears, which feed on the abundant *achupallas* plants in the *páramo*. There's also lots of trout in the lake and tributaries.

Hiking directions
Route 1 Descend below the ruins of the old town of Oyacachi, cross Río Oyacachi and find the trail on the right side of Río Huashuja, a very steep climb on a muddy trail in cloudforest. The valley opens up with views to the west of Cerro Casa Urcu, and to the east of Cerro Pusita. This wide valley is swampy in places and the stream is full of obsidian flakes which have eroded from obsidian flows in outcrops above. Follow the main drainage south to a pass at 4,100m. It takes 6 to 8 hours to get here from Oyacachi. There are views of Cayambe and Sara Urcu to the north and the Laguna Encantada to the south. It takes about 30 minutes to descend to the lakeshore. Camping next to the lake can be swampy, but there are some knolls that are dryer.

Route 2 From the hot springs in Oyacachi head up steep pastures to the right of Quebrada Piburja to a trail that enters very thick cloudforest. Lots of ducking and crawling for 300m eventually opens up to *páramo*. Cross this *páramo* and gain the ridge east of Cochaloma and Río Chalpi. Follow this ridge around to the pass or cut down to the Río Huashuja valley. It's about 7 to 8 hours to the lake. There are good views from the ridge.

PAPALLACTA LAKE DISTRICT

The Papallacta lake district contains hundreds of rocky peaks and glacially carved lakes. It is mostly *páramo* at high elevation, and lower down it is a mixture of grassy areas with remnants of cloudforest. The area is regularly burned by *campesinos* who have used it for hundreds of years for grazing their cattle. Still, the area supports white-tailed deer, Andean wolf, and Andean spectacled bear populations. The lakes were stocked by the military in the 1940s with rainbow trout, making it a fisher's paradise. We saw a local *campesino* hauling over 50 trout back to his home in Papallacta.

Although it is only about 2 hours' drive from Quito, typically rainy weather and a lack of infrastructure has limited recreational use of this area. This is changing as new roads are being built by EMAAP, the municipal water authority of Quito. An access road was recently bulldozed from Papallacta to the Laguna Parcacocha, and a road linking Oyacachi to Papallacta is currently under construction. The Ministerio de Ambiente, with the aid of the Nature Conservancy Council and US AID, have been working to provide long-term protection to the area, but this may prove a difficult task with easier vehicle access.

Trails exist, but cross-country travel is relatively straightforward with a compass, map, and proper gear. The area is wet and driving hail in a white-out is not uncommon. There are not many forested areas, so getting cover from one of these storms can be difficult. Occasionally you will run into a log-framed structure built by *campesinos*; a sheet of plastic could come in handy to drape over the beams of the logs to sit out a storm. (See *Papallacta Lake District map*, page 150.)

Papallacta Pass to Papallacta hike

Distance 13km round-trip
Altitude 3,250–4,370m
Rating Moderate
Time 5–7 hours
Start La Virgen
End Papallacta
Maps IGM 1:50,000 Oyacachi
Other essential notes This is a great day outing from Quito, with an optional overnight at the hot springs of Papallacta.

Hiking directions Take any bus heading to Baeza or beyond. Get off at the pass or at La Virgen, which is a shrine located precisely on the continental divide. Locate the antennas to the north and follow the unpaved side road to this summit (called Poterillos) passing several *páramo* lakes. There is a reserve guard station at the beginning of the road and you will need to pay the entrance fee if it is manned.

The views from Poterillos are some of the best in the Lake District. Follow the ridge trail northwest, then drop down steep grassy slopes on a trail to the east side of the Laguna Parcacocha. This is a nice spot to stop and perhaps swim if it is sunny. Follow this track past several lakes and eventually down though remnant cloudforest. Connect with the Río Papallacta road where there is another guard

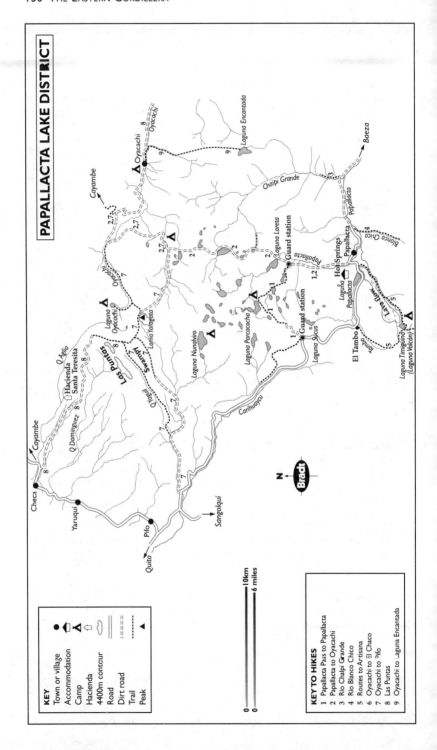

PAPALLACTA LAKE DISTRICT

KEY
Town or village
Accommodation
Camp
Hacienda
4400m contour
Road
Dirt road
Trail
Peak

0   10km
0   6 miles

KEY TO HIKES
1 Papallacta Pass to Papallacta
2 Papallacta to Oyacachi
3 Rio Chalpi Grande
4 Rio Blanco Chico
5 Routes to Artisana
6 Oyacachi to El Chaco
7 Oyacachi to Pifo
8 Las Puntas
9 Oyacachi to Laguna Encantada

station. Turn right and head down to the hot springs. The hike takes 5 to 7 hours. There are numerous buses back to Quito from the town of Papallacta.

The hot springs have recently been remodelled, with several pools, changing rooms, a hostel and *cabañas*, and a restaurant. You can make reservations in Quito at Termas de Papallacta (593 2 2557850) or in Papallacta (593 6 320620); rates range from $20 for a bunk-bed to $70 for a luxurious suite. The hostel also has an indoor thermal pool ($20 per night). Alternatively there are several more basic hostels in town ($5 per night). The main outdoor hot springs ($5 entrance) only see crowds on weekends, so you may well have them to yourselves midweek. They are the best hot springs we have found in Ecuador. The views of Antisana can be superb on a clear day. There is also a short interpretive nature trail above the springs.

Oyacachi to Sigsipamba hike

Distance 31km
Altitude 3,200–4,493m
Rating Moderate
Time 2 days
Start Oyacachi
End Sigsipamba
Maps IGM 1:50,000 Oyacachi and Sangolqui
Other essential notes Cross-country route from Oyacachi to the central valley.

Hiking directions This is a 2-day hike from the village of Oyacachi to the town of Pifo. For access see Oyacachi to El Chaco Hike. Follow the new road out of Oyacachi (not shown on IGM maps) to the Y junction just below the pass. Turn left on the road that contours up the broad Oyacachi valley. Pass a water diversion tunnel through a ridge (used to bring Oyacachi water to the thirsty mouths of Quito). After about an hour of walking from the intersection, reach the Río Oyacachi. From here there is no established trail, only thick brush and boggy ground. The way is clear, however, and the views are worth the work. It takes 2 to 3 hours to reach the head of the valley below Loma Yaragata. Climb west for 30 minutes to a grassy bench below steep slopes. One option from here is to hike to the north to the Laguna Oyacachi for a secluded camp spot.

Head south-southwest towards the slopes of Yaragata. You should encounter a trail that skirts the north side of this peak and the south side of a flat area known as El Tambo (only shown on 1:25,000 scale map). Along this horse trail are obsidian outcrops and interesting *páramo* plants. Eventually follow the trail to the saddle below Loma Yunguillas. Climb to the top of Yunguillas and follow the rocky ridge (no cliffs) southwest. Drop down to Quebrada Mullumica where a house is located. From here follow the road back to Pifo. From the Laguna Oyacachi to Quebrada Mullumica it is approximately 4 to 6 hours of steady walking. It is another 3 to 4 hours out to Sigsipamba, where you can get a bus back to Quito.

Alternatively, from Yunguillas you can also cross Loma Ingaraya and drop into the Quebrada Yanquil. There is no obvious trail, but you can follow cow paths down this broad U-shaped valley, which is a bit boggy. Where the stream valley becomes steep and the valley V-shaped, follow an irrigation ditch (in disuse) on the left side of the valley. Eventually crest the pastures of Loma Cole Pugra and follow the ridge down to the road. Walk down the cobbled road to the Quito-Papallacta road, arriving near the town of Pifo.

Las Puntas

Distance 26km round-trip to the first rock outcrops
Altitude 2,700–4,350m
Rating Moderate
Time 1–2 days
Start Checa
End Checa
Maps IGM 1:50,000 Oyacachi, El Quinche, Cangahua
Other essential notes Hike on a dirt track to some rocky peaks on the eastern side of the Central Valley.

The name of this serrated ridge of peaks is 'the points'. This area can be seen on a clear day from Hotel Quito, located only 28km east of the city, but oddly it is rarely visited. If you want to avoid the weekend crowds on Rucu Pichincha, Las Puntas will likely offer solitude. There are dozens of separate small peaks that offer good rock climbing and many opportunities for first ascents.

The rock consists of a layer of andesite covered by agglomerate (a mixture of lava cobbles and ash that were deposited and welded together while the material was still partially molten). The surrounding hillsides are covered by the ash deposits that fill the central valley. The upper agglomerate unit is knobbly, with many handholds and footholds, but they are not secure and placing protection is difficult.

Access To get to Las Puntas from Quito take a bus to El Quinche; these travel along Eloy Alfaro near Parque Metropolitano in Quito and head down to the valley. The bus goes through the towns of Cumbaya, Tumbaco, Puembo, Yaruqui, Checa and El Quinche. Get off at Checa, 1½ hours from Quito.

Hiking directions Walk out of town uphill, cross a railway line just beyond the village, and take the obvious cobbled road to the right, just before the main road turns sharply left. Stay on this main cobbled road up Loma Achachi to the Hacienda Santa Teresita (3,250m). It is possible to drive a 4WD vehicle as far as the Hacienda Santa Teresita, and – if the driver's feeling adventurous – to the top of Loma Grande in front of you. There is water at the *hacienda*, and this is the last good water before reaching the east side of Las Puntas. Stay on the cobbled road that continues to the right above the *hacienda*. Pass another small house before the road becomes black dirt. The road forks above this house; take the right fork that switchbacks up Loma Grande, passing through many barbed-wire gates (do not forget to close them after you pass). The left fork takes you to Quebrada Aglla, which is the valley to the north of Loma Grande, with what looks like good multiple-pitch crack climbing on the far side of the valley. The road reaches the top of the hill with views of Las Puntas. Continue on the road until it arrives at a gentle pass (4,115m). You can camp here, but there's no water. It is approximately 6 to 8 hours of walking to reach this point from Checa, or 1½ hours by car if the road and weather conditions are good. A track through the grass heads up towards the crags of Las Puntas Chiquito, which deteriorates to a cow path that contours around the base of the rocks. You will reach a grassy ridge and have to drop down below some rocky gullies, then climb to regain a saddle between Loma Puntas Chiquito and Loma Contrayerba. Crossing these gullies is a little tricky. The cliffs of Quebrada Aglla can be seen across the valley to the north, and there's an irrigation channel below you. From the saddle traverse on a cow path to the east side of Las Puntas. The trail is difficult to follow on this side and requires some bushwhacking through colourful *páramo* vegetation. There are many seeps on the east side for filling up with water.

From here you have many opportunities for hiking. You can return to Checa the way you came or down the Quebrada Aglla valley. You can continue to the south side of Loma Yaragala (4 to 5 hours) where there are small outcrops of obsidian. This is actually an archaeological site, an old collecting area for the trading of obsidian arrowheads and other tools to tribes all over Ecuador. A pleasant-looking lake for camping is located at the headwaters of the Quebrada Aglla, at the base of some cliffs, and can be seen from Las Puntas.

Las Puntas to Oyacachi hike

Distance 21km
Altitude 3,250–4,390m
Rating Moderate
Time 1–2 days
Start Las Puntas
End Oyacachi
Maps IGM 1:50,000 Oyacachi
Other essential notes Combine this hike with the Las Puntas hike to end up at hot springs in Oyacachi.

Hiking directions Traverse the east side of Las Puntas to Loma Ingaraya and crest the top of this exposed ridge to find the trail. Head south to Loma Yanguil, which looks like a large rock on the ridge. Just past this hill look for a trail heading east towards a flat swampy area known as El Tambo, and continue to the Oyacachi Valley. There is daily transport out of Oyacachi.

Other hikes in the Reserva Ecológica Cayambe-Coca
Río Salado hike It is possible to ascend the Río Salado starting at the bridge on the Baeza to Lago Agrio road, following a trail at least as far as the Río Cascabel.

Río Chalpi hike A trail heads up the east side of the Río Chalpi, with good cloudforest in abundance. It may be possible to reach the Laguna Encantada.

Bosque Protector Los Cedros It is a 5-hour walk to Bosque Los Cedros from Km75 (Guayacan) on the Baeza to Lago Agrio road.

Oyacachi to the Hacienda Piemonte hike You can walk north from Oyacachi, linking the villages of Gualimburo, Pisarubilla and Sayaro, and ending at the Hacienda Piemonte on the road to the refuge on Cayambe. This is a several-day hike over the *páramo*.

Río Blanco Chico You can walk up several kilometres through good cloudforest to an abandoned water gauging station. There are tapir tracks here, and good birding opportunities.

CERRO SARA URCO (4,676m)

With turned-out toes we went cautiously along the crisp arête, sharp as a roof-top, and at 13.30 stood on the true summit of Sara-Urco: a shattered ridge of gneiss – wonder of wonders, blue sky above – strewn with fragments of quartz and micaschist ... without a hint of vegetation.

Edward Whymper, 1892

Sara Urco (Corn Mountain) is one of Ecuador's few non-volcanic peaks and lies about 15km southeast of Cayambe peak. Despite its low altitude it is normally snow-capped, and many sources and climbers believe it to be higher than the given IGM elevation. It is surrounded by jumbled-up *páramo* which is either boggy or brushy and difficult to move through; hence, this is not a frequently climbed mountain. It is technically straightforward, however, and was first climbed in 1880 by Whymper and the Carrels, who seem to have got everywhere. December and January are the best climbing months; the rest of the year is wet. Route finding is challenging. A guide and/or a GPS is highly recommended.

Distance 42km round-trip
Altitude 3,600–4,676m
Rating Difficult
Time 3–5 days
Start La Dormida
End La Dormida
Maps IGM 1:50,000 Cerro Saraurcu and Cangahua
Other essential notes Climb the only non-volcanic peak with a glacier in Ecuador.

Access Access is the same as for Cayambe as far as the Hacienda Piemonte, after which you turn right (left leads to Cayambe) to a flat swampy plain called La Dormida where the approach hike begins. From the main square in the town of Cayambe you can hire a truck for $30 to take you to La Dormida. This ride takes about 1 hour. Follow the description for the drive to Nevado Cayambe until the Hacienda Piemonte Alto and the Reserva Ecologia Cayambe-Coca guard station. Here you need to turn right onto a dirt road. This road is not cobbled and may not be drivable during the wet season due to deep mud. The road eventually drops down to a plain called La Dormida and peters out on the north side of the plain.

Hiking directions From La Dormida you can see a ring of white cliffs and a waterfall to the east. There is usually a trail that heads though the basin – there's often a *campesino* around who can help you find the route – but if not, prepare yourself for a muddy crossing. There are some nice campsites in the quinua forests of La Dormida.

Once you cross La Dormida you must head up the right drainage (east of Loma Huagra Parada), following the white cliffs until there is a breach that can be ascended. On top of the cliffs is a boggy plain to the east. To the left is a large glacial lake named the Laguna Corazón by the locals, but unnamed on maps. From the upper boggy plain contour around the north side of a peak labelled 4,066 on the map. Cross a low pass and head across a small bog, and then drop down grassy slopes to the sinuous Río Volteado. It is best to stay north of the unnamed tributary during the descent. There is a dry campsite on this tributary 200m upstream of the confluence with the Río Volteado. La Dormida to the Río Volteado takes 5 to 7 hours.

From here route finding can be tricky. Head downstream along the Río Volteado for about 1km to a steep avalanche gully (and stream) on the east side of the valley, and then follow an indistinct trail to a grassy bench above. There are probably other ways to get up to the bench but thick cloudforest will slow you down. Once on the bench head south on a rolling and indistinct trail through bogs and *páramo* grass. About 3km south, begin to head southeast below peak 4,176. Follow a small valley up to a flat area. Cross this flat area then descend into a basin and climb the other side to the northwest of peak 4,104. Cross another flat area and drop steeply south into another basin, before descending a tapir trail next to a waterfall and turning left into a wide U-shaped valley with waterfalls at the headwaters. From here there are views of the steep southwest wall of Sara Urco. Follow the stream through a flat-bottomed valley to the first cascade and look for tapir trails that weave through the thick, reed-like vegetation. Ascend above this cascade and continue across a meadow to an upper waterfall. Look for trails on the left side of the waterfall. Above the upper waterfall head across *páramo* cushion plants to the left-most gully on the rock face in front of you. You should see a green lake on your right at the base of the southwest wall. Hike up the gully (if you are rock climbing you chose the wrong gully) to several glacial tarns. From here follow cairns up to a glacially polished bench. Traverse this bench right to the southwest side of the mountain, where there is a remnant glacier about 150m by 200m. You can avoid the glacier by heading around to the right of it and staying on rock. The glacier is low-angled but icy, so you will need crampons and an ice axe if you decide to climb it. At the top of the glacier follow a gully on the right to the summit ridge and traverse to the true summit. You should not need to do any rock climbing above Class 4. It is about 8 to 10 hours from the Río Volteado to the summit, so a camp below the summit would be logical. Mark completed this round-trip in one long day but returned at about midnight.

RESERVA ECOLÓGICA ANTISANA
Maps IGM 1:50,000 Cangahua and Cerro Saraurco

The Reserva Ecológica Antisana was established in 1994 by INEFAN to protect 120,000 hectares that include seven ecological zones ranging in elevation from high *páramo* to lowland rainforest. A large portion of the reserve is *páramo*, but like the Reserva Ecológica Cayambe-Coca, it protects largely untravelled Andean eastern slope terrain, including the Cordillera de Los Guacamayos, which connects with Parque Nacional Sumaco Napo-Galeras located in the Oriente. The centrepiece of the reserve is Volcán Antisana, a heavily glaciated volcanic peak. Also within the reserve is the Laguna Mica, a famous spot for trout fishers.

Co-ordinating with the Ministerio de Ambiente to promote and manage this reserve is the Fundación Antisana (FUNAN), a private non-profit organisation based in Quito. They maintain two field offices – one in Pintag for the high elevation region and the other in Borja for the low elevation region – for activity management in the reserve. In addition, FUNAN offers full-service accommodations in a large, well-equipped encampment at 4,000m on the *páramo* of Antisana. It is within a 5-hour hike of the traditional climbers' basecamp, and well-situated with respect to several points of interest in the reserve. The encampment is available to everyone but is not an open refuge. Stays must be arranged in advance and are open to group sizes of up to 30. The cost is fixed according to the group's size and needs. FUNAN can be contacted in Quito (593

2 2442302, (593 2 2430861); the office is located at Mariana de Jesús and Carvejal, above the San Gabriel church. (See map opposite.)

Volcán Antisana

Volcán Antisana (5,752m) is the fourth highest mountain in Ecuador, but is seldom seen by tourists because of its position some 55km southeast of Quito, well away from any main road. The broad summit contains four separate peaks which are, in descending order, the central, eastern, northeastern and southern summits. Their elevations are widely disagreed upon. These four summits represent the highest points of a crater rim; the crater itself is totally filled with glacial ice and doesn't appear to be active. For this reason Antisana is popularly supposed to be extinct, but volcanologists claim that its comparatively recent major eruptions indicate that the volcano is, in fact, still active. The 10km long lava flow near the Hacienda Pinantura, to the west of the mountain, is attributed to an eruption in around 1760, and the 6km long flow by the Laguna Papallacta, to the north of the mountain, dates from 1773. Both these flows originated from fissures in the sides of the volcano, thus a cone is absent. Some fumarolic activity still exists near the highest summit.

The climbing history of this mountain is predictable: it was another first ascent by Whymper and the Carrels in 1880. Whymper wrote that he could smell sulphurous fumes during the ascent. The lower peaks, however, are more of a challenge and did not see conquests until the 1970s, by various Ecuadorian climbers.

The access town of Píntag, with its cobbled streets and tiled roofs, is unusually attractive and the surrounding farmland green and beautiful. The *páramo* near Antisana is more varied than usual. Flowering puya plants are plentiful, providing nectar for the many hummingbirds, and there are even some rather subdued-looking *frailejones*. The further east or 'around the back' of the mountain you go, the more likely you are to see animals such as the white-tailed deer, mountain tapir, puma and spectacled bear. Lava fields are a fascinating feature of this area. Antisana itself is a splendid sight, with its four peaks covered in blue glaciers; to the west is Cotopaxi, showing its best profile.

A jeep road runs to the foot of Antisana. Very little traffic uses this track, which is in poor condition, making it ideal for hiking. Many people will choose to return by the same route, but it is possible to hike cross-country to Papallacta on the Quito–Lago Agrio road, or cross the *páramo* to Cotopaxi via Sincholagua.

Access The approach to the base of Antisana has presented some difficulties in recent years. EMAP (Quito water utility) has built a new paved road here, so driving from Píntag is a breeze with a normal car, but you still must obtain permission to pass through the locked gate at the Delgado family's *hacienda* (Hacienda Pintura). The other option is to walk/hitchhike, either along the same road from Píntag, or on the trail from Papallacta.

The guards of the Delgado family will send you back to Quito if you have not paid for permission to cross their land to get to the reserve. The cost for an entry permit currently is about $12 – call Jose Delgado (tel: 593 2 2435828; fax: 593 2 2462013) to make arrangements 2 weeks prior to entry. He may be convinced to give you a permit in a shorter period of time.

Buses leave from Plaza La Marin in Quito several times a day for the hour-long journey to Píntag through lovely scenery and pretty villages. In Píntag, you may decide to hire transport ($20) to go the 25km to the Hacienda El Hato (also known as the Hacienda Antisana). The road continues a considerable distance past the

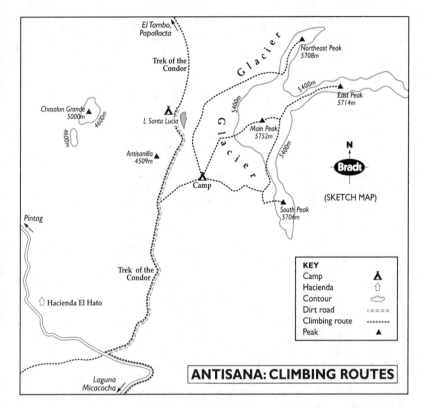

ANTISANA: CLIMBING ROUTES

hacienda to the Laguna Micacocha – a popular fishing lake. On foot from Píntag, head on the paved road to a gravel mine at the toe of lava flow, which is over 200 years old and covered with moss and shrubs. You have the choice of following a path across the lava for a while, continuing up the new road, or contouring around on the old road to the *hacienda*. If you decide to cross the lava you need to ask for directions to the trail since construction activity has altered the area. Along this trail there are beautiful little rock gardens between the chunks of lava, and all sorts of flowers can be admired. It's worth going out of your way to find a flowering *puya*, with its apple-green flowers. After about an hour of lava-leaping you will want to join the road. Look out for an easy access place on your right where the lava cliff is low and no scrambling is involved. Once on the paved road you simply keep walking past a string of beautiful lakes dammed by the lava flows and over several bridges. Continue up the road as it twists and turns through broad fields and *páramo*, and look out for short cuts if you're on foot.

About 25km by road from the Hacienda Pintura you'll pass the Hacienda El Hato (Hacienda Antisana). Another 3–4km due south is the Laguna Micacocha. To reach Antisana turn left, or northwest, on a rapidly deteriorating track. The area is flat pastureland and looks very eerie in low evening sunlight, with dozens of cattle skulls dotting the landscape. One route to the base is to follow the track for about 8km, where it peters out high in the *páramo* west of the mountain. From here head east for another 2km and make your basecamp close to the snowline. Another popular campsite is just below the south peak on a glacial moraine called the South Crespo. To get to the South Crespo camp, ford the Río Antisana in your 4WD – or, if you are less foolhardy, park and walk across the river. Follow the *páramo* up towards the south peak, staying on the south bank of the river. Camp at the toe of the glacier.

The weather is generally wet and cold. If your tent and raingear aren't waterproof you'll probably be miserable, and if you think they are waterproof you'll know for sure by the end of your hike. With Oriente weather conditions prevailing, the driest months are November through to February; the wettest months are June through to August.

Climbing Antisana

Antisana is one of the more difficult peaks in Ecuador to climb, and is dangerous because of its many crevasses and bad weather. It is not for the inexperienced. The lengthy access trek and the lack of a mountain refuge compound your problems; this is the highest peak in Ecuador with no hut, and you have to carry complete wet-weather camping gear and food for several days.

Main summit

Normal Route From the basecamp at the South Crespo, climb up to the glacier about half an hour away. Looking left you'll see the main summit of Antisana, the south peak to the right and a centre ridge separating the two. Head across and up the glacier aiming for the lowest point on this centre ridge. Because of constantly changing snow conditions there's no 'best way' to get there. You'll have to do a bit of route finding through the snow-fields (and crevasses) for the best route up to the ridge. This area should be wanded. Just before reaching the low point on the ridge, a glacier to the left leads to the main summit, ascending just below the ridge. Approaching the summit, stay east (right) of the ice walls on the southeast face. Keep nearer and parallel to the ridgeline, continuing up in a northeasterly direction as you traverse below the summit. Just as the northeast and east peaks come into view, head left (northwest) up to the main summit. The climb takes 7 to 8 hours in good conditions and without too many route-finding problems.

Direct Route Another route is to head straight up the glacier, but there are numerous crevasses and seracs to negotiate. The route steepens towards the summit, with possible vertical ice near the summit plateau.

South peak

This mixed rock/ice route was first climbed by an American team in the 1960s. It's a more difficult climb than the main summit and requires technical equipment, not to mention experience. To climb the south peak follow the route for the main summit to below the same low point on the centre ridge. From here you can see the rocky summit of the south peak to the right. Climb the snow-field which ascends right and leads to a high ridge below the summit. Set up camp at the top of the glacier just below the ridge. It's about a 4 to 6 hour climb from the basecamp.

The following day climb to the top of the ridge and follow it up to the rocky base of the summit. At the base, traverse right to a steep snow couloir and ascend it, angling up left to an obvious ramp of volcanic sand. Follow the ramp as it angles up and left. Caution is advised here as no belay is possible and a fall would be disastrous. Continue up the ramp to a rock chimney of 50m, where various sizes of rock protection will be needed for the ascent. Above the chimney there's another 30m of easy climbing to the top of the rock section. Here you'll come to the upper snow-field for the final traverse (right) to the summit. Allow about 6 to 7 hours to reach the summit and another 3 hours to get back to the snow camp. The following day will get you down to the basecamp and breathing easy.

East peak

This is probably the most difficult of the Antisana summits. You'll need the full regalia of ice gear, including screws and stakes, and even jumars would be helpful. Follow the same route up towards the main peak and set up camp about 50m below the summit. Here you'll find a flat area on the east slope just past the ice walls. A little farther up the snow-field is the ridge which connects the east summit with the main peak. On the second day follow the ridge towards the east summit to a high point called Pico Colgante (hanging peak) about an hour from camp. Here you'll see that 'hanging peak' gets its name from an extremely deep crevasse which cuts off the approach to the summit. Crossing it involves a rappel down and pendulum across to the lower summit ridge. Set up a fixed rope for the jumar/prussik exercise awaiting you on the return. After all that, begin the ascent of the summit ridge which drastically narrows, provides dramatic views of huge drops on either side, and forces you to sit and scoot along. To wrap up the trip to the summit, climb the 20m ice wall at the end of the ridge, which is angled at about 60 to 70°.

Northeast peak

This route was first climbed in 1972 by Santiago Rivadeneira, Leonardo Menses and Hugo Torres. It's not a particularly difficult climb, but some route-finding problems and steep snow/ice make it challenging. From the lower basecamp head left along the moraine until you're in line with the main summit. An alternative camp can be set up here as there's plenty of water available. The climb begins by ascending the glacier seen to the left of the main peak. Find the best route up to the ridge which separates the main summit from the northeast peak. Climb this ridge and follow it to the summit. A steep section of snow/ice, angled at about 50 to 60°, will have to be negotiated just below the summit. Allow about 6 to 8 hours to get to the top.

Antisana to Papallacta hike

Distance 12km
Altitude 3,360–4,400m
Rating Moderate–difficult
Time 6–8 hours
Start Laguna Santa Lucia
End Laguna Papallacta
Maps IGM 1:50,000 Papallacta
Other essential notes Cross-country, downhill *páramo* trek ending on a trail through a lava flow to reach the Laguna Papallacta.

From the Laguna Santa Lucia at the base of Antisana, hikers and climbers can follow the description (in reverse) to El Tambo to get to the Papallacta road (see *Antisana to Cotopaxi hike*, page 162). Those wishing to continue northwards directly to Papallacta will have to go cross-country. This is not easy as there are no paths, the countryside is rough, and the vegetation can be extremely dense, especially in the valley bottoms.

Hiking directions From the Laguna Santa Lucia head roughly north and to the right of peak 4,144. Cross several tributary stream valleys, staying well above the cloudforest to the west, passing to the right of peak 3,857. Continue contouring around several stream valleys until you are directly above an unnamed lake and can see pastures heading down to several huts. Do not be tempted to head down into the cloudforest.

From the mouth of the lake (northeast side) follow a faint trail downstream along the Río Tumiguina. This trail soon veers away from the river valley and through the lava flow to a gravel pit. This section of trail offers a great view of the lava flow and vegetation like you might expect to find in a Japanese garden. From the gravel pit a road leads to the Laguna Papallacta and the Quito–Lago Agrio road. If you wanted to do the hike in reverse, from Papallacta to Antisana, your main problem would be finding the beginning of the rough trail across the lava flow. Once on it, it is straightforward to follow to the lake, where you head up the slope and south to Antisana. This is a challenging and interesting route that requires maps, compass and route-finding ability.

Trek de Condor

> **Distance** 60km
> **Altitude** 3,600–4,400m
> **Rating** Moderate–difficult
> **Time** 3–5 days
> **Start** El Tambo
> **End** Limpiopungo
> **Maps** IGM 1:50,000 Papallacta, Laguna de Mica, Sincholagua
> **Other essential notes** Classic *páramo* trek by Antisana, Sincholagua, Rumiñahui and Cotopaxi.

More than a few seasoned trekkers claim that the Trek de Condor is one of the best in Ecuador. It certainly is one of the more challenging, being physically demanding and requiring some route-finding ability. It can also test one's capacity for inclement weather and mud-slogging, depending on the season. The hike takes you over the *páramo* past the peaks of Antisana, Sincholagua and finally Rumiñahui and Cotopaxi. There is a good chance you will also see a condor, hence the Ecuadorian name for the hike. It takes 4 to 5 days and there is a good chance of rain so come prepared.

Recently there have been problems with landowners between Antisana and Sincholagua, occasionally turning hikers back because they do not want them crossing their land. Enquire at SAE for updated conditions. Olmedo Mashqui (tel: 593 9 9249001; email: paso_del_inca@hotmail.com) runs a café below the Papallacta Pass (Oriente side) near El Tambo. He offers guiding services for the Trek of the Condor and claims he has had no problems with property owners in the past few years.

Access Take a bus from the Terminal Terrestre in Quito to Papallacta (ie: any bus going to Baeza or beyond). Cross over a 4,100m pass where there is a shrine to the Virgin Mary and the first impressive views of Antisana (this is the beginning of the Papallacta Pass to Papallacta hike). Tell the bus driver you want to get off at El Tambo, a broad river valley where the road makes a sharp bend about 4km before you get to the Laguna Papallacta. There are several houses at this bend and a kiosk. Pay the community entrance fee of $5 for foreigners or $2 for residents.

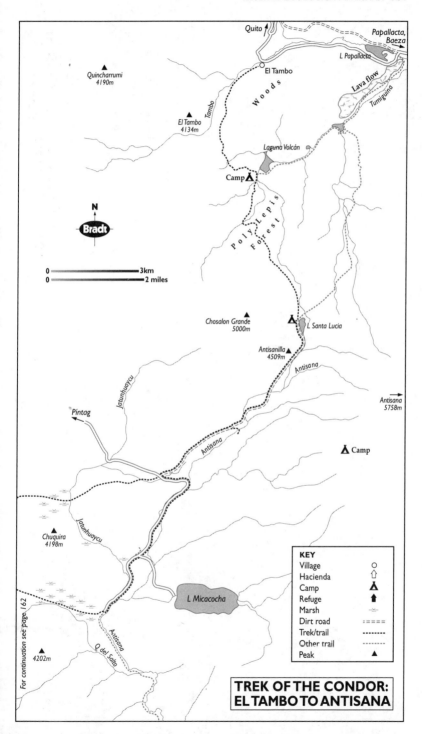

TREK OF THE CONDOR:
EL TAMBO TO ANTISANA

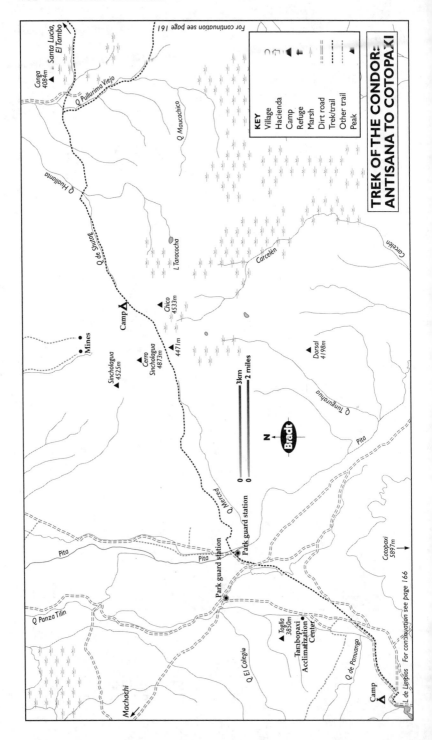

TREK OF THE CONDOR: ANTISANA TO COTOPAXI

For continuation see page 161

KEY
Village
Hacienda
Camp
Refuge
Marsh
Dirt road
Trek/trail
Other trail
Peak

Conga 4084m

Santa Lucia, El Tambo

Q. Pullurima Viejo

Q. Maucachico

Q. Huallanta

Q. de Shutos

L. Taracocha

Carcelen

Carcelen

Camp

Chico 4533m

4471m

Cerro Sincholagua 4873m

Sincholagua 4525m

Mines

Dorsal 4198m

Q. Tungurahua

Pita

3km

2 miles

0

0

N Bradt

Q. Marced

Pita

Pita

Park guard station

Park guard station

Catopaxi 5897m

Q. Panza Tilin

Q. El Colegio

Toglla 3850m

Tambopaxi Acclimatization Center

Q. de Pamuango

Camp

L. de Limpios

For continuation see page 166

Machachi

Hiking directions Pick up the main trail, which leads upstream on the north side of the Río Tambo. After half an hour jump across and continue up the south side of the river. There are numerous cattle trails. You'll be heading southwest up the Río Tambo valley for 3km until you reach the base of the long, flat-topped hill called El Tambo (4,134m). Here a more defined trail turns south, away from the river, and angles up through *páramo* and polylepsis forest to a hummocky pass area on the opposite side of the valley from the peak called El Tambo. Continue over the pass on a trail and head down in a southeasterly direction over grassy countryside for a couple of kilometres until you are within sight of the Laguna Tumiguina (also called the Laguna Vulcán). The trail descends steeply to the south end of the lake, where there is a gravel fan with some flat camping areas. It takes 3 to 4 hours to reach the Laguna Tumiguina from the start of the hike at the road in El Tambo.

There is a lava field at the north end of the lake that you can explore. This moon-like landscape offers a variety of interesting vegetation, including orchids. There is no trail across the lava and the rocks can be quite rough, so wear sturdy hiking boots and be prepared for a little scrambling. It is very time-consuming crossing the lava flow and there are many loose boulders. If the lake level is low, you can make a circuit around it, avoiding the rough surface of the lava flow.

On the second day the trail ascends from the Laguna Tumiguina to the Laguna Santa Lucia at the base of Antisana. It is important to find the correct trail from the lake; many people get lost. If you try to head directly up the slopes to the east of the lake you will be blocked by thick cloudforest. Instead, head upstream (south) from the lake for about 300m to the point where three rivers form a confluence. Ascend the well-defined trail between Quebrada Sunfohuaycu and the stream directly to the east. This trail switchbacks up grassy slopes, eventually crossing a narrow cloudforest band, where the trail becomes a muddy trough. Once above this cloudforest band follow the trail as it climbs around the northeast side of Antasanilla (shown as Loma Chosalongo Grande on the IGM map). You are also walking on a contour around a large basin to your left, avoiding descents. This section is featureless in terms of topography and it is very easy to get disoriented if there's any fog. The trail starts to peter out as the grassy vegetation changes to cushion-plants, but just head cross-country (it's a bit boggy) more or less in the direction of Antisana. This slope seems to go on forever, but eventually flattens out and becomes a jeep track a kilometre before you arrive at the Laguna Santa Lucia. This shallow lake is located between Antisana and the small rocky peaks of Antisanilla to the west. Camping by the lake is recommended for the views of Antisana, but it's somewhat exposed to the weather. If time allows, scramble up Antisanilla for excellent sunset views. There are herds of semi-wild horses in this area along with a number of lapwings, Andean gulls and perhaps a condor or two. The hike from the Laguna Tumiguina to the Laguna Santa Lucia takes 5 to 7 hours.

The next day offers easier walking on dirt tracks and soft *páramo* plants. Follow a faint jeep track, which eventually becomes a gravel road to the Y at the Hacienda Antisana. This is the area were hikers have had problems with landowners. Make sure you stay on the road, since that is a public right-of-way, and do not head off cross-country. At the Y turn left towards the Laguna Mica, follow the road that parallels the Río Jatunhuaycu southwest, then head west up the valley of Quebrada del Salto. Cross over a pass into the drainage of Quebrada Pullurima Viejo and descend. Towards the bottom of this valley find a trail that traverses (crossing a gravel road and water pipeline right-of-way) over to Quebrada Shutog, and hike up this broad valley to the base of Sincholagua. There are good camping spots below the headwall of this valley. This is also the best area to spot condors. This hike takes about 8 hours.

Climb out of the Quebrada Shutog to the southwest on a trail to a pass between Sincholagua and a peak labelled Chico (4,533m). Traverse to another pass between Sincolagua and an unnamed peak (4,471m). Descend into Quebrada Merced (there may be a sign here indicating the Cotopaxi park boundary) on a trail which then contours onto the north slope of the valley. Follow this trail down to the road next to the Río Pita. Cross the Río Pita on a concrete bridge and arrive at the park entrance gate, where you may be required to pay the entrance fee to the park. Plan on 6 hours from the Quebrada Shutog to the Río Pita.

From this entrance gate you can hike up the sparsely vegetated volcanic plain (along Quebrada Chilcahuaycu) where there are lots of places to camp. Continue to the Laguna Limpiopungu, which is 3 to 4 hours from the Río Pita. It is possible to extend your hike by picking up the trail to Mulaló (on the south side of Cotopaxi), which is described in the *Hiking around Cotopaxi* section (see pages 168–71).

El Tambo to Quincharrumi

Distance 10–18km
Altitude 3,600–4,225m
Rating Moderate–difficult
Time 8 hours to 2 days
Start El Tambo
End El Tambo or Laguna Muerte Pungu
Maps IGM 1:50,000 Papallacta, Pintag
Other essential notes Cross-country *páramo* trek.

Hiking directions This is a long day-hike from the village of El Tambo (approximately 3,600m) to a group of rocky peaks labelled Quincharrumi (approximately 4,200m). Start at El Tambo (the beginning of the Trek of the Condor) and follow the Río Tambo to its headwaters. The first part is pretty easygoing, except for quaking bogs. Later the terrain becomes swampy and uneven. You can walk around the south or the north side of El Tambo, then head over to the rocky peaks directly east. It is interesting to gain the sawtooth ridge of Quincharrumi. Try walking around the horseshoe-shaped basin to Lomas Cadena Shayana for a view of the Laguna Muerte Pungu. This lake was formed by a lava flow (18th century) from a crater still visible to the southwest of the lake. Return to the village of El Tambo the same way, or around the other side of the peak of El Tambo for variety.

You can also continue cross-country to the Laguna Muerte Pungu and out onto the road to Pintag. There is a guard station at the lake where you will be charged the entrance fee. Camping is possible and there are a few beds available at the station. It is a day's walk out to Pintag, but as you get further down the road, there are more possibilities for a ride. It is also possible to explore the area around Laguna Muerte Pungu as a day's outing; access is by private car or taxi, 30 minutes from Pintag.

PARQUE NACIONAL COTOPAXI AND SURROUNDINGS

Cotopaxi's shape is the most beautiful and regular of all the colossal peaks in the high Andes. It is a perfect cone covered by a thick blanket of snow which shines so brilliantly at sunset it seems detached from the azure of the sky.

Alexander von Humboldt, 1802

The Galápagos islands excepted, this is without doubt Ecuador's showpiece national park. There are picnic areas, camping sites, huts and a mountain refuge, making it somewhat similar to the national parks in North America and Europe.

The centrepiece of the park is Volcán Cotopaxi (5,897m), which lies about 55km south of Quito, and whose symmetrical cone can often be seen from the capital on a clear day. This active volcano is Ecuador's second highest mountain, and it has long been considered the highest active volcano in the world (although recent claims in favour of Tupungato, on the Argentine-Chilean border, cannot be discounted).

The history of Cotopaxi's activity is the most dramatic of all the volcanoes in Ecuador. Although other volcanoes may be more active geologically, Cotopaxi has caused the most death and destruction. Records of its eruptions date back to 1534, though it was undoubtedly active long before then. After a long period of dormancy, Cotopaxi erupted three times in 1742, destroying the town of Latacunga and killing hundreds of people and livestock. More eruptions followed in 1743, 1744 and 1766. A major eruption in 1768 again destroyed Latacunga, which had been rebuilt, with much loss of life and property. Almost a century of inactivity followed, but in 1853 Cotopaxi again began to display its awesome power and erupted frequently for several years. Four separate eruptions occurred in 1877 and the one of June 26 produced catastrophic lahars (avalanches of ice, snow, water, mud and rocks), one of which reached Esmeraldas on the Pacific coast, and another of which swept down on ill-fated Latacunga, wiping out the greater part of it yet again. This latter lahar was recorded as having reached the town in 30 minutes. Latacunga lies 35km southwest of Cotopaxi as the crow flies, but the lahar would have followed the lie of the land by a more circuitous route – the concept of a huge wall of volcanic and glacial debris sweeping towards you at some 90km per hour, or 25m per second, is impossible to comprehend. As Michael Andrews remarks in *The Flight of the Condor*, 'I find it very curious that Latacunga has been rebuilt repeatedly on its old site.' Frequent but minor eruptions continued for 8 years after this catastrophe. Since 1885 eruptions have been limited to two minor ones in 1903 and 1904, and a disputed one in 1942.

Cotopaxi showed some some signs of increased volcanic activity in 2001, evidenced by more small earthquakes below the mountain. This indicates magma (molten rock) is moving below the crater. This activity is being monitored by an array of seismographs operated by the Universidad Politecnica, but currently there is no imminent threat of eruptions, just a bit of snoring. Fumarolic activity also continues in Cotopaxi's crater, as anyone who has climbed the volcano will know.

Cotopaxi was first climbed in 1872 from the southwest by the German geologist Wilhelm Reiss, accompanied by Angelm Escobar, a Colombian. A few months later the German, Stübel, accompanied by four Ecuadorians (Jantui, Páez, Ramón and Rodriguez) logged the first Ecuadorian ascent. Edward Whymper, along with the Carrel cousins, spent a night on the summit in 1880 – a somewhat hazardous exercise bearing in mind the restless nature of the volcano at that time. Since then many successful ascents have been made and today the mountain is a popular destination for weekend mountaineers and tourists from Quito, as well as foreign climbers. Despite its relative simplicity, however, this is not a climb for the inexperienced, and beginners should avail themselves of professional guides.

The national park surrounding the volcano offers excellent hiking and camping opportunities as well as lesser peaks to climb. Rumiñahui (4,712m) and Morurco (c4,840m) lie within the park boundaries and the peaks of Sincholagua (4,898m) and Quilindaña (4,877m) are found just outside the park. There is talk of extending the park boundaries. Hiking a complete circuit around the base of

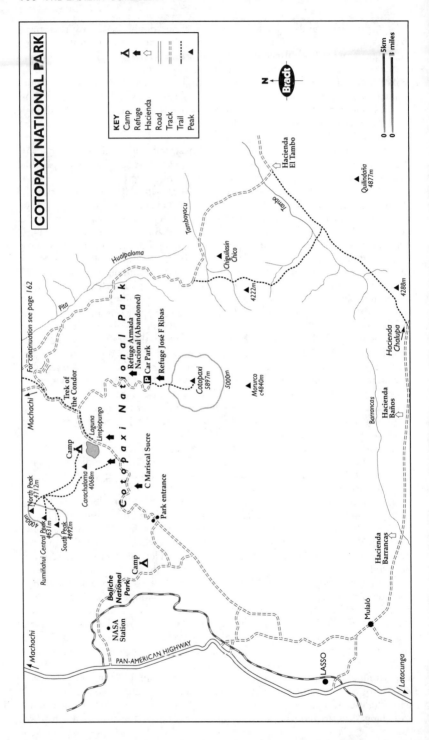

COTOPAXI NATIONAL PARK

KEY

Camp
Refuge
Hacienda
Road
Track
Trail
Peak

N

Bradt

0   5km
0   3 miles

Hacienda
El Tambo

Quilindaña
4877m

Chigualasin
Chico

Tamboyacu

Tambo

Hualpaloma

4222m

4288m

Pita

For continuation see page 162

Cotopaxi National Park

Refuge Armada
Nacional (Abandoned)
Car Park
Refuge José F Ribas

Cotopaxi
5897m

5000m

Hacienda
Chalupa

Machachi

Trek of
the Condor

Laguna
Limpiopungo

Morurco
c4840m

Hacienda
Baños

Barrancas

Camp

Corachaloma
4068m

C Mariscal Sucre

Cotopaxi National Park

North Peak
4712m

4000m

Rumiñahui Central Peak
4631m

South Peak
4692m

Park entrance

Camp

Boliche
National
Park

NASA
Station

Hacienda
Barrancas

Mulaló

Machachi

PAN-AMERICAN HIGHWAY

LASSO

Latacunga

Cotopaxi is a good 6 to 7 day trip in which all of the above peaks can be seen or climbed. (See *Cotopaxi map*, page 170.)

Access You can reach the museum and administration centre of the park from the El Boliche (closed to vehicles) or the Lasso entrances on the Pan-American Highway. There is no pubic transportation into the park, but it is easy to get to these turn-offs by taking a southbound bus from Quito. Hiking or climbing routes from the centre are described individually. El Boliche is about 1½ hours south of Quito and is also the turn-off to the Clirsen NASA minitrak station. This satellite tracking station is now owned and operated by the IGM to download satellite images. It is still marked with a huge sign and the tracking equipment is plainly visible from below. This entrance road is now closed to vehicles but accessible to hikers and mountain bikers.

To reach the park administration centre head to the main entrance just north of Lasso, marked by a wooden 'Parque Nacional Cotopaxi' sign. About 1km south on the Pan-American Highway, past the turn-off, is a small, rounded, grassy hill on the left; this useful landmark is reputedly a pre-conquest mound but no-one seems to know very much about it. Turn left onto the entrance road and immediately cross the railway tracks. The route to the park entrance station is clearly marked by arrows at all intersections. You meet up with the El Boliche entrance road before the park entrance station and continue to the park administration centre. This is about a 15km trip from the Pan-American Highway. This road is open to vehicular traffic and during the weekend you'll have little difficulty in hitchhiking into the park, but midweek there is less traffic. Alternatively, you can get off the bus at the railway station in the small village of Lasso and hire a taxi or *camioneta* to take you into the park. Sometimes there are taxis waiting at the park entrance turn-off.

It costs about $10 to hire a taxi to take you to the park administration centre, but many hikers opt to hire a ride to the Laguna Limpiopungo. If you're on foot you can arrive anytime, but if you're driving remember that the park entrance station is open only from 08.00 to 18.00. During weekends it is open longer, from 07.00 to 18.30. Outside these hours you must find someone to open the locked gate. You'll need your passport and a small fee is charged.

The Boliche entrance is closed to traffic but makes a pleasant walk. The turn-off is asphalted for the first 2km until it reaches the old tracking station, where it becomes a dirt road. There are signs most of the way, but stay right following the railroad tracks for ½km. You pass a railway station and then cross the tracks and continue to the Río Daule campsite, which is about 7km beyond the tracking station. This campsite has plenty of flat tent spaces, two small picnic shelters (unsuitable for sleeping in) and fireplaces. Drinking water is available from the river about 500m past the campsite, beyond a bend in the road. This is a good place to spend your first night.

The dirt road continues climbing gradually and 1–2km beyond Río Daule passes a hairpin bend with a camp by it; there is a stable and a thatched hut, but no water. After a further 1–2km take an unmarked left-hand turn (look for herds of llamas; the animals are being studied in the area) down the main road to the park entrance station (where a fee of $10 is charged). The Mariscal Sucre administration centre is 5–6km beyond the park entrance station and houses a museum with a small collection of flora and fauna, and has views of the mountain. It is about 15km from the museum to the climbers' refuge.

The rustic but elegant Tambopaxi Acclimatization Center (tel: 593 2 2224241/9 9448223, web: www.tambopaxi.com) is located about 3km north of the turn-off to the Cotopaxi refuge on the road to the Machachi entrance to the park. It costs about $15 per night for a comfortable bed and has great meals. Camping is possible. There is even a telescope for viewing Cotopaxi. This is also near one of the starting points for Rumiñahui.

Hiking around Cotopaxi

Distance Approximately 75km
Altitude 4,080m
Rating Moderate
Time 5–7 days
Start Lasso entrance to Cotopaxi
End Mulaló
Maps IGM 1:50,000 Machachi, Sincholagua, Cotopaxi, Mulaló
Other essential notes Circles around Cotopaxi, partly on dirt tracks and trails.

This is a beautiful and not too difficult hike which takes about a week and can be combined with ascents of some of the nearby peaks. A dirt road runs more than halfway around the volcano, but some cross-country hiking will be involved to complete the circuit. If you're a beginner and not confident of your abilities to hike without trails, you can do the dirt road sections and return the way you came. During weekends you will be able to hitchhike much of the way, but midweek you will probably find the jeep road deserted.

Hiking directions Your first step is to reach the park museum and administration centre by one of the two entrance roads described in *Access*. If you are on foot your first night's camp will probably be at Río Daule. On the second day you should reach the centre in 4 to 6 hours from Río Daule, and can then continue to one of the several nearby campsites.

The first campsite is some 2–3km along the road beyond the centre. There is a small sign and a turn-off to the left onto a small plain, where there are little picnic shelters, an outhouse, a recently built cabin, and water running from a pipe in the gully behind the campsite. On a clear day there are excellent views of Chimborazo about 100km to the south-southwest. This campsite provides one base for climbing Rumiñahui, but don't leave your gear here because it is not safe.

About 1km further down the road is a second camping site, also signed, but this time to the right. Again picnic shelters and a small cabin are available, but there is no running water.

Just beyond the turn-off to the second campsite there is a track off to the left of the road across a large plain to the Laguna de Limpios (also known as Limpiopungo) at about 3,800m. Around the lake you should watch for waterfowl and other birds, as well as the black Atelopus toad (see *Natural History* in *Chapter 3*). There is a trail around the back of the lake which will be described in *Climbing Rumiñahui* (see pages 173–5).

To continue your hike around Cotopaxi, go from the campsites past the Laguna Limpiopungo and along the road as it begins to curve further east around the north side of the mountain. Some 2–3km beyond the lake, you will see a signed road to the right leading up to the Cotopaxi climbers' refuge some 9km away (see *Climbing Cotopaxi*).

About 3km after the turn-off for the refuge the road forks. The track going straight on will eventually bring you to Machachi, over 20km away to the northwest. Take the right fork and curve northeast, east, and then southeast until you ford an unnamed river about an hour's walk beyond the fork. This point is about 8km from the lake and you could camp here, although it is rather exposed. It's better to continue southeast a further 8km on the gently climbing road around Cotopaxi to the next running water, which is usually at the stream crossing the road just above the area marked Mudadero on the IGM map. If this stream is dry, head left or west across flat pastureland to the Río Hualpaloma which flows all year. This camp gives good views of the northeastern flanks of Cotopaxi.

From this camp continue on the jeep road southeast and then south for about 1km to the point where (on the IGM map) the road stops and becomes a 4WD jeep track heading east. This place is easily identified because the track makes a hairpin bend into a small but steep-walled canyon. There is a locked gate near here that prevents car access to a consortium of *haciendas* that have set up a private nature reserve on the edge of the park. If you are on foot and do not plan to hunt or fish through their land there is no problem with access. Continue down the canyon and you'll soon come to the Río Tamboyacu; good camping is also possible here.

Now you have two choices. You can continue along the jeep road as it curves east, south, and finally back west to the Hacienda El Tambo. At about the halfway point there is a fork where you go right. Alternatively, you can forsake the jeep track and head south across somewhat boggy country. With the IGM maps and a compass this is quite easy. Head more or less south and pass a small conical hill (Chiguilasín Chico) to your left. Continue south across a plain (you should find a horse track) over a pass to the left of a flat-topped hill. On the other side of the pass you look down on the valley of the northwest branch of the Río Tambo. Follow the valley on the right-hand side southeast for several km, until you come to a large valley on your right (the southwest branch of the Río Tambo). From here and further up the southwest branch of the Río Tambo there are good views of Morurco (c4,840m and named Guagua Cotopaxi on the IGM map), Cotopaxi, Antisana and Quilindaña.

Climbers' note: Morurco can be approached from this area using an IGM map; Koerner (1976) writes that Morurco is a minor southern peak of Cotopaxi, has only been climbed once, and is reputed to be easy but interesting, with technical possibilities. Access is from the east and north around Cotopaxi. The snow cover is variable.

Cross the southwest branch of the Río Tambo (it is not difficult to ford). If you are coming from the Hacienda El Tambo there is a well-travelled trail to this branch, as shown on the map. Further upstream this trail is no more than a meandering animal track, but the Río Tambo valley is easy enough to follow. This area is also used as a base for climbs of Quilindaña (see page 179).

Heading southwest you will see a mountain with a steep rock face (Morro) about 7km away. The trail, or what you can find of it, follows the Río Tambo for 4–5km, and where one branch of the river turns west the trail continues southwest over a pass on the northwest side of Morro. Just before the pass is a large flat area which is the best place for a last camp.

Beyond the pass the trail continues clearly to the southwest for 1–2km and then joins a dirt road. A left turn takes you some 8–10km to the Hacienda Chalupa, which can be used as another basecamp for Quilindaña; a right turn takes you out to the Pan-American Highway. To get to the Pan-American Highway follow the road for some 7–8km past a white stone block marker for the Hacienda Baños. A

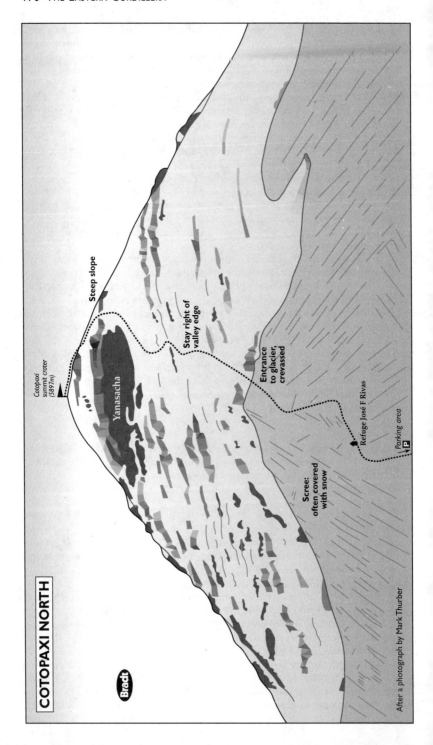

COTOPAXI NORTH

Bradt

Cotopaxi summit crater (5897m)

Steep slope

Yanasacha

Stay right of valley edge

Scree: often covered with snow

Entrance to glacier, crevassed

Refuge José F Rivas

Parking area

After a photograph by Mark Thurber

few hundred metres further on take a left fork, and after another few hundred metres go straight at a junction. There are no more major turns for the next 3 to 4 hours. Then you descend into the Río Barrancas valley where you could camp. Otherwise, climb up the other side and follow the trail another 3 to 4 hours into Mulaló, where you will find buses to Latacunga. There are many forks in the trail beyond the Río Barrancas; take the most used-looking trail and ask the many inhabitants for the way to Mulaló. It is possible to walk out on the road to Mulaló in one long, hard day; otherwise camp in the flat valley-bottom of Río Barrancas. There are no hotels in Mulaló and buses stop running before nightfall.

Volcán Cotopaxi (5,897m)

Not too long ago a German guidebook came out with a description of climbing Cotopaxi that pointedly said it was not a technical climb, and that no special equipment was necessary. Trying to convince its readers they could not climb in running shoes was practically impossible. The climb is not difficult, but is considered technical because of the equipment required for the ascent. Ropes, ice axes, crampons and wands are absolutely necessary. Experienced teams don't usually bother with protection, but less-experienced climbers may want to carry along a couple of snow stakes and deadmen.

The Cotopaxi area is blessed with the highest number of clear days per year in the Ecuadorian Andes, and thus climbs may be attempted year round. Cotopaxi is further west than Cayambe and Antisana, so it experiences the climate of the central highlands rather than of the Oriente. June and July are the driest months, but extremely high winds blowing continuously for days on end are not uncommon. December and January are almost as dry and much less windy. (See route diagram opposite.)

Access If you are a mountaineering party and want to reach the climbers' refuge quickly you'll need to hire a jeep or pick-up truck. This can be done in Lasso, 3km north of the park entrance, or in Latacunga's Plaza El Salto, where you will find an *estacionamento* where there are various transportation companies. A company which will do the trip for around $25 per pick-up truck is Cooperativa de Transportes Riberas del Cutuchi.

If you have your own vehicle or are on foot, follow gravel road for 45 minutes in a car to the park entrance gate, which is open from 08.00–15.00 for entering cars, but will stay open until 17.00 for those exiting. Continue for another 20 minutes to the turn-off for the climbers' refuge. The turn-off is at 3,830m; it is 8.5km to the parking area at 4,600m so you have to climb hard. The road is easy to follow; en route you pass the abandoned Armada Nacional refuge at 4,400m. It's old, small, damaged and rarely used. If you're on foot, the gully behind this refuge offers a short cut to the newer refuge; it takes at least an hour to get there with a pack. From the parking lot a trail leads up the sand to the new refuge. Though it looks close, with a heavy pack it will take at least half an hour to walk there.

The new José Ribas refuge was built in 1971 and extended in 1977. It has room for about 70 climbers in three dozen bunk-beds and on the floor, and boasts electricity, basic food supplies, running water, kitchen facilities, outhouses, a fireplace and lock-up facilities for your gear when you climb. It costs about $10 per night to stay here for non-residents, and half that for residents.

Tragically, on Easter Sunday 1996, an avalanche partially buried the refuge and dozens of tourists. The glacier above the refuge was probably weakened by an earthquake that shook the province of Cotopaxi several days prior to the avalanche. In the warm midday sun a huge portion of the ice wall broke loose. Since it was

Easter there were many day-trippers visiting the mountain. Although many were saved and those trapped in the refuge broke windows on the downhill side to climb to safety, over ten people died on the slope above the refuge. The refuge itself is located in a valley and is consequently more vulnerable to avalanches. It has since been remodelled with an escape door, and some avalanche deflection structures have been constructed upslope, but they would likely be ineffective for a big avalanche.

Normal Route The Normal Route (other routes are rarely climbed) takes 5 to 9 hours for the ascent and 2 to 4 hours for the descent. The snow becomes unpleasantly wet and soft by early afternoon, so you should begin the climb from the refuge between 24.00 and 02.00. The first hour of the climb takes you up the right side of a triangular scree slope which is sometimes snow covered. You need to climb onto the glacier at the apex of the scree slope (at about 5,100m) negotiating several crevasses. Once you are on the glacier you generally head south and up, but usually the 'trail' meanders. Although the mountain is well-crevassed, for the most part the crevasses are spectacularly large and open and thus easy to avoid. A route is usually well marked around the crevasses with wands and footprints – remember this is the most popular high climb in Ecuador. Above about 5,400m the crevasses are less pervasive and you begin a rather featureless snow plod towards the right side of a huge rock face called Yanasacha (literally 'black forest' in Quechua). There is a spot protected from the wind below a bergschrund just to the right of Yanasacha where you can rest before beginning the steep ascent to the crater rim. For the last 250m angle to the right and up the steep snow, then back to the left to the summit. Yanasacha will be to your left at first and then you will traverse above it just before summiting.

The classic round crater is over half a kilometre wide, and a circuit is possible. Steam can be seen escaping from vents in the centre and from the walls. Expeditions into the crater have been undertaken; the first was in 1972 when a Polish-Czech expedition spent 6 hours in the crater, and since then several Ecuadorians have repeated the venture.

An alternative route follows the standard climb up the glacier, but then traverses left to below Yanasacha. Here it turns right just below the rock face and climbs a long snow ramp to the summit. Several decades ago this was the more commonly used route, but a huge crevasse has since made it impassable.

Southern Route and Morurco
by Damaris Carlisle
This is another non-technical route to the summit and an approach to the southern spur of Morurco (called Guagua Cotopaxi on the IGM map). A tent is necessary. Wands are recommended since almost no-one climbs this route. The climb takes 2 to 3 days including the approach, or approximately 8 hours from basecamp to the summit.

Access Turn left onto a dirt road, just south of Lasso on the Pan-American Highway at the right turn-off for La Cienaga Hosteria, heading towards the small village of San Ramon. At the first junction turn left, pass several *haciendas*, then take a left at the next junction. In about 200m take a right turn and arrive in San Ramon. Continue through town; you should see a football field on the right. Follow a dry riverbed then turn left. The road becomes rather rocky and looks like it will fizzle out. Eventually you will come to a church. Take a very sharp right through some low gates. Stick to this road to Rancho María. The gates to the ranch are usually locked but there is a track to the left. Follow this up to the *páramo*. The vehicle should reach 3,400m, where there is a wide place to park. A drivable track continues a bit higher (1 hour).

Climbing Start hiking following the track that eventually peters out to a path up a valley. Halfway up the valley you come to a small dammed section where there is a natural spring and the last place to get water. Fill up!

Continue up the valley to where it opens out onto the *páramo*. From here you should have a view of Cotopaxi to the left and Morurco to the right. There is a small ridge in front of these two peaks with a distinctive big rock on the top. To get to Morurco you head straight for the distinctive big rock then over and down the ridge to the south. To reach Cotopaxi head to the left of the rock, skirting the ridge lower down. Once you come about level with the rock you will see a deep valley. Slide down a sandy scree slope, then cross to the other side of the valley. You can camp in this gully (4,400m). Three glacial tongues of Cotopaxi are visible in front of you.

Gain the ridge to the right of the campsite. The ridge becomes quite narrow, climbing between two tongues of the glacier. Cross onto the left tongue near the end of the ridge and head up the glacier, eventually reaching a large crevasse; skirt to the west of the crevasse. You should see fumeroles above you near the summit. Once past the crevasse head north to the crater rim near the south summit.

Cerro Rumiñahui (4,712m)

A geologist would place Rumiñahui in *Chapter 4, The Central Valley*, but it is included here because it is within the confines of Parque Nacional Cotopaxi. This long-extinct volcano is located 45km south of Quito and only 13km northwest of Cotopaxi. It is an easy ascent and has often been climbed; surprisingly, I could find no records of ascents prior to the 1950s. Although occasionally sprinkled with snow, it is normally a walk up with a rocky scramble at the top.

Rumiñahui is named after one of Atahualpa's famous generals and means 'face of stone'. Despite the name, one should remember that this stone is heavily laced with metal, so you should descend if an electric storm threatens. (See overleaf.)

Access The most well-known route begins from the Laguna Limpiopungo. The lake is quite shallow, and during the dry months it may be a bit scummy or even completely dry, but you'll find a path going around its east side and past a boggy area to the north. About 1km northwest of the lake you'll find possible camping spots with clean running water. This is not an officially designated campsite and has no facilities. The closest official camping spot is north of the road below Caracha Loma.

Climbing Cerro Rumiñahui
Central peak (4,631m)
From the campsite head west up a small, steep-sided valley, following the stream around to the northwest to a boggy plain below the mountain. Skirt this plain to the northeast and ascend the grassy ridge coming off the central peak. Once on the ridge swing west and head for the central peak; there is a bit of class 3 scrambling at the top. From the camp it should take 2 to 3 hours to get to the summit.

North peak (4,712m)
To get to the main north summit, a traverse across the summit ridge is not possible. You'll have to descend about halfway down, back towards the grassy ridge, to where

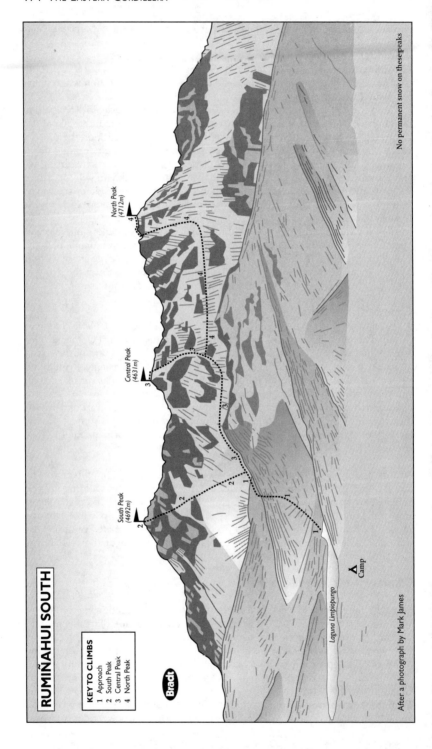

RUMIÑAHUI SOUTH

KEY TO CLIMBS
1 Approach
2 South Peak
3 Central Peak
4 North Peak

South Peak (4692m)

Central Peak (4631m)

North Peak (4712m)

No permanent snow on these peaks

Laguna Limpiopungo

Camp

Bradt

After a photograph by Mark James

you can see a number of narrow arêtes running up to the summit of the north peak. Traverse below these arêtes across rocky *páramo* until you come to the last major gully of reddish sand, which is the route to the summit ridge. This gully is just before the large rockface at the northern end of the mountain. Climb to the top of the summit ridge, cross it, and then drop down the western side. From here you should be able to scramble to the summit. Ascents from the eastern side are difficult. Except for the last few metres, which are on the usual rotten rock, the ascent is an easy scramble. Even if you don't quite make the top, the view is great.

South peak (4,696m)

Climbing the south peak involves some moderate technical rock climbing (class 5.5) and the proper technical equipment. The climb takes 4 to 6 hours depending on how well you've acclimatised. Walk to the north end of the boggy plain and begin a scramble up the flanks below the south peak. There are a number of routes up the centre of the summit pyramid, though the rock isn't all that great. For an excellent view into the crater, traverse right from the south summit base and head for the saddle on the ridge that separates the south and central peaks. There is an obvious grey sand slope leading up to this saddle. Up to here only a bit of careful scrambling is necessary. However, the rocky traverse across the ridge to either the south or central Peak will require some technical rock climbing. It's best to bring a rope and some protection if planning the traverse, and the route is certainly not for the inexperienced.

Other routes

Other approaches and routes are possible but less frequently climbed. Approaches are made from the northeast over the Filo Santo Domingo to the bottom of the last sandy gully described in the standard route. The rock face just north of this gully offers a technical rock route first climbed in 1972 by the Ecuadorian climbers Cruz, Reinoso and Berge. Ascents from the Machachi side (from the northwest) are also reportedly possible.

Cerro Sincholagua (4,873m)

Map IGM 1:50,000 Sincholagua

Sincholagua is an extinct volcano located 45km south southeast of Quito and 17km northeast of Cotopaxi, just outside the national park boundary. It is one of the many mountains first ascended by Edward Whymper and the Carrels in 1880. They climbed the northwest ridge and this is still considered the normal route. It used to be a well-glaciated mountain and the old IGM 1:50,000 Sincholagua map showed a permanent ice cap over 1.5km long. In common with other Ecuadorian peaks, however, the permanent snow line has receded over recent decades and today there is no permanent glacier, although after a heavy storm there is some snow cover. The climb is mainly a scramble, but the scree below the summit pinnacle is loose, except after a good snowfall and a cold night, when the gravel should be solidly frozen together.

Access Access is most frequently made from the south via Parque Nacional Cotopaxi, although access from Quito is also possible. Enter the national park as usual and continue around Cotopaxi on the dirt road described in *Hiking around Cotopaxi* (see pages 168–71). Go to the point on the road when you cross an unnamed river on a small bridge. If you're in a jeep continue beyond the bridge for about 3km, until you pass a perfectly cone-shaped hill on your right and a hillock

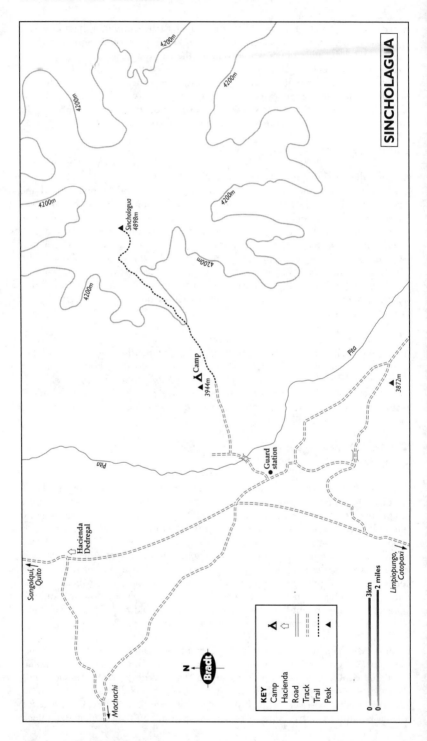

to your left. Look for an unmarked jeep trail which goes hard left and northwest. Follow this track for about 4–5km, then turn right on a side track which fords the Río Pita. If on foot you can go north cross-country from the bridge, and meet the track just before the right turn about 2km north of the bridge.

This point can be also be reached by 4WD from Quito. Head south on the Valle de los Chillos freeway to Sangolquí and continue to the village of Selva Alegre. Head south towards the Hacienda Patichupamba and continue south towards the Río Pita and Sincholagua. The road is difficult and unsigned, so ask everyone you meet for directions. It's 50–60km by bad road from Selva Alegre.

Once you've crossed the Río Pita head northeast up a ridge with vehicle tracks on it, past a survey marker (3,969m), until you meet a ridge running northwest. This will take half a day on foot from the river, but a 4WD vehicle will get some of the way up the hill. Camp is usually made near the junction of the two ridges (shown as Parquedero on the map) in order to make an early start the next day, whilst the rocks are still frozen together. Water is difficult to find along this ridge.

It is also possible to access the mountain from a road in Quebrada Yagüil on the north side of the mountain that leads to a gravel pit. You will need to do your own route finding in a 4WD vehicle and on the mountain to intersect with the route described below. (See map opposite.)

Climbing Sincholagua
Main peak (4,873m)
From the Parquedero continue up along the flatter ridge to the base of the rocks. Traverse left around and up the rocky peak to the northwest side of the mountain; the route should be cairned. Drop down to a scree or snow-filled basin and contour up on rocky shelves to a scree saddle below the summit pyramid. After a cold or snowy night the scree is usually frozen together, but otherwise the approach to the summit pyramid is difficult because of the loose scree. There is a short exposed pitch (25m) to the summit with fairly good rock. Head for the left skyline where there is a gully. The last 5m are not difficult but are very exposed. A descent by abseiling off the summit is sometimes made.

Pico Hoeneisen
For the rock climber, Pico Hoeneisen is a prominent 'lower peak' below the southeast peak of Sincholagua. It was first climbed by Miguel Andrade and Hugo Torres in 1972. You'll need a rope, obviously, and an assortment of nuts and chocks for this technical rock climb. The approach begins at the bridge off the Cotopaxi road, described previously in the *Access* section. From here you'll see the southeast ridge of Sincholagua, with the prominent rock outcrop or peak in the centre of the mountain. Cross the *páramo* northeast following a W-shaped *quebrada* as it ascends to the top of the *páramo*. Drop down from here to just below the base of the south ridge where there is good camping with plenty of water. Follow the *páramo* up from the camping area to the scree and continue along the ridgeline to the mountain. You'll come to a prominent wide ledge, highly visible from below, cutting across the south side of the mountain and intersecting the ridge. Follow the ledge around to the right side of the ridge and you'll come to a 15m chimney of good rock. A thin crack in the chimney will take small nuts. Ascending this, you'll next reach an overhanging section which is fairly difficult – 5.10 free, or maybe requiring some aid moves. The rock is loose at the top of this section. Here, the route traverses right to another small chimney of about 10m. At the top, you'll come to a triangular sand/snow slope which leads up to the summit. The route will have to be descended the same way with several abseils.

This is the twelfth highest peak in Ecuador, but is rarely visited because climbers tend to concentrate on the ten peaks over 5,000m. So much the better! In common with Rumiñahui and Cotopaxi, the weather is better than average; the driest months are June through to August.

Cerro Quilindaña (4,877m)
Map IGM 1:50,000 Cotopaxi

This extinct volcano lies just outside the park boundaries, about 16km southeast of Cotopaxi and 65km south southeast of Quito. It is an infrequently climbed, difficult and technical mountain that offers one of the most interesting rock-climbing routes in Ecuador. It was first climbed in 1953 by a large party of Ecuadorians, Colombians, Frenchmen and Italians.

Access There are two principal points of access: 1) from the main Cotopaxi National Park entrance to the Hacienda El Tambo, and 2) from the village of Alaquez (south of Lasso) to the Hacienda Chalupas.

El Tambo
El Tambo can be reached on foot or by 4WD vehicle as described in *Hiking around Cotopaxi* (see pages 168–71). The land south of Parque Nacional Cotopaxi is protected by the Fundacíon Páramo, which prohibits hunting and fishing. This road is gated at the headwaters of the Río Tamboyacu, so you either need to make arrangements with this organisation to get keys to the gate or travel by foot across the *páramo*. There is a good camping site just west of the *hacienda* near the river, or you can continue south towards several prominent *páramo* hills, hiking for about an hour. There is no trail, but just after dropping down, slightly past the hills, there will be a flat area with water which is good for camping and which has excellent views of Quilindaña. From here you could attempt the summit by leaving at about 05.00 to allow enough time for the return trip (hide any gear left behind, since *campesinos* travel though the area). Otherwise, you can continue the following day across the *páramo* to the obvious central (north) ridge that leads to the base of the mountain. At the top of the ridge on the northwest flank is a small unnamed lake southeast of Cerro Vetanillas, which is also suitable for camping. It is about 1½ to 2 hours up the ridge to the lake from the suggested *páramo* camp.

Hacienda Chalupas
The Hacienda Chalupas can usually be reached in a normal truck or car from Lasso or Latacunga. Head south from Lasso on the Pan-American Highway to the turn-off to Alaquez, then follow a dirt road to Cuchitingue. The road is located on the south side of a deep canyon. The Hacienda Chalupas (labelled Hacienda Pansachi on some maps) is a cement building with a grass roof. The caretakers can give you directions to Quilindaña. The trip from Lasso takes about 2 hours and costs $20. If the gate across the Río Pansachi is open you can cross the concrete bridge and drive up the dirt road up the ridge called Loma Ensillo. This road is passable with a 4WD vehicle in dry conditions. It also connects with the older road that passes through the Hacienda Baños (the owners currently do not allow the public to use this road) near the rocky hill called Morro. From here there is a trail that heads through a pass on the northwest side of Morro and drops down to a swampy basin. Cross a stream and head cross-country to the east (towards Quilindaña). Hike around the north side of the Laguna Yuracocha. Contour up the slope to the north and reach a

small unnamed lake, then reach the Laguna Verdecocha. Hike around the north side of this lake to camping spots on the west side of Quilindaña (the basecamp for the West Face Route). Alternately you can scramble up the moraine to the lake southeast of Cerro Ventanillas (basecamp for North Ridge Route).

Climbing Quilindaña
North Ridge
This route departs from the small lake south of Ventanilla, traversing left to an obvious couloir (which may be either snow- or sand-filled, depending on the recent weather). The couloir is the only access to the prominent left (northwest) ridge. Begin rock climbing directly up the ridge; the grade is slightly difficult at class 5.6/5.7. It's easy to pick out the line on the good, solid rock. The technical part ends where the ridge flattens out, and from here it's only another 150m of easy scrambling to the summit. Keep slightly to the right on the ridge as you approach the peak.

A little easier would be to cross the ridge rather than climb directly up, traversing to below the north rock face. The line up the face to the flat part of the ridge is straightforward class 5 climbing.

West face
This route is technically easier than the North Ridge but the lower portion of the route involves some rock climbing on very rotten rock. The strategy is to follow the orange-coloured scree gullies to the ridge crest to the south of the summit pyramid. Depart from the east end of the Laguna Verdecocha and ascend the moraine to the base of the rock. Skirt to the left and follow a gully to an obvious notch low on the west face. Scramble through this notch to a scree basin; to the left is a steep orange face (difficult to protect). Work right to a saddle. Continue right and climb up a slanting ramp to another saddle. Traverse right and climb a somewhat rotten and difficult-to-protect gully. This ends in a short chimney which opens on to another scree slope. Climb this to the saddle and then climb left on the summit ridge (easy class 5 but loose rock scramble) to the summit. There are about two pitches that should be protected; slings are sufficient. The climb from the lake to the summit will take about 4 to 5 hours.

PARQUE NACIONAL LLANGANATES
If you've heard of the Llanganates you've probably heard of treasure. From the time of the conquistadors it has been believed that treasure was buried here. The story is that when the last Inca, Atahualpa, was murdered by Pizarro, Atahualpa's general, Rumiñahui, hid the treasure from the Spaniards. Many eminent people have been convinced of its existence or have gone to look for it; they include the botanist Richard Spruce, the scientist and evolutionist Alfred Russel Wallace, George Dyott – the man who looked for Colonel Fawcett – and the British climbers Joe Brown and Hamish MacInnes. No-one has found the treasure yet, but a Swiss-German resident of Quito, Eugene Brunner, looked for almost half a century. He was convinced that he had found its location but at the time of his death, the treasure, estimated at 750 tons of gold, had yet to be recovered.

In 1996 the area was made a national park, though at present there is very little infrastructure or administration. Since it is such an inhospitable place, there are practically no development threats except a proposed road from Salcedo to Tena, which would be extremely difficult to construct.

If you want to look for the treasure yourself, you'll probably find it the most difficult trip of your life. The following description by Koerner in his (out of print) book *The Fool's Climbing Guide to Ecuador* (which the author freely admits to being a work of fiction and plagiarism!) explains why. Rob likes the succinctness of his description so much that he reprints it here.

> The Llanganatoo are a mysterious and almost impenetrable range to the northeast of Baños. Part of Atahualpa's gold is said to be hidden there, and people occasionally go off to look for it. You can too if your interest is to get hideously and hopelessly lost in 15-foot high, razor sharp pampas grass and continuous rain.

One route into the Llanganates is to follow in the footsteps of Valverde, a Spanish gentleman who claimed to know the location of the treasure on his deathbed and drew a treasure map for the King of Spain. The map is vague but he may have followed the route below. Please remember that it is really easy to get lost. The topography is confusing since there are many geographical features that are less than 40m high and that therefore do not appear on topo maps with 40m contour lines. Also, it is mostly foggy or raining, so it's often impossible to get a view of where you are located. Avoid flat areas since they may contain 'quaking bogs', where you will sink up to your knees or waist in muck. The Llanganates is the most difficult area in Ecuador to hike – people get lost and die. Wear only rubber boots, as hiking boots will get hopelessly wet and muddy. Bring a machete. The best months are December and January, when you might get a few days of sunny weather. A road heads up from Píllaro to Embalse Pisayambo (a large reservoir) where you can walk into the Llanganates more or less following way trails for several days. After that you are on your own. Hire a taxi in Píllaro to take you up to the Ministerio de Ambiente control point at the Laguna del Tambo ($25) where you may be asked to pay a park entrance fee. Continue by car to a bridge over Río Millin and find the trail shown on the map heading south. Head up the ridge and contour around to La Puerta. Below is 'the maze', where two English explorers once became hopelessly lost. Your goal is to get to the Laguna Aucacocha and not drop down into the cloudforests of the Río El Golpe. Keep your compass in hand and contour around the southern side of this flat quaking bog. It is easy to miss the lake completely; it is behind a hill. There is a trail on the hill on the north side of the lake. Continue up ridges to the Laguna El Cable. This is a good place to camp, a mere 8km from the road, but this is a long day in the Llanganates. There is a black peak to the east – you need to find a trail that contours on the north side of the peak. Follow the narrow and exposed ridge on the trail to the horseshoe basin that contains the Laguna Sogillas, a good place to camp at the end of your second day. From here you can contour on a way trail to Páramos de Soguillas and cut a trail through cloudforest down steep slopes to an interesting valley northwest of peak 4,257. Note the river in this valley has no outlet and probably drops into a cave. We have not got any farther than this, but there is a vast wilderness area to the east with rocky peaks and lakes. Again be careful; the difficulty of travel in this area cannot be overestimated.

Cerro Hermoso (4,571m)

Cerro Hermoso is an infrequently climbed peak in the centre of the Llanganates. Access to the basecamp is more difficult than the actual climb, which does not require any special equipment. On a clear day it lives up to it's name in English, Beautiful Mountain, as dark bedrock peaks jut above the surrounding *páramo* and cloudforest terrain. There may be a basic hut at the Laguna El Cable that was constructed of logs and *pambi* grass in around 1993, probably by treasure hunters. There are two standard routes into the Laguna El Cable. Most people access the peak on a trail across the *páramo* from the town of Pillaró, but a quicker route is from the town of El Triunfo. Mark recommends rubber boots for footgear, even

Distance 38km round-trip
Altitude 2,550–4,571m
Rating Difficult–very difficult
Time 5 days
Start Triunfo
End Triunfo or Laguna del Tambo
Maps IGM 1:50,000 Sucre
Other essential notes A difficult trek into the heart of one of the most remote ranges in Ecuador.

for the ascent of Cerro Hermoso. Also bring a light pair of gloves to protect your hands from getting cut by sharp grasses. Bright flagging will also help on your return journey if you are without guides. If possible, also bring a GPS.

Access El Triunfo is about an hour by bus or truck from Baños on a new gravel road which is not shown on the topographic map. The Ecológico Baños bus leaves at 06.00 and in the afternoon for El Triunfo. The fare is about $2. Trucks can be hired for $20. Once in El Triunfo there is a small store near the school, which is run by the Rodriguez family. Segundo Rodriguez lives across a field and can offer a basic room in his house. He is also an excellent source of information, since he has guided many expeditions into the Llanganates. He has maps and several books that clients have sent him on the scientists and treasure hunters who have explored the area.

Hiking directions The route to the Laguna El Cable at the foot of Cerro Hermoso is difficult to follow, especially beyond the Río Muyo, and it makes sense to hire guides. Many men in El Triunfo know the route since they have either been a porter on one of the many expeditions looking for the lost Inca treasure, or they have hunted deer and tapir in the *páramo* below the peak. Some good guides are Solomón Cunalata, Jaime Cumalata and José Luis Quispe. Segundo Rodriguez can recommend other reliable guides. Since Segundo is now 70 years old, it may be difficult to convince him to make the journey. You can call El Triunfo on the community phone at 03 740 109 to make prior arrangements with Segundo. Guides should cost between $15 and $20 per day, plus their food. The trip is difficult and they should be well tipped if they do a good job.

El Triunfo is located on the edge of Parque Nacional Llanganates. The Río Muyo is the route to Cerro Hermoso, which is travelled by settlers who have moved up the valley. There is a new road that heads up this valley about a kilometre from town and crosses the Río Muyo. Just before the bridge find a prominent cattle trail and follow this through pastures and forest on the east side of the river. This trail progressively becomes more faint upstream as there are fewer people and cows trafficking the route. About 3 hours from El Triunfo the trail alternates between jumping boulders in the river and steep ascents through forest to get around areas of rapids. About 5 hours from El Triunfo the trail crosses a medium-sized stream just below a confluence of two smaller streams. Several hundred metres uphill on the trail there may be a turn-off to the right that is cut out of the cloudforest. This trail ascends 800m, straight up to the *páramo*. The top of this climb is marked as peak 3,748 on the topographic map. This is where a guide would be useful, since it is easy to miss this turn-off, especially if the route has been overgrown. The climb is tiring since it is a muddy trough with overhanging branches and logs. If you cannot locate this trail it may be necessary to clear a new one with machetes. On a trail the climb takes 3 hours; double that time if you have to cut a new one. At the top the transition to *páramo* is an abrupt relief. There is a small pond to the northeast of peak 3,748 which makes for a good campsite.

From the pond there is a grassy and somewhat rocky peak to the northeast. Head cross-country through difficult grass and shrub vegetation to a pass just to the right of the peak. There does not seem to be a trail until you get near the pass. It is easier to stay on hills and out of the flat basin on the right. From this pass drop down to cloudforest on a trail and eventually to a larger, unnamed lake south of peak 3,986, which is also a good campsite. From the lake traverse around a bench northeast and then drop down to the Río Verde Grande just upstream of a confluence. There is a good campsite here and trout in the stream. From the Río Verde Grande climb up another slope to the right of a rocky peak. The trail here is hard to follow, but you need to continue to a pass where it becomes obvious again. Traverse over several small hills to just south of the pass west of peak 4,215. This is where the trail from Pillaró connects with the El Triunfo trail. A more well-travelled trail traverses over to the stream draining the Laguna El Cable and ascends to the lake. There is a basic hut here and areas to camp. It takes 5 to 6 hours from the pond below peak 3,748 to reach the Laguna El Cable.

Climbing Cerro Hermoso Drop down to the Laguna El Cable and walk around the south and west shores (counter-clockwise). Find the trail that heads up a bench to the right of a waterfall; there should be no rock climbing here. This trail climbs to an open valley. Ascend next to the stream to a small plain between Cerro Hermoso and peak 4,215. Once at the plain, head east up slabs following cairns. There are a few rock scrambles but no technical climbing requiring a rope. If it is cloudy the route may be hard to follow so watch for cairns carefully. Near the ridge crest there is a small pond not shown on the map. The highest peak is to the left. Scramble to the ridge and then north to the summit, which is marked by a cement monument. On a clear day the views are outstanding. The climb takes about 3 to 4 hours from the Laguna El Cable and the descent about 2 to 3 hours. It may also be possible to ascend the ridge south of the camp and to follow it to the summit.

Río Topo

Distance Approximately 12km round-trip
Altitude 3,150–3,950m
Rating Very difficult
Time 2–3 days
Start Laguna El Cable
End Laguna El Cable
Maps IGM 1:50,000 Sucre and San José de Poaló
Other essential notes You need to be able to crawl like a tapir, but there are great opportunities on this route to see large Andean mammals.

Hiking directions If you want more mud and wilderness head down to the Río Topo for chances to see tapir and other wildlife. From the pass where the two trails from Pillaró and El Triunfo meet you can head north down a drainage to the Río Topo. There are tapir trails but the route is very rough, with many crawls under low logs and thick grass to negotiate. Machetes are a necessity. It will take you most of the day to get down to the Río Topo. There was a small hut just above the confluence with the Río Topo in 1998, but it may be necessary to camp. There is also a thermal spring 30 minutes upstream along the Río Topo on the west bank. Look for interesting calcium deposits. The Río Topo is a large river and can be tricky to cross during high water. From here you can return to El Triunfo or continue cross-country to the Laguna del Tambo and Pillaro if you are feeling very adventurous; count on 3 to 4 days more of hiking.

Sacha Llanganates
Lou Jost

Distance 21km round-trip to ridge, unknown beyond!
Altitude 1,200–2,500m, unknown beyond!
Rating Very difficult
Time 5 days round-trip to the ridge
Start Topo
End Topo
Maps IGM 1:50,000 Mera and Río Negro
Other essential notes A true wilderness experience which requires a team of *macheteros* and porters.

The Sacha Llanganates are a virtually unknown and uninhabited mountain range between the Amazon basin and the Topo river, along the border between the Tungurahua and Pastaza provinces. Tropical lowland forest covers the flanks of this mountain range. The peaks rise to surprising heights; just how high no-one knows, since constant cloud cover has kept the highest peaks from being mapped! This is truly *terra incognita*. From the highest ridges it is possible to look down into lightning storms rolling across Amazonia, a stunning sight at sunset. There are many unusual plants endemic to the Sacha Llanganates, most of them only discovered in the last few years. Lou Jost has discovered over ten new orchid species in this range. It is not a place for the casual hiker, but it can be a very special experience for someone looking for uncharted cloudforest and possibly *páramo*.

These may be the wettest mountains in Ecuador, since they are constantly hammered by weather systems from the Oriente. They can be cold and windy from June to August. The nicest weather is from November to January. There are no permanent streams on the steep ridgeline of this hike, and it is sometimes necessary to collect rainwater. A long spell of clear weather may well force a hiker to turn back. A water pump/filter should be carried, since it may be necessary to extract water from very small puddles, seeps, or even bromeliads.

It would be wise to hire a local guide for this route, which was created by spectacled bears and enlarged by Lou Jost and his porters in 2001. Lou paid the bears some leftover rice to keep the trail open, but they are less than reliable trail maintainers. Mario Gamboa (tel: 593 9 7089197), Ali Araujo (ask for his very helpful family in Viscaya), or Klever (tel: 593 9 7633198) are all good guides for this trek. Do not expect the local people who live at the trailhead to know this path.

Hiking directions The path starts at the village of Topo (1,200m) between Puyo and Baños. For the first day it follows the beautiful Río Zuñac, first on the west bank and then crossing to the east bank. If it has been raining a lot, the river can still be crossed by walking on cables 6m above the river; these are all that remain of a bridge that was washed out by a massive flood. This is the critical route-finding day, as the well-used trail from town is left behind. You need to ford a large tributary of the Zuñac (about 1km south of Colonia La Union). There are nice campsites at this ford (but watch out for tent-cutter ants!). Here your guide must pick up the entrance to Lou's trail – which goes steeply upward on the north side of the tributary – or cut a new one. After a few hours the trail makes a sharp right-hand turn as it reaches a ridgeline at 1,900–2,000m. The path follows the gentle ridgeline eastward from here. After ½km it suddenly joins a large mountain and becomes much steeper. Turn right where the ridgeline hits the mountain (2,000m). There is a small spring off to the right. During dry periods this may be the last water source for the rest of the trip. Camp here, and load up with water.

The next day the trail continues upward and eastward, eventually reaching a confusingly flat marshy plateau (2,500m), which is thickly overgrown by giant swordgrass. This is where the trail gradually begins to turn northward onto the main ridge of the Sacha Llanganates. There is no water here, but its flatness makes it a good choice for a campsite. Perhaps one could dig holes in the marshiest parts in order to collect seepage water. Pray for rain.

From this point onward, if you have clear weather, you will have excellent views of Amazonia and the high Andes. Lou has travelled only a couple of days further along the main north–south ridge, which makes a series of gentle rises and falls. There are small seeps on the slopes below the trail, but they can be difficult to find, and they only run if there has been recent rain. A larger stream, which may be accessible in an emergency, can be heard off to the right after about a day and a half of hard hiking from the marshy plateau. At that point, the ridgeline hits a very steep mountain. That mountain forms a new ridgeline, which disappears into the blank areas of the map labelled 'nubes' ('clouds') on the IGM topographical maps. Only the bears know what is hidden there.

THE BAÑOS AREA

This resort town is popular for its thermal springs, splendid scenery, and pleasant climate. Many day-hikes can be made and the town is a good base for climbing Volcán Tungurahua and El Altar, as well as being the beginning of one of Ecuador's principal roads into the jungle.

The town's tourist attractions include several thermal baths (*piscinas*), a small museum, a zoo of Ecuadorian animals, and restaurants serving the typical Andean delicacy *cuy*, or roast guinea pig. Your hotel manager can direct you to all of these. By strolling down the main street in the morning you'll see the shop-keepers busy making taffy. A glob of the soft mixture is slung onto a wooden hook on the wall, then pulled repeatedly until it hardens. Although you can buy it in bars, it's much nicer to pay a few cents for a wispy piece of still-warm taffy.

Baños has a broad selection of lodging in most price ranges. Finding something to meet your needs will present no problem. The Residential Rosita (16 de Diciembre and Luis A Martinez, tel: 593 3 240396) is a good cheap hotel with kitchen facilities in some rooms. A nice mid-range hotel is El Marquez (Pasaje V Ibarra and Av Juan Montalvo, tel: 593 3 2740053), and a very nice, slightly more expensive hostel with great breakfasts is the Posada del Arte (Pasaje V Ibarra and Av Juan Montalvo, tel: 593 3 2740083).

Day-hikes from Baños

Baños lies at 1,800m in the valley of Río Pastaza, which flows from west to east. Good day-hikes may be made in the mountains to the north and in the foothills of Tungurahua to the south, as well as down the river valley to the east.

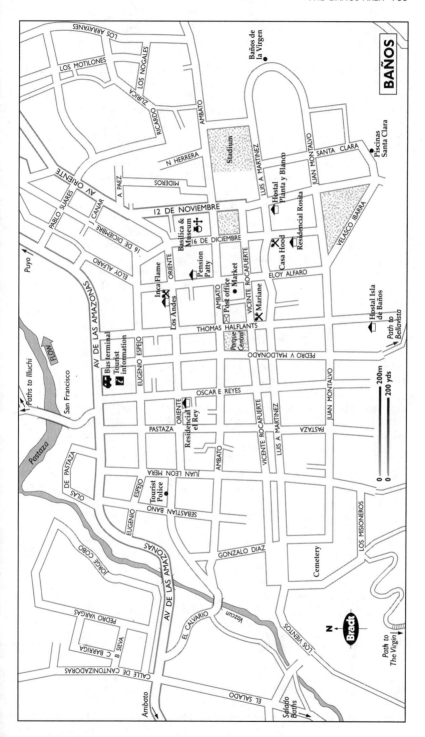

BAÑOS

To reach the steep hills on the north side of town you must cross the Río Pastaza on one of two bridges, the Puente San Francisco or the Puente San Martín, but once on the other side, directions become meaningless. There are so many paths to choose from that it's up to you how high and how far you climb. Just plan to cross one bridge going and the other coming back for variety. The trail to Puente San Francisco leaves from behind the sugar cane stalls by the main bus station, and after crossing the bridge becomes very steep. You can climb to the antennas at the top of the hill or follow the road up for fantastic views of Baños and Tungurahua. Or take a taxi across the bridge and up to the Patate–Triunfo road, with plenty of trails for hiking into the high mountains to the north. On a clear day you are rewarded with marvellous views of Tungurahua and Chimborazo, as well as of green cultivated fields, passion flowers, waterfalls, and the turbulent Río Pastaza.

The Puente San Martin lies 1km or so to the west of town. Walk out on the main westbound road, crossing a bridge. Keep going until you reach a right fork by a blue religious shrine just before the police checkpoint. Take this fork and walk less than 1km to the bridge. It crosses an impressive gorge and continues a few kilometres to the village of Lligua. At several points trails climb the hill to the right of the road so you can take your pick.

There is a small zoo near the bridge that houses an interesting collection of Ecuadorian species and a free-range, ridiculously tame tapir. The zoo keeper is interested in his job and will give you plenty of information, and will perhaps even let you into some of the cages for photographs.

If you prefer a day-hike with clearer directions and well-defined trails then head for the hills south of town. The hike to Pondoa and the Tungurahua climbing refuges on the slopes of Volcán Tungurahua is one idea (see *Tungurahua*, opposite). Another possibility is the hike to the village of Runtun, which consists of a luxury hotel and half-a-dozen buildings, one of which is a bar with a pool table! There are two trails to Runtun; the shorter of the two will take about 2 hours from Baños. Leave town by heading south on Calle Tomás Haiflans, which soon passes Escuela Pedro Vicente Maldonado. Just beyond the school the road becomes a footpath which climbs diagonally left up the hill towards a house with a huge cross plainly visible on the sky line. It's the only good trail so you can't miss it. It will take about 1 hour to reach the cross, with excellent views of Baños. The trail now doubles back to the right and towards the top of the hill until it reaches Runtun. Immediately before the village there is a fork; the left trail goes to the village (50m) and the right goes down to Baños. This alternative descent is rather longer than returning the way you came. On a clear day the views of Tungurahua from near Runtun are magnificent.

Finally, if you've had enough of running up and down steep mountain sides, you can walk, hitch or take a bus (marked 'Agoyan') about 6km to the once-famous Agoyan Falls (where the bus terminates). A new hydro-electric plant above the falls has altered their lovely character, though at times they will still be visible from the road. At the bus terminus you can continue through the tunnel (take the one on the right), walking or hitching a further 10km to the Río Verde Falls. There are many different cascades along the road, but the Pailon del Diablo at Río Verde are the most impressive. The views along the road are wonderful, as the steep walled Río Pastaza canyon slowly opens up into the Oriente. Once at the little village of Río Verde, walk through town and over the road bridge until you find a trail to your right, just by the last house in town. The trail leads steeply down to the Río Pastaza, which is crossed by a suspension footbridge from where you can view the falls. Better still, scramble right up to them on the steep and narrow path immediately before the footbridge. It is an exciting place; the constricted gorge reverberates with power and it is difficult to make yourself heard above the roar. This point is 20km from Baños and about as far as you can easily reach in a day and still hitch back to Baños. An alternative is to take one of the frequent buses (at least one per hour) that go east from the Baños terminal, and get off at Río Verde (20 minutes from Baños), Machay (25–30 minutes from Baños), or Topo (about 1 hour from Baños). At each of these small villages there are excellent trails north into rich cloudforest full of exciting birds and plants; enquire locally for more information.

Rock climbing

Just below the zoo in Baños, along the river, there are bolted routes on columnar andesite ranging in difficulty from class 5.9 to 5.12. The rock is reasonably solid and the bolt spacing is close enough to make leading safe. Many of the climbs crest out on overhangs. This rock-climbing area is a good destination for sport climbing.

Tungurahua (5,029m)

> The paths feather-lined and steep.
> Overhead a sky of mud.
> Then all of a sudden in the air the purest white lily of a tall volcano.
>
> Henri Michaux

Tungurahua is a beautiful and active snow-capped volcano situated about 10km south of Baños, and now part of Parque Nacional Sangay. The volcano was first climbed in 1873 by the Germans Wilhelm Reiss and Alfons Stübel.

The volcano became active again in 1999, spewing out large volumes of ash and incandescent boulders that rolled down the slope of the volcano – glowing at night. The town of Baños was temporarily evacuated for about six months, but it now appears to be back to normal despite continual eruptions, with an evacuation plan in place should the volcano spew material in the direction of town. Mark visits Baños regularly, but it's worth remembering that an eruption in 1711 totally destroyed the village, so take your chances! The last eruptive period lasted from 1916 to 1918, so it may settle down again in the next few years. A brief description of the climb is included in case the eruptions do subside, but climbers are currently (2004) not permitted to climb the volcano. You are, however, allowed to hike to the refuge and spend the night. Keep yourself up-to-date by checking the Smithsonian Global Volcanism Program and Universidad Politecnica webpages.

From a climber's point of view, Tungurahua is rather an anomaly. It has been described both as 'easy to access and to climb' and also 'one of the hardest climbs in Ecuador'. Both descriptions are correct because it is easy from a technical viewpoint, but it is also physically demanding, as it involves 3,200m of vertical ascent from Baños, at 1,800m.

Access To get to the refuge you can either go on foot or hire transport up to the park entrance, where you'll pay a park entrance fee and the $6 per night refuge fee. You may be able to arrange for a truck to make the trip for about $15.

Approach If going on foot, start your climb at the western entrance to Baños at a police checkpoint. Across the highway you'll see a dirt road bearing up and to the right. Walk up this road about 100m and turn right at a sign for Refugio Nicolás Martínez, where you'll pick up the trail which is very steep and narrow. It follows a ridge with fine views of Baños, and 1 or 2 hours' walking are needed to reach the small village of Pondoa. Stop at the Pondoa store and chat with the owner, who will

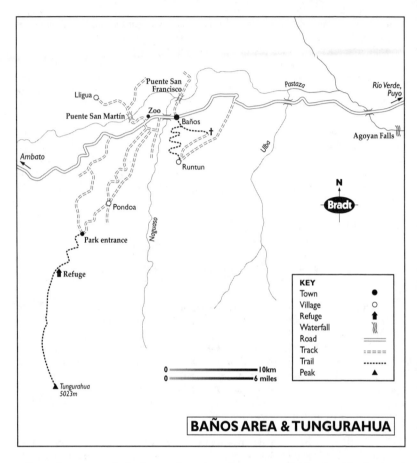

KEY
Town	●
Village	○
Refuge	🛉
Waterfall	〜
Road	
Track	=====
Trail	--------
Peak	▲

BAÑOS AREA & TUNGURAHUA

tell you how to reach the hut and can introduce you to the local guide, Sr Angel Perez, who has climbed the volcano dozens of times and is very experienced. He doesn't have much equipment to rent but can arrange mule hire and a guide if you wish. Only very basic supplies (beer, sardines and crackers) are available at the store.

It takes an hour or two to climb from Pondoa to the park entrance. If arriving by local transport, this is the end of the road, and the start of the final approach to the refuge. Often there are mules and horses available to help carry gear up to the refuge (about $10 per animal), but don't rely on it. If you definitely want to go with pack animals, then arrange it ahead of time.

Follow the cobbled road out of Pondoa (about 30 minutes' walking) to an obvious sharp left, which puts you on a well-worn dirt track leading to the park entrance. The trail up to the refuge begins about 100m past the entrance station to the left. It's quite steep in places and often muddy. At several points the trail goes through 'tunnels' of bamboo and other tropical vegetation. Expect to take from 3 to 5 hours getting to the refuge.

When you reach the refuge (built in the late 1970s) you will find floor space for about 18 people and a propane cooking stove. Water is obtained from a spring about 200m beyond the hut. There is no secure lock-up for packs etc. Many choose to carry their gear with them to the summit and avoid the risk of leaving it behind unattended. The altitude here is about 3,800m and the view of Chimborazo's east face is impressive. The refuge is on a ridge that was protected from eruptions and has now been reopened for overnight stays.

Climbing directions The climb from the hut to the top is best attempted in the early morning, before the summit snow becomes soft and slushy (assuming the volcano is not erupting and there is snow). A dawn start is adequate, but a pre-dawn start is often better. Note that the material on the slopes is likely to be very unstable since it has been recently deposited. Even if the volcano has become dormant, heavy rain could trigger deadly lahars (mud flows) on the flanks of the volcano. Stay out of gullies and on ridges. Also, volcanic gases can be deadly.

The descent from the summit back to Baños in one day is not easy, especially with heavy packs. It can be hot, depending on the season, and the steep trail makes it hard on the knees. It is, after all, 3,200m of downhill!

If the volcano is impossible to climb, arrange a trip to the opposite side of the Río Pastaza canyon to view a night-time eruption; there are tour agencies that offer these tours. Mark viewed some of the first and most spetacular eruptions in 1999 from a pasture that reminded him of Woodstock, complete with an international collection of drummers, dancers and other mystics coming to life with every eruption in the wee hours of the morning.

PARQUE NACIONAL SANGAY

Parque Nacional Sangay, which almost doubled in size in 1992 with the addition of 245,000 hectares to the south, includes vast tracts of high-altitude *páramo* and lush, lower level cloudforest. Its original, northern section is listed as a World Heritage site. Within the park and more specifically around the area of the Sangay volcano, there exists one of the last sizeable refuges for the mountain, or woolly mountain, tapir. This species is listed as endangered and until the last two decades the area supported a healthy population. Hunting is the major cause of the population decline, despite the laws prohibiting it. Many areas of the park are beginning to open up to hikers, with the implementation of new guidelines and services by the parks department. For now, though, Volcán Sangay, Tungurahua (described in the Baños section) and El Altar, all in the western zone of the park, remain the primary attractions for park visitors.

Although information can be obtained about the park in Quito at the Ministerio de Ambiente offices or at Fundacíon Natura, the main office for the park is located in Aloa. There should also be guard stations in Aloa (Volcán Sangay, El Placer), Atillo (Guamote-Macas Trail), Candelaria (El Altar), Pondoa (Tungurahua), and Río Negro (cloudforest).

El Altar (5,319m)

This, the fifth highest mountain in Ecuador, undoubtedly involves some of the most technical climbing and has one of the longest approaches. Situated some 170km south of Quito, El Altar is an extinct volcano which at one time was probably higher than Cotopaxi, but a huge ancient eruption almost totally destroyed the cone, leaving a steep-sided and jagged crater 3km in diameter. Despite repeated attempts by many climbers, including Whymper, the icy ramparts of El Altar withstood all assaults until July 7 1963, when an Italian expedition led by Marino Tremonti conquered the last unclimbed 5,000m mountain in Ecuador.

Indigenous legend dates the huge final explosion to 1460, but volcanologists agree that it must have been far more ancient. Today, the volcano is inactive. Nine separate sub-summits are recognised on its C-shaped crater. They have now all

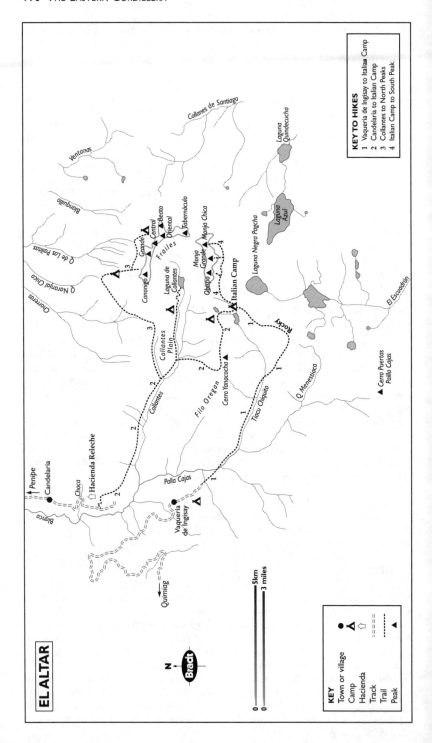

EL ALTAR

KEY TO HIKES
1 Vaquería de Ingisay to Italian Camp
2 Candelaria to Italian Camp
3 Collantes to North Peaks
4 Italian Camp to South Peak

KEY
Town or village ●
Camp △
Hacienda ⇧
Track = = =
Trail ••••••
Peak ▲

0   5km
0   3 miles

been climbed, although one of the Frailes was not conquered until 1979 by a team of six Ecuadorian climbers led by Luis Naranjo.

El Altar needs no translation into English and its various peaks all bear church-related names. The highest is El Obispo (the bishop), at 5,319m, but its height is much in dispute, with some authorities suggesting as much as 5,465m. This was the first peak to be climbed. The Italians, led by Tremonti, then played an important part in the conquest of the rest of El Altar's peaks. They returned in 1965 to conquer the second peak, El Canonigo (the canon), at 5,260m, and in 1972 achieved the first ascent of El Fraile Grande (the great friar). The three other Fraile peaks were all climbed for the first time by Ecuadorian teams. Bernado Beate, Jacinto Carrasco and Rafael Terán were the summit climbers in two of those first ascents. La Monja Grande (the great nun), the third highest peak at 5,160m, was climbed by a US-Japanese team in 1968 and the remaining two peaks, La Monja Chica (the little nun) and El Tabernaculo (the tabernacle) fell to a German team in 1972. The extremely difficult north face of Obispo was climbed from within the crater by a French/Ecuadorian team in 1984. The ascent of this grade VI rock face took 6 days to complete.

In October 1995, the nine summits of El Altar were climbed for the first time in one expedition. The team consisted of four Ecuadorian mountaineers – Osvaldo Freile and Gabriel Llano climbed all nine summits. They started at the Italian Camp and climbed counter-clockwise for 23 days, ending in the Collantes Plain. The loads were carried across the glaciers on sleds. This difficult feat was a watershed in Ecuadorian mountaineering and still awaits a repeat.

This volcano is obviously not a jaunt for the beginning climber, but a backpacking trip is very rewarding. There is a grey-green crater lake called, curiously, the Laguna Amarilla (yellow lake), and from the edge of the crater backpackers can listen to the hanging glaciers crack and rumble, and catch glimpses of enormous ice slides. Condors are also seen around here. El Altar is protected as part of the Parque Nacional Sangay.

It is rainy for most of the year, with June and July being the wettest months. The best times to go are from late November through to early February, with the majority of successful ascents having been made around Christmas and New Year. I have seen one report published in Ecuador which claims that the El Altar region receives 14,600mm (that's about 48ft!) of precipitation annually. Although I find this hard to believe, it does indicate that the region is wet ... very wet.

On October 13 2000 at 05.00, the face of Monja Grange collapsed into the Laguna Amarillo of El Altar, causing a wave of water and debris to rush over the western lip of the crater onto the Collantes Plain. This debris flow continued down the canyon of the river, arriving upstream of the town of Penipe and temporarily damming the Río Penipe. The summit lost as much as 50m of elevation. The Collantes Plain is now covered with boulders and the canyon walls are scoured and still unstable all the way to the Río Penipe. Nine people and about 100 livestock perished in this tragedy. Mark remembers a trout farm just below Candeleria that was completely washed away by the debris flow. Amazingly, Candelaria and the trail up to the lake were not impacted except on the Collantes Plain.

Access From Quito's Terminal Terrestre, take a bus via Ambato to Riobamba. Locate the Terminal Oriente in Riobamba and get a bus to Penipe (1 hour), from where you can walk (4 hours) or hire a truck to take you the 15km to the small town of Candelaria. There are several buses a day that make the trip all the way up to Candelaria from Riobamba and vice-versa; check with Transporte Bayushig in Riobamba for current schedules or ask in Penipe.There is also a driver who will

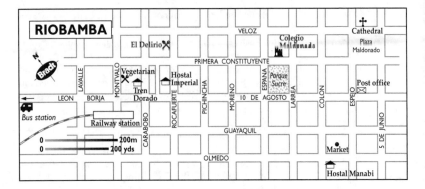

take you in his pick-up truck from Penipe to Candelaria and the Hacienda Releche. Ask around the main plaza for Ernesto Haro. He charges about $12 one-way and will pick you up for the return trip at a pre-arranged time if you wish.

In Candelaria there is a small store with very basic food supplies, and they may be able to suggest somewhere you can sleep. There are also mules available to pack your gear up to the base of the mountain. Return pick-up times can be arranged.

The Hacienda Releche (tel: 593 3 2960848 in Riobamba, 593 3 949761 at the hostel) is now a hostel and is a good base for excursions up to El Altar. They charge $6 a night, plus $3 for breakfast and $5 for dinner. A recommended guide is Sergio Chiriboga; he charges $10 per day for guiding and $10 per day per mule. They also offer cabins (Rancho de Limpiopungo) at the Collantes Plain for $6 per night, and an extra $5 for use of the gas stove.

Hiking to the crater and beyond

Distance 25km round-trip to crater
Altitude 3,150–4,200m
Rating Moderate
Time 2 days
Start Releche
End Releche
Maps IGM 1:50,000 Guano, Palitahua and Volcán El Altar
Other essential notes Hike to the crater lake of El Altar, with great views of the surrounding peaks and the possibility of seeing condors.

Hiking directions From Candelaria continue along the road for about 2km until you come to a light green building with a Parque Nacional Sangay sign, which is the ranger station. For a modest charge, you can overnight in the ranger cabin (with toilets and cooking facilities) before continuing on. Pay your park fee and follow this road up a steep hill, across a stream and past the Hacienda Releche. The beginning of the hike can be confusing, but there are arrows which indicate the correct path. Switchback up the trail until it contours along the midslope of the ridge all the way to the Collantes Plain, about 4 to 5 hours from the Hacienda Releche. The plain is covered with boulders from the recent collapse of Monja Grande in 2000, so stay to the left for easy walking up to the trees at the base of the crater, where you can camp out of the wind. Edward Whymper did just that in 1880.

From the Collantes Plain there are three basic choices – assuming, that is, that you wish to do anything at all. You can go east and visit the crater; you can go south to climb the southern peaks (including Obispo, the highest) or do some backpacking in a beautifully wild and trackless area with many lakes; or you can go north to climb the northern peaks (including Canonigo, the second highest) and do some backpacking in this area, which is little explored. A challenging and adventurous hike would be to go all the way around the back of the mountain – it is rarely done.

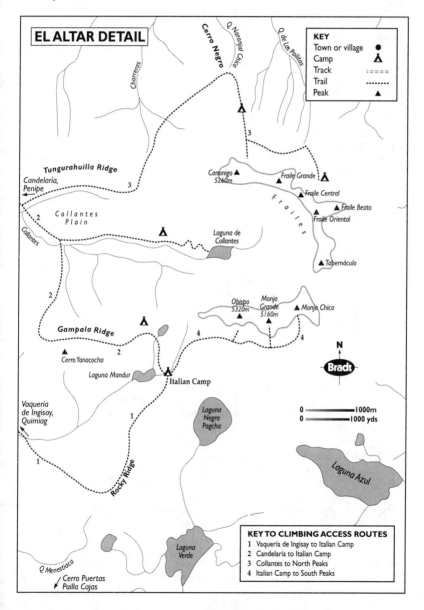

The best route from the Collantes Plain to the rim of the crater is up along the wooded ridge on the left of the outlet canyon (follow cow paths). It takes about 3 hours for the round trip from the bottom. There are rewarding views of the peaks and hanging glaciers which frequently send small avalanches into the lake.

For the return trip, consider hiking to the Hacienda Puelazo via Vaquería de Ingisay.

Climbing Obispo and the southern peaks

Access The best approach is via the *hacienda* of Vaquería Ingisay and the Cordillera de Mandur. From the end of the road it is a mere 4 hours with mules, plus 2 hours carrying packs to the Italian Camp. From Riobamba or Baños get a bus to Cubijíes or Químiag. In Cubijíes you can hire a taxi (4WD not necessary) to transport you up to the *hacienda* of Vaquería Ingisay, or the end of the road where there is a water diversion project. Expect to pay about $10 for the vehicle – it is about an hour's drive on a gravel road.

Approach You can hire mules near the *hacienda* – ask for José Colcha Mandsanda. It may take a few hours to organise, so it is best to plan an overnight stay here so that you are assured of making it to the Italian Camp the next day. The mules can take you to within 2–3km of the camp. The route is muddy so rubber boots are recommended. Try to get the mule driver to take horses up the Cordillera de Mandur as far as they can get before encountering rocky terrain. The best route is to cross to the east side of the Río Paila Cajas (also called Río Blanco) and head straight up to a way trail that contours above cloudforest and into the Río Tiacu Chiquito valley. Head across tussocky terrain to the head of the valley, cross to the south side of Río Tiacu Chiquito and climb the steep grassy slopes to the ridge crest of Cordillera de Mandur. On the ascent avoid the cliffs near the waterfall; stay far right where there are no cliffs. Walk up the rocky ridge to the Italian Camp (4,550m), with obvious tent platforms in a notch with a 5m high spire. The camp is sometimes buried in snow. The Laguna de Mandur is located west and the Laguna Negra Pagcha is southeast of the camp. The Italian Camp has an inordinate amount of rubbish around the tent platform; please help clean up this once pristine spot. A small spring can be found about 100m down on the west side of the ridge or you can melt snow.

An alternative and more arduous route is from the Collantes Plain. From the plain head south and climb up to Filo de Oregan. The cliffs of Cerro Yanacocha look impenetrable, but there is a gully marked with cairns between the peaks marked as 4,548 and 4,685 on the IGM map. An easier route is to head right from the beginning of the Collantes Plain and climb the steep grass to a ridge where you will find a trail. There are spectacular views of El Altar, Tungurahua, Carihuairazo and Chimborazo. Contour on the north side of Cerro Yanacocha and the south side of the peak 4,685 until you get to a green lake with an ice fall above. For some reason this lake is not shown on the map, perhaps because old aerial photos were used from when glacial ice was present. There are some nice camp spots above this lake.

Follow the outlet stream of this lake downstream towards the Laguna Mandur, but before arriving at the lake shore contour below and eventually up some gravely ledges and gullies to the Cordillera de Mandur, where the Italian camp is located in a notch. This route is cairned but may be difficult to follow; the tricky part is finding the right gully up to the ridge. Be careful of rockfall. Realistically, with heavy packs it is two days to the Italian camp following this approach. (See route diagram opposite.)

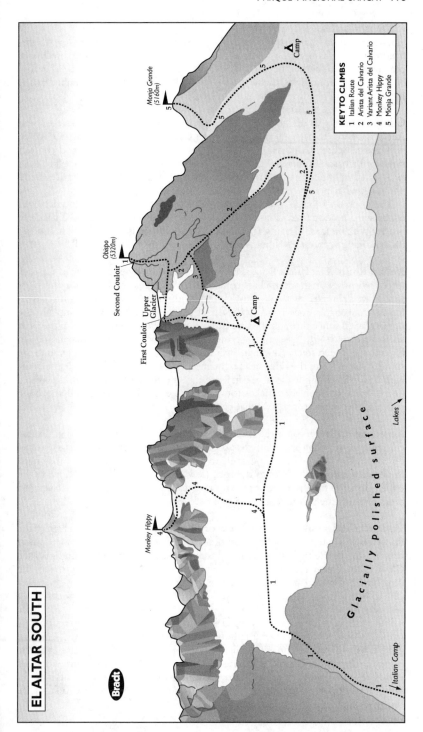

EL ALTAR SOUTH

Bradt

KEY TO CLIMBS
1 Italian Route
2 Arista del Calvario
3 Variant Arista del Calvario
4 Monkey Hippy
5 Monja Grande

Monja Grande
(5160m)

Obispo
(5320m)

Second Couloir

First Couloir Upper
Glacier

Monkey Hippy

Camp

Camp

Camp

Lakes

Glacially polished surface

Italian Camp

Climbing Obispo

There are three main routes up Obispo which are described below. Snow conditions are changing on Obispo, thus making route finding on this technical peak necessary. It should be noted that the Italian Route is rarely climbed because of poor snow conditions in the first couloir. When the Italians climbed it the gullies were full of snow – now it is a mixed route with rotten rock.

For all routes continue up the ridge from the Italian Camp for about 30 minutes, until you get to a gully of rotten rock (there are a couple of tent platforms here) that heads right and down to a glacially polished plain covered with gravel debris. Continue north to the lower glacier, and ascend and contour right to the base of Obispo. You can also make a camp here, though the peak can be reached in one long day. Any route from the Italian Camp will take at least 12 hours round-trip.

The rock on Obispo is poorly consolidated volcanic breccia – boulders and cobbles in a mud matrix. Consequently it is easy to pull blocks out and difficult to protect rock pitches. Slinging large protruding boulders is often the best you can do. Climbing without a helmet is stupid because of the risk of rockfall.

Italian Route The Italian Route climbs the wide and obvious couloir in the rock to the left of the main peak. This couloir is now a mixed rock-and-ice climb (or should we say mixed dirt-and-snow climb). With heavy snow covering it is easier. It passes through a rock band to the upper glacier to the left of Obispo and the upper glacier. Once through the first couloir, traverse the upper glacier to the right until you reach the base of a second couloir (rock or snow depending on conditions), much steeper and narrower than the first. This gully brings you to the summit ridge. From the ridge head right and you'll be faced with a moderate 30m-high rock wall which is the final barrier to the summit. This final pitch is class 5.5 or 5.6, but the rotten rock makes it much more difficult. It is exposed above the crater, and very airy (or should that be hairy?!).

Arista de Calvario Route To avoid the first couloir of the Italian Route, continue around the base of the rock below the upper glacier to the west side of an obvious ridge. Follow up a snow gully to get on the *arista* or ridge. You may need to negotiate a moat to get onto the rock (low class 5) and follow the ridge to the upper glacier. There may be some crevasses to negotiate on the upper glacier in order to reach the second couloir. From here follow the Italian Route.

Variant of Arista de Carvario Route or Hidden Couloir From the base of the first couloir on the Italian Route find a white dike forming a diagonal couloir heading to the right. This scramble and low class 5 route joins the Arista de Calvario route near the base of the upper glacier. This route perhaps provides the most straightforward and fastest access to the upper glacier.

Monkey Hippy

To the left of Obispo is a pyramid-shaped peak on the ridge affectionately named Monkey Hippy, after a famous Ecuadorian brand of peanuts. This is a good warm-up climb from the Italian Camp. Head straight up the glacier to the ridge to the right of Monkey Hippy; you may need to negotiate some 60°-plus slopes to avoid crevasses. It is also possible to climb the rock, but it looks difficult to protect. You can do this climb in about 5 hours round-trip from the Italian Camp.

Climbing Monja Grande, Monja Chica and Tabernaculo

To climb the other southern peaks you have to continue from the base of Obispo around the south side of the mountain along the foot of the glacier. Ecuadorian climbers are now using an upper route that traverses across the glaciers. These routes involve technical ice climbing and are more difficult than the routes up Obispo.

Climbing Canonigo and the Northern Peaks

From the Collantes Plain head northeast over the Tungurahuilla ridge, where there are possible campsites. Continue to the next ridge, Cerro Negro, where a basecamp is made. Mules from Candelaria can reach this point in 2 days – or perhaps one long hard one.

From the basecamp on Cerro Negro ridge traverse the glacier which lies to the northeast of Canonigo, the second highest peak of Altar. Head towards the base of a small ridge which leads to a minor eastern summit of Canonigo. Difficult mixed climbing takes you up the western side of this small ridge, and you then curve around the crater towards the summit west of you. A bivouac is often necessary. Canonigo is less frequently climbed than Obispo and is more difficult.

To climb the other northern peaks, the four Frailes, continue around the bottom of the northern glaciers to a camp in the cirque of the Frailes. These peaks have had very few ascents.

Volcán Sangay (5,230m)

Maps IGM 1:50,000 Volán El Altar and Palitahua. For more detail, the 1:25,000 Cerros Negros and the Laguna Pintada are useful. There are some map errors near the Laguna Mandur.

In many ways Sangay is the most difficult and dangerous mountain to climb in Ecuador. It is said to be the most continuously active volcano in South America and the constant shower of red hot rocks and ash make all attempts to climb it an exceedingly hazardous venture. Furthermore it is situated in a very remote region and several days of hard travel are required to reach its base. The volcano is found in the southern central part of the largely inaccessible Parque Nacional Sangay, some 200km south of Quito.

The height of Sangay is usually given as 5,230m, but constant activity periodically alters this. The shape of the cone and the number of craters are also constantly changing. The volcanologist Minard L. Hall recorded three main craters and several smaller ones during investigations in 1976.

The first recorded eruption was in 1628 but it was doubtless active before that date. The next 100 years were apparently quiet, but since 1728 the volcano has been erupting almost continuously. In 1849 the Frenchman, Sebastian Wisse, explored the area and counted 267 strong explosions within one hour. A short spell of inactivity occurred from 1916 to 1934 and it was during this time that the volcano was first ascended. The US climbers Robert T and Terris Moore, Paul Austin and Lewis Thorne reached the summit on August 4 1929. Attempts since then have claimed the lives of several climbers, including two British mountaineers who died in 1976, as recorded in the book *Sangay Survived* by Richard Snailham. Despite the constant eruptions and danger, however, several successful ascents by Ecuadorian climbers have been reported in the '70s and '80s. On September 16 1982, Helena Landázuri, of the Fundación Nature, became the first woman to reach the summit. Since then, the volcano has seen quite a few successful attempts, both by expeditions and individual climbers. (See map overleaf.)

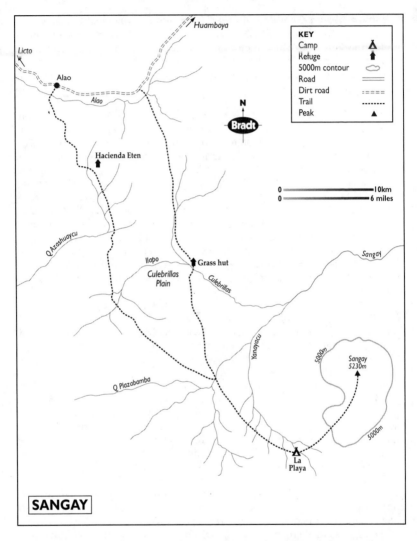

KEY

Camp	▲
Refuge	▲
5000m contour	◯
Road	———
Dirt road	=====
Trail	·········
Peak	▲

SANGAY

Access Hiring a guide is essential. You could probably get to the basecamp at La Playa with no problem, but finding your way across the lower flanks of the volcano at 02.30 presents some really time-consuming considerations. The route finding on the descent is no less difficult. Few guides will accompany you to the summit (each will adamantly declare he has a wife and children to think about!) but a guide will get you to the start of the climb and wait there for your return. There are about 25 guides in an association based in San Antonio across the river from Aloa. The core of this group are Roberto and Carlos Cas. Another well-recommended guide is José Baño Masa, who lives in Alao on the south side of the river. Ask anyone in the village for directions to his house. You can also stay the night there. He charges about $10 a day, depending on the size of the group. Food must be provided for the guide and any porters that may be hired, in addition to the wages paid. Be sure to bring enough for everyone.

It has been recently reported that locals with a knowledge of the area are setting themselves up as guides, but are ill-equipped, stand rigidly on a $10-a-day fee for guiding and speak no English. This may be in reaction to the Ministerio de Ambiente beefing up the park headquarters, adding more staff, and infusing the system with improvements (with much credit due to Fundación Natura and the US Peace Corps), making it appear as if charging more is justified. Most of them do know the route and can get you in, but be prepared to bargain fiercely.

The initial stages of the approach are simple: take one of the many buses from Quito's Terminal Terrestre to Riobamba. Taxis can be hired to make the Riobamba–Alao trip for about $35. There is daily transport from Riobamba or Licto (20km south southeast of Riobamba) to Alao.

Alao is a small village which boasts a few small shops where basic last-minute supplies may be purchased. You can stay at the Ministerio de Ambiente guard station for about $2 per night, located on the main road about 1km beyond the turn-off to Alao. There are showers, occasional hot water, a stove and bunks. The long-time park guard Juan Velastegui can provide up-to-date information on the hike.

Hiking and climbing directions There are two established routes into La Playa at the base of Sangay. The Eten/Plazapamba route takes 3 to 4 days, and mules can travel most of the way to the mountain. The shorter Culebrillas route takes 3 days, but you can use pack animals only on the first day.

Eten/Plazapamba route

Distance Approximately 35km
Altitude 3,160–5,230m
Rating Difficult
Time 6–7 days
Start Alao
End Alao
Maps IGM 1:50,000 Llactapamba de Aloa and Volcán Sangay
Other essential notes Great trek to the base of the active volcano Sangay in the middle of the reserve, if not an active climb to the summit. Pack animals possible to Playa.

It may require some time in Aloa to arrange the pack animals. This route begins from the Hacienda Eten, which is almost a day's hike from Alao. From Eten you head more or less south along the Quebrada Azashuaycu and camp in an area known as Escaleras, continuing the next day in a roughly southeasterly direction to Plazabamba. The going is very up and down as you constantly climb rises and cross rivers. In one day alone there are fourteen river fordings. The vegetation here, however, is not too thick. Plazabamba is a large, flat, low area which can be seen from quite a distance. There is a simple shelter which is easy to find in the flat plain. This is as far as the mules will be taken unless the trail is dry (Dec/Jan). From here the mule-driver/guide will help you carry your gear to the basecamp at La Playa, but the going is difficult.

From Plazabamba, there is more vegetation and the terrain becomes increasingly ridged and difficult. There are many streams and small rivers to ford. The La Playa basecamp is approximately east-southeast of Plazabamba. Although you are now close to the mountain, almost constant cloud makes a sighting infrequent.

Culebrillas route

Distance Approximately 27km
Altitude 3,160–5,230m
Rating Difficult
Time 5–6 days
Start Aloa
End Aloa
Maps IGM 1:50,000 Llactapamba de Aloa and Volcán Sangay, 1:25,000
IGM topo for the zone around the volcano, CT-NIV Río Culebrillas.
Other essential notes Great trek to the base of the active volcano Sangay
in the middle of the reserve, if not an active climb to the summit. Pack
animals possible to Culebrillas.

This shorter route requires you to carry in your own gear. Pack animals can go part of the way in, but not far enough to justify using them. Because this route is shorter – only 2 to 3 days to basecamp – hiring porters to carry extra gear might be more practical than dealing with mules. From Alao the first day's hike goes to the river junction of the Culebrillas, taking anywhere from 8 to 12 hours depending on the trail conditions. The track crosses the Filo de Miliciano (almost 1,000m of ascent and descent). The Culebrillas Plain has a couple of grass huts for shelter if you don't feel like setting up a tent. If the weather is good, you'll see magnificent views of Sangay.

From Culebrillas head along a trail across Río Ramos and onto another plain with numerous cow paths. Head towards a forest and find the trail that leads up a slope and pass to the south (3,740m). The following day gets you to the Yanayacu river camp in about 4 to 6 hours. If the weather conditions were perfect, and your physical condition nearly that, you could probably make it to La Playa basecamp in one very long day. However, it's more realistic to plan on camping at Yanayacu after a day of wading through streams and crossing numerous bogs. From here to La Playa the route goes up and down constantly, through thick, rough vegetation that can cut the hands. A pair of light gloves will provide some protection. The La Playa area, at 3,600m, is reached after about 4 to 6 hours of walking from Yanayacu. On the southwest side of the mountain, this basecamp is an obvious red lava flow flanked by streams. There is a flattish platform of several hundred square metres in size which is used for the camp. Set up tents as close to the mountain as possible. There are signs of previous camps.

In 1995, with the aid of Fundacíon Natura, the World Wildlife Fund and the US Peace Corps, a refuge was constructed at La Playa. It measures 3m by 5m, with no sleeping pads, but can accommodate eight to ten people. There is a wood stove (but not much wood around the refuge) and a nearby latrine.

At the basecamp you may hear numerous explosions, but the activity in the last few years has lessened. Clouds often obscure the volcano during the day, making night-time viewing the best option. Although it is hard work to reach this point, you are still not in danger from falling rocks. The ascent to the summit can be made in some 8 hours, but changing conditions make it impossible to give a standard route. For quite some time there have been three craters on the summit, with all three active at different times and to different degrees. One friend who went in to climb was told by an experienced Ecuadorian climber that the north crater was inactive and that rocks only fell down the western face. When he got there, all three craters were active and, though there were a considerable number of rocks being blown down the west side, he found that debris was coming down all visible faces at one time or another. Another couple of friends who climbed the peak reported that red hot rocks the size of Volkswagen Beetles were being blasted out of the volcano on the north and west sides of the cone. To the south and east, only small rocks were coming down and most of these were loosened by the vibration of the eruptions and thawing by the sun. The moral of the story is that it is difficult to predict the conditions. Any descriptions will be out of date by the time you get to Sangay and inaccurate information is more dangerous than none at all. However a few general points can make a summit attempt less risky:

• Find out from your guide where the majority of rocks have been falling lately and take some time to observe for yourself.
• Most recent successful attempts have gone up the southeast face which is smooth and virtually featureless. There is no glacier, only firm, compacted snow in places.
• Remember that all routes to the summit can be dangerous. Some climbers have made it to the top without any rocks falling around them, but the risk is real.
• Move as quickly up and back down the slopes as possible and keep your head up, always looking for missiles coming your way.

An early start – about 02.30 – is essential to minimise the danger from rockfall and to make the going quicker on firm snow.

Your guide will take you to the highest point on the base above a *páramo* ridge. Be sure to have him wait for you there. Carry a compass so as not to get lost on the way back down in the invariable morning fog. Crampons and an ice axe may or may not be necessary, but it's best to bring them. The climb is not technical, but it's quite steep in parts, and it's difficult to avoid falling on your backside on the way down. Wearing two pairs of old trousers will protect you from the sharp lava rock, which rips clothes, and skin, easily. A helmet and sturdy, work-type gloves are also advised for safety. A rope is not recommended as it would severely limit your ability to dodge falling rocks. There are no good maps covering the region.

Even if you're not planning to climb, a hike to the basecamp can be a tremendous experience, especially if the weather is good. For both hiking and climbing, a good selection of waterproofs is a must, including rubber boots for the muddier sections of the trail. Attempts on the summit and hikes into the area can be made year round, but December to February are the driest months as a rule. July and August are the wettest, but other months are also very rainy.

Other routes have been reported as well. Chris Bonington was there in 1966 and records his experiences in his book *The Last Horizon*. He climbed up from the southeast via the Río Upano and Río Volcán. It took him 9 days and he wrote '...every foot of the way had to be hacked from the impenetrable entanglement presented by the undergrowth.' Doesn't sound like much fun! He also reports his ice axe turning a dull yellow-green because of the sulphurous fumes.

El Placer

El Placer is located in the western part of the park about 27km from Alao. This area was previously inhabited by settlers up until the 1980s, but it's now abandoned and overgrown with native vegetation. There is a basic and dry, ten-person refuge with a fire pit in an adjacent room. A small stove is recommended, since there is no wood cache and the wood around the refuge is usually wet. The area offers natural hot springs which are perfect for bathing, excellent trout fishing, and superb

Distance Approximately 55km round-trip
Altitude 2,850–3,950m
Rating Difficult
Time 3–4 days
Start Aloa
End Aloa
Maps IGM 1:50,000 Alao Llagtapamba and Volcán Altar, 1:25,000 IGM topo for the zone around the volcano, CT-NIV Río Culebrillas.
Other essential notes Hike on an abandoned road over a *páramo* ridge to a trail in the cloudforest that leads to hot springs.

birdwatching. Spectacled bear and mountain tapir are at home in the dense vegetation.

It's a 2-day (or marathon 1-day) trip from Alao, following the old jeep trail to Huambaya, a former community in the centre of the park, which was expelled in its entirety after the area received national park status.

Hiking directions Take the main road east out of Alao (locals can point it out) and follow it along the clearly defined track. You stay in the valley of the Río Aloa and after 4 to 5 hours cross the concrete bridge over the river. There is a small herder's hut here which would make a good camping spot. If you have access to a 4WD vehicle you can sometimes drive this far in the dry season, but only if the persistent landslides have been cleared. The distance is about 15km of gradual uphill going.

From the Río Aloa bridge continue climbing along the track 4½km up to the Laguna Negra (3,950m), a small lake which is at the pass and often fogged in. From here, descend the old road which switchbacks down the slope; there are some short cuts, but you may get lost, so it's recommended that you stay on the road. You can rent horses in Alao to take you as far as the site known as Magdalena (indistinct grassy area at 3,500m, with a sign), about 2 to 3 hours below the pass. It is another 3 to 4 hours of difficult hiking through overgrown cloudforest on a muddy switchbacking trail to reach El Placer (2,900m). Be sure to check at the ranger station in Alao about the condition of this section of the trail, as it can get overgrown and difficult to follow. Although this final section is challenging, the flowering plants, birds and occasional views make it worthwhile.

Be cautious of leaving your gear at the refuge at El Placer because a lot of locals use the area for fishing and have been known to take a few things. It's best to leave your gear in bushes if you plan an extended visit to fish or to soak in hot springs.

From the refuge you can walk 300m (20 minutes) on a very muddy trail to a river where trout fishing can be done. The turn-off for the trail to the hot springs is about 100m back along the trail that you came down to reach the refuge, and about 10m beyond a waterfall. The trail is on the right; follow it for 350m to reach a large waist-deep pool with pleasant temperatures ranging between 102°F and 105°F. The pool has a sandy bottom with cement walls on one side.

The hike out of El Placer can be gruelling; allow up to 5 hours to reach the beginning of the old road in Magdelena. The remainder of the return hike takes about the same time as it did on the way in.

The best months for hiking in the area are November through to January, although raingear and mud boots should be packed even during this 'dry' season. Abundant rain and cloudy conditions make the rest of the year predictably miserable for visitors.

Beyond El Placer It is possible to continue from El Placer, crossing the park from Aloa to the town of Palora in the Amazon basin. We quote Shane McCarthy, former Peace Corps volunteer working in the park: 'Below El Placer, for those hikers liberally endowed with energy, determination, time, and a fairly high threshold for pain and misery, there is a great bushwhack route that crosses the park longitudinally, exiting in the Amazon basin and connecting with the Puyo–Macas road. This route provides the opportunity to take in all of the existing life zones in the park, enjoy the thermal pool at El Placer, observe an incredible array of wildlife, and explore ground and historic sites such as the ghost town of Huamboya, rarely seen by human eyes.' With this said, the hike takes 7 to 10 days, depending on how many *macheteros* you have in the group. Shane says you should most definitely hire a guide, or he recommends 'updating your will and insurance policy'. The only time it makes sense to do the hike is from December to February when the rivers are low.

THE ATILLO AREA

The hike described in this section originates in the Atillo area and traverses across rough páramo past high lakes. There are a number of other possibilities using topo maps including the not-quite-completed road to Macas. You can invent one of your own treks using the IGM maps for the area. The region is wide open for adventure and exploration.

This is an area for experienced campers, hikers and mountaineers who want to get as far off the beaten track as possible.

Access The following access information covers the possible routes to Atillo, which is approached from the main city of Riobamba.

Take a bus from Quito's Terminal Terrestre. From Riobamba you can either go the Riobamba–Cebadas–Atillo route to Atillo, or via the new, more direct Riobamba–Guamote–Atillo road. Transport is scarce beyond both Cebadas and Guamote, but the road from Guamote is more direct and in better condition.

If you choose the newer route, Guamote is situated just off the Pan-American Highway, about an hour south of Riobamba. You can take the bus direct from Riobamba, or any bus heading south and ask the driver to let you off at the village entrance. The best place to stay in Guamote is Residencial Turismo Guamote, which costs about $3 per night. There are several basic restaurants in town. Not many visitors come to Guamote, so the locals are very friendly. If you bump into Milton Arguello Rivera, the director of the local high school, he may invite you to share some rum and songs with his friends. Getting from Guamote to Atillo is easiest done by hiring a truck (expect to pay about $35 for the trip). Thursday is market day in Guamote, and transport in general is much easier to come by, as few vehicles make the trip on other days.

For the Cebadas option, Cooperativa de Transportes Unidos (CTU) bus has service from Riobamba (Barrio El Dolorosa) to Cebadas. There are no places to stay in the village of Cebadas but plenty of options for camping. There are usually pick-up trucks that make this trip from Cebadas and it is likely normal bus service will be initiated in the near future. Enquire in Cebadas.

Atillo to Achupallas

Very few established hikes in Ecuador combine cross-country navigating across high *páramo* and around remote lakes with isolated villages where simple footpaths provide the only means of access. This 3- to 5-day hike goes into an area rarely visited by any outsider, let alone gringo trekkers. For this reason, it is a unique and

> **Distance** 45km
> **Altitude** 3,320–4,300m
> **Rating** Moderate to difficult
> **Time** 3–5 days
> **Start** Atillo
> **End** Achupallas
> **Maps** IGM 1:50,000 Totoras and Alausí
> **Other essential notes** This hike across *páramo* has great views of lakes, Alpine mountains and indigenous villages, and is one of Mark's favourites.

spectacular area to explore. On the other hand, it sets up a fragile situation which demands a level of responsibility from the intruder. Practising sound environmental and ecological techniques means not only preserving the natural beauty around you by treading lightly, but treating those cultures with whom you come into contact with equal care. Sweets and loose change tossed out liberally serve no purpose other than to corrupt. As an old-time American hiker once said, 'Take only photographs and leave only footprints.' There is a lot of wet ground so bring rubber boots for hiking. (See map opposite.)

Access Refer to the Access directions for the Atillo area (previous page).

Hiking directions Because of the lengthy approach, you are likely to be arriving in Atillo in the early afternoon. For camping, you can continue past Atillo and look for a suitable spot along Río Atillo. Better still, and time allowing, you could continue for another half hour to just below the Laguna Atillo, or for another 2 to 3 hours to the Laguna Iguan. Atillo is a spread-out community and the residents are suspicious of visitors. Since this area is part of Parque Nacional Sangay, locals on horseback may ask you for written permission to enter this area. To avoid this problem you can pay the entrance fee at the Ministerio de Ambiente offices in Quito, or pay on the spot.

The route follows the road out of the village for about 5 minutes, until the Laguna Atillo comes into view. The road continues up along the north shore, but as soon as you see the lake, drop south, crossing a small creek just below the road and heading through a pasture towards Río Atillo, about half an hour away. From the road you'll spot two prominent hills before Laguna Atillo. Head for the right-hand hill and you'll find camping possible between the hill and the river. If continuing on, find the best place to cross the river and then begin the climb up the middle valley (you'll see three valleys coming down into the Laguna Atillo) to the Laguna Iguan, about 1 hour away. There's no trail, but cattle tracks are everywhere. The going is easy up this steep valley, following the left-hand side of the creek, which flows from the lake. The Laguna Iguan Cocha is beautiful, situated in a big bowl with stunning views looking back to the mountains. There is obvious camping on the southeast side of the lake. A picturesque waterfall at the south end completes the scene. At night the place comes alive with the lights of a million fireflies and noisy frogs singing in chorus.

The next day involves a very rugged stretch, heading cross-country up the *páramo*. The going is wet and awkward across tussocks, or spongy clumps of vegetation, heading up to the Laguna Pocacocha, 2 hours away. Animal trails can be found occasionally to make the going a little easier, but you can't rely on them. Take a compass bearing before starting out. The route follows a wide valley with a

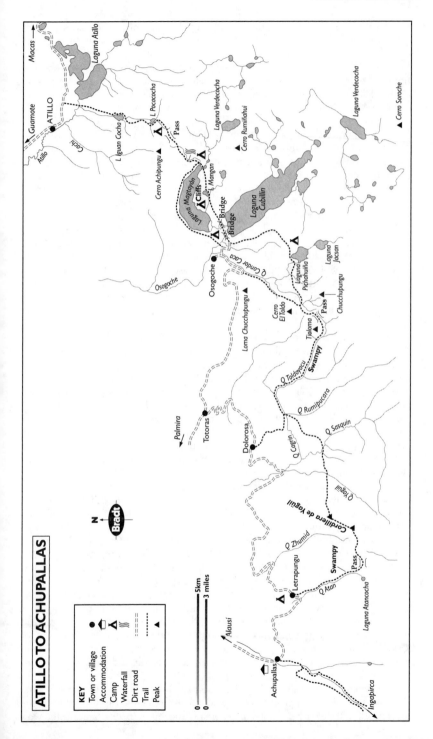

creek from Pocacocha flowing through it; keep far right on the flanks as you climb up to the lake. The area around the Laguna Pocacocha is lovely and is good for camping.

From the Laguna Pocacocha, the route climbs up to a pass at 4,300m, about 2 hours away. Again, take a compass bearing before continuing. Stay on the right side of the valley as you skirt the Laguna Pocacocha, and follow the creek as the route ascends. About halfway up the valley, the creek begins to branch out and following it will not be reliable. At this point look up towards the only grassy pass and spot a huge, rectangular-shaped rock leaning at an angle to the right. Head for this and cross the pass which is about 50m above.

An interesting side trip from the pass would be to climb Cerro Achipungo, only 360m higher. The climb is easy to the top, following the ridge up to the summit.

From the pass, it's fairly obvious where to go, but it's best to take a compass bearing on the easternmost point of the Laguna Magtayán. You can see two smaller lakes from the pass, and could also take a compass bearing on these. The descent follows a narrow creek through a marshy area which funnels down to an obvious notch. Before you get to this notch find a pass to the right and follow a cattle trail down to a large rockfall. In this section you get glimpses of the Laguna Magtayán and Osogoche. Follow a stream around to the eastern end of the Laguna Magtayán. The last 200m is a little tricky. A steep grassy chute almost literally drops you down to the lake. Hanging on to the tall grass and sliding on your backside is one method that works. It's about 2 hours from the top of the pass down to the lake. Camping near its eastern end is ideal.

The following day you have two options, skirting the right or left sides of the Laguna Magtayán. The trail on the right is straightforward and takes you to the community of Osogoche. The more interesting route on the left side heads up to a pass above a rocky cliff that blocks travel along the lake shore. Climb high early and contour over to the pass about 1 hour away. From this pass you see two lakes, the Laguna Mangan and an unnamed lake. A cow path skirts to the right of the unnamed lake. This is a good camping spot. It's then a question of easy walking across (still more) *páramo*, with the trail becoming more distinct as you continue southwest past the small lake. Cross the outlet stream of the lakes and contour around a grassy ridge until the Laguna Cubillín comes into view. Make your way west to the point between lakes Magtayán and Cubillín. There are spectacular views of the entire area here, with lots of lakes and small settlements.

(For the truly adventurous, an extra day or two could be set aside for exploring the southwest end of the Laguna Cubillín. From the map it would appear to be an incredible area, with lots of little lakes and rocky bluffs.)

The trail heads for a small settlement at the north end of Cubillín lake, but the villagers here have learned to beg from the few strangers passing through. It may be better to keep a little distance. There are foot bridges across both streams, but they are also easily waded. Once across both streams, head for the road leading into Osogoche. The villagers here are also unaccustomed to visitors and may be persistent about wanting gifts/money. As with the last community, it might be easier to avoid the village altogether, and to skirt south instead, picking up the road leading out of town. You can camp about 15 minutes to half an hour out of Osogoche, near a stream, depending on how long or short a day you choose. There is daily traffic from Osogoche to Totoras in the morning, and you can arrange to buy a meal in Osogoche.

You could continue by walking the road to Achupallas, but a more interesting route is through the high country. Head up the ridge on the west side of the Laguna Cubillín over peak 4,008 and Loma Chugchuyacu. The basin to the west does not contain two lakes as shown on the IGM map! Cross the basin and head southwest to the Laguna Pichahuiña, a good spot to camp, with opportunities to see condors. Walk around the north side of the Laguna Pichahuiña and head for Cerro El Toldo, a grassy hill to the west. Reach the pass between Cerro El Toldo and Tioloma and contour around to the pass on the southeast side of Tioloma. Drop down into the grassy U-shaped valley of Quebrada Toldoyacu. This valley is boggy because for most of it there is no stream channel, so water flows through the vegetation instead. Turn left at Quebrada Cagrín. We found a good camp spot next to Quebrada Rumipucará.

It is an easy walk from here on an established track south of Loma Yurac to the Achupallas road. If you have an extra day, heading up the rocky ridge of Cordillera de Yagüil is highly recommended for the views. Head downstream slightly and contour around Loma Santa Ana. Cross Quebrada Sasquin and find a trail on the right side of Quebrada Tiucuhuaycu that eventually crosses the ridge with the same name. Descend to Quebrada Yagüil where there is a colourful community of *chozas*. Find a water pipeline on the other side and follow it uphill to a water tank. Continue to the rocks above. From here there are spectacular views of Cerro Soroche, a seldom seen – let alone climbed – peak 20km to the east. Cerro Soroche is very Alpine-looking and is sometimes covered with snow fields. Head southwest around Cerro Atán on a trail. The walking along the ridge is quite pleasant. We crossed a pass and descended the right side of Quebrada Atán to the village of Letrapunga, but you can also continue to Atilla Puga and descend directly into Achupallas, thus avoiding the road all together. The Laguna Atancocha is beautiful, but too swampy to camp next to; there are places to camp above 3,920m, next to the stream. Below this elevation the valley sides are steep. You could also arrange to stay in the village of Letrapungu.

In Achupallas there are no hotels or restaurants, but you may be able to stay in the school. Contact Jorge Merchan or Alonso Zea (both on the main square near the church) for meals or a bed. Transport is available to Alausí, about 2 hours away. Trucks leave at 07.00 for Alausí and return at around lunch time. You can also get a truck to Alausí for about $20. Even better continue along on the Inca road to Ingapirca.

THE INCA ROAD TO INGAPIRCA

Distance Approximately 38km
Altitude 3,100–4,300m
Rating Moderate
Time 3 days
Start Achupallas
End Ingapirca
Maps IGM 1:50,000 Alausí, Juncal, and Cañar, or you can get by with IGM 1:100,000 Cañar
Other essential notes One of the classic Ecuadorian treks along an Inca road through the *páramo* to the Inca ruins of Incapirca.

At the height of its power the Inca Empire extended from northern Ecuador to central Chile. This huge area was linked by a complex system of well-made and maintained roads, the longest of which stretched over 5,000km from Quito to Talca, south of Santiago in Chile. This was the greatest communication system the

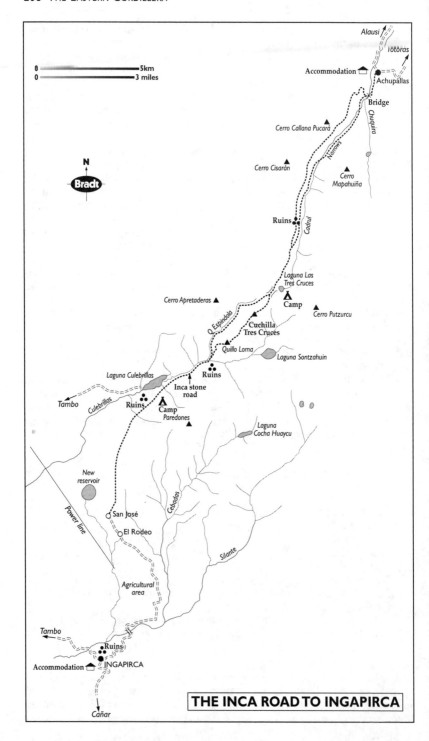

THE INCA ROAD TO INGAPIRCA

world had known, greater even than the roads of the Roman Empire. Although today the road is in a state of disrepair and in many areas the route has been lost or forgotten, it is still possible to find and walk along some remnants of this marvellous road system. There is a popular segment of this trail system at the southern end of the Central Valley which leads to Ingapirca, the most important Inca ruin in Ecuador. This 2- to 3-day hike is a fascinating glimpse of an Andean rural life which has changed little in hundreds of years.

Access The nearest major town to the beginning of the hike is Alausí, where there are several cheap hotels. It is situated just off the Pan-American Highway, 290km south of the capital. Buses go there from Terminal Terrestre in Quito, but it may be easier first to go to Riobamba and then change to an Alausí bus at Riobamba's Terminal Terrestre. From Alausí you can get an early start, taking any southbound bus on the Pan-American Highway and asking to be let off at La Moya, about 10km from Alausí. (You can camp in La Moya by the swimming pool, with a nearby spring for clean drinking water.) When you reach La Moya, stand by the left fork of the road junction just past the bridge to hitch a ride up a steep and spectacular mountain road to the village of Achupallas, some 12km away. There are also several trucks a day that leave Alausí at around noon bound for Achupallas. Either way you should be able to get from Alausí to Achupallas in a few hours. A more direct, yet more expensive, alternative is to hire a truck in Alausí (near the Hostal Tekendama) to take you to Achupallas. This takes about an hour to an hour and a half and drivers charge between $5 and $7 per person for the trip.

Hiking directions In Achupallas head for the white arch below the plaza; take the track left (to the south) of the arch and soon pass the cemetery on your right. There are two options: follow the low road along the river, or the high road below cliffs on the right side of the Río Cadrul valley. To take the high road, after you cross the river on a bridge, switchback up the hillside on the road. Eventually the road/track heads up the valley. The other option is to follow footpaths on the other side of the bridge (there are several options – it's best to ask locally) along the west side of the Río Cadrul. Some 30 to 40 minutes out of town you re-cross the river on another footbridge and then follow the east bank of the Río Cadrul (marked as Quebrada Gadrui on some maps). You are headed for a rocky narrow in the stream between a pyramidal hill to your left (Cerro Mapahuiña, 4,365m) and a flat-topped hill to your right (Cerro Callana Pucará).

As you get closer to this narrow you will see a well-defined notch which you will have to climb. This is interesting as the trail goes up through a hole in the rock: it's a very tight squeeze and it can be difficult to pass your pack through. Soon after the notch you should cross the river (it can be jumped in dry season) to climb to the upper trail on the far side. The Inca road contours along the west side of the Cadrul valley as it becomes more U-shaped and open. At 3,900m you reach the foundations of an Inca town. Within several kilometres you reach the Laguna Las Tres Cruces (by now you are on the Juncal 1:50,000 map). To get to this lake takes about 6 hours of steady hiking from Achupallas, but you can find flat spots near the stream to camp earlier if you wish. The area around the lake is boggy, so it is best to camp on the bluffs next to the inlet or outlet streams.

The following day you follow the trail up beyond the lake and across a pass to the southwest. There is a shallow seasonal pond near the pass and a pile of stones marking the way (probably Incan). There are two paths beyond the pass – an upper road along the Cuchilla Tres Cruces or a boggier route in the valley of Quebrada Espíndola. For the upper Inca road, contour up the ridge crossing some worn rocks. Much of the road is deeply eroded and seems like a streambed in places. Below you is the valley of the Quebrada Espíndola, and the lower road is plainly visible. Walk along the top of this ridge and admire the wonderful views as you follow it to its final peak, Quillo Loma. To your left is wild trackless countryside with many lakes, the largest of which is the Laguna Sontzahuín. This area would doubtless provide several days of excellent camping off the beaten track.

The trail becomes quite distinct again at the top of the ridge and then descends as a rocky path to the left of Quillo Loma to the lush and boggy valley bottom beyond where it meets the lower trail. You can quite clearly make out the remains of the old Inca road as a straight line in the grass at the bottom of the valley. At the point where the road crosses the stream you'll find the remains of the foundations of an Inca bridge. This stream has to be crossed; it's best to take off your boots and wade across. There is an obvious trail on the left-hand side of the Quebrada Espíndola which leads you past the southeastern shores of the Laguna Culebrillas and to some Inca ruins known as Paredones (ruined walls) on a bluff above the lake.

Although it is only an easy half day from the Laguna Las Tres Cruces to Paredones, this is an excellent place to camp, relax and enjoy the countryside. To preserve the area, campsites should be set up near the ruins rather than in them, and you should make an effort to carry out or burn rubbish you find around the ruins.

The ruins themselves consist of a large main structure whose walls are still more or less standing; there are three main rooms and two smaller ones. The stonework is crude compared to Ingapirca and the famous Peruvian ruins, and there is no evidence of typical Inca features such as trapezoidal niches. Around this main structure are the tumbled remains of several smaller buildings. Animal life is rather limited; there are caracara hawks and cinclodes. Flowers are prolific, however, and you can expect to see gentians, lupins and daisies, among others.

The final day brings you to the ruins of Ingapirca. The walk will take you some 4 to 5 hours, which thus leaves you with enough time to explore the ruins and then reach a town to spend the night.

From Paredones head southwest on the Inca road, which here is at its full width of about 7m. The trail soon swings south and continues straight across the countryside, but it is extremely boggy. The scenery is rather eerie, with huge boulders strewn around like a giant's playthings. Frogs whistle repetitively and brooks bubble up from underground. You pass a new reservoir on your right that is not shown on any maps. After 2 or 3 hours the Inca road becomes difficult to follow. Head for the village of San José and take a right turn on a dirt track to the village of El Rodeo. From here follow the road to Ingapirca, which should now be in view. It seems closer than it is since you need to contour around several valleys. The terrain shows increasing signs of cultivation and habitation. You end up walking past fields and houses to a road which leads to the ruins themselves.(See Inca Road to Ingapirca map, page 208.)

Ingapirca

This area was occupied by the Cañaris for some 500 years before the construction of the Inca site. In the 1490s the Inca Huayna Capac conquered the area now known as Ecuador and soon after the construction of Ingapirca (in Quechua, Inca walls) began. Its existence has long been known about by academics, and the plan drawn by La Condamine in 1739 was accurate enough to be used as a basis for the modern excavations of the ruins which began in the late 1960s.

Ingapirca, with its close fitting, mortarless stonework and typical trapezoidal windows and niches, is the finest example of imperial Inca construction in the country, and was evidently built by stone masons trained in Cuzco. The precise functions of the site can only be guessed at, but archaeologists think that the most evident and well-preserved structure, an elliptical building known as the temple of the sun, had religious or ceremonial purposes. The less well-preserved buildings were probably granaries or store houses, and part of the complex was almost certainly used as a *tambo*, or stopping place, for the runners taking messages along the Inca road from Quito to Tomebamba (present-day Cuenca).

Ingapirca is 3,160m above sea level. An entrance fee of about $4 is charged. There is a new visitors' hut and entrance station, along with an excellent site museum. It is funded by the Banco Central and is well laid out, with many interesting maps and exhibits. A brochure in English is also available for a dollar, with decent photos and text. The nearby village of Ingapirca has several basic stores, restaurants and hostels. One recommendation is the hostel and restaurant Inti Huasi, owned by Julia Serrano, whose father has been a guide at the ruins for more than 25 years. Buses leave every 3 hours for the Pan-American Highway, until 16.00. A truck costs about $10 for the trip to El Tambo. There are also basic hotels in Cañar, about 17km from Ingapirca and on the Pan-American Highway.

GIMA TO NUEVA TARQUI

Distance Approximately 60km
Altitude 880–3,450m
Rating Difficult
Time 3–4 days
Start Gima
End Nueva Tarqui
Maps Gima, Amazonas and Gualaquiza
Other essential notes Hike from the southern Sierra to the Oriente, passing through friendly villages.

This well-worn but physically demanding mule trail is testament to the tenacity of poor Ecuadorians seeking a better life on unsettled lands at the foot of the Andes. Most of the hike follows the Río San Miguel de Cuyes (Saint Michael of Guinea Pigs River) along which there are several communities built-up entirely without road access. One wonders at the number of mule trips required to lay down a concrete playing field, build a cinderblock church, and span a stream with a tin-roofed bridge. These people have worked hard to carve out a civilised life in the wilderness. Most of the families arrived from the Sierra town of Gima, crossing the Cordillera Moriré (I Will Die Ridge) and clearing the forested mountain slopes to make pasture for cattle. Sections of the valley were too steep to clear and some good primary forest remains near the trail. A road from Gima was started by some well-meaning US Peace Corps volunteers in the early 1970s and now switchbacks a few kilometres below Cordillera Moriré where it ends in deep mud. The farmers below are still waiting for it to be extended down their valley to the Oriente town of Gualaquiza. They claim it would be a much quicker route than the current road from Cuenca. Once you walk this trail you will understand why it may be many years before a road is completed.

Before the current wave of settlement, this area was likely a wilderness crossed and hunted with trepidation, separating two very different and at times conflicting cultures, the lowland Shuar and the highland Quechua. The valley may have been a trading route, but there are no known ruins along the route, so it probably was never heavily populated. The modern villages in the headwaters are all Quechua, but Shuar influence increases downstream. Everyone seems to speak Spanish.

It is curiously warm at higher elevations (around 2,500m). The crest of the Andes is relatively low (3,400m) here, which may explain the presence of warm Amazon air. Above the pastoral valleys the forests are relatively intact. Distant peaks such as Cerro El Altar and Cerro Manga Urco are in untouched wilderness. Locals say there are monkeys, tapirs and Andean spectacled bears in the area. Encouragingly, the Quechua claim not to hunt them.

The headwaters of many streams and rivers in the area are a tea colour, from the tannin in the water. The soils here are poorer than in the northern Sierra and form a thin blanket over high-grade metamorphic rock. The groundwater is generally low in dissolved solids and sediment, and instead seeps out rich in the organic tannin produced by plants. Natural landslides are evident from the scars on the mountain slopes, a process accelerated by forest clearing.

Although this trail is the lifeline for about a thousand people (several days a week traders walk up from the town of La Florida to buy cattle and trade with the villagers) very few gringos have travelled this route. The people are courteous and friendly, but they're also curious, and may suspect that you are looking for gold.

This walk is less interesting than others from a natural history perspective, but it is culturally compelling. It offers a window into the process of colonisation in Ecuador, and the works and unfulfilled dreams of its settlers. The area is unique and beautiful, and it's perhaps worth spending a few extra days here to get to know one of the villages and hike up a mountainside into primary forest.

Weather and times to go The dry summer months are September to March, but the best months are November and December. It can get cold over the Cordillera Moriré, but the rest of the hike is moderately warm.

Equipment Bring raingear and rubber boots. The trail is a bit rocky so you might opt for wet feet and heavy leather hiking boots instead. The trail is obvious and heavily travelled, so a machete is unnecessary. It is possible to camp, but to save weight you could sleep at the schools in the communities. There is plenty of water, but bring iodine pills. There are a few basic stores in Gima, but it's best to buy food in Cuenca.

Access Gima is easily accessed from Cuenca by a bus that leaves from Feria Libre at Avenida Las Americas y Ramijio Crespo at 06.00 and 13.00. The trip takes about 1½ hours. Gima is an interesting colonial village with a phone service and several small restaurants, and shops in which to buy food and other provisions. It is worth stopping by the orchid greenhouses of the Bosque Protector de Tambillo. Several leaders of the community of Gima have started a sustainable orchid business, harvesting from 215 known orchid species in a protected forest along the route you will be walking. There is no regular transport service to Cordillera Moriré, but ask around the plaza if anyone is heading out that way, or hire a pick-up truck for about $15. Since the road deteriorates on the other side of the Cordillera, the truck drivers only take you as far as the crest. It is also possible to do the hike in reverse from Nueva Tarqui, but it's more difficult since it is uphill.

Hiking directions Starting at the crest of Cordillera Moriré follow the road down to hummocky terrain with cloudforest shrubs. There is a short cut that eliminates a switchback on the descent but we missed it. You reach the road head in about 2¹/₂ hours. The forest to your left is the Bosque Protector de Tambillo, where the orchids are harvested. From here the trail climbs up and down over the small hills, passing to the left of Cerro Guachupalas. Another 1¹/₂ hours of hiking takes you to an intersection: the right fork descends to Espíritu Playa; the left fork descends to San Miguel de Cuyes. Taking the left fork, descend to a stream crossing the Río Boradel. Descend the ridge for 1¹/₂ hours to re-cross the Río Boradel on a covered bridge near the confluence with Río Moriré. Traverse and descend the trail steeply to a suspension bridge over the Río Moriré. Ascend and traverse pastures on the trail to the village of San Miguel de Cuyes. It takes about 7 to 8 hours to walk from the crest of Cordillera Moriré to San Miguel de Cuyes. There is a grade school and church here, which you can probably arrange to stay in – be sure to offer to pay for the privilege.

The village of Amazonas is about 2 hours from San Miguel de Cuyes and also has places to sleep. There is a fork just before the town; make sure you take the left fork to pass through the town. From Amazonas it is about an hour to Ganazhuma, a pleasant village on the other side of the Río San Miguel de Cuyes. Here there is also a school and several stores in which to buy snacks and colas. An interesting side trip would be to head up to Los Angeles from Ganazhuma and explore the forests to the south.

The river valley of the Río San Miguel de Cuyes below Ganazhuma narrows and there are very few houses. Plan to make it all the way to La Florida, which is a good 7 hours of difficult hiking. The trail descends in and ascends out of the numerous gorges of tributary streams flowing into the Río San Miguel de Cuyes. The views are excellent of the other side of the valley (including the waterfall Chorrera San Vicente) and the interesting covered bridges over the streams. In an emergency you could sleep on one of the bridges.

About 2km outside of La Florida the trail flattens out and the village also has a school where you can sleep under the porch. From La Florida it is about 30 minutes to La Punta, where *rancheras* arrive in the early morning and afternoon to transport people back to Nueva Tarqui, which is about a 20 minute drive away. Frequent *rancheras* make the 1 hour trip from Nueva Tarqui to Gualaquiza, where there are several hotels and restaurants to choose from. Buses from Gualaquiza head north to Macas (9 hours), south to Loja (8 hours) and over the cordillera to Cuenca (8 hours).

SARAGURO

Saraguro is home to the Cañari indigenous group, who fiercely resisted the Inca conquest and to this day maintain cultural independence and pride. Sunday is market day, with a chance to see the distinctive Canári dress and perhaps buy some pigs, vegetables and handicrafts. The countryside around Saraguro is well worth exploring. You can hike to the caves of Sinincapa, 2km outside of town, where there are several pools, including the Inca's bathtub. Take the road north out of town and ask for directions. Getting to the Virgencaca waterfall, located on the Río Huaylashi, takes a full day on foot. There are two possible routes – Tuncarta–Tambopamba–Oñacapa or Namarin–Tambopamba–Oñacapa – both on jeep tracks. The falls are about a mile down from Oñacapa and it's best to have someone show you the way. You can climb Puglla from Saraguro or Cerro de Areos from the village of Manu. Not many travellers visit this area and there are many more day-hikes to be discovered. You can easily arrange a home stay with a Cañari family or try the Residencia Armijos in Saraguro.

Saraguro to Yacuambi trek
Mike Kraft

> **Distance** 37km
> **Altitude** 1,000–3,400m
> **Rating** Moderate
> **Time** 2–3 days
> **Start** Saraguro
> **End** Yacuambi
> **Maps** IGM 1:50,000 Saraguro and San José de Yacuambi
> **Other essential notes** This Sierra to Oriente route follows a pre-Columbian trail still used by Saraguro cattle ranchers.

This 2- to 3-day hike from Saraguro to Yacuambi is the premier Andes to Amazon trek in southern Ecuador. From the pastures and farmland of the indigenous Quechua highlanders, through a lake region surrounded by rocky peaks and chilly *páramo* meadows, and descending to the jungle town of Yacuambi, the old trading route promises hikers a wide range of natural beauty and cultural richness.

Equipment Even in the summer months of November and December, you can count on rain at some point along the trail. That means waterproof tents and full raingear. Be careful to keep the contents of your pack dry. Warm headgear, gloves and heavy sleeping bags are a must for camping in the *páramo*. Hiking boots are fine, but anyone who can handle the lesser degree of comfort might take a hint from the locals and tackle the trail with rubber boots. You may get blisters, but at least your feet will stay dry.

Access The trek begins near the town of Saraguro, which is easily accessed from the southern Sierra cities of Loja (1½ hours) or Cuenca (3 hours). Food and basic supplies can be picked up in Saraguro. Buses frequently depart from the central park; take one northbound on the Pan-American Highway towards Cuenca. Ask to be dropped off in the village of Urdaneta, only a few kilometres north of Saraguro. The other transportation option is getting to Urdaneta by pick-up truck which should cost less than $5. Pick-up trucks are easily found in the streets around the central park or market, and most drivers are familiar with the trailhead leading to Yacuambi. For a few dollars more the driver may be willing to take you along the rough road leading off the Pan-American Highway to the beginning of the footpath. Otherwise, villagers can point the way, which leads east from the highway.

Hiking directions The first few kilometres of the trail are a seldom-travelled dirt road which leads past mud-brick farmhouses, small garden plots, and pasture land dotted with shepherds and flocks of sheep. The government plans to eventually construct a road directly linking Saraguro and Yacuambi; consequently, the initial section of the trail is scarred by the early stages of construction. This road will reportedly follow the old trail described herein, so the opportunity to experience this trek may disappear in the distant future. Since the harsh terrain favours the interests of hikers (rather than road construction crews) it will probably be a number of years before a road finally replaces this enchanting trail.

At the time of writing (spring 2003), the developed part of the road ends at a small footbridge. About 100m after this bridge, hikers arrive at a grove of tall pine trees and a fork in the trail. Follow the wider path to the left, which begins to climb steeply uphill. As you ascend, the farmland and pastures will shortly give way to classic Andean *páramo*, and the trail itself undergoes a dramatic change as well. This route dates from the days of the Inca Empire, and the path looks every bit as old as its 500 years. Nearly 2m wide in areas, parts of the trail are paved with large interlocking stones, worn smooth (and slippery in the rain, as we learned) by centuries of human and livestock traffic. The *páramo* section of the trail is occasionally travelled by the Saragurans, riding horses up to the highlands from Yacuambi. These intrepid walkers are often dressed only in cut-off jeans and T-shirts. It is not uncommon for locals, even without horses, to tackle the entire trail in one very long day.

Grumbling about bad weather aside, the wild fluctuations that characterise the *páramo* climate usually provide intermittent clear and dry periods. In November and December, the best months for the hike, the entire trek is often rain-free. With clear skies, views along the trail are breathtaking, with sweeping vistas of the Andes' eastern peaks and the wide central valley to the west. Throughout the highlands, the trail is easy to follow as it snakes along the mountainsides.

As you progress through the highlands, you will cross two stone bridges, located 4 to 5 hours from the beginning of the old path. The first bridge crosses Río San Antonio, tumbling down a rocky streambed in a crashing series of rapids and small waterfalls. About an hour later, you cross the Río Negro. On a high plain about an hour from the Río Negro, the trail splits, at the only significant junction on the highland trail. The trail on the left leads eventually to the jungle village of Tutupali, about 10km north of Yacuambi. Continue to the right to travel directly to Yacuambi.

From the junction, you will soon pass Cerro La Voladora to the left, one of the most notable rock formations along the trail. The summit is topped by a huge boulder, which some say appears to be flying when seen from a distance; hence the peak's name, which means 'the flying mountain' in Spanish. After passing Cerro La Voladora, hikers arrive at the lake district, where brilliant, blue-green *lagunas* shine like jewels in the stark *páramo* landscape. The first group of three lakes lies a few hundred metres to the south of the trail, and offers a promising side trek. Hikers (or at least those undeterred by local legends that the lakes are haunted and swallow up trespassers) may wish to head off across the soggy *páramo* to explore the lakes and the vast trackless area surrounding them.

About half an hour after passing these lakes, the trail threads between two more lakes; one to the left, and – a short distance later – another smaller pond directly to the right of the trail. These lakes lie at the foot of the Cerro Condorcillo, which towers over the trail to the north, and marks the highest point on the trek.

Shortly after Cerro Condorcillo, you begin the long descent into the jungle. The weather becomes noticeably warmer as you descend the eastern slopes of the Andes, as warm air rises up from the Oriente. From the heights of the final mountain pass, you see the lush green mountain-tops of the Andes-Amazonian transitional zone, afloat in an endless sea of clouds rolling in from the lowlands. After about an hour's descent, the trail crosses another stone bridge, over the Río Corral Huaycu.

There are a number of good reasons for camping near the Corral Huaycu bridge. Nice campsites abound on patches of level, grassy meadow surrounding the bridge, and the river offers a good, easily accessed water supply. What makes this campsite special, however, is watching the first rays of the morning sun explode over the sprawling Amazon basin.

From the Río Corral Huaycu, a hike of about 8 hours leads down to Yacuambi, so start early if you want to reach town by the end of the day. Within half an hour of the bridge crossing, you will enter the misty confines of the cloudforest and begin a long, meandering ridge hike. Views from the ridge-tops are, again, stunning, as the mountainsides drop precipitously to the jungle below. Many species of birds are abundant, and local hunters report tapirs and the odd monkey troop in the cloudforest. However, extreme vigilance and plenty of luck are needed if you hope to see any of the larger animals.

The hiking on this final day is almost entirely downhill, and your knees (and almost everything else) will be sore by the end of the day. Luckily, though, plenty of inspiration to push on is found in the vistas across the jungle hills. Notable is the towering waterfall across the valley, tumbling out of the mountains into the Río Garcelan. About 2 to 3 hours into the morning you will start to see signs of civilisation, including cleared jungle pastures and the occasional isolated farmstead. Around this area you will encounter another trail junction. The main route to Yacuambi is on the left, and the smaller branching trails along the way that lead into the pastures and farms are to be avoided.

Upon entering this inhabited agricultural area, local people will be able to point you in the right direction if confusion arises. One generous Saraguran woman insisted that our group stop by her farmhouse for a few cups of *chicha* (a thick, lightly alcoholic drink made from fermented yucca or corn), to fortify us for the remaining hours of the hike. We happily obliged.

Continuing along the mountainside and passing a few scattered homes, you will pass a small school building. Proceed past the school for another hour or so, and you will arrive at another, older schoolhouse to the left of the trail. From here begins the final 2-hour descent into Yacuambi, along a series of jungle switchbacks leading down the mountain. The trail is straightforward, though it does pass through a steep area which recently had a landslide, so careful footing is required. Arriving at a small cluster of homes at the bottom of the mountain, hike for another 15 minutes to a suspension bridge over the Río Yacuambi. The river is a welcome site, and hikers will be grateful for a chance to cool off and clean up with a quick dip. From the bridge, a gravel road leads into the town of Yacuambi, about 30 minutes further on.

Buses depart from the central park in Yacuambi to Zamora every 2 hours or so. Buses from the Cooperativa Zamora leave for the city of Zamora throughout the day, and two buses from the Cooperative Cariamanga depart Yacuambi for Loja at 22.00 and 04.30. The 22.00 bus continues from Loja back to Saraguro, native home of many of the inhabitants of the Yacuambi valley.

THE VILCABAMBA VALLEY AND PARQUE NACIONAL PODOCARPUS

The Vilcabamba valley, located in the southern province of Loja, is an area of rolling hills and lush vegetation that ranges from tropical montane cloudforest to stark *páramo*. The valley, at 1,500m, is surrounded by forested mountains nearing an altitude of 3,500m. With the dramatic snow-capped volcanoes attracting the majority of attention in the central and northern parts of the country, this beautiful area is often overlooked by hikers. Access is from the city of Loja which, being the commercial centre of the province, is served by buses from all parts of the country. There is also an airport about an hour away, with daily flights (except on Sunday) from Quito and Guayaquil. Vilcabamba is about 45 minutes by road south of Loja. Buses leave frequently from Azuay and Guerrero on the west side of Loja, across the river.

The Vilcabamba Valley

Vilcabamba has for many years been famous as the 'Valley of Longevity'. Based on a single anthropological study done some years ago, international attention was drawn to the valley inhabitants who supposedly lived to be well over 100 years old. The excellent climate and simple, unhurried lifestyle in this peaceful valley were said to be major contributing factors. Further scientific research has failed to substantiate the initial research, but the legend persists and gives the area a certain claim to fame.

The valley is popular with travellers looking for a place to take it easy. The village of Vilcabamba is a small town, and horses can be rented for excursions into the countryside. There are some charming places to stay, one of the most popular being the cabañas of Madre Tierra. The simple bungalows, rustic sauna (with mud baths), home-cooked, mostly vegetarian meals, and gardens of colourful flowers make it an excellent base for hikes around the area. Owner Jaime Mendoza and Canadian wife Durga are wonderful people and excellent sources of information. About 4km south of town, the cheaper and equally friendly Cabañas Río Yambala are run by Charlie and Sarah (tel: 593 7 2580299, email: rioyambala@yahoo.com). Day-hikes and longer excursions are only limited by one's imagination. The IGM 1:50,000 Vilcabamba map shows a number of trails, and local backpackers can suggest many more.

One short trip worth making is to the local zoo. It's about a 20-minute walk out of the town centre. Follow the road on the north side of the plaza and go east, crossing a bridge and continuing uphill. The road angles to the right (southeast) and you'll follow it until it reaches a junction, with a school on the right. Take the smaller dirt road on the right and continue downhill until you see the zoo sign. The collection of animals – including monkeys, spectacled bears, ocelots and a variety of large birds – is somewhat interesting, but what makes the trip worthwhile is the large greenhouse devoted solely to the cultivation of orchids. There are over 30 varieties – some quite rare – which have been collected from areas throughout the province.

Cerro Mandango

Distance 5km
Altitude 1,560–2,022m
Rating Easy–moderate
Time 3–4 hours
Start Vilcabamba
End Vilcabamba
Maps IGM 1:50,000 Vilcabamba
Other essential notes A pleasant half-day-hike up a peak to the west of Vilcabamba.

A popular day-hike is the climb up Cerro Mandango, a rocky peak just to the west of town. From the main plaza in Vilcambamba, walk south on the main highway for about 10 minutes, to a gravel road on the right and a house with terracotta roofing. Walk though a gate and find the trail at the back of the house. Continue up towards Mandango, passing powerlines until you reach the ridge and the first white cross. Most people stop here and enjoy the views, since the rest of the trail is a bit exposed.

To continue to the summit, follow the trail along the ridge to the left until you reach a cliff, then traverse around the right side of the mountain. Reach a gully in about 5 minutes and then climb to a left-traversing trail, which is very exposed. Finish with a steep climb up to the summit. It is about 30 minutes from the first cross to the second cross on the summit. The descent to town takes less than an hour.

For more demanding excursions, Parque Nacional Podocarpus, found just to the north of Vilcabamba, is a magnificent hiking area with much potential.

Parque Nacional Podocarpus

Parque Nacional Podocarpus was established by the Ministerio de Agricultura y Ganaderia on December 15 1982. The park is now managed by the Ministerio de Ambiente, with help from numerous organisations, including the Embassy of Holland, The Nature Conservancy, Conservation International, and about a dozen local NGOs, Arco Iris being the most active. This park, along with Cajas, are examples of local conservation successes in Ecuador – the people living around the park respect and value it. Most of the mining activities were removed from the park in 1994, and areas in the buffer zone are being reforested by concerned landowners. The dollars generated by ecotourism have played a large role in convincing the general population that conservation makes sense.

Podocarpus is the scientific name for a type of conifer tree – the only one native to Ecuador. This huge tree can occasionally be found with trunks of 3m in diameter and growing up to 40m in height. However, its fine, rose-coloured wood is highly prized, and the pressure of logging has resulted in the elimination of this magnificent conifer from much of the Ecuadorian sierra. Today the majority of the remaining reserves now exist within the park's boundaries.

The park spans an area of 146,280 hectares, much of which is unspoiled cloudforest between the highland city of Loja and the city of Zamora in the Oriente. Divided by the Cordillera El Nudo de Sabanilla mountain range, the park ranges in altitude from 1,000m to 3,600m. Six distinct life zones, from Amazonian rainforest to high Andean *páramo*, provide suitable habitats for a wide array of plants and animals. It is, for example, one of the few remaining protected areas for the elusive spectacled bear. Other mammals found in the park include the mountain tapir, the sloth, the Andean wolf (which is actually a fox) and the puma. The birdlife is especially noteworthy, with such species as guans, toucans, woodpeckers, flycatchers, swifts, tanagers, hummingbirds and parrots much in evidence.

There are three principal entrances into the park. The Cajanuma Park Station is approached from Loja on the western side of the park, the San Francisco visitors' centre is approached from the north side of the park, and the Bombuscara Park Station is located on the Zamora side in the Oriente. All three locations have basic refuges or cabins where small groups can sleep or set up tents nearby. The offices of the Ministerio de Ambiente are located in Loja on Sucre and Imbabura (tel: 593 7 2585421, email: podocam@impsat.net.ec).

Fundación Ecológica Arco Iris has a strong interest in preserving the forests of Podocarpus and southern Ecuador. They have education programmes for children, assist scientists, and are working to keep mining interests out of the park. They also own several reserves, including Tambo Negro, a dry forest near the Peruvian border. Arco Iris is one of the most serious NGOs in Ecuador working for conservation. For more information on hikes in the Loja area contact their offices in Loja. Office locations can be obtained at the Ministerio de Ambiente office in Loja.

Weather and times to go Being so heavily forested, with a broad range of elevations running from the highlands to the edge of the Oriente, the weather within the park is a combination of many climatic zones. This mainly means that when it's raining in the highlands from February through to April, it rains in

Podocarpus, and when it's raining in the Oriente from May through to August, it rains in Podocarpus. And of course even during the dry season it can rain! The best month for visiting either side of the park is November, with a somewhat dry period of grace between September and January. On the Cajanuma side the rain is a major impediment; due to the altitude it is quite cold and potentially hypothermic. On the Zamora side this is less of a problem. Here the rain is just wet and refreshing, rather than a major bother.

Equipment If it's not already obvious, good raingear is an essential part of the equipment list, along with the usual tent, stove, sleeping bag, etc. Sturdy, waterproof jungle boots are best, but you can temporarily mistreat you feet and get by with simple rubber boots (*botas para agua*). Bring plenty of plastic bags to keep spare clothes and other items dry.

Maps Along with the rather vague yet functional map of the park available from the Ministerio de Ambiente office, the 1:100,000 IGM Gonzanamá map gives a good overview of the Vilcabamba side of the park, and the 1:50,000 maps of Ríos Sabinilla and Vilcabamba will serve for the hikes. On the Zamora side, the 1:50,000 maps of Zamora and Cordillera de Tzunantza cover a fair bit of the area but cannot be purchased at IGM.

Cajanuma Ranger Station park entrance
Access The turn-off to the Cajanuma Park Station is only 10km outside of Loja, on the main road to Vilcabamba. You can take one of the numerous Loja–Vilcabamba buses or hire a taxi for about $6. The entrance fee is $10 for foreigners and $2 for residents, which needs to be paid at the entrance gate near the turn-off. The road winds up a ridge for 8km, into cloudforest and to the park station, with great views of the Loja valley. This makes a good 2-hour walk, since the only traffic would be other hikers visiting the park.

Hikes within the area At the ranger station, there are several short hiking trails, one of which takes you up through temperate forests full of mountain tanagers to a prominent ridge for some beautiful views over the valley. There is a refuge with gas stoves and they charge $3 for foreigners and $2 for residents. There are also four cabins which can be rented for $3 per person.

There are four principal trails, which start at the station and are well marked. The Oso de Anteojos trail is a short 400m interpretive trail. The Bosque Nublado trail is a slightly longer trail (700m) with some good views.

El Mirador trail

Distance 5km
Altitude 2,800–3,400m
Rating Moderate
Time 4 hours
Start Cajanuma ranger station
End Cajanuma ranger station
Maps IGM 1:50,000 Río Sabinilla
Other essential notes A great day-hike through cloudforest and up into *páramo*, with views of Loja.

The El Mirador trail is a 5km trail that climbs up to the *páramo* and loops back around to the station. The first half of the trail is moderately steep, but manageable with children, but the descent on the second half has a very steep section where scrambling is required. The total hiking time is about 4 hours. Good birding opportunities abound, and include the chance to see chestnut-bellied cotinga, masked mountain tanager, neblina metaltail, mouse-coloured thistletail and bearded guan.

Laguna de Compadre

Distance 30km round-trip
Altitude 2,800–3,350m
Rating Moderate–difficult
Time 2 days
Start Cajanuma ranger station
End Cajanuma ranger station
Maps IGM 1:50,000 Río Sabanilla
Other essential notes A great day-hike through cloudforest and up into *páramo*, with views of Loja.

A longer hike (14.6km) requiring an overnight camp heads up to the Laguna de Compadre, which is actually several lakes in a high *páramo* setting. A steep trail with great cloudforest vegetation leads up from the ranger station, crosses the cordillera and finally gets you to the lakes at 3,200m in about 6 to 8 hours. Follow the beginning of the El Mirador trail and at the Y, just after reaching the open *páramo*, take a right and follow the muddy track to the lake. Beyond, the trail is marked, but it is important to stay on the spine of the cordillera as trails branch off the main trail. From here there are views of the Vilcabamba valley and the uncut watershed of the Río Sabinilla.

There are other, longer and more adventurous excursions possible; enquire in Loja at the Ministerio de Ambiente offices (located in Loja, on Sucre and Imbabura).

San Francisco station
Access The San Francisco station is a new and well-kept lodge on the road between Loja and Zamora (Km 22).

Hiking There are several short trails to explore here, including the Sendero Los Romerillos – which passes by several Podocarpus trees – the Sendero Bosque Nublado, the Sendero Las Golondrinas, and the longer Sendero de Los Colonos. Arrangements can be made to stay here with the Ministerio de Ambiente office in Loja (see above).

Bombuscara ranger station park entrance
Access This entrance is located outside of Zamora on the eastern side of the park. The vegetation is much more tropical here and the climate more tolerable. From Loja you can take a bus; Transportes Viajeros or Transportes Loja both make the 2 to 3 hour trip several times a day. The ride across the cordillera and the drop down to the Oriente side is spectacular. Zamora has a few simple places to stay, Hostal Seyma ($3.50) just off the plaza being one of the best. You can also go directly to the park entrance (the easiest way to get there is to hire a taxi) and walk the 20 minutes

to the refuge to camp there. Before leaving Zamora, however, it would be best to stop at the Ministerio de Ambiente office, which is on the main road just as you enter Zamora. Look for a large Ministerio de Ambiente sign on the right. Here you can get a map, pay your entrance fee and talk with the park guardians.

Hiking around the area For birdwatchers, the Bombuscara area is especially exciting. You don't have to wander far from the guard station to see an incredible variety of bird species. There are numerous day-hikes to explore including the Green Jay, the Higuerones, the Mirador, the Poderosa Waterfall, the Chimosa Waterfall and the Campesino trails. There is a photocopied map available – as well as information on longer excursions – at the park offices.

QUEBRADA HONDA

Distance 21km
Altitude Approximately 1,320–2,700m
Rating Moderate
Time 2–3 days
Start Quebrada Honda
End Tapala
Maps IGM 1:50,000 Yangana, Valladolid
Other essential notes A pleasant hike through cloudforests and villages south of Podocarpus.

Quebrada Honda is a deep valley surrounded by cloudforest peaks just beyond the southern boundary of Parque Nacional Podocarpus. This area was originally colonised 30 years ago when a rough trail linked the valley to the village of Yangana, but parts of the trail are protected by the Fundación Conservacion Jototoco, named after a new species of bird discovered here in the late 1990s. Fundación Conservacion Jototoco also runs an upscale lodge a few kilometres down the road from the beginning of the hike near Tapichalaca. Reservations can be arranged at offices in Quito: Pasaje Eugenio Santilla N 34-248 y Maurian, PO Box 17-16-337; tel: 593 2272013; email: fsornoza@pi.pro.ec.

The vegetation next to the Quebrada Honda and on the mountain-tops is largely intact, although some hillslopes have been cleared for cattle grazing. The road from Loja to Zumba skirts the headwaters of this basin providing relatively easy access. The charm of this hike is the people who live along the route, and the views of the surrounding cloudforest peaks. During the rainy season (December–July) the trail is very muddy, a factor which is made worse by the horse traffic dragging boards of mahogany out to the road to be sold to lumber traders. The route is also hilly. We were told the hike is much easier during the dry season.

This a great spot for birding mid-elevation forest (1,500–2,500m) and is a favourite spot for orchid collectors. There are also Andean spectacled bears, woolly mountain tapirs, monkeys and deer in the undisturbed areas of forest.

Access There are several buses a day that travel from Loja to Zumba. The beginning of the trail is approximately 50km south of Vilcabamba near the Casa Communal of Quebrada Honda. This is where mules arrive with lumber to sell to the lumber traders that drive back to Loja.

Hiking directions The trail/dirt road begins on the opposite side of the road where there is a community house. Head up a short incline and continue on an eroded roadbed for about 30 minutes, until it begins switchbacking down to Quebrada Honda on a deeply entrenched trail (in places it's up to 7m deep with cloudforest vegetation growing over the top of the trail – virtually a tunnel!). It takes about 2 hours to reach the crossing of Quebrada Honda. Wade across the stream and climb to pastures on the far side. The trail goes up and down along the left back in the forest and pasture, but it's very obvious. Arrive at a group of houses on a flat area, which is the community of Quebrada Honda. The locals are very friendly people, and you may be able to stay in the church or in the local school.

Continue along the main trail to the village of Palmeras. There's lots of up and down; if in doubt ask the locals where trail is. Just above Palmeras is a major intersection; turn right here, with a water tank below you. Head through Palmeras, taking in the good views. As the trail gets wider, with some spur trails, stay on the main path as it heads down to the bridge across the Quebrada Honda. Continue to follow the steep switchbacks up through forest, then contour across the grassy slopes to Tapala, where there is a road. You can stay at the store owned by Luz Maria Guoma, where the trail enters town. Buses head out from here in the evenings, but there may also be some truck traffic. From here it's about 1 hour to Valladolid, where you can stay at Residencial Sur Oriente and from where you can catch numerous buses back to Loja (4 hours).

The Oriente

If you are wise and know the art of travel, let yourself
go on the stream of the unknown and accept whatever
comes in the spirit in which the gods may offer it.

Freya Stark

The Oriente is the name given to Ecuador's
Amazonia, a huge lowland area east of the Andes and
comprising 36% of Ecuador's total territory. Popularly
known as 'the jungle', the region is properly referred to
as 'tropical rainforest'. Dense, hot, and wet, just as one
would expect it to be, the Oriente was largely unexplored
and untravelled until the oil boom of the 1960s. Now four roads penetrate the
region and access is relatively straightforward.

Without a doubt, the most fascinating aspect of the Oriente is its incredible
variety of flora and fauna. This is partly due to the so-called edge effect. This means
that any region where two different ecological zones are in sharp juxtaposition will
have a greater variety of species than a region where two ecological zones gradually
merge. The dramatic drop of the Andes to the Oriente is sudden enough to produce
this effect. Over 700, or half, of Ecuador's bird species have been recorded in the
Oriente; this is roughly equivalent to all of the species found in the United States.
About 3,000 species of butterfly are known in Ecuador; this represents an incredible
15% of the world's known butterflies. Sloths, armadillos, and anteaters are present,
all members of the strange Edentate family which is found only in the Americas. On
a single 10-day trip into the Oriente (admittedly to a remote region) Rob saw six
different species of monkey. And, of course, there are countless insects, many of
which still prove to be new to science when classified. The trees and plants are no
less varied and interesting; the giant buttressed ceibal tree, the chonta palm covered
with thousands of needle-sharp thorns, and the blossoms muskily scenting the
forest, all contribute to this fascinating natural wilderness.

Ecuador, the land of volcanoes, even manages to produce a couple of volcanoes
perched on the very edge of the lowlands. Rearing out of the rainforest, they are the
active Reventador (3,562m) and the presently dormant Sumaco (3,732m). Both
mountains have slopes dropping within 25km to high Amazonian forests at 1,200m.

Although roads now penetrate the lowlands, and airstrips occasionally puncture
the rainforest, some of the most satisfying journeys into the jungle can still be
made by dugout canoe and on foot. This section describes a variety of trips to
different areas, with an emphasis on hiking and paddling in dugouts.

THE MISAHUALLÍ AREA

For the traveller with a limited amount of time, a trip to the small river port of
Misahuallí on the Río Napo will give a good glimpse of the Oriente.

The journey begins at Baños, the prettily situated gateway town to the Oriente (see *The Baños area* in *Chapter 6*, page 184). From here you take a bus to Puyo which is the capital of the lowland province of Pastaza. Only 66km away from Baños, it lies just 950m above sea level. The winding gravel road follows the Río Pastaza valley and, as it drops, you can appreciate the rapidly changing vegetation and the many waterfalls (one of which cascades from an overhanging cliff onto the road – a damp experience in a pick-up truck!). From the narrow confines of the Río Pastaza gorge, the first sudden sighting of the Amazonian plains is breathtaking. There is an obligatory passport control in Shell-Mera, some 15km before Puyo.

From Puyo, if the weather is clear, you can view various snow-capped peaks rising over 4,000m above you and only 50km distant. Sangay is sometimes visible, exploding away some 65km to the southwest. Several buses a day leave Puyo for Tena. Get off the bus at Puerto Napo, some 75km beyond Puyo and 7km before Tena. From Puerto Napo, frequent pick-up trucks act as a bus service to Puerto Misahuallí, at the end of the road 11km away.

Now you're in the tropical lowlands, just 600m above sea level. It's amazing to realise that only 80km away to the northwest, Antisana towers over 5,000m above you, whilst the mouth of the Amazon at Belém lies over 3,000km to the east, with no higher ground in between.

Just 20 years ago, Puerto Misahuallí was no more than a huddle of huts, but the oil boom, the new road, and tourism have enlarged it to over a thousand inhabitants. It is still a very sleepy little port, however, boasting only very basic hotels and restaurants. Sometimes gaily painted dugout canoes powered by modern outboard motors arrive at Misahuallí's sandy beach, loaded down with cargoes varying from bananas to parrots. Most produce now goes by way of the new Tena–Coca road, however, and river traffic has slowed to a trickle. Nevertheless, occasionally gold panners still come into town to sell gold dust, and hardy colonists may arrive in the port trying to sell their corn, papayas and other produce.

Just a generation ago, the region east of here was the territory of the indigenous people known as the Aucas, which in Quechua means 'savage'. The term Auca is considered derogatory and has been discarded for the more favoured term, Huaorani (also spelled Waorani), which means 'the people' in their native language. In 1956 five missionaries were killed by the Huaorani. Oil was discovered about ten years later and the outpost of Coca began to grow into an important oil town. Killings by both settlers and indigenous people continued into the '60s, but by the '70s the situation had stabilised, with the Huaorani withdrawing to remote regions of the jungle, as they have done for centuries to avoid genocidal conflicts. In 1983 a reservation of 66,570 hectares was set aside for them in a remote region where, for the time being, they are able to continue life in a relatively traditional manner. Nevertheless, some Huaorani are now undergoing the painful change from their simple livelihoods to a 21st-century existence, a process which is so rapid that it proves very traumatic and often fatal to many primitive peoples. In May 2003 a tribal conflict in which one group of Huaorani attacked another group may have resulted in over 20 deaths.

The Huaorani are now governed by an organisation called ONHAE, which requires all guides entering their territory to have a permit. They are attempting to develop tourism as a sustainable alternative to Huaorani entering the labour force of the Oriente as low-paid workers. A highly motivated Canadian – Randy Smith – has helped them in this effort and recently published a manual for ecotourism for the Huaorani and other indigenous groups. The title of this book is *Manual de Ecotourism, Para Guias y Comunidades Indigenas de La Amazonia Ecuatoriana*. This book is also useful for travellers, since it has an excellent appendix on Huaorani, Quechua, Shuar, English, Spanish and Latin names for species found in the jungle.

Jungle trips

Even if you don't normally take organised tours, some of the tours offered in Misahuallí are both inexpensive and worthwhile. Many outfitters are available (there are too many to list here). The SAE office in Quito or other travellers can tell you of recommended outfitters. Tours range from 1-day walks in the nearby jungles to 10-day trips reaching close to the Peruvian border. Usually a minimum of five people are needed (more for longer trips), but there are plenty of gringos in Misahuallí looking for companions. Food, transportation and accommodation are provided for $25–40 a day, depending on the difficulty and duration of the trip. It must be remembered that the immediate area has been colonised, so you won't see much in the way of monkeys, peccaries and so on. Local wildlife is limited to birds and insects which are varied and colourful. A trip along the river near Misahuallí often produces sightings of egrets, vultures, toucans, anis, tanagers, caciques and oropendulas. On guided trips, keep your eyes open for well-camouflaged stick insects, fist-sized toads, armies of ants, and hosts of colourful butterflies. Ask to be shown the Achiote (*Bixa orellana*), a plant which is crushed to produce a red paint for body decorations, and a vine containing water fit to drink. A good guide will be able to show you much you would have missed on your own, particularly if you ask many questions and convey your interest and enthusiasm.

If you can get a group together and take a longer tour you will see more wildlife. These tours are not for the soft traveller, but you'll certainly see monkeys, caiman, macaws and parrots, and with any luck pacas, capybaras, anteaters, armadillos, peccaries, and who knows, maybe even a tapir or a jaguar?

CONTINUING INTO THE ORIENTE

The best-preserved rainforest is downstream of Coca on the Río Napo and downstream of Lago Agrio on the Río Aguarico. These trips require more time and expense to visit. There are reserves in this area: the Reserva Produccíon Faunistica Cuyabeno, Parque Nacional Yasuní and the Reserva Ecológica Limoncocha. These reserves harbour some of the most diverse ecosystems in the world, but are currently being degraded by illegal colonisation, African palm plantations, hardwood harvesting and illegal trading in forest animal species. Ten years ago oil companies could have been added to this list, but now they have become proactive promoters of conservation. Outside of these reserves are lands that are owned by colonists and indigenous groups, and about a dozen private reserves usually associated with tourism. There is much lip service paid to ecotourism in the Oriente, and many communities have decided to follow a path of development that incorporates elements of ecotourism in their land-use planning and hunting practices. This is particularly true of indigenous communities who have a tradition of living in balance with the rainforest ecosystem. Efforts to conserve lands outside the reserves is evidence that tourism has a positive impact to these once isolated areas. As you travel through the boomtowns of Coca, Shushufindi and Lago Agrio you will be reminded of the American West in the previous century – roaming the streets are outlaws, Columbian refugees, oil workers, hard-working colonists, indigenous people and a few tourists. Your visit to an indigenous village or a jungle lodge strengthens the conservation ethic in the Oriente.

Access

One interesting way to get to Coca from Misahuallí is to continue downriver by motorised dugout canoe for the 6-hour journey to the town of Coca and beyond, but with the new Tena–Coca road, regular river transportation has been reduced. It can be costly to hire an unscheduled canoe to make the trip. This part of the Río Napo has long been travelled and settled, so don't expect to see monkeys and 'wild Indians', but you will see dramatic views of the forest and many birds, including parrots. Easier and less expensive is to take the bus from Quito or Tena to Coca.

From Coca daily buses head north to Lago Agrio, another jungle town produced by the oil boom. It is the most eastern city in Ecuador and the capital of the province of Sucumbíos. From Lago Agrio a gravel road follows the oil line to Quito, some 265km and 10 hours away by bus. The road passes the active volcano Reventador (3,562m) and the village of Baeza, both described later in this chapter, and continues past Volcán Antisana (5,752m) and the village of Papallacta (see *Chapter 6*, page 159) before reaching Quito.

Regular flights from both Lago Agrio and Coca return to Quito, and buses travel from Puerto Misahuallí to Quito via Tena (there are several a day). Tena is the capital of the Napo province. Good views are often had of the dormant volcano Sumaco (3,732m) about 50km north-northeast. From Tena buses continue on the road north which runs parallel to the Andes, passing through Archidona and on to Baeza, nearly 100km away. Archidona is famous as being the centre from which you can visit the large cave complex of Jumandi. Unfortunately, the stalactite hunter and phantom spray painter have reached the caves before you, and they are now a rather sorry sight.

Jungle trips

For any jungle trip you will need to travel by canoe downriver. You have the choice of arranging a stay with an indigenous family, travelling with a guide on an extended canoe trip, or visiting a lodge. Although from the air much of this area appears to be wild country, the forest is criss-crossed by numerous trails. If you are not accustomed to travelling in the rainforest it is best to arrange trips with guides from Quito, Coca or Lago Agrio. You can contact Whymper Torres and Luis García, who are two native guides well recommended for trips on the Napo and Aguarico. Randy Smith also works closely with the Huaorani as a guide. There are a dozen established lodges from which you can explore the forest by canoe and on day-hikes accompanied by native guides, and usually English-speaking translators. The advantage of a lodge is that after a day of walking you can come back to a shower, a clean bed, and good food. Some of the best lodges on the Ríos Napo and Aguarico are Yachana Lodge, La Selva, Sacha Lodge, Napo Wildlife Centre (Añangu), Sanisla, Yuturi and Paradise Huts. It is best to book trips to these lodges in Quito. Information on lodges can be obtained at the SAE in Quito. An excellent source of written information on the Napo region is *The Ecotourist Guide to the Ecuadorian Amazon* edited by Rolf Wesche and available at the IGM offices (3rd floor) or at the SAE.

The Napo Wildlife Centre is a new, first-class lodge jointly operated by the local indigenous community (Centro Kichwa Anangu) and EcoEcuador (which belongs to the International Tropical Nature NGO network). This lodge is located on the banks of the blackwater lake Añangucocha, inside Parque Nacional Yasuní. They have protected over 5,000 hectares from hunting and other activities. There are eight very comfortable individual cabins, with hot water and a dining area. All waste water is treated in a carefully designed artificial wetland.

Spectacular wildlife viewing opportunities include giant river otters on a small stream near the lodge, enormous black caimans in the lake, ten species of monkeys, observation blinds at two parrot clay licks, and hundreds of bird species. The endangered Amazonian manatees are also found in the lake, but their quiet habits, while eating bits of the abundant floating vegetation, make them hard to see. Community members know their forest very well and one (Jiovanny Rivadeneyra) is a world-renowned bird guide.

Trips begin with a flight to Coca, then a 2-hour motorised canoe ride on the Río Napo, and finally a 2-hour trip in a dugout canoe paddled by the community members to Añangucocha.

There are a variety of hiking and paddling routes. One trail links the lake of Añangucocha with the Río Napo in unflooded mature rainforest and takes approximately 2 hours. A set of trails also leads into the primary forest behind the parrot observation blinds. Another trail makes a ½km loop on the west side of the hill where the lodge is located. A new 15km trail is being developed which will connect the lodge with the Río Tiputini. Paddling can be done on the kilometre-wide lake, on the flooded streams which flow into it and on the Río Añangu, which flows to the Río Napo. Wildlife observation is great in the morning, since the community does not allow motorised canoes. More information can be obtained at www.ecoecuador.org.

Other interesting areas to visit along the wide Río Napo are the other lagunas: Limoncocha, Pañacocha, Challuacocha and Yuturi. These oxbow lakes have very high bird, fish and mammal diversity. Most of the people living on the Napo downstream of Coca are Quechuas and are accustomed to tourism. You can actually drive to the Laguna Limoncocha and stay at the park station or in the town of Limonocha. A boat trip combined with a walk can occupy 2 days. It is also possible to travel down the Ríos Tiputini and Curaray from the Vía Auca which heads south from Coca. These narrow and sinuous rivers offer days of views of primary rainforest and wildlife, but require more than a week of sometimes uncomfortable travel in a canoe, and some pretty remote camping.

The Aguarico is a smaller river than the Napo, and so travelling on it you are closer to the shore and have a better chance of seeing wildlife. You can reach the Aguarico by taking a taxi from Lago Agrio to Poza Honda or Chiritza, from where you can catch a canoe downstream. Some of the Secoya (eg: San Pablo) and Cofán communities welcome visitors. The Quechua, Siona, Shuar and colonial communities are more reserved and generally should not be visited unless they are set up for tourism.

There is one Quechua community that will cater to hikers, however, and that is Pucapeña. From this community there is a tough 2-day hike that crosses from the Río Aguarico to the Río Napo that gets you into primary forest. Bring rubber boots, as you will be wading through streams and mucking around in the mud. It begins in Pucapeña, on the Río Aguarico, and ends in the small settlement of Pañacocha on the Río Napo. You will pass through the Bosque Protector Pañacocha. Contact Franklin Grefa in Pucapeña – he has guided a few people on this *pica* (ill-defined trail through the forest). Once in the town of Pañacocha, try to get up to the Lagunas de Pañacocha for a chance to see freshwater dolphins and caiman.

The Río Aguarico eventually cuts through the centre of the Reserva Producción Faunística Cuyabeno. It meets the Napo at the international border near the town of Rocafuerte, and continuing on to Perú is an option; it is about 3 days to Iquitos.

A final note about the weather: it can rain year round, but June through to August seem to be the wettest months around Misahuallí. November and December have the least rain. During these times the Río Napo could be either too high or too low to make a boat trip.

REVENTADOR (3,562m)

Distance 20km
Altitude 1,400–3,562m
Rating Difficult
Time 3–4 days
Start INECEL Camp near Cascada San Rafael
End INECEL Camp near Cascada San Rafael
Maps IGM 1:50,000 Reventador. An IGM air photo of the peak which is extremely detailed and useful can also be purchased.
Other essential notes Reventador is currently erupting (2003), so route changes are likely, and it may even be too dangerous to climb.

Reventador is a unique geological and ecological landscape to visit. Its recent eruptive history and its location on the edge of the Oriente have created interesting landforms and habitats that are changing extremely rapidly. An intriguing project would be to come back in 20 years and compare your notes and impressions to your initial visit – they are likely to be radically different.

This volcano is currently erupting and extremely dangerous to climb. The refuge is still present and most of the trail is intact but there are new lava flows and periodic ash eruptions. It is likely, however, that this volcano will evolve into a dormant status again in the next few years. Check its status with SAE or the Smithsonian Global Volcanism Program (www.volcano.si.edu).

Reventador lies 90km east-northeast of Quito. Its name means exploder and this volcano has been frequently active as far back as records go – the first recorded eruption was in 1541. For many years little was known about the area, and it was not until 1931 that an Ecuadorian, L Paz y Miño, visited the area to study it and map it for the first time. It remained relatively inaccessible until the building of the trans-Ecuadorian oil pipeline began in the late 1960s. This in turn prompted the construction of a road from Baeza to the new oil boomtown of Lago Agrio, and it is from this all-weather road that access to Reventador is made.

Reventador consists of an outer crater 2–3km across within which is an imposing 1,000m-tall resurgent volcanic cone. This andesitic strato-volcano erupted catastrophically, blowing away much of the summit and leaving only the flanks of a volcano that once rivaled Chimborazo in height. Since Reventador lies to the east of the main crest of the Andes on the edge of the Oriente, it must have been a truly awesome sight, a glaciated peak towering over the rainforest.

The south rim of the volcano is missing, which indicates large-scale debris flows broke the rim, depositing material in the Río Quijos valley. Outcrops of unconsolidated lahars (chaotic mixtures of boulders, gravel and volcanic sand) can be observed from the road and on the approach to the peak. This material is not stable, so landsliding has created a chaotic landscape of steep ridges. The opening on the south rim also provides an outlet for lava flows from the active cone, some of which have reached to within 1½km of the road.

The central cone is in the process of rebuilding the volcanic edifice and seems to follow a cycle of 25 years between eruptions. The kind of lava it produces when it is erupting is extremely viscous and breaks into large blocks as it cools, forming vast fields of boulders with ankle-breaking crevices. This makes walking to the summit an extremely slow and difficult process of hopping from one mossy boulder to the next.

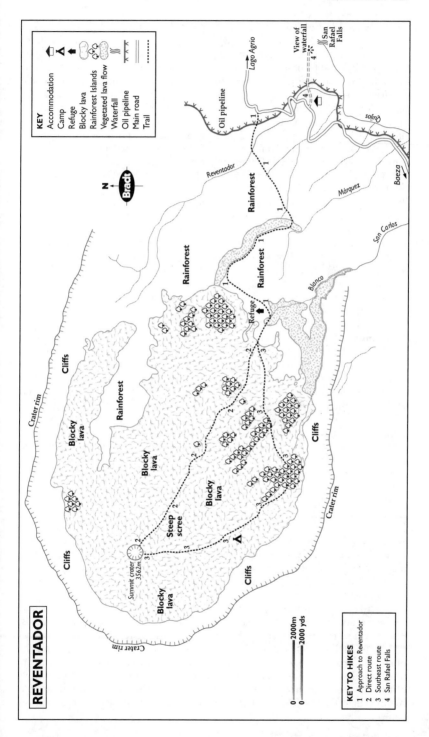

REVENTADOR

KEY
- Accommodation
- Camp
- Refuge
- Blocky lava
- Rainforest Islands
- Vegetated lava flow
- Waterfall
- Oil pipeline
- Main road
- Trail

N
Bradt

Lago Agrio

View of waterfall

San Rafael Falls

Oil pipeline

solino

Reventador

Rainforest

Márquez

Baeza

Rainforest 1

Rainforest

San Carlos

Blanco

Crater rim

Cliffs

Rainforest

Refuge

Blocky lava

Blocky lava

Cliffs

Blocky lava

Steep scree

Summit crater 3562m

Blocky lava

Cliffs

Crater rim

Crater rim

0 ————— 2000m
0 ————— 2000 yds

KEY TO HIKES
1 Approach to Reventador
2 Direct route
3 Southeast route
4 San Rafael Falls

The recent lava flows are now re-vegetating with mosses and shrubs. As the soil develops, the cloudforest will eventually cover these lava flows – at least until another hot lava flow restarts the process. Remnant islands of cloudforest vegetation can still be observed where lava did not cover the old soil surface. It is interesting to compare the quietness on the relatively barren lava flows to the familiar sounds of birds and insects within these small, ecologically isolated islands. Also, when you are on the summit of the cone, the roots of the volcano can be seen in the layers exposed in the cliffs on the inside of the old crater rim – there are alternating strata of andesite flows and lahars representing previous eruptions.

The volcano is currently erupting and at the time of writing (2004) a climb to the summit is not recommended. The top of the cone has a small crater, approximately 100m across. If you do decide to climb make your visit very short since hydrogen sulphide fumes are toxic and an eruption from the summit cone is likely to kill you. It is highly advisable to check with locals of SAE in Quito for current conditions before attempting this climb (See *Reventador* map, previous page.)

Weather and times to go A friend who lives in the Lago Agrio area claims to have driven the Lago Agrio–Quito road dozens of times, but has only seen Reventador twice, even though it is only 8km from the road as the crow flies. It's probably fair to say, then, that the area is very wet and usually cloudy. The wettest months are June and July, and the best are September through to December, but you can still expect daily showers at any time of year.

Equipment The trail to the lava flows quickly becomes overgrown so a machete is necessary. During the 'dry' season, insects aren't a major problem but repellent should be brought during the wetter months. A waterproof tent is a must. My preferred clothing is raingear (Gore-Tex) over T-shirt and shorts, with a dry shirt and pair of trousers kept in plastic bags for camp and tent wear. It does not get too cold, so a sweater and a light sleeping bag or blanket are sufficient for the evening. The trail is muddy in places. Sturdy leather boots for ankle-twisting lava blocks are a must. The Ecuadorian knee-high rubber boots (*botas para agua*) are quite suitable for the approach, though not entirely comfortable. A spare pair of trainers for camp and tent wear mean your feet can dry out occasionally. A large selection of plastic bags is a must for keeping things dry. A compass and topographic map are also absolutely necessary. If you are leaving gear at the refuge, bring a padlock to secure your things in a locker. Bring extra water bottles, too, because if you camp high on the peak you will be waterless. Lastly, be responsible and carry out all of your litter.

Access Catch a bus from Quito's Terminal Terrestre through Baeza to Lago Agrio. Although you will only be going two-thirds of the way to Lago Agrio you may be charged the full fare at the bus station. Tell the bus driver you are going to Cascada San Rafael (San Rafael Waterfall). The bus journey is very interesting and worth a description.

The road descends from Quito through several growing suburbs, and is paved for 70km, until just before Papallacta, on the other side of the crest of the Andes. The ascent to this Andean crest takes you up a broad valley with cliffs above, on which condors are very occasionally spotted. Also, about halfway up, the remnants of an Inca Trail can be seen if you know what you are looking for. The pass at the top of the Eastern Cordillera is at 4,100m and is marked by an altar to the Virgin Mary. The road then drops to the lake of Papallacta, formed when a lava flow from Antisana dammed the Río Papallacta. The hike from Papallacta to Cotopaxi begins here.

Just before the village of Papallacta, over 60km from Quito, is a turn-off to the left with a sign for a hostel and thermal baths which are some of the best in the country. The road then continues to drop through enchantingly beautiful cloudforest with many strange plants and colourful birds. Approximately 100km from Quito the road forks; you follow the left fork and proceed through the villages of Borja and El Chaco, from where you may get your first views of Reventador. There are also frequent views of the Río Quijos on your right. About 150km from Quito you cross the Río Salado, which is a major landmark. Ten kilometres further on you cross the Río Malo (the starting point for the route used when Reventador was active). 170km from Quito you arrive at a little cement-block hut with an INECEL sign, at a turn-off to your right which leads to the Cascada San Rafael. About 500m down this road there is a complex of buildings originally constructed for a planned hydro-electric diversion around the falls. The complex is now run nominally as a tourist hotel by Hotel Quito, but hardly anyone uses it. Since the bus ride from Quito is 5 to 6 hours, you can stay here and get information on where the trail starts from the guard. Cheaper options are several basic hotels in the town of El Chaco, 45km before Cascada San Rafael, and the Hotel Amazonas, 13km beyond the Cascada San Rafael in the village of El Reventador.

Climbing Reventador

The climb takes 3 to 5 days round-trip and is physically demanding but not technically difficult. If you decide to hire a guide for the climb, there are some local guides available. Guillermo Vasquez was involved in chopping the original trail and knows the area well. He lives close by the school in the Pampas area, 2–3km before Cascada San Rafael. Luis 'Lucho' Viteri can be found in Baeza and Edgar Ortiz in the Hotel Amazonas in the village of El Reventador.

Finding the beginning of the hike is a little tricky and colonisation in the area results in new trails that lead to pastures, so it is always good to ask locals. On the main road, continue 5 minutes beyond the turn-off to the INECEL camp to the bridge over Río Reventador. From here continue 15 minutes uphill until the pipeline crosses the road. Here you can turn left next to the pipeline up a steep hill, or continue 5 minutes up the road to the next stream (1,520m) and follow a trail west up a pasture to the pipeline on the hill crest. It is recommended to follow the trail, as it has steps. Whichever route you take, the important thing is to find a wood ladder over the pipeline just before it heads up a very steep incline. Cross over the ladder and head northwest, staying to the right of a wood shack in a flat field. There is a vague trail in the grass that soon enters forest where it becomes more defined. You should be heading towards a grove of palm trees on a ridge in the distance. Soon you will reach a small stream choked with cobbles; jump across and look for the trail several metres upstream. A few minutes later the trail forks; stay left, as the right fork heads up to new pastureland. If the trail gets steep you are on the wrong branch. Soon descend to Río Reventador, with great bedrock pools for bathing. Wade across this stream and find the trail slightly upstream marked by a cairn. The trail skirts the right side of a pasture and re-enters forest. You come to an overlook which has been constructed for views of the Río Quijos.

Now the trail is relatively easy to follow. It ascends over two ridges with well-constructed steps, crossing several small streams, and then ascends to the toe of a vegetated lava flow. Here the surface of the trail changes from mud to awkward boulders. The trail works it way northwest up the southwest side of this lava flow and then heads southwest across the forest to Río Blanco (not named on the IGM map) where the refuge is located (2,050m). If you do not get lost, count on 3 to 4 hours from the road to the location of the destroyed refuge next to recent debris flows from the volcano.

The refuge was built in 1994 and was a great place to spend the first night, but alas mother nature took it from us during the eruptions of 2002. Now you must find a camping spot. It is strongly recommended to camp away from the recent debris flows, since a heavy rain could trigger a a new flood of volcanic debris.

You can attempt the peak from here in one long day or set up a high camp at the base of the cone. It is 9 to 12 hours of walking round-trip, depending on how comfortable you are with hopping the mossy boulders. Remember, once it gets dark finding your way on the lava flows is nearly impossible. The problem with camping at the base of the cone is that there is no water on the lava flows, you need to carry all your water with you from the location of the destroyed refuge. You should have a minimum of five litres per person, per day.

In front of the destroyed refuge, wade across the 3m-wide stream known as the Río Blanco (slightly white from dissolved solids in the groundwater leaving the volcano) and head generally northwest on a trail across a swampy area and up a steep vegetated hill. About 40 minutes from the location of the destroyed refuge you reach the edge of the blocky lava flow (2,150m) with an open view of the cone 4km in the distance. There is an obvious and abrupt change in vegetation to moss and shrubs and the spot should be marked by wooden poles. Here you have two alternatives.

Note These routes are likely to have changed due to new lava flows in 2002.

Direct Route Head directly for the summit cone across the lava blocks. If the summit cannot be seen head northwest. There is a vague trail that can be followed to the base of the cone which is distinguished by crushed moss and occasional cut shrubs. Orientation during a clear day is easy but in fog or at night you could easily spend hours or even days wandering around the lava flows. Mark your ascent route for easy return. After cresting over several low ridges pass to the left of an island of cloudforest. Follow a 30m-high ridge to the left of a dry stream bed to the base of the cone, head up a silver (mossy) slope to the left of another small cloudforest island, and then traverse right into a dry stream bed. It takes 2 to 3 hours to reach this point from the toe of the lava flow. This is a reasonable place to camp, though you may need to flatten a spot for the tent (2,630m). From here the trail steepens, but the footing is easier and after another 2 to 3 hours of following a rocky gully you will reach the summit rim (3,500m). Watch out for rockfall. Near the crater rim are steaming fumaroles and the soil is warm. The actual summit (3,562m) requires a short jaunt around to the west side of the rim. The total time from the refuge to the summit is 6 to 8 hours. The descent to the wood poles takes 3 to 4 hours.

Southeast Route From the edge of the lava flow head west across several ridges of rough, blocky terrain – this is slow going. After about an hour reach a smooth lava flow covered with spongy moss. Continue up the flow crossing below a thick forest onto blocky lava again. Cross the lava and find a stream bed heading west; follow it upstream to the saddle between the old rim and the cone. This is a good place to camp. It takes 3 to 4 hours to reach the saddle from the poles. The summit is easily reached by following the stream northwest and then north to the south side of the crater rim: 1 to 2 hours of hiking. The descent to the wood poles takes 3 to 4 hours.

The view from the top of the desolate, steaming crater is worth the muddy, slippery effort; it is a beautiful, empty, chaotic place which few people visit. When you arrive back at the San Rafael camp it's also worth making the ½-hour hike down to an overlook of the San Rafael Waterfalls on the Río Quijos.

PARQUE NACIONAL SUMACO-NAPO GALERAS

The wilderness surrounding Volcán Sumaco has so far mostly escaped colonisation and oil development and is now protected in Parque Nacional Sumaco-Galeras. The park is rarely visited by foreigners and Ecuadorians alike, so the area is mostly un-trailed and difficult to travel through. Several scientific expeditions have visited the area and discovered endemic species. The wildlife does not appear to be frightened by people, which indicates it is not often hunted. A difficult but rewarding adventure would be to cross this park over a period of several weeks, perhaps climbing Cerro Negro or Cerro Pan de Azucar, two peaks that have no records of being visited. There are also plans to put in a trail to the top of Galeras, a limestone mountain just north of the Río Napo, with many endemic species and caves.

Volcán Sumaco (3,732m)

Distance 40km round-trip
Altitude 1,480–3,732m
Rating Difficult
Time 3–4 days round-trip
Start Pacto Sumaco
End Pacto Sumaco
Maps Pavayacu and Volcán Sumaco
Other essential notes A climb of the rainforest volcano Sumaco.

The jewel of the park is the recently active Volcán Sumaco. This anomalous volcano rises from the jungle 60km east of the main crest of the Andes. The route to the summit passes through an intact elevation gradient of vegetation from 1,300m to 3,700m with undisturbed lowland rainforest, cloudforest, and – close to the summit – *páramo* vegetation. On a clear day from the summit crater you can see several of the major glaciated peaks of the Andes including El Altar, Tungurahua and Chimborazo, as well as the Río Napo snaking through the lowland rainforest. The non-technical route takes 4 to 6 days round-trip, and involves much machete work and route finding. We do not know of anyone who has climbed it without a guide.

The volcano has been known to Europeans since the Spanish conquest, when Francisco de Orellana recorded its presence in 1541 after he saw it from the Río Napo during the first stages of his historic first descent of the Amazon. However, its isolated, forest-bound position and generally wet weather have made it one of Ecuador's least known volcanoes.

Although some sources consider Sumaco to be extinct, the few records we have of it indicate that it is an active volcano. Jiménez de la Espada, who made the first ascent in 1865, found a gullied, 100m wide crater blown open to the south. In 1925, the British climber George Dyott climbed Sumaco and recorded that the crater was 210m wide with no signs of cracks or gullies. This indicates that an eruption must have occurred between the years 1865 and 1925, but the volcano's

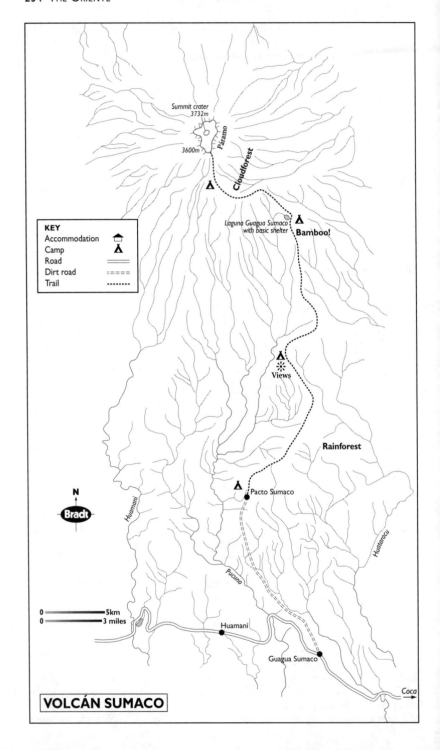

KEY

Accommodation	⌂
Camp	⛺
Road	───
Dirt road	=====
Trail	-----

Summit crater
3732m

3600m

Páramo

Cloudforest

Laguna Guagua Sumaco
with basic shelter

Bamboo!

Views

Rainforest

N

Bradt

Huamaní

Huataracu

Pacto Sumaco

Pucuno

0 ─── 5km
0 ─── 3 miles

Huamaní

Guagua Sumaco

Coca

VOLCÁN SUMACO

isolated position prevented this phenomenon from being recorded by any observer. This theory is supported by the fact that Sumaco has a conical shape which, in an environment promoting severe erosion, indicates that activity must have occurred within the last few hundred years. At present there appears to be no activity whatsoever, but volcanologists still consider Sumaco to be potentially active. Dyott also collected several rock samples that he sent to Columbia University for analysis. They proved to be geo-chemically distinct to all other volcanoes in Ecuador, indicating that the lavas of Sumaco have a different origin than the lava of other Ecuadorian volcanoes. (See map opposite.)

Access Take a bus from Quito's Terminal Terrestre to Coca along the relatively new Loreto road, getting off in the small village of Guagua Sumaco. This trip takes 6 to 7 hours, so it is best to leave early in the morning so that you have time to arrange a guide for the following day. You can also take a bus to Tena, getting off at the Y at the roadside village of Narupa. From here buses pass on their way to Coca every 1 to 2 hours. Huamani is 1½ hours from Narupa.

Guagua Sumaco is a little roadside village with several stores offering basic supplies, and from here a new spur road leads to the colonial town of Pacto Sumaco. There is occasional transport up this road to Pacto Sumaco (it takes half an hour) or you can arrange a truck for about $5; this saves you 3 hours of walking. The park entrance fees are collected in Pacto Sumaco.

You might want to stop in Huamani (15 minutes before Guagua Sumaco) to contact the best-known guide in the area, Don Francisco Chimbo, a Quechua in his sixties who has the body of a 40-year-old. He has guided many groups to the summit but is getting older and may no longer be able to do the trip, but he can recommend someone else. There is a growing group of guides in Pacto Sumaco as well. The charge is about $10 a day. The IGM topographical maps are of limited use, since you are under the canopy most of the time and the trail can get overgrown in places, so again we recommend using a guide.

Equipment Try to travel light and expect to get wet. You need to be prepared for humid warm weather and close to freezing weather on the summit (see *Reventador*, pages 228–33).

Climbing Sumaco

From Pacto Sumaco you follow a trail constructed of cut logs for about 2 hours, crossing pasture and second growth forest with several intersections. The area is confusing; it's a good idea to hire a guide to show you the way. In another hour (after you leave the cut logs) you reach the top of a hill called El Mirador. At El Mirador a trail cuts to the right and drops down to a water source and cleared area for camping. Back up at the Mirador, the trail to the summit continues more or less straight, dropping steeply down before going up again. You hike for about an hour and a half through lowland jungle before the trail rises steadily through thick bamboo. If you don't have to do much cutting you should reach the small lake filling a parasitic cone on the flanks of Sumaco (called Guagua Sumaco, the unnamed lake near peak 2,525m on map) in about 7 to 9 hours of hiking from Pacto Sumaco. There are two intermediate camp sites between El Mirador and the lake, but the lake makes a great camping spot. There may be some basic shelter or poles for tarps, but do not count on it. The views and birding are great from this camp. The lake is said to be home to a large serpent, so don't ask your guide to go for a swim.

Follow a trail along the ridge, eventually droping down to a saddle between peak 2,870m and Volcán Sumaco. Begin climbing the cone of Sumaco and break out of the forest onto *páramo* (3,250m) and climb the grassy slopes to the summilt ridge (3 to 4 hours from the saddle). Once on the *páramo* ridge you need to drop off it to the right to a another small saddle and make a short climb of the summit cone. There is a small pond at the bottom of the crater and an orange communication hut below the northeast side of the cone. It is possible to camp at the summit.

Note The summit of Sumaco seems close from the lake, but you must climb over several ridges before you reach the base of the peak. From the lake camp, you can reach the summit in just under 6 hours with light packs. It takes 5 hours to return to the lake camp, so if you plan to do the whole thing in a day, a 06.00 start or earlier is necessary. There is also a clearly marked campsite in the jungle about 2½ to 3 hours up from the lake camp and about 2 hours before you break out into the *páramo*.

THE BAEZA AREA
Baeza is a small but historical town in the eastern foothills at 1,400m. It was on an ancient trade route even before the conquest. The coming of the Spaniards elevated it to the position of a mission settlement, but nowadays no vestiges remain of its past. It is a very quiet place with one basic hotel and a couple of cheap restaurants. It is surrounded by steep hills which could provide days of hiking and exploration. We describe one day-hike here, but armed with the IGM 1:50,000 Baeza map you could have several to choose from.

Buses pass through Baeza several times a day to and from Tena. If you are on the Quito–Lago Agrio route, you have to walk about 1.5km up the road from the Baeza turnoff. Baeza is about 100km by road from Quito.

Baeza to communication towers

Distance 8km round-trip
Altitude Approximately 1,900–2,400m
Rating Easy
Time 3–4 hours
Start Baeza
End Baeza
Maps IGM 1:50,000 Baeza
Other essential notes A nice birding walk above Baeza with views of the Río Quijos valley.

This is a pleasant hike up the steep gravel road to the communication towers above town, and it boasts excellent birding. Head up the road from the old section of Baeza (north section of town) past some fields, and then switchback up the road to the communication towers (about 1½–2 hours). There is usually a guard there who can point you in the direction of other hikes into the forest.

THE MACAS AREA
Though a small town, Macas is the capital of one of the largest provinces in Ecuador, Morona-Santiago. Its history goes back at least four centuries; it was an

important Spanish missionary and trading settlement linked with the highlands by a trail still in existence. Despite its provincial capital status, Macas had remained a very isolated town until recently. It now has an airport with daily flights to and from Quito, and the recently constructed road north to Puyo now gives this jungle city two means of access to the Sierra. At one time its only link with the rest of Ecuador was the southbound road through Sucua to Cuenca, some 10 hours away by bus.

The Oriente east of Macas is perhaps the least explored region in the entire country. It is the home of the Shuar and Achuar, famous for their expertise (no longer practised) at shrinking the heads of their enemies. There is a major Shuar centre in Sucua which is partially run by indigenous people, and which plays an important part in both recording and encouraging traditional lifestyles as well as aiding the Shuar people in the difficult process of entering 21st-century life, which they seem to be doing with more success than many groups. Nevertheless, some semi-wild groups still exist deep in the forests.

Many of the Shuar and Achuar communities have strict control on access. Do not try to enter remote communities (no road access) unless you have obtained permission from the indigenous organisations that represent these communities. Several international oil companies have been trying to get into these areas for years and have been resisted fiercely – people have been kidnapped and threatened with death.

From Macas, trails are marked on the maps which penetrate deeply into the Oriente, reaching extremely remote villages. The trails are not often used, as small aircraft are the main means of communication with Macas, and river travel is used between the villages. There is one trail which can easily be walked in a day from Macas.

From Macas cross the Río Upano by a simple bridge to Sevilla Don Bosco, a Salesian mission. From here, head south along the road, roughly following the eastern river bank. This dirt road slowly deteriorates into a side track impassable to vehicles. You will pass cultivated areas and indigenous huts and perhaps be invited to try some of their *yucca chicha*. This drink is made by the women masticating the yucca and then spitting the contents of their mouths into a bowl of water, which is left to ferment; the process is started by the ptyalin in saliva. It takes some time (and a lack of imagination) to develop a taste for this sour, gruel-like drink which is served cold in large gourds. One is normally expected to drink the whole gourd in one or two gulps.

Some 4 hours from Sevilla Don Bosco you come to the small indigenous centre of San Luis, where you can buy soft drinks if you're not up to *chicha*. San Luis is almost the halfway point to Sucua. If you do get all the way to Sucua, you could return to Macas by one of the frequent buses joining the two towns.

Another interesting, but very tough hike, would be to cross the Cordillera Cutucu from Logroño to the village of Yaupi. Locals claim the hike is only 3 days, but plan on it taking a week. Make sure you have permission from the Shuar Federation controlling this area.

The Western Lowlands and Pacific Coast

Here I am, safely returned over those peaks from a journey far more beautiful and strange than anything I had hoped for or imagined – how is it that this safe return brings such regret?

Peter Matthiessen

West of the Andes and stretching to the Pacific Ocean lies some of Ecuador's most valuable agricultural land. Although this is good for the Ecuadorian economy, it means also that much of the lowland forest has been destroyed, along with the accompanying wildlife. The best places to see the western forests are the slopes of the Andes or in the coastal ranges, as the terrain is too rough for agriculture. More and more trails are being cut into these areas which can be used for backpacking or horse trips. These forests are hot, humid and thickly covered with vegetation, so they require a temperate character. The three most visited protected areas on the coast are the Reserva Ecolóloca Mache-Chindul, Parque Nacional Machalilla and Cerro Blanco.

A good variety of sea and shore birds is found on the coast. The southern coast has mangrove swamps but is nevertheless rather scrubby and dry, as is the Santa Elena Peninsula west of Guayaquil. Rainfall here is comparatively low and falls mainly from January to April. Further north there is more rainfall, more vegetation, and a longer rainy season, from January to June, and on the far northern coast it sometimes rains during the 'dry' season. Good areas for birdwatching in the south are found at Jambelí, which is a low-lying island off Puerto Bolívar near Machala, the capital of the province of El Oro. From Machala frequent buses do the short trip to Puerto Bolívar, where motor boats can be hired to cruise among the swamps, estuaries and islands of the area and where you can see large flocks of pelicans and other sea birds. In the Santa Elena Peninsula are found many fishing villages and tourist resorts, such as Playas and Salinas. These are often used as bases for walks along the beach, although overnight backpacking trips aren't normally done.

The northern coast is perhaps richest in coastal birdlife because of the heavier rainfall and vegetation. There are also various resort towns you can use as a base for coastal hiking.

RESERVA ECOLÓLOCA MACHE-CHINDUL

The coastal ranges of Mache-Chindul near the city of Esmeraldas have received considerable attention from the conservation community ever since the late Al Gentry and Ted Parker surveyed the area for the Rapid Assessment Program from Conservation International. This area of coastal premontane wet forest is isolated from the Andes, but it's rugged topography (300–800m) and coastal climate create a dense fog that sustains the sort of cloudforest vegetation usually restricted to higher elevations. Because of the isolation of the range there is a high degree of plant endemism which has stimulated botanists from around the world to collect and catalogue these species which one day may have economic value. The reserve also harbours jaguars, the umbrella bird, and abundant populations of the threatened mantled howler monkey.

Fundación Jatun Sacha first set up a private reserve (Bilsa) in this area in 1994 and every year adds land to their 2,500-hectare holding. Unfortunately there are extreme development pressures from logging companies and colonists, the latter primarily from the province of Manabí, who are rapidly deforesting the area. The ex-director of INEFAN, Jorge Barba, declared this area a Reserva Ecológica in July 1996, just as he was leaving office, much to the delight of the international and Ecuadorian conservation community. The status of the reserve is controversial with the logging companies and the colonists, however, and it remains to be seen whether the reserve will receive the protection it deserves.

Access The easiest way to visit the area is by arranging a stay at the Jatun Sacha research station located a day's drive and walk from the town of Quinindé. Take a bus from Quito towards Esmeraldas and get off in Quinindé (about 4 hours from Quito). There are several cheap hotels in Quinindé, including Paraiso ($3 per night) and Hotel Sans ($9 per night). From Quinindé you can get a truck from the petrol station Cinco Esquinas towards the settlement of Herrera, a town about 25km from the reserve. In the wet season (January to June) you can only get as far as La Y by private truck; it's an additional 3 to 4 hour walk to the reserve. As conditions become dryer (September to December) you can sometimes actually drive to the reserve, but do not count on it.

The facilities are mostly set up for volunteers, scientists and students, but an interested tourist could make arrangements to stay there. Reservations need to be made through Jatun Sacha in Quito (tel: 593 2 2441592 or 2250976) and advance warning is appreciated. There is room for 40 people and non-Ecuadorian visitors pay $20 per night, which covers room and board.

Bilsa to Muisne

Distance Approximately 40km
Altitude 0–600m
Rating Moderate to difficult
Time 3 days
Start Bilsa
End Puerto Nuevo
Maps Muisne, Puerto Nuevo, Viche, El Mamey, El Mirador, Rosa Zárate Norte
Other essential notes A walk across the Mache-Chindul range to the coast.

Hiking directions There are numerous day walks from the Bilsa research station. It is possible to join a park guard on his rounds of the forest, or perhaps a scientist if you are willing to help with research.

A longer overnight trip is to hike from Bilsa to the coastal village of Muisne – crossing the coastal range. It is best to arrange a guide for this, since the area is isolated and it is easy to get lost. You will pass through primary forest and Chachi communities – the Chachi are one of the few coastal indigenous groups remaining in Ecuador.

From Bilsa walk west to the colonist town of Mono (3 to 5 hours). The trail is frequently travelled and if you leave early you can usually find someone who will accompany you along the trail. You pass through small farms and secondary growth forest. It is possible to sleep in the school in Mono or with a family. Although the people of this village do not ask for money, it is polite to buy some food for your host.

The next day, walk northwest to the Río Sucio drainage and eventually to the Chachi community of San Salvador. This is a long day through primary forest and could be broken into 2 days of walking if necessary. You can hire a guide from Mono for this section. In San Salvador you can stay in the Casa Comunal. Since this community is lower in elevation (200m above sea level) you should have a mosquito net.

The last day you walk west to Puerto Nuevo (4 to 6 hours). You do not really need a guide for this section since there are enough people along the way to ask for directions. There may be a new road to Puerto Nuevo, so there will be some sort of transport out to Muisne or beach towns to the north.

RESERVA ECOLÓGICA MANGLARES-CHURUTE
The Reserva Ecológica Manglares-Churute preserves a 35,000 hectare area of mangrove swamps and the coastal forest of the Cordillera Churute next door to Guayaquil. The reserve was declared in 1979, since much of the coastal mangrove swamps were and are being converted into shrimp ranches and coastal forests and are heavily logged. The ecosystem of the swamps supports a rich and diverse variety of marine fauna and is an important breeding area for some fish species. The forests of the Cordillera Churute are dry tropical forests, like those in Parque Nacional Machalilla, and they contain numerous endemic tree species. The reserve is largely undeveloped but can be accessed from the water (Río Guayaquil) or the land (the Guayaquil-Machala road).

The easiest way to access the reserve is to take a bus south from Guayaquil towards Machala and get off at the settlement of Cooperativa El Mate. Here you can arrange transport to the park guard on the Río Churute, who can then take you by canoe into the mangrove swamps. Alternatively, you can hike through the Cordillera Churute up to Cerro El Mate and on to the lake of El Canclón, where there is a population of endangered and endemic ducks. Not many travellers visit this reserve, but it would make a interesting day excursion.

Maps You can probably get by without a map in the mangrove swamps since you will be guided, but the IGM 1:50,000 Laguna El Canclón map covers most of the Cordillera Churute in the park.

PARQUE NACIONAL MACHALILLA
Parque Nacional Machalilla is located on the central coast between Jipijapa to the north and Manglaralto to the south. It was established in 1979 to protect 55,000 hectares of an endangered tropical dry forest ecosystem, unique coastal and island resources, and important pre-Columbian archaeological ruins and artefacts. For much of the year the vegetation seems dead, but it springs to life when the January rains arrive. It is very hot and dry most of the year.

The park entrance ticket should be purchased in the town of Puerto Lopez. There are also restrictions on hiking because of joint land titles with communities within the park, so you may need to hire a local guide. Having said this, it is worth a visit if you are on the coast, if only for the park's diversity of birds and its unique dry forest vegetation. Several areas within and near the park are described below.

Los Frailes

Distance Approximately 40km
Altitude 0–600m
Rating Moderate to difficult
Time 3 days
Start Bilsa
End Puerto Nuevo
Maps Muisne, Puerto Nuevo, Viche, El Mamey, El Mirador, Rosa Zárate Norte
Other essential notes A walk across the Mache-Chindul range to the coast.

Los Frailes are three beautiful beaches and rocky headlands connected by a trail. The entrance gate to the beach is about 1km south of the town of Machalilla. The beaches are reached by walking/driving 2km down a dirt road. A short, self-guided nature trail heads north to a lookout and then back to the entrance gate.

Agua Blanca
Agua Blanca is the largest present-day settlement within the park and was built over a pre-Columbian site of the Manta culture. Originally known as Señorio de Salangomé, this pre-Columbian capital city served as the political and administrative centre for the area. A large part of this ancient settlement has been excavated and an impressive site museum, constructed with traditional materials, is located in the centre of the modern village. In order to visit the museum and archaeological ruins of Agua Blanca an additional fee must be paid to the community (about $4). There is a rather grungy sulphur spring near the town and trails that take you past the ruins. Several families in Agua Blanca are accustomed to taking in people for overnight stays, especially when they are planning to hike or ride up to the San Sebastian cloudforest area of the park.

San Sebastian
In the heart of the park is an undisturbed example of pre-montane forest near the community of San Sebastian. This dense vegetation includes tall trees and palms, and supports howler monkeys, white-tailed deer, ant-eaters, iguanas and numerous bird species. In order to visit the area you need to hire a guide and mules from the community of Agua Blanca, as you are not allowed to go independently. It is better to make arrangements for the hike in Agua Blanca rather than at one of the agencies in Puerto Lopez, since your money then goes directly to the community and supports the idea of the park. We recommend the guide Enrique Ventura – he seems to have a good knowledge of the fauna and pre-Columbian ruins. In San Sebastian, you can camp or stay in a wooden house owned by two brothers who make a living from tourism and collecting Tagua nuts. It may also be possible to do this hike from the town of El Pital.

Isla de La Plata

The Isla de La Plata is a small island (2km by 4km) located 24km off the coast, but still protected within the park. It has locally been dubbed the 'poor folk's Galápagos' since it is much cheaper and easier to visit. It is home to some of the same species found in the Galápagos Islands such as sea lions, sea turtles, red-billed tropic birds, waved albatrosses, three species of boobies and long-tailed mockingbirds. Between June and October you might spot a migrating humpback whale. A day tour of Isla de La Plata can be arranged from the waterfront in Puerto Lopez; camping is not allowed on the island without special permission. The boat trip to the island takes about 1½ to 2 hours each way and costs about $25 (excluding the park entrance fee). There are two loop trails on the island that are easily walked in the 4 hours you are there. It is also possible to snorkel on the coral reefs that surround the island. You can even dive out here; the only licensed operation is Exploromar in Puerto Lopez.

Ayampe to Puerto Lopez

Distance Approximately 25km
Altitude 0–200m
Rating Easy
Time 8 hours
Start Ayampe
End Puerto Lopez
Maps Puerto Lopez, Olón, Pedro Pablo Gomez
Other essential notes A walk up the Ayampe river valley which has great birding; it finishes on a dirt road to Puerto Lopez.

This long day-hike or more leisurely 2-day walk is outside the park, but offers great views of open humid forest with excellent birding opportunities. It also makes a good mountain bike trip, since it is all on dirt tracks. It is best to bring drinking water, as it is usually hot. You will be wading through a shallow river so wear footgear you do not mind getting wet, like sandals or trainers.

Hiking directions Begin the hike in the small community of Ayampe (just south of Alandaluz resort) at the mouth of the Río Ayampe on the main coastal road. The Río Ayampe is the only river that flows year-round from the park and you will notice water trucks filling up for delivery of fresh water to communities along the coast. The track follows the riverbed upstream, and sometimes is the riverbed! It tucks through giant bamboo groves and past small wetlands in a lush river valley where there are herons, parakeets and kingfishers. After 3 to 4 hours of walking you reach a turn-off on the left to Cantalopiedra, an organic farm that supplies food to the Alandaluz Ecological Resort and which makes a good spot to stop for lunch. About 300m beyond Cantalopiedra you reach a gravel road where a right turn takes you to the village of Guale and eventually to the main coastal highway. A left turn takes you on a dirt road to Puerto Lopez. Along the back road to Puerto Lopez you pass through occasional *fincas* and good humid forest. Río Blanco is another 3 to 4 hours beyond Cantalopiedra, and a good place to sleep if you want to visit a rural village. There is a small store and a public water source here. Puerto Lopez is about 2 to 2½ hours beyond Río Blanco and there is often traffic on this portion of the hike. You are not in the park on this hike so you do not need to pay an entrance fee or hire a guide.

Julcuy to Agua Blanca

Distance 27km
Altitude 100–835m
Rating Moderate
Time 1–2 days
Start Julcuy
End Paved road 5km beyond Agua Blanca
Maps Jipijapa, Pedro Pablo Gómez and Puerto Lopez and Delicias
Other essential notes A hike across the coastal range of Machallila to the archaeological sites at Agua Blanca.

Access About 11km south of Jipijapa on the main road to Guayaquil is a turn-off for the village of Guarango. Have the bus let you off at the small settlement of San Dimas on the main road. From here it's a short (three dusty kilometres) walk to the small village of Guarango. Beyond (west of) the village, along the mostly unused jeep trail, the valley narrows as the track heads north around a steep hill, then south again. Two hours after leaving the main road, you'll come to the village of Julcuy. Here there are several examples of pre-Columbian *alvaradas* constructed to catch the infrequent rainwater runoff in this semi-desert area.

Hiking directions The trail runs southeast through the village leading up towards a notch in the cliffs. About 1km beyond Julcuy, the track drops down to the river valley and enters a deep gorge. Both waterbirds and raptors abound here, and the stream has both fish and freshwater shrimp. Once past Julcuy you are in Parque Nacional Machalilla.

After about an hour the trail and the riverbed separate, although they will continue to criss-cross regularly. There are a couple of springs along the way and several small clusters of houses. It is possible to hike through to Agua Blanca in one very long hot day (about 9 to 10 hours from the main road), but much more pleasurable is to take two leisurely days looking at the birds and plants. From May to November it's usually dry and this hike can be done without a tent.

The 5km hike from Agua Blanca to the coastal highway can be done in an hour along a gravel road, or you can find a dirt track on the left side of the river that takes you through shaded brush and comes out on the highway several hundred metres south of the guard station. Here frequent buses pass, going south to the fishing village of Puerto López and north to the village of Machalilla.

Cerro Blanco

Barely 20 minutes out of Guayaquil, heading west towards Salinas, is the huge cement operation of Cemento Nacional. The name conjures up images of industrialisation with all its negative aspects, such as habitat destruction, soil erosion, air pollution, constant chugging of machinery and the like. Cemento Nacional, however, has done a contrary thing. It has set aside much of its property as an ecological reserve, which may eventually become a national park. The lowland vegetation here ranges from dry forest on the northern flanks to scrub and kapok to the south. Despite being practically a stone's throw from the largest city in Ecuador, Cerro Blanco is home to an amazing variety of wildlife. Puma, jaguar, jaguarundi, ocelots, howler monkeys, coatis and peccaries are representative of some of the mammals. The list of birds in the area is equally impressive – there are owls, grey hawks, crane hawks, snail kites, chacalacas, and a wide variety of waterfowl, to name just a few. You can go in for the day or camp in the reserve.

To get to the Bosque Protector Cerro Blanco catch a bus to Salinas and get off at the entrance marked by a large white sign that says 'Entrada Bosque Protector Cerro Blanco' just before reaching the Balrosa Río cement plant. Taxis from Guayaquil cost between $7 to $10. The park is open between 08.30 and 17.00 and the entrance fee is about $1.

There is a new campground near the visitors' centre, with tent pads, tables and cooking grills, as well as bathrooms with running water. The camping fee is about $5 per night. The reserve has two trails. The Quebrada Canoa is a short loop through a ravine with permanent pools of water and abundant aquatic life. The other trail is the Buenavista, a 3 to 4 hour round-trip up to forest and lookouts over the mangrove swamps. A backcountry trail is planned for overnight hikers wishing to visit the core of the reserve. Canoe trips can be arranged through the mangrove swamps.

More information on the area can be obtained from Fundación Natura, D Sucre 401 and Rosendo Avilés in Guayaquil; tel: 2441793.

Appendix 1

LANGUAGE

With the exception of a few small, remote, indigenous groups, everyone speaks Spanish in Ecuador, including the Andean indigenous people, although for them it is a second language, after Quechua. Other European languages are rarely understood except in the major tourist agencies and first-class hotels. Therefore it is essential that you learn some basic Spanish; take heart, it is an easy language to learn.

Quechua, though widely spoken in the highlands, is a difficult language to learn and dialects tend to vary greatly from area to area, so unless you are an avid linguist you're better off learning some Spanish.

Spanish

The following list of words and phrases will get you started:

Greetings

good afternoon	*buenas tardes*
good evening/night	*buenas noches*
good morning/day	*buenos días*
goodbye	*adios*

Essential phrases

Where are you going?	*A donde va?*
Where are you coming from?	*De donde viene?*
I'm passing through	*Estoy paseando*
May I camp?	*Puedo acampar?*
Where is the trail to…?	*Donde está el camino por…?*
How are you?	*Como está?*

General vocabulary

please	*por favor*	baggage	*equipaje*
thank you	*gracias*	bath	*baño*
yes	*sí*	bus	*bus, colectivo*
no	*no*	pick-up truck	*camioneta*
		road	*carretera*
bad	*malo*	room (in hotel)	*habitación*
good	*bueno*	train	*ferrocarril, tren*

Climber's and hiker's vocabulary

above	arriba	landslide	derrumbe
altitude	altura	left	izquierda
aqueduct	acequia	meadow	pampa
ascent	subida	moraine	morena
backpack	mochila	mountain	cerro
below	abajo	(without snow)	
bivouac	vivac	mountain	nevado
boots (climbing)	botas (de andinismo)	(snow peak)	
bridge	puente	mountaineer	andinista
camp	campamento	mule	mula
carabiners	mosquetones	muleteer	arriero
climb (down)	bajar	needle	aguja
climb (up)	escalar, ascender	north	norte
close (to)	cerca	pass	paso, abra,
cold	frio		porta-chuelo, punta
crampons	grampones	peak	pico
crevasse	grieta	plain (plateau)	pampa
(to) cross	cruzar, atravesar	point (minor peak)	punta
distant	lejos	rain	lluvia
east	este	ravine	quebrada
face	cara	right	derecha
fixed rope	cuerda fija	river	río
fog	niebla	rock	roca
forest	bosque	rope	cuerda, soga
freeze	congelar	route	ruta
glacier	glaciar	snow	nieve
hail	granizo	south	sur
hammer	martillo	straight ahead	derecho, recto
highlands	sierra	summit	cima, cumbre
hill	loma	swamp	pantano
house	casa	tent	carpa
hut (climbers')	refugio	trail	sendero
ice	hielo	valley	valle
ice axe	piolet	village	pueblo
ice screw	tornillo	waterfall	cascada
lake	lago, laguna	west	oeste

Appendix 2

ELEVATIONS

The height of a mountain is a constant source of interest to climbers and non-climbers alike. Upon returning from a climb, one is often asked 'How high is it?' before being questioned about the difficulty, duration, or equipment needed for the ascent. In lesser-known areas, the question 'How high is it?' is not easily answered. Maps are often sketchy or inaccurate, and different sources come up with various possible heights for the same mountain. Perhaps one of these is correct, perhaps none.

For the sake of consistency, we have used what appears to be the most accurate source for the elevations in this book. These are from the 1999 Instituto Geográfico Militar (IGM) 1:1,000,000 maps of Ecuador. Many other sources are available, and even different maps from the institute have a variety of elevations. The following table lists various given elevations of Ecuador's major peaks – take your pick.

Sources

1 IGM 1:50,000 series maps, various years
2 *Montaña* magazine, Colegio San Gabriel, Quito, No 11, June 1975
3 *The Fool's Climbing Guide To Ecuador and Peru* Michael Koerner, 1976
4 *El Volcanismo en El Ecuador* by Minard L Hall, 1977
5 Ecuador 1:1,000,000 by Kevin Healey, ITM Publishing, Canada, 1993
6 IGM 1:1,000,000 map, 1999

	1	2	3	4	5	6
Chimborazo	6,310	6,310	6,310	6,267	6,310	**6,310**
Cotopaxi★	5,880+	6,005	5,897	5,897	5,758	**5,897**
Cayambe		5,840	5,790	5,790	5,790	**5,790**
Antisana★	5,753	5,750	5,704	5,705	5,758	**5,752**
El Altar★		5,404	5,404	5,319	5,319	**5,319**
Iliniza Sur	5,248	5,305	5,305	5,266	5,263	**5,248**
Sangay★		5,323	5,230	5,230	5,230	**5,230**
Iliniza Norte	5,126	5,116	5,116		**5,126**	
Carihuairazo		5,106	5,116	4,990	5,020	**5,020**
Tungurahua★		5,087	5,016	5,016	5,023	**5,029**
Cotacachi		4,966	4,939	4,939	4,939	**4,944**
Sincholagua	4,893	4,988	4,893	4,898	4,893	**4,898**
Quilindaña	4,760+	4,919	4,878	4,898	4,788	**4,877**
Guagua Pichincha★	4,784	4,850	4,839	4,794	4,794	**4,675**
El Corazón	4,788	4,810	4,788	4,786	4,788	**4,788**
Chiles	4,768	4,720	4,712	4,720	4,723	**4,723**
Rumiñahui	4,712	4,757	4,712	4,722	4,712	**4,712**
Rucu Pichincha	4,680+	4,787	4,787	4,698	**4,627**	
Sara Urco		4,725	4,710		**4,428**	

	1	2	3	4	5	6
Imbabura	4,560	4,630	4,630	4,630	**4,609**	
Hermoso		4,571		4,571	**4,571**	
Puntas				4,452	**4,452**	
Atacazo	4,463	4,470	4,457	4,457	4,463	**4,463**
Pasochoa	4,199	4,220	4,255	4,199	4,200	**4,199**
Sumaco★		3,828	3,828	3,828	3,732	**3,732**
Reventador★		3,485	3,485	3,485	3,562	**3,562**

All heights are in metres.
★ signifies active or potentially active volcanoes.
Elevations used in this book are shown in heavy type.

Appendix

FURTHER READNG

This lists all the books we referred to in preparing this guide and a few more besides. We have tried to give as much variety as possible. Books published in Ecuador, and a good selection of English books about Ecuador, are available at Libri Mundi, Casilla Postal 3029, Quito. Many of the Spanish-language books are available at the Abya-Yala bookstore next to the Universidad Católica in Quito.

General South American guidebooks

The South American Handbook Footprint Handbooks, England. Updated annually, this 1,000 plus page book is the best overall guide to Latin America. Expensive, but worth every penny to anyone planning on spending a long time in Latin America.

Ecuador & the Galápagos Islands – a travel survival kit Rob Rachowiecki. Lonely Planet, Australia. Updated regularly. The best general guide to Ecuador.

Ecuador Insight Guides, 1996. Beautiful photographs and good background essays.

Ecuador – A Bird's Eye View Jorge Anhauzer, 1999. Photographs from all over Ecuador taken from an ultralite plane.

Haciendas of Ecuador Barry W Barker, Earthworld Press, 1994. Description of upmarket *haciendas* in northern Ecuador which have been converted into hotels.

Guidebooks for the outdoors

Trekking in Ecuador Robert & Daisy Kunstaetter, Mountaineers Press, 2002. Several of the hikes are repeats of those found in this book, but there are some new routes.

Ecuador: A Climbing Guide Yossi Brain, Mountaineers Press, 2000. This pocket-sized guide provides some additional technical routes by author Yossi Brain, who tragically died in a climbing accident in Bolivia in 1999.

Montañas Del Sol Marcos Serrano, Iván Rojas and Freddy Landazuri, Campo Abierto, 1994. Spanish-language climbing guide to mountaineering in Ecuador.

The Ecotourist's Guide to the Ecuadorian Amazon edited by Rolf Wesche, University of Ottawa and TR&D, 1995. Excellent guide to ecotourism in the Napo Province, with some hikes described.

Guía Para Excursiones en Automovil a Traves del Ecuador Arthur Weilbauer, Quito, 1985. Available in Spanish, German and English. An invaluable guide to all the major and most minor roads in Ecuador. Available only in Ecuador.

Walking the Beaches of Ecuador J G Cardenas and K M Greiner, Quito, 1988. The authors describe how they walked or jogged the entire Ecuadorian coastline.

Trekking in the Central Andes R Rachowiecki, G Caire and G Dixon, Lonely Planet, 2003. Only four Ecuadorian treks and no climbs arecovered, but the title is useful for hikers who want to continue into Peru and Bolivia.

General mountaineering and exploration

Andes del Ecuador Jorge Anhauser, Imprenta Mariscal (Quito), 2000. Coffee-table book – great photography of major peaks taken from an ultralite plane.

Travels Amongst the Great Andes of the Equator Edward Whymper, 1891. Worth getting hold of – this book describes the 1880 expedition which first climbed Ecuador's highest peak, and made seven other first ascents. Available in several recent reprints by other publishers.

Sweat of the Sun, Tears of the Moon, A Chronicle of an Inca Treasure Peter Lourie, University of Nebraska Press, 1998. Interesting accounts of historical and modern searches for the lost Inca treasure of the Llanganates.

El Gran Viaje Marcos Jiménez de la Espada, Francisco de Paula, Manuel Almagro and Juan Isern, Abya-Yala (Quito), 1998.

Latin America by Bike – A Complete Touring Guide Walter Sienko, Mountaineers Press, 1993. A few rides in Ecuador are described.

Llanganati Jorge Anhalzer, Imprenta Mariscal (Quito), 1998. First-hand account of crossing the Llanganatis on foot to the Oriente (the eastern lowlands).

Andes Jorge Anhalzer, Imprenta Mariscal (Quito), 1997.

Personal Narrative of the Travels to the Equinoctial Regions of the New Continent Alexander von Humboldt and Aime Bonpland. Various editions. Again, difficult to find, but fascinating reading for anyone interested in the historical aspects of Latin American exploration.

Sangay Survived Richard Snailham, Hutchinson, 1978 (now out of print). The story of a six-man British scientific expedition to Sangay volcano which ended disastrously when an eruption killed or injured most of the members.

En Los Altos Andes del Ecuador Hans Meyer, and translated Jonás Guerrero, Abya-Yala (Quito), 1993. Originally published in German as *In den Hoch-Anden von Ecuador*, Berlin, 1907.

Ecuador: A Travel Journal Henri Michaux

The Fool's Climbing Guide to Ecuador and Peru Michael Koerner, Buzzard Mountaineering, 1976. Out of print but an early cult classic.

Natural history and vulcanology

Megadiverse Ecuador Luis Coloma and Santiago Ron, PUCE (Quito), 2002. Photos and text on animals of Ecuador.

A Field Guide to the Families and Genera of Woody Plants of Northwest South America (Colombia, Ecuador, Peru) Alwyn H Gentry and Adrian G Foryth, University of Chicago Press, 1996. The classic tome on trees in Ecuador; a must for amateur botanists.

Actividad Volcánica y Pueblos Precolombianos en el Ecuador Patricia Mothes, Abya-Yala (Quito), 1998. Acedemic studies of volcanic effects on pre-Columbian cultures in northern Ecuador.

Los Antiguas Paisajes Forestales del Ecuador Fernando Hidalgo Nistri,. Abya-Yala (Quito), 1998. Interesting historical accounts of once forested areas in the Andes.

Contribuciones para el Conocimiento Geológico de la Región Volcánico del Ecuador Augusto N. Martínez Holguín, Abya-Yala (Quito), 1994. Academic studies of volcanoes of Ecuador.

Mammals of the Neotropics: The Central Neotropics – Ecuador, Peru, Bolivia, Brazil John F Eisenberg and Kent H Redford, University of Chicago Press, 2000. Good guide with pictures of mammals from the neotropics; the majority are found in Ecuador.

Murciélagos del Ecuador Luis Albuja, Fundacyt (Quito), 1999. Definitive book on Ecuadorian bats.

El Paisaje Volcánico de la Sierra Ecuadoriana Patricia Mothes, Corporación Editora Nacional (Quito), 1991. Study of Ecuadorian volcanoes.

El Agua en el Ecuador: Clima, Precipitaciones, Escorrentia Pierre Pourrut, ORSTROM (Quito), 1995. Technical overview of climate, precipitation and rivers of Ecuador.

The March 5, 1987, Ecuador Earthquakes: Mass Wasteing and Socioeconomic Effects The National Research Council, National Academy Press, 1991. Study of the destructive 1987 earthquake in the Reventador area.

Historia de los Teremotos y las Erupciones Volcánicas en el Ecuador (siglos XVI–XX) J Kolberg, N Martinez, L E Whimper, L T Wolf and L A Yturralde Taller de Estudios Andinos (Quito), 2000. Historical accounts of volcanic eruptions by famous climbers and explorers.

Volcan Pichincha Erupciones, Destruciones e Invenciones Tamara Estupiñán Viteri, Banco Central del Ecuador (Quito), 1998. Study of the volcanism of Pichincha.

Riesgos Naturales en Quito. Lahares, aluviones y derrumbes del Pichincha y del Cotopaxi Pierre Peltre, Coporacion Editora Nacional, Quito, 1989. Technical studies on geologic risks to Quito.

Fauna del Ecuador Erwin Patzelt, Banco Central del Ecuador, Quito, 1989. In Spanish; particularly useful for mammals, reptiles and amphibians.

Flora del Ecuador Erwin Patzelt, Banco Central del Ecuador, 1985. In Spanish and out of print, but there is talk of a new edition.

The Andes Tony Morrison, Time-Life Books, 1975. A beautiful book covering the whole Andean chain; Ecuador's mountains are not forgotten, with superb photographs of Cotopaxi and Sangay.

Land Above the Clouds Tony Morrison, Deutsch, 1974. This book also deals with the whole Andean chain, with an emphasis on its wildlife. Recommended.

The Flight of the Condor Michael Andrews, Collins, 1982. Subtitled *A Wildlife Exploration of the Andes*, this well-illustrated book contains an excellent chapter on Ecuador.

Ecuador: Snow Peaks and Jungles Arthur Eichler, English translation, Cromwell, NY, 955. There's also a bilingual edition by Eichler, published in Quito, 1970. Although some of the information is rather inaccurate, the excellent photographs make this book well worth looking at.

Ecuador – in the Shadow of the Volcanoes, Ediciones Libri Mundi, 1981. Available in English, Spanish, German and French. A coffee-table book, with many superb photos.

El Volcanismo en El Ecuador Minard L Hall, IPGH, Quito, 1977. In Spanish; mainly of interest to the volcanologist – the best work on the subject.

Neotropical Rainforest Mammals – A Field Guide Louise H Emmons, University of Chicago Press, USA, 1990. A detailed and well-illustrated guide to the mammals of Amazonia and the Central American rainforests. Recommended.

Tropical Nature Adrian Forsyth and Ken Miyata, Scribners, New York, 1984. Sub-titled *Life and Death in the Rainforests of Central and South America*, this book is a great introduction to the natural history of the rainforest.

A Neotropical Companion John C Kricher, Princeton University Press, USA, 1989. Sub-titled *An Introduction to the Animals, Plants, and Ecosystems of the New World Tropics*, this book is just as good as the one listed above. Both are recommended.

Ecuador and its Galápagos Islands: The Ecotraveler's Wildlife Guide David L Pearson and Les Beletsky (eds), Academic Press, 2001. This well-illustrated book provides a general overview of the most common and important birds, mammals, amphibians, reptiles and insects.

Galápagos Wildlife: A Visitor's Guide David Horwell and Pete Oxford, Bradt Travel Guides, 1999. A pocket-sized guide and souvenir to the wildlife of the islands, with full-colour photographs and details of individual walks.

Ornithology

A Guide to the Birds of Ecuador R Ridgely and P Greenfield, Cornell University Press, 2001. This is the definitive guide to birds in Ecuador. Excellent two-volume guide that took almost 30 years to complete.

Common Birds of the Amazon Canaday and Jost, Libri Mundi, Quito, 1997

An Annotated List of the Birds of Mainland Ecuador Robert Ridgely, Paul Greenfield and Mauricio Guerrero, CECIA, Quito, 1998

South American Birds – A Photographic Aid to Identification John S Dunning, Harrowood Books, USA, 1987. 1,400 birds illustrated and 2,700 described in this book, which covers water- as well as landbirds.

Birding Ecuador Clive Green, 2nd edition, 1996. Available from the American Birding Association; tel: 1 (800) 834 7736; fax: (719) 578 9705, PO Box 6599, Colorado Springs, CO 80934, USA. Detailed account of birding trips in Ecuador with useful checklists, sketch maps and access details of many birding hotspots in Ecuador.

Birds of Ecuador Crespot, Greenfield & Matheus, FEPROTUR, Quito, 1990. A locational checklist.

Health

Medical Handbook for Mountaineers Peter Steele, Constable, London. Pocket-sized yet detailed.

Medicine for Mountaineering James Wilkerson, Mountaineers Press, 2001. Comprehensive first-aid manual for outdoor medical emergencies.

Mountaineering Medicine – A Wilderness Medical Guide Fred T Darvill MD, Wilderness Press, USA, 1992. A 100-page booklet worth carrying on hiking and backpacking trips.

Miscellaneous

El Niño in History: Storming Through the Ages César N Caviedes, University of Florida Press, 2001. Explains the El Niño effect.

Parques Nacionales del Ecuador Jorge Anhauzer, Imprenta Mariscal, Quito, undated. Pictures of wildlife and mountains from national parks in Ecuador.

La Selva Culta Simbolismo y Praxis en la Ecología de los Achuar Phillipe Descola, Abya Yala, Quito, 1986. Study of the Achuar culture.

El Clima y Sus Características en El Ecuador Carlos Blandin Landivar, IPGH, Quito, 1976. A Spanish-language book on the meteorology of Ecuador.

El Mundo Perdido de Los Aucas (The Lost World of the Aucas) K D Gartelmann, Quito, 1978. A multi-lingual book with many colour photographs describing one of the least known and least accessible indigenous tribes of Ecuador.

Humboldt and the Cosmos Douglas Botting, Sphere Books, London. A biographical account of one of the best known early explorers of Ecuador and South America.

The Conquest of the Incas John Hemming, Harcourt Brace, USA, 1970. A thorough and exceptional work on the subject.

In the Eyes of My People Pablo Cuvi, Dinediciones/Grijalbo, Ecuador, 1988. Difficult to find outside of Ecuador, but highly recommended once you get there. Sub-titled *Stories and photos of journeys through Ecuador*, this book is written by an Ecuadorian who both loves his country and knows how to write. The photos are some of the best I've seen of Ecuador and its people.

Ecuador – Fragile Democracy D Corkill and D Cubitt, Latin American Bureau, UK, 1988. A look at historical patterns and current trends in Ecuadorian politics.

Amazon Crude Natural Resources Defense Council, USA, 1991. A hard-hitting look at the environmental and social problems caused by oil drilling in the Amazon.

The Panama Hat Trail Tom Miller, Vintage Departures, NY, 1988; reprinted by National Geographic, 2001. A well-written account of Miller's search for Panama hats in Ecuador – Ecuadorian life is well described.

Two Wheels and a Taxi Virginia Urrutia, Mountaineers Press, USA, 1987. Ms Urrutia was 70 when she cycled around Ecuador with a local cab driver for logistical support.

Diez Cuentistas Ecuatorianas (Ten Stories From Ecuador), Libri Mundi, Quito, 1990. Ten short stories by Ecuadorian writers, in Spanish with English translations.

Manual de Ecotourism: Para Guías y Comunidades Indigenas de la Amazonia Ecuatoriana Randy Smith, Abya-Yala, Quito, 1996. Good species lists in the appendix in several indigenous languages.

Savages Joe Kane, Vintage Books, 1995. Describes the lives of the Huarani (formerly known as Auca) Indians of the Amazon, and how their remote culture was changed by the discovery of oil in their Amazonian territories.

Amazon Stranger: Rainforest Chief Battles Big Oil Mike Tidwell, Lyons and Burford, 1996. Based on the true story of the son of American missionaries who was raised with the Cofan tribe and eventually became their chief.

Living Poor Moritz Thomsen, Eland, 1989. An account of working for the US Peace Corps in coastal Ecuador during the 1960s.

For a complete bibliography of Ecuador get hold of a copy of *Ecuador* by David Corkhill, in the World Bibliographical Series from Clio Press, Oxford

Periodicals

Montaña The magazine of the San Gabriel climbing club, Quito. The oldest established mountaineering magazine in Ecuador, appearing at irregular intervals. In Spanish with some English mountain descriptions.

Campo Abierto Quito, Ecuador. A small mountaineering magazine begun in 1982. Spanish language.

Websites

The following websites provide information about Ecuador:

www.saexplorers.org The best source of current information, with useful trip reports online

www.ecuadorexplorer.com EcuadorExplorer.com is a complete and highly visited guide to Ecuador. Get up-to-date, accurate travel information on everything you'll need to plan your trip, like maps, tours, hotels, national parks, work/volunteer opportunities and Spanish schools.

The Best of Ecuador can been found at **www.thebestofecuador.com**

National Newspaper El Comercio **www.elcomercio.com** Daily news in Spanish.

Ecuadorian Ministerio de Turismo **www.vivecuador** General tourist information on Ecuador.

Ecuadorian Ministerio de Ambiente **www.ambiente.gov.ec** Information on protected areas in Ecuador.

Bradt Travel Guides

Africa by Road	£13.95	London: In the Footsteps of	
Amazon	£14.95	the Famous	£10.95
Antarctica: A Guide to the Wildlife	£14.95	Madagascar	£13.95
The Arctic: A Guide to Coastal		Madagascar Wildlife: A Visitor's	
Wildlife	£14.95	Guide	£14.95
Azores	£12.95	Malawi	£12.95
Baltic Capitals: Tallinn, Riga,		Maldives	£12.95
Vilnius, Kaliningrad	£11.95	Mali	£13.95
Botswana: Okavango Delta,		Mauritius	£12.95
Chobe, Northern Kalahari	£14.95	Montenegro	£12.95
British Isles: Wildlife of Coastal		Mozambique	£12.95
Waters	£14.95	Namibia	£14.95
Cambodia	£11.95	North Canada: Yukon, Northwest	
Cape Verde Islands	£12.95	Territories, Nunavut	£13.95
Cayman Islands	£12.95	North Cyprus	£11.95
Chile & Argentina: Trekking		North Korea	£13.95
Guide	£12.95	Palestine with Jerusalem	£12.95
China: Yunnan Province	£13.95	Paris – Lille – Brussels: The Bradt	
Croatia	£12.95	Guide to Eurostar Cities	£11.95
East & Southern Africa:		Peru & Bolivia: Trekking Guide	£12.95
Backpacker's Manual	£14.95	River Thames: In the	
Eccentric America	£12.95	Footsteps of the Famous	£10.95
Eccentric Britain	£11.95	Rwanda	£13.95
Eccentric France	£12.95	Seychelles	£12.95
Eccentric London	£12.95	Singapore	£11.95
Ecuador, Peru & Bolivia:		South Africa: The Bradt	
Backpacker's Manual	£13.95	Budget Travel Guide	£11.95
Eritrea	£12.95	Southern African Wildlife	£18.95
Estonia	£12.95	Sri Lanka	£12.95
Ethiopia	£13.95	St Helena, Ascension &	
Falkland Islands	£13.95	Tristan da Cunha	£14.95
Gabon, São Tomé & Príncipe	£13.95	Switzerland: Rai, Road, Lake	£12.95
Galápagos Wildlife	£14.95	Tanzania	£14.95
The Gambia	£12.95	Tasmania	£12.95
Georgia	£13.95	Tibet	£12.95
Ghana	£12.95	Uganda	£11.95
Iran	£12.95	USA by Rail	£12.95
Iraq	£13.95	Venezuela	£14.95
Kabul: Mini Guide	£9.95	Your Child's Health Abroad	£8.95
Latvia	£12.95	Zambia	£12.95
Lithuania	£12.95	Zanzibar	£12.95

CLAIM YOUR HALF-PRICE BRADT GUIDE!

Order Form

To order your half-price copy of a Bradt guide, and to enter our prize draw to win £100 (see overleaf), please fill in the order form below, complete the questionnaire overleaf, and send it to Bradt Travel Guides by post, fax or email. Post and packing is free to UK addresses.

Please send me one copy of the following guide at half the UK retail price

Title	*Retail price*	*Half price*

Please send the following additional guides at full UK retail price

No	*Title*	*Retail price*	*Total*
...	....	....	......
...	....	....	......
...	....	....	......

Sub total	......
Post & packing outside UK	......
(£2 per book Europe; £3 per book rest of world)	
Total	......

Name . . . .

Address . . . .

Tel. . . . .   Email . . . .

☐ I enclose a cheque for £. . . . . . . made payable to Bradt Travel Guides Ltd

☐ I would like to pay by VISA or MasterCard

    Number . . . .   Expiry date . . . .

☐ Please add my name to your catalogue mailing list.

Send your order on this form, with the completed questionnaire, to:

Bradt Travel Guides/CHE
19 High Street, Chalfont St Peter, Bucks SL9 9QE
Tel: +44 1753 893444 Fax: +44 1753 892333
Email: info@bradt-travelguides.com
www.bradt-travelguides.com

WIN £100 CASH!

READER QUESTIONNAIRE

Win a cash prize of £100 for the first completed questionnaire drawn after May 31 2004.

All respondents may order a Bradt guide at half the UK retail price – please complete the order form overleaf.

(Entries may be posted or faxed to us, or scanned and emailed.)

We are interested in getting feedback from our readers to help us plan future Bradt guides. Please complete this quick questionnaire and return it to us to enter into our draw.

Have you used any other Bradt guides? If so, which titles?. . . . .

. . . .

What other publishers' travel guides do you use regularly? . . . .

. . . .

Where did you buy this guidebook? . . . .

What was the main purpose of your trip to Ecuador (or for what other reason did you read our guide)? eg: holiday/business/charity etc. . . . .

. . . .

What other destinations would you like to see covered by a Bradt guide?

. . . .

Would you like to receive our catalogue/newsletters?

YES / NO (If yes, please complete details on reverse)

If yes – by post or email?. . . . .

Age (circle relevant category) 16–25   26–45   46–60   60+

Male/Female (delete as appropriate)

Home country. . . . .

Please send us any comments about our guide to Ecuador or other Bradt Travel Guides. . . . .

. . . .

. . . .

. . . .

Bradt Travel Guides

19 High Street, Chalfont St Peter, Bucks SL9 9QE, UK
Telephone: +44 1753 893444 Fax: +44 1753 892333
Email: info@bradt-travelguides.com
www.bradt-travelguides.com

Index

*Page numbers in bold refer to major entries;
those in italics indicate maps*